Latest Research in Computational Intelligence and Soft Computing

Volume I

Latest Research in Computational Intelligence and Soft Computing Volume I

Edited by **Tom Halt**

LANRYE INTERNATIONAL

New Jersey

Published by Clanrye International,
55 Van Reypen Street,
Jersey City, NJ 07306, USA
www.clanryeinternational.com

Latest Research in Computational Intelligence and Soft Computing
Volume I
Edited by Tom Halt

International Standard Book Number: 978-1-63240-329-2 (Hardback)

Printed in the United States of America.

Contents

Preface

Soft computing is a subject that is used in the science of computers. It is basically used to refer to the problems in the field of computer science whose solutions are mostly unpredictable and always have a probability value of zero to one. This field came into existence in early 1990s with a huge impact on computer sciences. The perfect example of a soft computing model is the human mind. It becomes pertinent to note here, that soft computing is absolutely tolerant of approximation and uncertainty, unlike hard computing. Moreover, there's a huge difference between possibility and soft computing.

Earlier applied computational approaches were used to model and analyze only simple systems. But due to advancement in the fields of biology, medical science, humanities, management, and numerous others, the need for soft computing and applied computations gained significant attention. Applied computation and soft computing deals with problems like imprecision, uncertainty, partial truth, and approximated values to achieve practicability, robustness, and above all low solution cost. The soft computing process is mostly used when the information about the problem is highly limited and not even available sometimes.

Instead of organizing the book into a pre-formatted table of contents with chapters, sections and then asking the authors to submit their respective chapters based on this frame, the authors were encouraged by the publisher to submit their chapters based on their area of expertise. The editor was then commissioned to examine the reading material and put it together as a book.

I especially wish to acknowledge the contributing authors, without whom a work of this magnitude would definitely not be realizable. I thank them for allocating their very scarce time to this project. Not only do I appreciate their participation, but also their adherence as a group to the time parameters set for this publication.

Editor

State-of-the-Art Review on Relevance of Genetic Algorithm to Internet Web Search

Kehinde Agbele,[1] Ademola Adesina,[1] Daniel Ekong,[2] and Oluwafemi Ayangbekun[3]

[1] *Department of Computer Science, Soft Computing and Intelligent Systems Research Group, University of the Western Cape, Private Bag X17, Bellville, Cape Town, South Africa*
[2] *Department of Mathematical Sciences (Computer Science Option), Ekiti State University, Ado-Ekiti, PMB 5363, Ado-Ekiti, Ekiti State, Nigeria*
[3] *College of Information and Communication Technology, Crescent University, Abeokuta, Ogun-State, Nigeria*

Correspondence should be addressed to Kehinde Agbele, agbelek@yahoo.com

Academic Editor: Cheng-Jian Lin

People use search engines to find information they desire with the aim that their information needs will be met. Information retrieval (IR) is a field that is concerned primarily with the searching and retrieving of information in the documents and also searching the search engine, online databases, and Internet. Genetic algorithms (GAs) are robust, efficient, and optimized methods in a wide area of search problems motivated by Darwin's principles of natural selection and survival of the fittest. This paper describes information retrieval systems (IRS) components. This paper looks at how GAs can be applied in the field of IR and specifically the relevance of genetic algorithms to internet web search. Finally, from the proposals surveyed it turns out that GA is applied to diverse problem fields of internet web search.

1. Introduction

There is a virtual explosion in the availability of electronic information. The advent of the Internet or World Wide Web (WWW) has brought far more information than any human being can absorb. The goal of IR systems is to assist user to organize and store such information and retrieve useful information when a user submits a query to the IR systems. To resolve this problem, many research communities have implemented diverse techniques such as full text, inverted index, keyword querying, Boolean querying, knowledge-based, neural network, probabilistic retrieval, genetic algorithm, and machine learning. Now, increasing numbers of people use web search engines which enable them to access any kind of information from the Internet in order to formulate better, well-informed decisions. However, the ability of search engines to return useful and relevant documents is not always satisfactory. Often users need to refine the search query several times and search through large document collections to find relevant information.

But, according to [1], the results returned by the search engine may not be relevant to the users' information needs and, hence users need to modify and reformulate their queries.

The focus of IR is the capability to search for information relevant to individual user's needs within a documents collection which is relevant to the user's query. According to [2], the authors stated that user is in need of information. The work reported in Agbele et al. [3] describes access to information as an important benefit that can be achieved in many areas including socio-economic development, education, and healthcare. In healthcare, for example, access to appropriate information can minimize visits to physicians and period of hospitalization for patients suffering from chronic conditions, such as asthma, diabetes, hypertension, and HIV/AIDS. Agbele method examines the opening of health information system based on ICT as one fundamental healthcare application area, especially within the context of the Millennium Development Goals to improve the management and quality of healthcare for development at

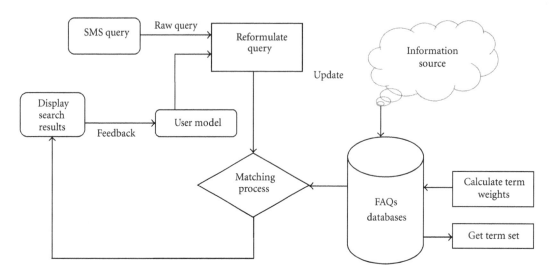

FIGURE 1: Important Processes in Web Information Retrieval-framework.

lower cost. It is the responsibility of a user to formulate query and send the query to the search engine (or IRS).

IR system searches for the matches in the document databases and, thus, retrieves search results of the matching process. However, based on the relevance, the user will then evaluate and display the search results. The relevance of the document is very important to the user. If the user feels that it is a relevant document, he finishes the search while else user continues to search in the document database by reformulating the query until the relevant documents that will satisfy users' information needs are retrieved.

GA is a probabilistic algorithm simulating the process of natural selection of living organisms and finally coming up with an approximate solution to a problem [4–6]. In GA implementation, the search space is composed of candidate solutions (called individuals or creatures) to an optimization problem to evolve better solutions; each represented by a string is termed chromosome. Each chromosome has an objective function value, called fitness. A set of chromosomes together with their associated fitness is called a population. This population, at a given iteration of the genetic algorithm, is called a generation. In each generation, the fitness of every individual in the population is evaluated from the current population based on their fitness value and modified to form a new population. The new population is then used in the next iteration of the algorithm.

GA terminates when either a maximum number of generations has been produced or a satisfactory fitness level has been reached for the population. If the algorithm has terminated due to a maximum number of generations, a satisfactory solution may or may not have been reached. The working of the genetic algorithm depends upon the constraint of how well we choose our initial random keywords.

The rest of the paper is organized as follows: Section 2 discusses important processes within IR components while Section 3 reviews the relevance of GAs to Internet web search and its applications in IR. Section 4 gives the conclusion.

2. Components of an Information Retrieval System

In the framework for IR as depicted in Figure 1, the user gives a mobile SMS-query (raw query) and the query is reformulated in order to improve the predicted relevance of the retrieved document. The reformulated query is searched against the databases. The IR system searches for the matches in the document databases and, thus, retrieves search results of the matching process. Based on the relevance, the user will then display the search results. The relevance of the document is very important to the user. If the user feels that it is a relevant document, he finishes the search while else user continues to search in the document database by reformulating the query until the relevant documents that will satisfy users' information needs are retrieved. Hence, user query reformulations will apply by updating its model. A user model is a stored knowledge about a particular user. A simple model consists usually of keywords describing user's area of interest. Sort those documents according to TFIDF approach. The documents which have the high retrieval status value (RSV) are considered as the top ranked documents.

The two main components in the proposed IR system framework are document databases and reformulated query processing system. The document databases stores the databases related to documents and the representations of their information contents based on TFIDF approach. An SMS-query keyword term is also associated with this component which automatically generates a representation for each document by extracting the frequency of the SMS-query keyword terms from the document contents. The reformulated query processing System consists of two subsystems: Searching-Matching Unit and Displaying-Ranking Unit.

Searching unit allows user to search the documents from the document database, and matching unit does a comparison of all documents against the user's query. To improve the predicted relevance of the retrieved document, the reformulated query is searched against the databases. Searching-Matching unit does a thorough search and finds out which documents match the user query. This unit retrieves almost all the documents that match either part or whole of the entire query, that is, the unit retrieves relevant amid nonrelevant documents. Displaying unit displays the search results based on relevance of the documents to user information needs, and ranking unit ranks the document according to the relevance of the user query. Displaying-Ranking unit does a detailed display of search results and find out which documents have high RSV to be considered as the top ranked documents. Therefore, IR system ranks the documents according to the RSV between document and the query. If a document has got high RSV, that document is closer to the query.

Generally, IR system ranks the list of documents in the descending order. After processing the query effectively, the top most relevant documents are retrieved, and it is given to the user. Though relevance feedback is one of the processes in an IR system that seeks to improve the system's performance based on a user's feedback, it modifies queries using judgments of the relevance of few, highly-ranked documents and has historically been an important method for increasing the performance of IR systems. Specifically, the user's judgments of the relevance or nonrelevance of some of the documents retrieved are used to add new terms to the query and to reweigh query terms. For example, if all the documents, that the user judges as relevant contain a particular term, then, that term may be a good one to add to the original query. It is made known that relevance feedback has improved the system's overall performance by 60% to 170% for different document collections [7]. Given the apparent effectiveness of relevance feedback techniques, it is important that any proposed model of information retrieval includes these techniques.

3. Literature Review

In designing GA, there are three main components which had to be taken into consideration [8]. This research study presents an application of GA as relevant feedback method aiming to adapt keywords weights. In the following, we shall give the three main components; the first one is coding the problem solutions; subsequent is to find a fitness function that can optimize the performance, and, finally, the set of parameters includes the population size, population structure, and genetic operators. Genetic algorithms are generally used for solving timetabling [9], stock marketing [10], and job scheduling [11] problems. A Genetic Algorithm (GA) is used as a powerful tool to search solutions in the domain of relevant features and is suitable for the IR for the justifications discussed in [12, 13].

Ever since the advent of the public network Internet, the quantity of available information is rapidly rising. One of the most important uses of this public network is to find information. In such a huge and unstable information collection, today's greatest problem is to find relevant information. It is necessary to improve the existing search agents. Diverse proposals that use GAs in Internet search with this aim are put forward.

According to [14], proposed the problems of existing internet search engines are examined, and, hence, the need for a novel design is warranted. To make search engines work more efficiently, new thoughts on how to improve existing Internet engines are presented, and then an adaptive technique for Internet metasearch engines with a multiagent, especially the mobile agent, is presented. In the technique, the understanding between stationary and mobile agents is used as an indication to make it more competence. However, the metasearch engine gives the user needed documents based on the multiagent mechanism. The combination of the results obtained from the search engines in the network is done in parallel. In this regards, a feedback mechanism gives the metasearch engine the user's suggestions about the found documents, which leads to a new query using a genetic algorithm.

Reference [15] proposed a new technique that, given a keyword query, on the fly generates new pages, called composed pages, which include all query keywords. The composed pages are generated by extracting and mending together relevant pieces from hyperlinked Web pages and retaining links to the original Web pages. To rank the composed pages, both the hyperlink structure of the original pages and the associations between the keywords in each page are considered. The proposed technique is used to evaluate heuristic algorithms to efficiently generate top composed pages.

Reference [16] uses GAs for user modelling of adaptive and exploratory behaviour in an information retrieval system. Maleki Dizaji choices of the underlying genetic operators are mentioned as a major drawback in the use of GAs. However, GA is primarily used to solve optimization problems; their use for information retrieval is gaining ground.

Reference [17] proposed an improved GA which solves the issues in two-generation competitive genetic algorithm. So, it changes the selection technique of the simple genetic algorithms and improves search efficiency, but local best search ability cannot be improved. The proposed algorithm does the adaptive adjustment of the mutation probability and the position of crossover and mutation probability in chromosomes.

According to [18] they surveyed an effective GA that monitor the success of internet database management system by combining functionality, quality, and complexity of query optimizer for finding good solutions to the problem.

Also [19] they proposed a framework for web mining, the applications of data mining and knowledge discovery techniques to data collected in WWW, and a genetic search for search engines. The authors defined an evaluation function that is a mathematical formulation of the user request to define a steady state GA that evolves a population of pages with binary tournament selection. This approach chooses one crossover position within the page randomly and exchanges the link after that position between both individuals (web pages).

According to [20] they proposed a class-based internet document management and access system, ACRID; it uses machine learning techniques to organize and retrieve Internet documents. The knowledge acquisition process of ACRID automatically learns the classification knowledge from classified-internet documents into one or more classes. The two-phase search engine in ACRID will use the hierarchical structure for responding to user queries.

According to [21] they proposed and applied a dynamically terminated GA to generate page clippings from web search results. The page clipping synthesis (PCS) search method applies a dynamically terminated GA to generate a set best-of-run page clippings in a controlled amount of time. In the proposed approach the dynamically terminated GA yields cost-effective solutions compared with solutions reached by conventional GAs.

According to [22] they proposed an intelligent personal spider approach for Internet searching. The authors implemented Internet personal spiders based on best first-search and GA techniques. The used GA applies stochastic selection based on Jaccard's fitness, with heuristic-based crossover and mutation operators. These personal spiders dynamically take a set of user's selected starting homepages in the web, based on the existing links and keyword indexing.

According to [23] they proposed the use of genetic programming (GP) to derive approach for the combination of three different sources of evidence for ranking documents in the web search engines. The initialization method of the approach defines the method to create the initial population. Two methods can be adopted, grow or full, which represent small changes in the algorithm to construct the trees. The approach is useful for coping with search engines that can request diverse forms of queries for submission.

Consequently, there has been an increasing interest in the application of GA tools to IR in the last few years. The machine learning concept [24], whose aim is the design of system able to automatically acquire knowledge by themselves, seems to be interesting [22]. GAs are not specifically learning algorithms, but also offering a powerful and domain-independent search ability that can be used in many learning tasks, since learning and selforganization can be considered as optimization problems in many cases. As a result of this reason, the applications of GAs to IR have increased in the last few years. Among others, in the following, we shall examine some of the diverse proposals made in these fields in the last few years.

3.1. Clustering of Document and Terms. In this field, two approaches have been applied for obtaining user-oriented document clusters. According to [25], look for groups of terms appearing with similar frequencies in the documents of collection. The authors consider a GA grouping the terms without maintaining their initial order. The main features of the GA are as follows.

(i) Representation scheme: two different coding schemes are considered to include division-assignment and separator methods.

(ii) Initial population: the first generation of the chromosomes depends on the chosen coding, and the rest of individual are randomly generated.

(iii) Operators: each operator has an application probability associated and is selected spinning the roulette. Different crossover and mutation operators are used.

(iv) Fitness function: a measure of the relative entropy and Pratt's measure are two proposals adopted.

3.2. Matching Function Learning. The objective of matching function learning is to use a GA to generate a similarity measure for a vector space IR system to improve its retrieval efficiency for a defined user. This constitutes new relevance feedback beliefs since matching functions are adapted instead of queries. In this regards, two different variants have been proposed in the specialized literature.

(i) Automatic similarity measure learning: according to [26, 27], they introduced a GA that automatically learn a matching function with relevance feedback. Besides, the similarity functions are represented as trees and a classical generational scheme; the usual GA crossover are considered.

(ii) Linear combination of existing similarity functions: [28] propose a new weighted-matching function, which is the linear combination of different existing similarity functions. The weighting parameters are estimated by a genetic algorithm based on relevance feedback from users. The authors use real coding, a classical generational scheme, two-point crossover, and Gaussian noise mutation. Finally, the algorithm is tested on the Cranfield collection.

Automatic Document Indexing. The applications in this area adapt the descriptions of the documents in the documentary base with the aim of facilitating document retrieval in the face of relevant queries. According to [28] they propose a GA to derive the document descriptions. They choose a binary coding scheme where each description is a fixed length and a binary vector. The genetic population is composed of diverse descriptions for the same document. The fitness function is based on calculating the similarity between the current document description and each of the queries (for which the document is relevant or nonrelevant) by means of the Jaccard's index and, then, computing the average adaptation values of the description for the set of relevant and nonrelevant queries. In Gordon work, GA is considered quite unusual as there is no mutation operator, and the crossover probability is equal to 1. With regard to the selection scheme, the number of copies of each chromosome in the new population is calculated and dividing its adaptation value by the population average. Also [29] propose an algorithm for indexing function learning based on GA, whose aims to obtain an indexing function for the key term weighting of a documentary collection to improve the IR process.

Query Learning. This is the most extended group of applications of genetic algorithms in information retrieval. Every proposal in this group use genetic algorithms either like a relevance feedback method or like an Inductive Query By

TABLE 1: Comparison of Diverse Proposals that use genetic algorithm for internet search.

Diverse proposals	Reason for GA	Chromosomes	Fitness function adopted	Genetic operators used
(Eissa and Alghamdi, 2005) [30]	Genetic algorithm is used to optimize the profiles whereas the relevance feedback is used to adapt it.	Represent a gene as a term, an individual as a document and the population as the profile.	$F(P_i) = k \sum S(D_{Pk}, P_i)/\#D_p$.	Selection.
(Vallim and Coello, 2003) [31]	Combines user's feedback to new documents retrieved by the agent with a genetic algorithm.	Individuals represented by a query vector and its adaptation rate.	$Q = Q + \alpha f$ $F(Q) = f + \beta f$.	Two point crossover and Mutation operator.
(Li et al., 2000) [32]	Realize the scheduling strategy of agent manager.	Search space is represented as weight field in the search engine. Field are search parameters.	Adaptation function $\Phi(\text{agent}) = \Gamma(f, p, c, u, t)$.	One point Cross over and Single point Mutation.
(Caramia et al., 2004) [33]	Select a subset of original pages for which the sum of scores is large.	Chromosomes represent subsets of pages of bounded cardinality. Each page is a gene.	$Ff(c) = \alpha \cdot t_1(C) + \beta \cdot t_2(C) + \gamma \cdot t_3(C)$.	Single point crossover.
(Rocio et al., 2008) [34]	Evolving lofty quality query.	Chromosome is represented as a list of terms where each term corresponds to a gene.	Fitness $(q) = \max(\sigma(c, d_i))$ $d_i \varepsilon A_q$.	Roulette Wheel Selection, Single point crossover, One point mutation.
(Abe et al., 1999) [35]	For evolving information retrieval agents.	Genes are represented by the search parameters.	$F = (\text{SH/MH} + \text{SI/MI}) * (1 - \text{ST/TL}) + (1 - \text{ME/MM})$.	Selection uses ranking strategy, Uniform crossover, and Single Point Mutation.
(Martin-Bautista et al., 1999) [36]	Adaptive internet information retrieval.	Each gene represents a fuzzy subset of the document set by means of a Keyword term and number of occurrences in a document.	$f_i^j = f_i^{j-1} + P_i^j - L_i^j$ where $P^i j$ and $L^i j$ is the pay off of life tax and chromosome number respectively.	Random selection, Double point Crossover, Random Mutation.
(Marghny and Ali, 2005) [19]	Steady state genetic algorithm for optimizing web search.	Initial population is generated by heuristic creation operator which queries standard engines to obtain pages.	Fitness function evaluates web pages is a mathematical formulation of Link quality, Page quality and Mean quality function.	Binary tournament selection, Single point crossover.
(Cheng et al., 1998) [22]	GA implemented as a spider to find most relevant home pages in the entire internet.	Chromosomes represent all input home pages in a set.	Jaccard's coefficient function.	Heuristic based cross over, Simple mutation.
(Lin et al., 2002) [20]	Improving the searching performance.	Initial population represented by binary coding selected at random.	$F_d = (F_{\max} - F_{\min})/F_{\text{aver}}$.	Fitness proportion selection, Adaptive adjusting crossover, Mutation operation range.
(Fan et al., 2003) [37]	Genetic Programming to the ranking function discovery problem leveraging the structural information of HTML documents.	Chromosomes represent html pages.	The fitness evaluation of each ranking tree is done at the level multiple queries. $P_{\text{Avg}} = \sum_{i=1}^{T\,\text{Re}\,l} P_i/T\,\text{Re}\,l$, $P_i = i/\text{Rank}_i$.	Single point Crossover, One point Mutation.

TABLE 1: Continued.

Diverse proposals	Reason for GA	Chromosomes	Fitness function adopted	Genetic operators used
(Milutinovic et al., 2000) [38]	Genetic search algorithms enable intelligent and efficient internet searches.	Chromosomes represent set of input Web sites given by a user.	Jaccard's Function.	Topic Mutation, Spatial Mutation, Temporal Mutation.
(Koorangi and Zamanifar, 2007) [14]	Query reformulation in search engine.	Initial population consists of first five keywords of the user dictionary.	CHK fitness function.	One point crossover, Inversion mutation operator.

Example (IQBE) algorithm. The fundamental of relevance feedback lies in the fact that either users normally formulate queries composed of terms, which do not match the terms (which used to index the relevant documents to their needs) or they do not provide the appropriate weights for the query terms. The operation mode is involving and modifying the previous query (adding and removing terms or changing the weights of the existing query terms), with taking into account the relevance judgements of the documents retrieved by it, and constitutes a good way to solve the latter two problems and to improve the precision, and especially the recall of the previous query [39].

Therefore, IQBE was proposed as "a process in which searchers provide sample documents (examples), and the algorithms induce (or learn) the key concepts in order to find other relevant documents" [22]. This technique is a process for assisting the users in the query formulation process performed by machine learning techniques. It works by taking a set of relevant (and optionally, nonrelevant documents) provided by a user and applying an offline learning process to automatically generate a query describing the user's information needs. Besides, [40] propose a GA for learning queries for Boolean IR system. Although the authors introduce concept approach as a relevance feedback algorithm, the experimentation is actually closer to IQBE framework.

According to [41] they propose a similar GA to that of [25]. They use a real coding with the two-point crossover and random mutation operators (besides, crossover and mutation probabilities are changed throughout the GA run). The selection is based on a classic generational scheme where the chromosomes with a fitness value below the average of the population are eliminated, and the reproduction is performed by Baker's mechanism.

A comprehensive comparison of the diverse proposals prepared by different authors is summarized in Table 1.

4. Conclusion

This paper has dealt with the fundamentals of the information retrieval and genetic algorithm. Issues that can be solved using Genetic Algorithm and research areas in Internet web search are discussed in this paper. It also deals with diverse proposals in Internet web search which are promising and growing research areas. This paper examines the relevance

of genetic algorithm in diverse fields of internet web search some applications of genetic algorithms to information retrieval and a survey of the research works done in Internet web search area have been examined carefully, and the results so far have, thus, been very promising and encouraging.

References

[1] F. G. Erba, Z. Yu, and L. Ting, "Using explicit measures to quantify the potential for personalizing search," *Research Journal of Information Technology*, vol. 3, no. 1, pp. 24–34, 2011.

[2] R. Baeza-Yates and B. Ribeiro-Neto, *Modern Information Retrieval*, Addison Wesley, New York, NY, USA, 1999.

[3] K. Agbele, H. Nyongesa, and A. Adesina, "ICT and information security perspectives in E-health systems," *Journal of Mobile Communication*, vol. 4, pp. 17–22, 2010.

[4] J. H. Holland, *Adaptation in Natural and Artificial Systems*, The University of Michigan Press, Ann Arbor, Mich, USA, 1975.

[5] K. A. DeJong, *An Analysis of the Behaviour of a Class of Genetic Adaptive Systems*, University of Michigan, 1975.

[6] D. E. Goldberg, *Genetic Algorithms in Search, Optimization, Machine Learning*, Addison Wesley, 1989.

[7] G. Salton and C. Buckley, "Improving retrieval performance by relevance feedback," *Journal of the American Society for Information Science*, vol. 41, no. 4, pp. 288–297, 1990.

[8] L. M. Schmitt, "Fundamental study, theory of genetic algorithms," *Theoretical Computer Science*, vol. 259, no. 1-2, pp. 1–61, 2001.

[9] K. Milena, "Solving timetabling problems using genetic algorithms," in *Proceedings of the IEEE 27th International Spring Seminar Electronics Technology: Meeting the Challenges of Electronics Technology Progress*, vol. 1, pp. 96–98, 2004.

[10] L. Lin, L. Cao, J. Wang, and C. Zhang, "The applications of genetic algorithms in stock market data mining optimization," in *Proceedings of the Capital Market*, CRC, Sydney, Australia, 2000.

[11] W. Ying and L. Bin, "Job-shop scheduling using genetic algorithm," in *Proceedings of the IEEE International Conference on Systems, Man and Cybernetics*, pp. 1994–1999, October 1996.

[12] J. F. Frenzel, "Genetic algorithms, a new breed of optimization," *IEEE Potentials*, vol. 12, pp. 21–24, 1993.

[13] L. Tamine, C. Chrisment, and M. Boughanem, "Multiple query evaluation based on an enhanced genetic algorithm," *Information Processing and Management*, vol. 39, no. 2, pp. 215–231, 2003.

[14] M. Koorangi and K. Zamanifar, "A distributed agent based web search using a genetic algorithm," *International Journal of*

Computer Science and Network Security, vol. 7, no. 1, pp. 65–76, 2007.

[15] R. Varadarajan, V. Hristidis, and T. Li, "Beyond single-page web search results," *IEEE Transactions on Knowledge and Data Engineering*, vol. 20, no. 3, pp. 411–424, 2008.

[16] S. Maleki-Dizaji, *Evolutionary learning multi-agent based information retrieval systems [Ph.D. thesis]*, Sheffield Hallam University, 2003.

[17] J. Cheng, W. Chen, L. Chen, and Y. Ma, "The improvement of genetic algorithm searching performance," in *Proceedings of 1st International Conference on Machine Learning and Cybernetics*, pp. 947–951, Beijing, China, November 2002.

[18] M. Sinha and S. V. Chande, "Query optimization using genetic algorithms," *Research Journal of Information Technology*, vol. 2, no. 3, pp. 139–144, 2010.

[19] M. H. Marghny and A. F. Ali, "Web mining based on genetic algorithm," in *Proceedings of the AIML O5 Conference*, CICC, Cairo, Egypt, December 2005.

[20] S. H. Lin, M. C. Chen, J. M. Ho, and Y. M. Huang, "ACIRD: intelligent Internet document organization and retrieval," *IEEE Transactions on Knowledge and Data Engineering*, vol. 14, no. 3, pp. 599–614, 2002.

[21] L. C. Chen, C. J. Luh, and C. Jou, "Generating page clippings from web search results using a dynamically terminated genetic algorithm," *Information Systems*, vol. 30, no. 4, pp. 299–316, 2005.

[22] H. Cheng, C. Yi-Ming, R. Marshal, and Y. Christopher, "An intelligent personal spider (agent) for dynamic Internet/Intranet searching," *Decision Support Systems*, vol. 23, no. 1, pp. 41–58, 1998.

[23] T. P. C. Silva, E. S. de Moura, J. M. B. Cavalcanti, A. S. da Silva, M. G. de Carvalho, and M. A. Gonçalves, "An evolutionary approach for combining different sources of evidence in search engines," *Information Systems*, vol. 34, no. 2, pp. 276–289, 2009.

[24] T. Mitchell, *Machine Learning*, McGraw-Hill, 1997.

[25] A. M. Robertson and P. Willett, "Generation of equifrequent groups of words using a genetic algorithm," *Journal of Documentation*, vol. 50, no. 3, pp. 213–232, 1994.

[26] M. Gordon, "Probabilistic and genetic algorithms for document retrieval," *Communications of the ACM*, vol. 31, no. 10, pp. 1208–1218, 1988.

[27] W. Fan, M. D. Gordon, and P. Pathak, "Discovery of context-specific ranking functions for effective information retrieval using genetic programming," *IEEE Transactions on Knowledge and Data Engineering*, vol. 16, no. 4, pp. 523–527, 2004.

[28] P. Pathak, M. Gordon, and W. Fan, "Effective information retrieval using genetic algorithms based matching functions adaptation," in *Proceedings of the 33rd Annual Hawaii International Conference on System Siences (HICSS '00)*, January 2000.

[29] W. Fan, M. D. Gordon, and P. Pathak, "Personalization of search engine services for effective retrieval and knowledge management," in *Proceedings International Conference on Information Systems (ICIS '00)*, Brisbane, Australia, 2000.

[30] F. Eissa and H. Alghamdi, "Agent based information retrieval system," in *Proceedings of the International Conference Proceedings*, pp. 265–279, 2005.

[31] M. S. Vallim and J. M. A. Coello, "An agent for web information dissemination based on a genetic algorithm," in *IEEE, International Conference on Systems, Man and Cybernetics*, vol. 4, no. 5–8, pp. 3834–3836, 2003.

[32] W. Li, B. Xu, H. Yang, W. C. Chung, and C.-W. Lu, "Application of genetic algorithm in search engine," in *Proceedings of the Proceedings of the International Conference on Microelectronic Systems Education (MSE '00)*, pp. 366–371, IEEE, 2000.

[33] M. Caramia, G. Felici, and A. Pezzoli, "Improving search results with data mining in a thematic search engine," *Computers and Operations Research*, vol. 31, no. 14, pp. 2387–2404, 2004.

[34] L. Rocio, L. Cecchini, M. Carlos, Lorenzetti, G. Ana, and M. Nelida, "Using genetic algorithms to evolve a population of topical queries," *Information Processing and Management*, vol. 44, no. 6, pp. 1863–1878, 2008.

[35] K. Abe, T. Taketa, and H. Nunokawa, "An efficient information retrieval method in WWW using genetic algorithms," *ICPP Workshops*, pp. 522–527, 1999.

[36] M. J. Martin-Bautista, H. Larsen, and M. A. Vila, "A fuzzy genetic algorithm approach to an adaptive information retrieval agent," *Journal of the American Society for Information Science*, vol. 50, no. 9, pp. 760–771, 1999.

[37] W. Fan, M. D. Gordon, P. Pathak, W. Xi, and E. A. Fox, "Ranking function optimization for efficient web search By genetic programming, an empirical study," Department of Computer Science of Virginal Tech, Florida Universities, 2003.

[38] V. Milutinovic, D. Cvetkovic, and J. Mirkovic, "Genetic search based on multiple mutations," *IEEE Computer*, vol. 33, no. 11, pp. 118–119, 2000.

[39] V. Rijsbergen, *Information Retrieval*, Butterworth, 2nd edition, 1979.

[40] M. P. Smith and M. Smith, "The use of genetic programming to build Boolean queries for text retrieval through relevance feedback," *Journal of Information Science*, vol. 23, no. 6, pp. 423–431, 1997.

[41] J. J. Yang and R. R. Korfhage, "Query modification using genetic algorithms in vector space models," *International Journal of Expert Systems*, vol. 7, no. 2, pp. 165–191, 1994.

2

Emotion-Aware Assistive System for Humanistic Care Based on the Orange Computing Concept

Jhing-Fa Wang, Bo-Wei Chen, Wei-Kang Fan, and Chih-Hung Li

Department of Electrical Engineering, National Cheng Kung University, Tainan 70101, Taiwan

Correspondence should be addressed to Jhing-Fa Wang, wangjf@mail.ncku.edu.tw

Academic Editor: Qiangfu Zhao

Mental care has become crucial with the rapid growth of economy and technology. However, recent movements, such as green technologies, place more emphasis on environmental issues than on mental care. Therefore, this study presents an emerging technology called orange computing for mental care applications. Orange computing refers to health, happiness, and physiopsychological care computing, which focuses on designing algorithms and systems for enhancing body and mind balance. The representative color of orange computing originates from a harmonic fusion of passion, love, happiness, and warmth. A case study on a human-machine interactive and assistive system for emotion care was conducted in this study to demonstrate the concept of orange computing. The system can detect emotional states of users by analyzing their facial expressions, emotional speech, and laughter in a ubiquitous environment. In addition, the system can provide corresponding feedback to users according to the results. Experimental results show that the system can achieve an accurate audiovisual recognition rate of 81.8% on average, thereby demonstrating the feasibility of the system. Compared with traditional questionnaire-based approaches, the proposed system can offer real-time analysis of emotional status more efficiently.

1. Introduction

During the past 200 years, the industrial revolution has caused a considerable effect on human lifestyles [1, 2]. A number of changes occurred [3] with the rapid growth of the economy and technology, including the information revolution [3], the second industrial revolution [4], and biotechnology development. Although such evolution was considerably beneficial to humans, it has caused a number of problems, such as capitalism, utilitarianism, poverty gap, global warming, and an aging population [1, 2]. Because of recent changes, a number of people recognized these crises and appealed for effective solutions [5], for example, the green movement [6], which successfully creates awareness of environmental protection and leads to the development of green technology or green computing. However, the green movement does not concentrate on body and mind balance. Therefore, a solution that is feasible for shortening the discrepancy between technology and humanity is of utmost concern.

In 1972, the King of Bhutan proposed a new concept that used gross national happiness (GNH) [7] to describe the standard of living of a country, instead of using gross domestic product (GDP). The GNH has attracted considerable attention because it measured the mental health of people. Similar ideas were also proposed in other works. For example, Andrew Oswald advocated Happiness Economics [8] by combining economics with other research fields, such as psychology and sociology. Moreover, a book entitled "Well-Being" [9], which was written by Daniel Kahneman (a Nobel Prize winner in Economic Sciences in 2002) explained the fundamentals of happy psychology. The common objective of those theories is to upgrade the living quality of humans and to bring more happiness into our daily lives. Recently, the IEEE launched the humanitarian technology challenge (HTC) project (http://www.ieeehtc.org/) [10] by sponsoring resource-constrained areas to build reliable electricity and medical facilities. Such an action also highlights the importance of humanistic care. Similar to the HTC project, Intel has supported a center for aging services technologies

(CAST) (http://www.agingtech.org/), and its objective is to accelerate development of innovative healthcare technologies. Several academic institutes responded to the trend and subsequently initiated medical care research, such as the "CodeBlue" project at Harvard University [11] and "Computers in the Human Interaction Loop" (CHIL) at Carnegie Mellon University [12]. Inspired by those related concepts [1, 2, 6, 8–12], this study devised a research project for studying the new interdisciplinary "Orange Technology" to promote health, happiness, and humanistic care.

Instead of emphasizing the relations between environments and humans, as proposed by green technology, the objective of the orange computing project is to bring more care or happiness to humans and to promote mental wellness for the well-being of society.

Orange computing is an interdisciplinary field that includes computer science, electrical engineering, biomedical engineering, psychology, physiology, cognitive science, and social science.The research scope of orange computing contains the following.

(1) Health and security care for the elderly, children, and infants.

(2) Care and disaster relief for people in disaster-stricken areas.

(3) Care for low-income families.

(4) Body-mind care for people with physiological and psychological problems.

(5) Happiness indicator measurement and happiness enhancement.

To demonstrate the concept of orange computing, a case study on a human-machine interactive and assistive system for emotion care was investigated in this study. The proposed system is capable of recognizing human emotions by analyzing facial expressions and speech. When the detected emotion status exceeds a threshold, an alarm will be send to a doctor or a nurse for further diagnosis and treatment.

The remainder of this paper is organized as follows: Section 2 introduces the orange computing models; Section 3 presents a discussion of a case study on the emotion recognition system for care services; Section 4 summarizes the performance of the proposed method and the analysis results; lastly, Section 5 offers conclusions.

2. Related Work and Orange Computing Concept

Orange computing originates from health informatics, and it contains two research topics: one is physiological care and the other psychological care. Both of the two topics focus on enhancing humans' physical and mental health, enriching positive emotions and finally bring more happiness to others [13, 14]. The physiological and psychological care models of orange computing are similar to the health model in medical expert systems [15, 16], which have been well developed and commonly used in health informatics over several decades.

In a medical expert system, when a user inputs a query through the interface, the system can automatically search predefined knowledge databases and consult with relevant experts or doctors. After querying databases or merging opinions of experts, the system subsequently replies to the user with an appropriate response. In traditional medical expert systems, database querying and feedback usually involve semantic understanding techniques and delicate interface design [17–19], so that users do not feel inconvenient during the process. However, in some telemedical care systems, such as [20], knowledge databases and feedback mechanisms are replaced with caregivers for better interactivity. Recently, expert systems have gradually integrated knowledge-based information management systems with pervasive computing [21]. Although such systems have been prototyped and modeled in several studies [22, 23], they have not been deployed. However, the abovementioned ideas have spurred the development of orange computing.

Happiness informatics, or the happiness model, is the key characteristic of orange computing. Similar to the health model, the happiness model also requires a user input and a predefined database. The input is commonly measured from the biosignals or behavior of a user, for example, facial expressions, emotional speech, laughter, body gestures, gaits, blood pressure, heartbeat rates, electroencephalograms (EEGs), electrocardiograms (ECGs), and electromyograms (EMGs) [24, 25]. With such information, the happiness model can help users evaluate their emotional status in various applications. Nevertheless, it is quite challenging to determine the manner in which to combine those data and determine emotional status [26–28].

3. Case Study

This section demonstrates a technological application for daily humanistic care in home environments. The system uses contactless multimodal recognition techniques to measure positive emotion degree of users. The recognition results can be logged into the database and sent to analysts for further processing. As shown in Figure 1, the ambient devices of the proposed system include multiple audiovisual sensors, a service robot, and a smart TV. The robot is a self-propelled machine with four wheels and serves as a remote agent between users and the server. To interact with users, it is equipped with audiovisual sensors, loudspeakers, and a touch screen. Similar to the robot, the TV is also used for interacting with users.

After the ambient sensors receive signals from users, data are subsequently sent to a processing server through a cloud network. The workflow of the data processing procedures comprises three stages, as follows: the first and second stages are the audiovisual recognition, and the last stage is the feedback stage. The detail of each stage is described as follows.

3.1. Visual Recognition. At the image processing stage, as shown in Figure 2, after video streams are captured by the camera, Haar-like features [29] are extracted and sent to

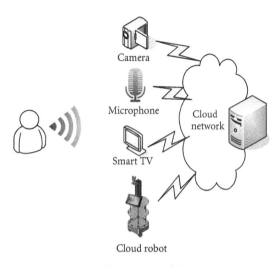

FIGURE 1: Framework of the system.

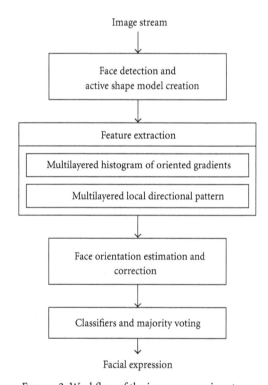

FIGURE 2: Workflow of the image processing stage.

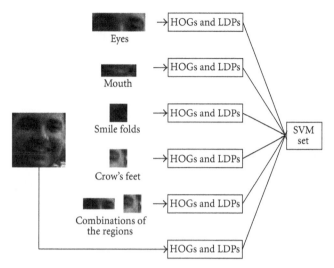

FIGURE 3: Concept of multilayered histogram of oriented gradients and multilayered local directional patterns (the facial image is extracted from the MPLab GENKI database).

to the weight of a coordinate, and θ be edge directions. The histogram of oriented gradients can be expressed as follows:

$$
\begin{aligned}
G_{x,y}^{\text{Horizontal}} &= 2f(x+1,y) - 2f(x-1,y) + f(x+1,y+1) \\
&\quad - f(x-1,y+1) + f(x+1,y-1) \\
&\quad - f(x-1,y-1), \\
G_{x,y}^{\text{Vertical}} &= 2f(x,y+1) - 2f(x,y-1) + f(x+1,y+1) \\
&\quad - f(x+1,y-1) + f(x-1,y+1) \\
&\quad - f(x-1,y-1), \\
W_{x,y} &= \left(\left(G_{x,y}^{\text{Horizontal}} \right)^2 + \left(G_{x,y}^{\text{Vertical}} \right)^2 \right)^{1/2}, \\
\theta_{x,y} &= \tan^{-1} \left(\frac{G_{x,y}^{\text{Horizontal}}}{G_{x,y}^{\text{Vertical}}} \right).
\end{aligned}
\tag{1}
$$

After gradients are computed, a histogram of edge directions is subsequently created to collect the number of pixels that belongs to a direction.

Unlike pyramid histogram of oriented gradients, which concentrates on fixed rectangular shapes inside an image, the proposed MLHOGs are modeled by object-based regions of interest (ROIs), such as eyes, mouths, noses, and combinations of ROIs. Furthermore, each objected-based ROI has a dedicated classifier for recognizing the same type of ROIs. A concept example of multilayered histogram of oriented gradients and multilayered local directional patterns is illustrated in Figure 3.

Similar to the proposed MLHOGs, our study also develops a new texture descriptor called "Multilayered Local Directional Pattern" for enhancing recognition rates. Such multilayered directional patterns are computed according to

AdaBoost classifiers [29] to detect user faces. Subsequently, the system uses the Active Shape Model, which was proposed by Cootes et al. [30], to model facial regions. Thus, facial regions can be represented by a set of points using the point distribution model.

A novel feature called "Multilayered Histogram of Oriented Gradients" (MLHOGs) is proposed in this study to generate reliable characteristics for estimating facial expressions. The MLHOGs are derived from Histograms of Oriented Gradients (HOGs) [31] and Pyramid Histograms of Oriented Gradients (PHOGs) [32]. Let $f(x, y)$ represent the pixel of coordinate x and y, G denote gradients, W refer "edge responses" of pixels, which are based on the same concept of Jabid's feature, "Local Directional Patterns (LDPs)" [33]. The difference is that the proposed method focuses on patterns at various ROI levels. Computation of multilayered local directional patterns is listed as follows:

$$\mathbf{R}_\psi = \mathbf{F} * \mathbf{M}_\psi, \tag{2}$$

$$\varepsilon_\psi = \sum_{\forall \text{block}_{3\times3}} \text{LDP}_{\text{Binary Code}}\left(\mathbf{R}_\psi\right), \tag{3}$$

where $\mathbf{F}$ is the input image, $\mathbf{M}$ means eight-directional Kirsch edge masks like Sobel operators, $\mathbf{R}$ stands for edge responses of $\mathbf{F}$, ψ represents eight directions, and ε is the number of edge responses in a designated direction. Before the system accumulates the edge responses of $\mathbf{R}$ using (3), an LDP binary operation [33] is imposed on $\mathbf{R}$ to generate an invariant code. A one-by-eight histogram is adopted to collect the edge responses in the eight directions. In the proposed multilayered local directional patterns, only edge responses in objects of interest are collected, so that the histogram differs from ROIs to ROIs.

In addition to upright and full frontal faces, this work also supports roll/yaw angle estimation and correction. The active shape model can label facial regions. Relative positions, proportions of facial regions, and orientations of nonfrontal faces can be measured properly with the use of spatial geometry. Once the direction is determined, corresponding transformation matrices are applied to the nonfrontal faces for pose correction.

At the end of the image processing stage, multiple Support Vector Machines (SVMs) are used to classify facial expressions. Each of the SVMs is trained to recognize a specific facial region. The classification result is generated by majority voting.

3.2. Audio Recognition.
Audio signals and visual data have a considerable effect on deciphering human emotions. Therefore, the audio processing stage focuses on detecting emotional speech and laughter to extract emotional cues from acoustic signals. The workflow at this stage is illustrated in Figure 4.

First, silence segments in audio streams are removed by using voice activity detection (VAD) algorithm. Subsequently, an autocorrelation method called "Average Magnitude Difference Function" (AMDF) [34] is used to extract phoneme information from acoustic data. The AMDF can effectively estimate periodical signals, which are the main characteristics of speech, laughter, and other vowel-based nonspeech sounds. The AMDF is derived as follows:

$$\tau^* = \arg\min_\tau \text{AMDF}(\tau),$$

$$\text{AMDF}(\tau) = \sum_{t=0}^{T-t-1} |S(t) - S(t+\tau)|, \tag{4}$$

where S represents one of the segments in the acoustic signal, T is the length of S, t denotes the time index, and τ is the shifting length. After $\text{AMDF}(\tau)$ reaches the minimum, a

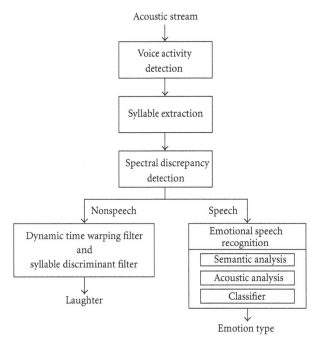

FIGURE 4: Workflow of the audio processing stage.

phoneme $P = [S(\tau^*), S(\tau^*+1), \ldots, S(2\tau^*)]$ can be acquired by extracting indices from $S(\tau^*)$ to $S(2\tau^*)$.

Algorithm 1 expresses the process of syllable extraction when phonemes of a signal are determined.

In the next step, to classify signals into their respective categories, energy and frequency changes are used as the first criteria to separate speech from vowel-based nonspeech because spectral discrepancy of speech is relatively smaller in most cases.

Compared with other vowel-based nonspeech, the temporal pattern of laughter usually exhibits repetitiveness. To detect such patterns, this study uses cascade filters, which consist of a Dynamic Time Warping (DTW) filter [35] and a syllable discriminant filter, to compute similarities of the input data. With the use of Mel-frequency cepstral coefficients (MFCCs), the Dynamic Time Warping filter can find out desired signals by matching them with the samples in the database. The signals that successfully pass through the first filter are subsequently input to the second filter. The syllable discriminant filter compares each input sequence with predefined patterns by using the inner product operation. When the score of an input is higher than a threshold, the input is labeled as laughter.

For emotional speech recognition, this study follows previous works [36–38] and extracts prosodic and timbre features from speech to recognize emotional information in voices. Tables 1 and 2 show the acoustic features used in this system.

In addition to the acoustic features, this study also uses the keyword spotting technique to detect predefined keywords in speech because textual data offer more emotion clues than acoustic data. After detecting predefined keywords in utterances, the system iteratively computes the association

```
Initialization
    designating the beginning phonemes P_start;
For each phoneme P_m
begin
    If Similarity (P_start, P_m) < δ_Similarity
        If Distance (P_{m-1}, P_m) > δ_Distance
            m is the end of asyllable;
end
```

ALGORITHM 1: Algorithm for syllable extraction.

TABLE 1: Timbre features.

Type	Parameter
1st–3rd formants	Frequency
	Mean
	Standard deviation
	Medium
	Bandwidth
Spectrum related	Centroid
	Spread
	Flatness

TABLE 2: Prosodic features.

Type	Parameter
Pitch and energy related	Maximum value
	Minimum value
	Mean
	Medium
	Standard deviation
	Range
	Coefficients of the linear regression
Duration related	Speech rate
	Ratio between voiced and unvoiced regions
	Duration of the longest voiced speech

degree between the detected keyword and each emotion category.

Let i represent the index of the emotion categories; j denote the index of the detected keyword in the sentence corpus; ω_j refer to the detected keyword; $\Gamma(\omega_j, c_i)$ represent the occurrence of ω_j in category c_i; $\Gamma(\omega_j)$ denote the number of sentences containing (ω_j).

The association degree can be defined as

$$e_i(\omega_j) = \frac{\Gamma(\omega_j, c_i)}{\Gamma(\omega_j)} \times \frac{\sum_i \Gamma(\omega_j, c_i)^2}{\Gamma(\omega_j)^2}, \quad (5)$$

where the first part of the equation is the weighting score, and the second part is the confidence score of ω_j (see [39] for detailed information). The textual feature vector is subsequently combined with the acoustic feature vector and sent into a classifier (AdaBoost) for training and recognition.

3.3. Feedback Mechanism. After completion of the audio-visual recognition stage, the system generates three results along with their classification scores. One of the three results is the detected facial expression, another is the detected vocal emotion type, and the other is laughter. The classification scores are linearly combined with the recognition rates of the corresponding classifiers and finally output to users. Additionally, the recognition result is logged in the database 24 hours a day. A user can browse the curve of emotion changes by viewing the display. The system is also equipped with a telehealthcare module. Personal emotion status can be sent to family psychologists or psychiatrists for mental care. The service robot can serve as an agent between the cloud system and users, providing a remote interactive interface.

4. Experimental Results

This study conducted an experiment to test audiovisual emotion recognition to assess the performance of our system. Only positive emotions, including smiling faces, laughter, and joyful voices, were tested in the experiment.

At the evaluation of the facial expression stage, 500 facial images containing smiles and nonsmiles were manually selected from the MPLab GENKI database (http://mplab.ucsd.edu/). The kernel function of the SVM was the radial basis function, and the penalty constant was empirically set to one. Furthermore, 50% of the dataset was used for training, and 50% was used for testing. During the evaluation of laughter recognition, a database consisting of 84 sound clips was created by recording the utterances of six people. Eighteen samples from these 84 clips were the sound of people laughing. After removing silence parts from all of the clips, the entire dataset was subsequently sent into the system for recognition. For emotional speech recognition, this research used the same database as that in our previous work [39]. The speech containing joyful and nonjoyful emotions was manually chosen and parsed to obtain their literal information and acoustic features. Finally, these features were inputted into an AdaBoost classifier for training and testing.

Figure 5 shows a summary of the experimental results of our system, in which the vertical axis denotes accuracy rates,

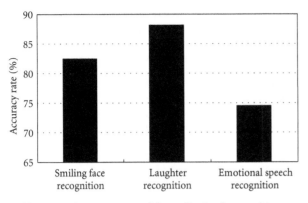

FIGURE 5: Accuracy rates of the audiovisual recognition.

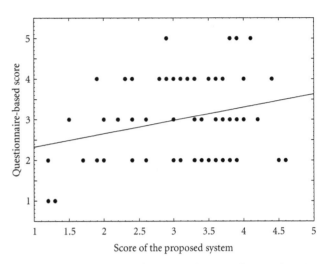

FIGURE 6: Correlation test of the scores between the questionnaire approach and the proposed system. The horizontal axis represents the evaluation result of the proposed system, whereas the vertical axis means the result of the questionnaire. The slope of the regression line is 0.33, and Pearson's correlation coeffcient is 0.27.

and the horizontal axis represents recognition modules. As shown in the figure, the accuracy rate of smile detection can reach 82.5%. The performance of laughter recognition can also achieve an accuracy rate as high as 88.2%. Compared with smile and laughter recognition, although the result of emotional speech recognition reached 74.6%, such performance is comparable to those of related emotional speech recognition systems. When combined with the test result of emotional speech recognition, the overall accuracy rate can reach an average of 81.8%.

The following experiment tests whether the proposed system can help testees remind and evaluate their emotional health status as caregivers do. During the experiment, total ten persons were selected from the sanatorium and the hospital to test the system for a week. The age of the participants ranges from 40 to 70 years old. The audiovisual sensors were installed in their living space, so that the emotional data can be acquired and analyzed in real time. For privacy, the sensors captured behavior only during 10:00 to 16:00. To avoid generating biased data, each testee was not aware of the locations of the sensors and the testing details of the experiment. Furthermore, after the system analyzed the data, the medical doctors and nurses helped testees complete questionnaires. The questionnaire contained total ten questions, nine of which were irrelevant to this experiment. The remaining question was the key criterion that allowed the testees to give a score (one(unhappy)–five(happy)) to their daily moods.

The questionnaire scores are subsequently compared with the estimated emotional status of the proposed system. To obtain the estimated emotional score, the proposed method firstly calculates the duration of smiling face expressions, joyful speech, and laughter of the testees. Next, a ratio can be computed by converting the duration into a one-to-five rating scale based on the test period.

The correlation test in Figure 6 shows performance of the questionnaire approach and the proposed system. The vertical axis represents the questionnaire result, whereas the score of the proposed system is listed on the horizontal axis. All the samples are collected from the testees. Closely examining the scatterness in this figure reveals that Pearson's correlation coefficient reaches as high as 0.27. This implies that our method is analogous with the questionnaire-based

approach. Moreover, two groups of the scores in the linear regression analysis reflect a linear rate of 0.33. Above findings indicate that the proposed method can allow computers to monitor users' emotional health, subsequently assisting caregivers in reminding users' psychological status and saving more human resources.

5. Conclusion

This paper presents a new concept called orange computing for health, happiness, and humanistic care. To demonstrate the concept, a case study on the audiovisual emotion recognition system for care services is also conducted. The system uses multimodal recognition techniques, including facial expression, laughter, and emotional speech recognition to capture human behavior.

At the facial expression recognition stage, multilayered histograms of oriented gradients and multilayered local directional patterns are proposed to model facial features. To detect patterns of laughing sound, two cascade filters consisting of a Dynamic Time Warping filter and a syllable discriminant filter are used in the acoustic processing phase. Furthermore, when classifying emotional speech, the system combines textual, timbre, and prosodic features to calculate association degree to predefined emotion classes.

Three analyses are conducted for evaluating recognition performance of the proposed methods. Experimental results show that our system can reach an average accuracy rate of 81.8%. Concerning the feedback mechanism, data from the real-life test indicate that our method is comparable to the questionnaire-based approach. Additionally, correlation degree between two methods is as high as 0.27. The above results demonstrate that the proposed system is capable of recognizing users' emotional health and thereby providing an in-time reminder for them.

In summary, orange computing hopes to arouse awareness of the importance of mental wellness (health, happiness, and warming care), subsequently leading more people to join the movement, to share happiness with others, and finally to enhance the well-being of society.

Acknowledgments

This work was supported in part by the National Science Council of the Republic of China under Grant no. 100-2218-E-006-017. The authors would like to thank Yan-You Chen, Yi-Cheng Chen, Wei-Kang Fan, Chih-Hung Li, and Da-Yu Kwan for contributing the experimental data and supporting this research.

References

[1] M. C. Jensen, "The modern industrial revolution, exit, and the failure of internal control systems," *Journal of Applied Corporate Finance*, vol. 22, no. 1, pp. 43–58, 1993.

[2] F. Dunachie, "The success of the industrial revolution and the failure of political revolutions: how Britain got lucky," *Historical Notes*, vol. 26, pp. 1–7, 1996.

[3] Y. Veneris, "Modelling the transition from the industrial to the informational revolution," *Environment & Planning A*, vol. 21, no. 3, pp. 399–416, 1990.

[4] J. Hull, "The second industrial revolution: the history of a concept," *Storia Della Storiografia*, vol. 36, pp. 81–90, 1999.

[5] P. Ashworth, "High technology and humanity for intensive care," *Intensive Care Nursing*, vol. 6, no. 3, pp. 150–160, 1990.

[6] P. Gilk, *Green Politics is Eutopian*, Lutterworth Press, Cambridge, UK, 2009.

[7] S. B. F. Hargens, "Integral development—taking the middle path towards gross national happiness," *Journal of Bhutan Studies*, vol. 6, pp. 24–87, 2002.

[8] A. J. Oswald, "Happiness and economic performance," *Economic Journal*, vol. 107, no. 445, pp. 1815–1831, 1997.

[9] D. Kahneman, E. Diener, and N. Schwarz, *Well-Being : The Foundations of Hedonic Psychology*, Russell Sage Foundation Publications, New York, NY, USA, 1998.

[10] K. Passino, "World-wide education for the humanitarian technology challenge," *IEEE Technology and Society Magazine*, vol. 29, no. 2, p. 4, 2010.

[11] K. Lorincz, D. J. Malan, T. R. F. Fulford-Jones et al., "Sensor networks for emergency response: Challenges and opportunities," *IEEE Pervasive Computing*, vol. 3, no. 4, pp. 16–23, 2004.

[12] A. Waibel, "Speech processing in support of human-human communication," in *Proceedings of the 2nd International Symposium on Universal Communication (ISUC '08)*, p. 11, Osaka, Japan, December 2008.

[13] J.-F. Wang, B.-W. Chen, Y.-Y. Chen, and Y.-C. Chen, "Orange computing: challenges and opportunities for affective signal processing," in *Proceedings of the International Conference on Signal Processing, Communications and Computing*, pp. 1–4, Xian, China, September 2011.

[14] J.-F. Wang and B.-W. Chen, "Orange computing: challenges and opportunities for awareness science and technology," in *Proceedings of the 3rd International Conference on Awareness Science and Technology*, pp. 538–540, Dalian, China, September 2011.

[15] Y. Hata, S. Kobashi, and H. Nakajima, "Human health care system of systems," *IEEE Systems Journal*, vol. 3, no. 2, pp. 231–238, 2009.

[16] K. Siau, "Health care informatics," *IEEE Transactions on Information Technology in Biomedicine*, vol. 7, no. 1, pp. 1–7, 2003.

[17] K. Kawamura, W. Dodd, and P. Ratanaswasd, "Robotic body-mind integration: Next grand challenge in robotics," in *Proceedings of the 13th IEEE International Workshop on Robot and Human Interactive Communication (RO-MAN '04)*, pp. 23–28, Kurashiki, Okayama, Japan, September 2004.

[18] P. Belimpasakis and S. Moloney, "A platform for proving family oriented RESTful services hosted at home," *IEEE Transactions on Consumer Electronics*, vol. 55, no. 2, pp. 690–698, 2009.

[19] L. S. A. Low, N. C. Maddage, M. Lech, L. B. Sheeber, and N. B. Allen, "Detection of clinical depression in adolescents' speech during family interactions," *IEEE Transactions on Biomedical Engineering*, vol. 58, no. 3, pp. 574–586, 2011.

[20] C. Yu, J.-J. Yang, J.-C. Chen et al., "The development and evaluation of the citizen telehealth care service system: case study in Taipei," in *Proceedings of the 31st Annual International Conference of the IEEE Engineering in Medicine and Biology Society (EMBC '09)*, pp. 6095–6098, Minneapolis, Minn, USA, September 2009.

[21] J. B. Jørgensen and C. Bossen, "Executable use cases: requirements for a pervasive health care system," *IEEE Software*, vol. 21, no. 2, pp. 34–41, 2004.

[22] A. Mihailidis, B. Carmichael, and J. Boger, "The use of computer vision in an intelligent environment to support aging-in-place, safety, and independence in the home," *IEEE Transactions on Information Technology in Biomedicine*, vol. 8, no. 3, pp. 238–247, 2004.

[23] Y. Hata, S. Kobashi, and H. Nakajima, "Human health care system of systems," *IEEE Systems Journal*, vol. 3, no. 2, pp. 231–238, 2009.

[24] Y. Gizatdinova and V. Surakka, "Feature-based detection of facial landmarks from neutral and expressive facial images," *IEEE Transactions on Pattern Analysis and Machine Intelligence*, vol. 28, no. 1, pp. 135–139, 2006.

[25] R. A. Calvo and S. D'Mello, "Affect detection: an interdisciplinary review of models, methods, and their applications," *IEEE Transactions on Affective Computing*, vol. 1, no. 1, pp. 18–37, 2010.

[26] C. Busso and S. S. Narayanan, "Interrelation between speech and facial gestures in emotional utterances: a single subject study," *IEEE Transactions on Audio, Speech and Language Processing*, vol. 15, no. 8, pp. 2331–2347, 2007.

[27] Y. Wang and L. Guan, "Recognizing human emotional state from audiovisual signals," *IEEE Transactions on Multimedia*, vol. 10, no. 4, pp. 659–668, 2008.

[28] Z. Zeng, J. Tu, B. M. Pianfetti, and T. S. Huang, "Audio-visual affective expression recognition through multistream fused HMM," *IEEE Transactions on Multimedia*, vol. 10, no. 4, pp. 570–577, 2008.

[29] P. Viola and M. Jones, "Rapid object detection using a boosted cascade of simple features," in *Proceedings of the IEEE Computer Society Conference on Computer Vision and Pattern Recognition*, pp. I511–I518, Kauai, Hawaii, USA, December 2001.

[30] T. F. Cootes, C. J. Taylor, D. H. Cooper, and J. Graham, "Active shape models-their training and application," *Computer Vision and Image Understanding*, vol. 61, no. 1, pp. 38–59, 1995.

[31] N. Dalal and B. Triggs, "Histograms of oriented gradients for human detection," in *Proceedings of the IEEE Computer Society Conference on Computer Vision and Pattern Recognition (CVPR '05)*, pp. 886–893, San Diego, Calif, USA, June 2005.

[32] A. Bosch, A. Zisserman, and X. Munoz, "Representing shape with a spatial pyramid kernel," in *Proceedings of the 6th ACM International Conference on Image and Video Retrieval (CIVR '07)*, pp. 401–408, Amsterdam, Netherlands, July 2007.

[33] T. Jabid, M. H. Kabir, and O. Chae, "Local Directional Pattern (LDP)—a robust image descriptor for object recognition," in *Proceedings of the 7th IEEE International Conference on Advanced Video and Signal Based Surveillance (AVSS '10)*, pp. 482–487, Boston, Mass, USA, September 2010.

[34] C. K. Un and S.-C. Yang, "A pitch extraction algorithm based on LPC inverse filtering and AMDF," *IEEE Transactions on Acoustics, Speech, and Signal Processing*, vol. 25, no. 6, pp. 565–572, 1977.

[35] J.-F. Wang, J.-C. Wang, M.-H. Mo, C.-I. Tu, and S.-C. Lin, "The design of a speech interactivity embedded module and its applications for mobile consumer devices," *IEEE Transactions on Consumer Electronics*, vol. 54, no. 2, pp. 870–876, 2008.

[36] S. Casale, A. Russo, G. Scebba, and S. Serrano, "Speech emotion classification using Machine Learning algorithms," in *Proceedings of the 2nd Annual IEEE International Conference on Semantic Computing (ICSC '08)*, pp. 158–165, Santa Clara, Calif, USA, August 2008.

[37] C. Busso, S. Lee, and S. Narayanan, "Analysis of emotionally salient aspects of fundamental frequency for emotion detection," *IEEE Transactions on Audio, Speech and Language Processing*, vol. 17, no. 4, pp. 582–596, 2009.

[38] N. D. Cook, T. X. Fujisawa, and K. Takami, "Evaluation of the affective valence of speech using pitch substructure," *IEEE Transactions on Audio, Speech and Language Processing*, vol. 14, no. 1, pp. 142–151, 2006.

[39] Y.-Y. Chen, B.-W. Chen, J.-F. Wang, and Y.-C. Chen, "Emotion aware system based on acoustic and textual features from speech," in *Proceedings of the 2nd International Symposium on Aware Computing (ISAC '10)*, pp. 92–96, Tainan, Taiwan, November 2010.

3

Aware Computing in Spatial Language Understanding Guided by Cognitively Inspired Knowledge Representation

Masao Yokota

Department of System Management, Fukuoka Institute of Technology, Fukuoka 811-0295, Japan

Correspondence should be addressed to Masao Yokota, yokota@fit.ac.jp

Academic Editor: Keitaro Naruse

Mental image directed semantic theory (MIDST) has proposed an omnisensory mental image model and its description language L_{md}. This language is designed to represent and compute human intuitive knowledge of space and can provide multimedia expressions with intermediate semantic descriptions in predicate logic. It is hypothesized that such knowledge and semantic descriptions are controlled by human attention toward the world and therefore subjective to each human individual. This paper describes L_{md} expression of human subjective knowledge of space and its application to aware computing in cross-media operation between linguistic and pictorial expressions as spatial language understanding.

1. Introduction

The serious need for more human-friendly intelligent systems has been brought by rapid increase of aged societies, floods of multimedia information over the WWW, development of robots for practical use, and so on. For example, it is very difficult for people to exploit necessary information from the immense multimedia contents over the WWW. It is still more difficult to search for desirable contents by queries in different media, for example, text queries for pictorial contents. In this case, intelligent systems facilitating cross-media references are helpful and worth developing. In this research area so far, it has been most conventional that conceptual contents conveyed by information media such as languages and pictures are represented in computable forms independent of each other and translated via so-called "transfer" processes which are often ad hoc and very specific to task domains [1–3].

In order to systematize cross-media operation, however, it is needed to develop such a computable knowledge representation language for multimedia contents that should have at least a good capability of representing spatiotemporal events perceived by people in the real world. For this purpose, mental image directed semantic theory (MIDST) has proposed a model of human mental image and its description

language L_{md} (Language for mental-image description) [4]. This language is capable of formalizing human omnisensory mental images (equal to multimedia contents, here) in predicate logic, while other knowledge description schema [5, 6] are too coarse or linguistic (or English-like) to formalize them in an integrative way as intended here. L_{md} is employed for many-sorted predicate logic and has been implemented on several versions of the intelligent system IMAGES [4, 7] and there is a feedback loop between them for their mutual refinement unlike other similar theories [8, 9].

As detailed in the following sections, MIDST was rigidly formalized as a deductive system [10] in the formal language L_{md}, which is remarkably distinguished from other work (e.g., [5, 8]). However, its application to computerized systems is another thing because computational cost of logical formulas is very high in general. In fact, however, the deductive system contains a considerable number of theses or postulates much easier to realize in imperative programming (e.g., in C) than in declarative programming (e.g., in Prolog) because L_{md} expressions normalized by atomic locus formulas are very suitable to structure and operate in table so-called Hitree [11]. Conventionally, it is as well convinced that hybrid computation based on both the programming paradigms is more flexible and efficient than that based on only one of them. This is also the case for each version of IMAGES so far and therefore the author has been promoting to replace declarative programs with imperative ones considering the benefit of L_{md} expression. This paper focuses as well on the hybrid computation guided by L_{md} expression and 3D map data, here so-called partially symbolized direct knowledge of space (PSDKS), in cross-media operation between linguistic and pictorial expressions as spatial language understanding. That is, static spatial relations among objects as 3D map data for imperative programming are utilized as well as those in L_{md} for declarative programming.

The remainder of this paper is organized as follows. Section 2 presents the omnisensory mental image model and its relation to the formal language L_{md}. Section 3 describes representation of subjective spatial knowledge in L_{md}. In Sections 4 and 5 are sketched several cognitive hypotheses on mental images for their systematic computation. Section 6 describes the systematic cross-media operation based on L_{md} expression. Section 7 gives the details of direct knowledge of space. In Section 8, is described an example of cross-media operation by IMAGES. Some discussion and conclusion are given in the final section.

2. Mental Image Model and L_{md}

An attribute space corresponds with a sensory system and can be compared to a certain measuring instrument just like a barometer, thermometer or so, and the loci represent the movements of its indicator. A general locus is to be articulated by "Atomic Locus" over a certain absolute time interval $[t_i, t_f]$ as depicted in Figure 1 and formulated as (1) in L_{md}, where the interval is suppressed because people are not aware of absolute time (nor always consult a chronograph).

$$L(x, y, p, q, a, g, k). \qquad (1)$$

This is a formula in many-sorted predicate logic, where "L" is a predicate constant with five types of terms: "Matter" (at "x" and "y"), "Value (of Attribute)" (at "p" and "q"), "Attribute" (at "a"), "Pattern (of Event)" (at "g"), and "Standard" (at "k"). Conventionally, Matter variables are headed by "x", "y," and "z."

This formula is called "Atomic Locus Formula" whose first two arguments are sometimes referred to as "Event Causer (EC)" and "Attribute Carrier (AC)," respectively, while ECs are often optional in natural concepts such as intransitive verbs. By the way, hereafter, the terms at AC and Standard are often replaced by "_" when they are of little significance to discern one another. The parameters "g" and "k" cannot be denoted explicitly in Figure 1 because their roles vary drastically depending on its interpretation.

The intuitive interpretation of (1) is given as follows.

> "Matter " x " causes Attribute " a " of Matter " y " to keep $(p = q)$ or change $(p \neq q)$ its values temporally $(g = G_t)$ or spatially $(g = G_s)$ over an absolute time-interval, where the values " p " and " q " are relative to the standard " k "."

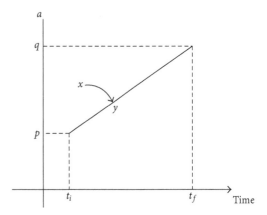

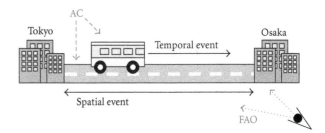

FIGURE 1: Graphical interpretation of Atomic Locus—the curved arrow indicates the abstract effect from "x" to "y."

FIGURE 2: FAO movements and Event types.

When $g = G_t$ and $g = G_s$, the locus indicates monotonic change or constancy of the attribute in time domain and that in space domain, respectively. The former is called "temporal change event" and the latter, "spatial change event," which are assumed to correspond with temporal and spatial gestalt in psychology, respectively. For example, the motion of the "bus" represented by (S1) is a temporal change event and the ranging or extension of the "road" by (S2) is a spatial change event whose meanings or concepts are formulated as (2) and (3), respectively, where "A_{12}" denotes the attribute "Physical Location". These two formulas are different only at the term "Pattern."

(S1) The bus runs from Tokyo to Osaka.

$$(\exists x, y, k)L(x, y, \text{Tokyo}, \text{Osaka}, A_{12}, G_t, k) \land \text{bus}(y). \qquad (2)$$

(S2) The road runs from Tokyo to Osaka.

$$(\exists x, y, k)L(x, y, \text{Tokyo}, \text{Osaka}, A_{12}, G_s, k) \land \text{road}(y). \qquad (3)$$

The difference between temporal and spatial change event concepts can be attributed to the relationship between the Attribute Carrier (AC) and the Focus of the Attention of the Observer (FAO). To be brief, FAO is fixed on the whole AC in a temporal change event but runs about on the AC in a spatial change event. Consequently, as shown in Figure 2, the bus and the FAO move together in the case of (S1) while FAO

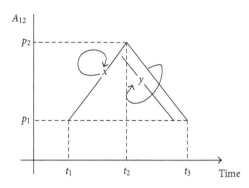

FIGURE 3: Conceptual image of "fetch."

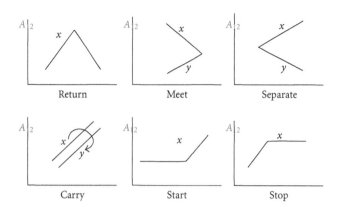

FIGURE 4: Event patterns of physical location (A_{12}).

solely moves along the road in the case of (S2). That is, *all loci in attribute spaces correspond one to one with movements or, more generally, temporal change events of FAO.*

Articulated loci are combined with tempological conjunctions, where "SAND ($\wedge_0$)" and "CAND ($\wedge_1$)" are most frequently utilized, standing for "Simultaneous AND" and "Consecutive AND", conventionally symbolized as "$\sqcap$" and "$\cdot$," respectively. The formula (4) refers to a temporal change event depicted as Figure 3, implying that "x" goes to some location and then comes back with "y" and corresponding to such a verbal expression as "x fetches y from some location":

$$(\exists x, y, p_1, p_2, k) L(x, x, p_1, p_2, A_{12}, G_t, k)$$

$$\cdot \left(L(x, x, p_2, p_1, A_{12}, G_t, k) \sqcap L(x, y, p_2, p_1, A_{12}, G_t, k) \right)$$

$$\wedge x \neq y \wedge p_1 \neq p_2. \tag{4}$$

As easily imagined, an event expressed in L_{md} is compared to a movie film taken through a floating camera where both temporal and spatial extensions of the event are recorded as a time sequence of snapshots because it is necessarily grounded in FAO's movement over the event. This is one of the most remarkable features of L_{md}, clearly distinguished from other knowledge representation languages (KRLs).

The attribute spaces for humans correspond to the sensory receptive fields in their brains. At present, about 50 attributes and 6 categories of standards concerning the physical world have been extracted from thesauri. Event patterns are the most important for our approach and have been already reported concerning several kinds of attributes [4, 7]. Figure 4 shows several examples of event patterns in the attribute space of "physical location (A_{12})."

3. Representation of Subjective Spatial Knowledge

MIDST can provide human knowledge pieces with flat L_{md} expressions as human mental images, not concerning whether they are concepts meant by certain symbols (i.e., semantic) or not. Therefore, such a distinction is not denoted explicitly hereafter. There are assumed two major hypotheses

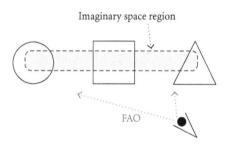

FIGURE 5: Row as spatial change event.

on mental image. One is that mental image is in one-to-one correspondence with FAO movement as mentioned above. And, the other is that it is not one-to-one reflection of the real world. It is well known that people perceive more than reality, for example, so-called "Gestalt" in psychology. A psychological matter here is not a real matter but a product of human mental functions, including Gestalt and abstract matters such as "society" and "information" in a broad sense. For example, Figure 5 concerns the perception of the formation of multiple objects, where FAO runs along an imaginary object so called "*Imaginary Space Region (ISR).*" This spatial change event can be verbalized as (S3) using the preposition "between" and formulated as (5) or (6), corresponding also to such concepts as "row," and "line-up," where A_{13} denotes the attribute "Direction".

Employing ISRs and the 9-intersection model [12], all the topological relations between two objects can be formulated in such expressions as (7) or (8) for (S4), and (9) for (S5), where "In," "Cont," and "Dis" are the values "inside", "contains" and "disjoint" of the attribute "Topology (A_{44})" with the standard "9-intersection model (K_{9IM})," respectively. Practically, these topological values are given as 3×3 matrices with each element equal to 0 or 1 and therefore, for example, "In" and "Cont" are transposes each other. That is, Cont = In^T.

(S3) The square is between the triangle and the circle.

(S4) Tom is in the room.

(S5) Tom exits the room.

$(\exists x_1, x_2, x_3, y, p, q)$

$(L(\_, y, x_1, x_2, A_{12}, G_s, \_) \sqcap L(\_, y, p, p, A_{13}, G_s, \_))$

$\cdot (L(\_, y, x_2, x_3, A_{12}, G_s, \_) \sqcap L(\_, y, q, q, A_{13}, G_s, \_))$ (5)

$\land \; \mathrm{ISR}(y) \land p = q \land \mathrm{triangle}(x_1)$

$\land \; \mathrm{square}(x_2) \land \mathrm{circle}(x_3),$

$(\exists x_1, x_2, x_3, y, p)$

$(L(\_, y, x_1, x_2, A_{12}, G_s, \_) \cdot L(\_, y, x_2, x_3, A_{12}, G_s, \_))$

$\sqcap L(\_, y, p, p, A_{13}, G_s, \_) \land \mathrm{ISR}(y)$ (6)

$\land \; \mathrm{triangle}(x_1) \land \mathrm{square}(x_2) \land \mathrm{circle}(x_3),$

$(\exists x, y) L(\mathrm{Tom}, x, y, \mathrm{Tom}, A_{12}, G_s, \_)$

$\sqcap L(\mathrm{Tom}, x, \mathrm{In}, \mathrm{In}, A_{44}, G_t, K_{9\mathrm{IM}}) \land \mathrm{ISR}(x) \land \mathrm{room}\,(y),$ (7)

$(\exists x, y) L(\mathrm{Tom}, x, \mathrm{Tom}, y, A_{12}, G_s, \_)$

$\sqcap L(\mathrm{Tom}, x, \mathrm{Cont}, \mathrm{Cont}, A_{44}, G_t, K_{9\mathrm{IM}})$ (8)

$\land \; \mathrm{ISR}(x) \land \mathrm{room}(y),$

$(\exists x, y, p, q) L(\mathrm{Tom}, \mathrm{Tom}, p, q, A_{12}, G_t, \_)$

$\sqcap L(\mathrm{Tom}, x, y, \mathrm{Tom}, A_{12}, G_s, \_)$

$\sqcap L(\mathrm{Tom}, x, \mathrm{In}, \mathrm{Dis}, A_{44}, G_t, K_{9\mathrm{IM}}) \land \mathrm{ISR}(x)$ (9)

$\land \; \mathrm{room}(y) \land p \neq q.$

With a special attention, the author has analyzed a considerable number of spatial terms over various kinds of English words such as prepositions, verbs, adverbs, and so forth, categorized as "Dimensions," "Form," and "Motion" in the class "SPACE" of the Roget's thesaurus [13], and found that almost all the concepts of spatial change events can be defined in exclusive use of five kinds of attributes for FAOs, namely, "Physical location (A_{12})," "Direction (A_{13})," "Trajectory (A_{15})," "Mileage (A_{17})," and "Topology (A_{44})."

4. Hypothetical Operations upon Mental Images

People can transform their mental images in several ways such as mental rotation [14]. Here are introduced and defined 3 kinds of mental operations, namely, "reversing," "duplicating," and "converting."

4.1. Image Reversing. It is easy for people to imagine the reversal of an event just like "rise" versus "sink." This mental operation is here denoted as "R" and recursively defined as O_R, where χ_i stands for a image. The reversed values p^R and q^R depend on the properties of the attribute values p and q. For example, $p^R = p$, $q^R = q$ for A_{12}; $p^R = -p$, $q^R = -q$ for A_{13}; $p^R = p^T$, $q^R = q^T$ for A_{44}.

O_R:

$$\left(\chi_1 \cdot \chi_2\right)^R \iff \chi_2^R \cdot \chi_1^R,$$

$$\left(\chi_1 \sqcap \chi_2\right)^R \iff \chi_1^R \sqcap \chi_2^R,$$ (10)

$$L^R(x, y, p, q, a, g, k) \iff L\left(x, y, q^R, p^R, a, g, k\right).$$

4.2. Image Duplicating. Humans can easily imagine the repetition of an event just like "visit twice" versus "visit once." This operation is also recursively defined as O_n, where "n" is an integer representing the frequency of an image χ.

O_n:

$$\chi^n \iff \chi \quad (n = 1),$$

$$\chi^n \iff \chi \cdot \chi^{n-1} \quad (n > 1).$$ (11)

4.3. Image Converting. We can convert temporal and spatial change event images each other and this is the reason why it is easy for us to understand instantly such an expression as (S2). This mental operation is here denoted as "C" and recursively defined as O_C, which will help a robot to cope with such a somewhat queer expression as "The road jumps up at the point. Be careful!".

O_C:

$$\left(\chi_1 \cdot \chi_2\right)^C \iff \chi_1^C \cdot \chi_2^C,$$

$$\left(\chi_1 \sqcap \chi_2\right)^C \iff \chi_1^C \sqcap \chi_2^C,$$ (12)

$$L^C(x, y, p, q, a, g, k) \iff L\left(x, y, p, q, a, g^C, k\right),$$

where $g^C = G_s$ for $g = G_t$ and $g^C = G_t$ for $g = G_s$.

5. Hypothetical Properties of Mental Images

Properties or laws of mental images as spatial knowledge pieces are formalized in L_{md} and introduced as postulates and their derivatives in a deductive system [10] to be employed in theorem proving there. Here are described two examples of such postulates, namely, "Postulate of Reversibility of Spatial Change Event" and "Postulate of Partiality of Matter."

5.1. Postulate of Reversibility of Spatial Change Event. As already mentioned in Section 2, all loci in attribute spaces are assumed to correspond one to one with movements or, more generally, temporal change events of the FAO. Therefore, the L_{md} expression of an event is compared to a movie film recorded through a floating camera over the event. And this is why (S6) and (S7) can refer to the same scene in spite of their appearances, where what "sinks" or "rises" is the FAO as illustrated in Figure 6 and whose conceptual descriptions are given as (13) and (14), respectively, where "A_{13}," "↑," and "↓" refer to the attribute "Direction" and its values "upward" and "downward" (practically as 3D unit vectors), respectively.

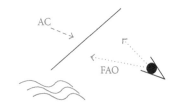

FIGURE 6: Slope as spatial change event.

(S6) The path *sinks* to the brook.

(S7) The path *rises* from the brook.

$$(\exists y, z, p) L(\_, y, p, z, A_{12}, G_s, \_) \sqcap L(\_, y, \downarrow, \downarrow, A_{13}, G_s, \_)$$
$$\wedge \operatorname{path}(y) \wedge \operatorname{brook}(z) \wedge z \neq p, \tag{13}$$

$$(\exists y, z, p) L(\_, y, z, p, A_{12}, G_s, \_) \sqcap L(\_, y, \uparrow, \uparrow, A_{13}, G_s, \_)$$
$$\wedge \operatorname{path}(y) \wedge \operatorname{brook}(z) \wedge z \neq p. \tag{14}$$

Such a fact is generalized as P_{RS} (postulate of reversibility of spatial change event), where χ_s and χ_s^R are an image and its "reversal" for a certain spatial change event, respectively, and they are substitutable with each other because of the property of "$\equiv_0$." This postulate can be one of the principal inference rules belonging to people's common-sense knowledge about geography.

P_{RS}:

$$\chi_s^R \cdot \equiv_0 \chi_s. \tag{15}$$

This postulation is also valid for such a pair of (S8) and (S9) as interpreted approximately into (16) and (17), respectively. These pairs of conceptual descriptions are called equivalent in the P_{RS}, and the paired sentences are treated as paraphrases each other.

(S8) Route A and Route B separate at the city.

(S9) Route A and Route B meet at the city.

$$(\exists p, y, q) L(\_, \operatorname{Route\_}A, p, y, A_{12}, G_s, \_)$$
$$\sqcap L(\_, \operatorname{Route\_}B, q, y, A_{12}, G_s, \_) \wedge \operatorname{city}(y) \wedge p \neq q, \tag{16}$$

$$(\exists p, y, q) L(\_, \operatorname{Route\_}A, y, p, A_{12}, G_s, \_)$$
$$\sqcap L(\_, \operatorname{Route\_}B, y, q, A_{12}, G_s, \_) \wedge \operatorname{city}(y) \wedge p \neq q. \tag{17}$$

Of course, P_{RS} is as well applicable to such an inference that "if x is to the right of y, then y is to the left of x," which is conventionally based on a considerably large set of such *linguistic* axioms as (18) regardless of *time*. Furthermore, it is notable that there are an infinite number of directions without good correspondence with single words such as "right."

$$(\forall x, y) \operatorname{right}(x, y) \supset \operatorname{left}(y, x),$$
$$(\forall x, y) \operatorname{under}(x, y) \supset \operatorname{above}(y, x). \tag{18}$$

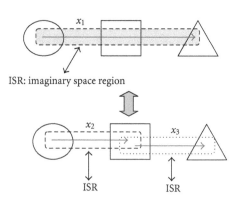

ISR: imaginary space region

FIGURE 7: Partiality of ISR—the arrows represent the directions of FAO.

5.2. Postulate of Partiality of Matter. Any matter is assumed to consist of its parts in a structure (i.e., spatial change event) and generalized as P_{PM} (postulate of partiality of matter) here. For example, Figure 7 shows that an ISR x_1 can be deemed as a complex of ISRs x_2 and x_3.

P_{PM}:

$$(\forall y, x_1, p, q, a, k) L(y, x_1, p, q, a, G_s, k)$$
$$\cdot L(y, x_1, q, r, a, G_s, k). \supset_0. (\exists x_2, x_3) L(y, x_2, p, q, a, G_s, k)$$
$$\sqcap L(y, x_3, q, r, a, G_s, k),$$

$$(\forall y, x_2, x_3, p, q, a, k)$$
$$L(y, x_2, p, q, a, G_s, k) \sqcap L(y, x_3, q, r, a, G_s, k)$$
$$. \supset_0. (\exists x_1) L(y, x_1, p, q, a, G_s, k) \cdot L(y, x_1, q, r, a, G_s, k). \tag{19}$$

We often refer to parts of an image especially for deductive inference upon it. For example, we can easily deduce from Figure 7 (Top) the two facts "the square is to the left of the triangle" and "the circle is to the left of the square." As its reversal, we can merge these two partial images into one meaningful image such as Figure 7 (Bottom). That is, P_{PM} is very useful to compute static spatial relations that are expressed by English spatial terms and conventionally formalized by a large set of such *linguistic* axioms as (20) regardless of *time* just like the case of P_{RS}. Furthermore, it is notable that the reversals of these axioms (i.e., $(\forall x, y, z)$ between $(y, z, x) \supset w(y, x) \wedge w(z, y)$) do not always exist in good correspondence with words (e.g., "left" for the predicate w).

$$(\forall x, y, z) \operatorname{left}(y, x) \wedge \operatorname{left}(z, y) \supset \operatorname{between}(y, z, x),$$
$$(\forall x, y, z) \operatorname{under}(y, x) \wedge \operatorname{under}(z, y) \supset \operatorname{between}(y, z, x). \tag{20}$$

Besides its orthodox usage above, P_{PM}, in cooperation with P_{RS}, can be utilized for translating such a paradoxical sentence as "The Andes Mountains run north and south." into such a plausible interpretation as "Some part of the Andes Mountains run north (from somewhere) and the other part run south."

6. Cross-Media Translation

As easily understood by its definition, an atomic formula corresponds with a pair of snapshots at the beginning and the ending of a monotonic change in an attribute. Viewed from pictorial representation, temporal and spatial change events correspond to animated and still pictures, respectively. Furthermore, the L_{md} expression of a spatial change event as the locus of FAO can be related to the sequence of pen-down and pen-up in line drawing. This section describes cross-media translation in general, focusing on that between text and map, one kind of still picture, as the core of spatial language understanding.

6.1. Functional Requirements. Systematic cross-media translation here is defined by the functions (F1)–(F4) as follows.

(F1) To translate source representations into target ones as for contents describable by both source and target media. For example, positional relations between/among physical objects such as "in", "around." are describable by both linguistic and pictorial media.

(F2) To filter out such contents that are describable by source medium but not by target one. For example, linguistic representations of "taste" and "smell" such as "sweet candy" and "pungent gas" are not describable by usual pictorial media although they would be seemingly describable by cartoons, and so forth.

(F3) To supplement default contents, that is, such contents that need to be described in target representations but not explicitly described in source representations. For example, the shape of a physical object is necessarily described in pictorial representations but not in linguistic ones.

(F4) To replace default contents by definite ones given in the following contexts. For example, in such a context as "There is a box to the left of the pot. The box is red. ...," the color of the box in a pictorial representation must be changed from default one to red.

For example, the text consisting of such two sentences as "There is a hard cubic object" and "The object is large and gray" can be translated into a still picture in such a way as shown in Figure 8.

6.2. Formalization. According to the MIDST, any content conveyed by an information medium is assumed to be associated with the loci in certain attribute spaces and in turn the world describable by each medium can be characterized by the maximal set of such attributes. This relation is conceptually formalized by (21), where Wm, Am_i, and F mean "the world describable by the information medium m," "an attribute of the world," and "a certain function for determining the maximal set of attributes of Wm," respectively,

$$F(Wm) = \{Am_1, Am_2, \ldots, Am_n\}. \tag{21}$$

There is a hard cubic object

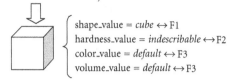

shape_value = *cube* ↔ F1
hardness_value = *indescribable* ↔ F2
color_value = *default* ↔ F3
volume_value = *default* ↔ F3

The object is large and gray

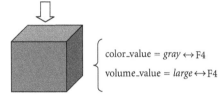

color_value = *gray* ↔ F4
volume_value = *large* ↔ F4

FIGURE 8: Systematic cross-media translation.

Considering this relation, cross-media translation is one kind of mapping from the world describable by the source medium (ms) to that by the target medium (mt) and can be defined by the following equation:

$$Y(S_{mt}) = \psi(X(S_{ms})), \tag{22}$$

where S_{ms}: maximal set of attributes of the world describable by the source medium ms, S_{mt}: maximal set of attributes of the world describable by the target medium mt, $X(S_{ms})$: L_{md} expression about the attributes belonging to S_{ms}, $Y(S_{mt})$: L_{md} expression about the attributes belonging to S_{mt}, and ψ: function for transforming X into Y, so called, "L_{md} expression paraphrasing function."

The function ψ is designed to clear all the requirements (F1)–(F4) by inference processing at the level of L_{md} expression.

6.3. L_{md} Expression Paraphrasing Function ψ. In order to realize the function (F1), a certain set of "*Attribute paraphrasing rules (APRs),*" so called, are defined *at every pair of source and target media.* The function (F2) is realized by detecting L_{md} expressions about *the attributes without any corresponding APRs* from the content of each input representation and replacing them by *empty events* [10].

For (F3), *default reasoning* is employed. That is, such an inference rule as defined by (23) is introduced, which states if *X is deducible and it is consistent to assume Y then conclude Z*. This rule is applied typically to such instantiations of X, Y, and Z as specified by (24) which means that the indefinite attribute value "p" with the indefinite standard "k" of the indefinite matter "y" is substitutable by the constant attribute value "P" with the constant standard "K" of the definite matter "$O\#$" of the same kind "M":

$$X \circ Y \longrightarrow Z, \tag{23}$$

$$\{X/(L(x, y, p, p, A, G, k) \land M(y))$$

$$\land (L(z, O\#, P, P, A, G, K) \land M(O\#)),$$

$$Y/p = P \land k = K, Z/L(x, y, P, P, A, G, K) \land M(y)\}. \tag{24}$$

TABLE 1: APRs for text-picture translation (A_{12}: physical location, A_{13}: direction, A_{17}: mileage, A_{10}: volume, A_{11}: shape, A_{32}: color, A_{44}: topology).

APRs	Correspondences of attributes (text : picture)	Value conversion schema (text ↔ picture)
APR-01	$A_{12} : A_{12}$	$p \leftrightarrow p'$
APR-02	$\{A_{12}, A_{13}, A_{17}\} : A_{12}$	$\{p, d, l\} \leftrightarrow p' + l' d'$
APR-03	$\{A_{11}, A_{10}\} : A_{11}$	$\{s, v\} \leftrightarrow v' s'$
APR-04	$A_{32} : A_{32}$	$c \leftrightarrow c'$
APR-05	$\{A_{12}, A_{44}\} : A_{12}$	$\{p_a, m\} \leftrightarrow \{p'_a, p'_b\}$

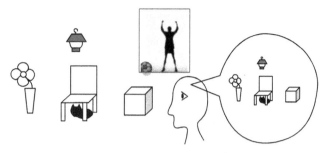

FIGURE 9: Scene of a room and its live image in human.

The function (F4) is realized quite easily by memorizing the history of applications of default reasoning.

6.4. Attribute Paraphrasing Rules for Text and Picture. Five kinds of APRs for this case are shown in Table 1 where $p, s, c, \ldots$ and $p', s', c', \ldots$ are linguistic expressions and their corresponding pictorial expressions of attribute values, respectively. Further details are as follows.

(i) APR-02 is used especially for a sentence such as "The box is 3 meters to the left of the chair." The symbols p, d and l correspond to "the location of the chair," "left," and "3 meters," respectively, yielding the pictorial expression of "the location of the box," namely, "$p' + l' d'$."

(ii) APR-03 is used especially for a sentence such as "The pot is big." The symbols s and v correspond to "the shape of the pot (default value)" and "the volume of the pot ("big")," respectively. In pictorial expression, the shape and the volume of an object is inseparable and therefore they are represented only by the value of the attribute "shape", namely, $v' s'$.

(iii) APR-05 is used especially for a sentence such as "The cat is in the box." The symbols p_a, p_b and m correspond to "the location of the desk," "the location of the cat," and "in," respectively, yielding a pair of pictorial expressions of the locations of the two objects.

7. Direct Knowledge of Space

Partially symbolized direct knowledge of space (PSDKS in short) introduced here is one of the data structures for imperative programming in IMAGES as well as Hitree [11]. PSDKS is a map for directional and metric relations among objects while Hitree is intended to be a complete substitute of L_{md} expression. That is, the relation between L_{md} expression and PSDSK is what is formalized by APR-02 in Table 1. For example, consider the scene of a room shown in Figure 9, where the FAO is posed on the formation of the flower-pot, box, lamp, chair, and cat. PSDKS here does not mean any kind of live image perceived by a human (or snapshot by a system) at a time point but somewhat abstract 3D map resulted from its recognition as depicted in Figure 10.

That is, PSDKS is defined as a set of points representing the 3D locations (i.e., A_{12}) of the involved objects linked to the corresponding L_{md} expression and therefore directly reusable for computation without recognizing them unlike the memory of their live image or snapshot.

In turn, consider verbalization of the PSDKS. In this case, any system must be forced to articulate it in accordance with existing word concepts and may utter such a set of sentences (S10)–(S13). These are to be generated from such L_{md} expressions as (25)–(28), respectively, where I_n, Fp, Ch, Bx, Lp and Ct stand for ISR, flower-pot, chair, box lamp, and cat, respectively.

(S10) The chair is 3 meters to the right of the flower-pot.

(S11) The flower-pot is 6 meters to the left of the box.

(S12) The lamp hangs above the chair.

(S13) The cat lies under the chair.

$$L(\_, I_1, \text{Fp}, \text{Ch}, A_{12}, G_s, \_) \sqcap L(\_, I_1, \rightarrow, \rightarrow, A_{13}, G_s, \_)$$
$$\sqcap L(\_, I_1, 3m, 3m, A_{17}, G_s, \_), \tag{25}$$

$$L(\_, I_2, \text{Bx}, \text{Fp}, A_{12}, G_s, \_) \sqcap L(\_, I_2, \leftarrow, \leftarrow, A_{13}, G_s, \_)$$
$$\sqcap L(\_, I_2, 6m, 6m, A_{17}, G_s, \_), \tag{26}$$

$$L(\_, I_3, \text{Ch}, \text{Lp}, A_{12}, G_s, \_) \sqcap L(\_, I_3, \uparrow, \uparrow, A_{13}, G_s, \_), \tag{27}$$

$$L(\_, I_4, \text{Ch}, \text{Ct}, A_{12}, G_s, \_) \sqcap L(\_, I_4, \downarrow, \downarrow, A_{13}, G_s, \_). \tag{28}$$

Even only for directional and metric relationships between two objects out of the five objects in Figure 10, there can be at least 20 ($=_5 P_2$) expressions in English including (S10)–(S13) that correspond with such formulas in conventional logic as (29)–(32), respectively.

$$\text{right}(\text{Ch}, \text{Fp}, 3\_\text{meters}), \tag{29}$$

$$\text{left}(\text{Fp}, \text{Bx}, 6\_\text{meters}), \tag{30}$$

$$\text{above}(\text{Lp}, \text{Ch}), \tag{31}$$

$$\text{under}(\text{Ct}, \text{Ch}). \tag{32}$$

FIGURE 10: PSDKS resulted from the live image in Figure 9.

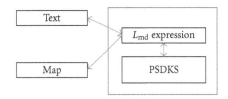

FIGURE 11: Text-map operation via L_{md} expression and PSDKS.

This fact implies that conventional declarative programs must employ numerous theses including the axioms (18) and (20) even for solving rather simple problems associated with this scene such as "What is between the box and the flower-pot?". The meaning of this question is conventionally notated as (33). However, it must be noted that the axioms like (18) and (20) cannot be applied to the assertions (29)–(32) for the answer to this question (i.e., $?x$).

On the contrary, it is much easier to search in the PSDKS for the event pattern specified by the L_{md} expression (34) for the question. This formula, a locus of FAO, can be procedurally interpreted as the command "Find "$?x$" by scanning *straight* from the *box* to the *flower-pot*." In case of understanding (S10)–(S13), the system is to apply APR-02 to (25)–(28) and synthesize the partial scenes into one whole scene similar to (not always the same as) the PSDKS shown in Figure 10, that is to say, *reconstructed* direct knowledge of space:

$$between(?x, Bx, Fp), \tag{33}$$

$$(L(\_, y, Bx, ?x, A_{12}, G_s, \_) \cdot L(\_, y, ?x, Fp, A_{12}, G_s, \_))$$
$$\sqcap L(\_, y, p, p, A_{13}, G_s, \_). \tag{34}$$

At summarization of this section, PSDKS is very much compact in memory size compared with conventional declaration about space and L_{md} expression can systematically indicate how to search PSDKS for an event pattern.

8. Implementation

IMAGES-M, the last version of intelligent system IMAGES, has recently adopted the multiparadigm language Python in place of PROLOG to facilitate both declarative and imperative programming. IMAGES-M is one kind of expert system with five kinds of user interfaces besides the inference engine (IE) and the knowledge base (KB) as follows.

(i) Text Processing Unit (TPU).

(ii) Speech Processing Unit (SPU).

(iii) Picture Processing Unit (PPU).

(iv) Action Data Processing Unit (ADPU).

(v) Sensory Data Processing Unit (SDPU).

These user interfaces can mutually convert information media and L_{md} expressions in the collaboration with IE and KB, and miscellaneous combinations among them bring forth various types of cross-media operations. The further details about mutual conversion between language and picture can be found in other papers (e.g., [15, 16]).

FIGURE 12: Transactions between human user and IMAGES-M while text understanding, map composition and question-answering on the map (At headers: "u…" = human user, "s…" = IMAGES-M).

The methodology mentioned above has been implemented on IMAGES-M for spatial language understanding. Here, distinguished from others, spatial language understanding is defined as cross-media operation between spatial language and map such as mutual translation and question-answering between them. The author has confirmed that the hybrid program in Python employing L_{md} expression mainly and PSDKS auxiliarily as shown in Figure 11 is much more flexible and efficient than the previous one [4] in PROLOG for solving problems expressed in spatial language.

Here is presented an example of cross-operation between text and picture performed by IMAGES-M.

IMAGES-M understood the human user's assertions or questions and answered them in picture or word. Figure 12 shows the transactions exchanged between the human user and the system, where the headers "u…." and "s…." stand for the human user's inputs and the system's responses,

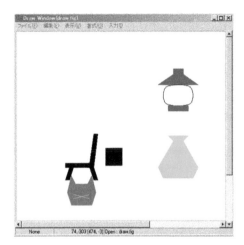

FIGURE 13: Map finally composed by IMAGES-M for u0001–u0006.

respectively. IMAGES-M can accept 3 kinds of natural language besides English, namely, Japanese (e.g., u0002, u0008 and s0029), Chinese (e.g., u0007 and s0026 in Pinyin) and Albanian (e.g., u0003, u0010 and s0035) as shown in Figure 12, where

    u0002 = "The cat is 1 m under the chair,"

    u0003 = "The cat is red,"

    u0008 = "What is between the chair and the pot?,"

    s0029 = "Box,"

    u0007 = "Is the cat red?,"

    s0026= "yes,"

    u0010 = "Is the box between the cat and the lamp?,"

    s0035 = "yes."

The map shown in Figure 13 was the final version of those which IMAGES-M composed at each of the user's assertions. IMAGES-M interpreted the assertions u0001–u0006 into L_{md}, and in turn into map and PSDKS (exactly, reconstructed PSDKS), where the system updated them assertion by assertion, responding so by s0002–s0022. In the process of text to map, default reasoning about color, and so forth. was performed in such a way as shown in Figure 8, where only the default locations of the objects within the map are significant for PSDKS.

On the other hand, during the question-answering (i.e., u0007-s0035), IMAGES-M translated each of the user's questions (i.e., u0007–u0010) into L_{md} and consulted the reconstructed PSDKS about Location (A_{12}) within the map or the corresponding L_{md} expression about the other attributes such as Color (A_{32}). In this process, the postulates P_{RS} and P_{PM} were utilized as procedures in Python, which could reduce remarkably the number of axioms such as (18) and (20) that are necessarily employed in conventional systems.

9. Discussion and Conclusion

MIDST is still under development and intended to provide a formal system, represented in L_{md}, for natural semantics of space and time. This formal system is one kind of applied predicate logic consisting of axioms and postulates subject to human perceptive processes of space and time, while the other similar systems in Artificial Intelligence [17–19] are objective, namely, independent of human perception and do not necessarily keep tight correspondences with natural language. This paper showed that L_{md} expressions can contribute to aware computing of spatial relations leading to representational and computational cost reduction in aid of Partially Symbolized Direct Knowledge of Space (PSDKS) while some further quantitative elaboration is needed on this point.

The author has already reported that cross-media operation between texts in several languages (Japanese, Chinese, Albanian, and English) and pictorial patterns like maps were successfully implemented on IMAGES-M [4]. As detailed in this paper, IMAGES-M has recently adopted the multiparadigm language Python in place of PROLOG to facilitate both declarative and imperative programming, and the author has confirmed that the hybrid program in Python employing L_{md} expression mainly and PSDKS auxiliary is much more flexible and efficient than the previous one in PROLOG for solving problems expressed in spatial language. To our best knowledge, there is no other system (e.g., [20, 21]) that can perform cross-media operations in such a seamless way as described here. This leads to the conclusion that L_{md} has made the logical expressions of event concepts remarkably computable and has proved to be very adequate to systematize cross-media operations. This adequacy is due to its medium-freeness and its good correspondence with the performances of human sensory systems in both spatial and temporal extents while almost all other knowledge representation schemes are ontology-dependent, computing- unconscious or spatial-change-event unconscious (e.g., [8, 9]).

The author deems that aware science or technology is still on the way to maturation and therefore that now it should foster various kinds of approaches. The model of human cognition employed in MIDST is formalized based on declarative knowledge representation in symbolic logic which has almost been discarded in this research area so far and instead certain approaches based on procedural knowledge representation has been prevalent. The author's very intention here is to present some prospective possibility of his original theory MIDST in aware science. The example presented in Section 8 is rather simple but one of the most complicated spatial relations displayable in this version of the intelligent system IMAGES-M because it was programmed exclusively to check the efficacy of PSDKS. Another extended version of the system is now under construction and some examples of further complicated human-system interaction in natural language have already been presented in another paper [15].

Our future work will include establishment of learning facilities for automatic acquisition of word concepts from sensory data [7] and human-robot communication by natural language under real environments [22].

Acknowledgment

This work was partially funded by the Grants from Computer Science Laboratory, Fukuoka Institute of Technology and Ministry of Education, Culture, Sports, Science and Technology, Japanese Government, nos. 14580436, 17500132, and 23500195.

References

[1] A. Yamada, A. Yamada, H. Ikrda et al., "Reconstructing spatial image from natural language texts," in *Proceedings of the 15th International Conference on Computational Linguistics (COLING '90)*, Nantes, France, 1992.

[2] P. Olivier and J. Tsujii, "A computational view of the cognitive semantics of spatial expressions," in *Proceedings of the 32nd annual meeting on Association for Computational Linguistics (ACL '94)*, Las Cruces, New Mexico, 1994.

[3] G. Adorni, M. Di Manzo, and F. Giunchiglia, "Natural language driven image generation," in *Proceedings of the 10th International Conference on Computational Linguistics (COLING '84)*, pp. 495–500, 1984.

[4] M. Yokota and G. Capi, "Cross-media operations between text and picture based on mental image directed semantic theory," *WSEAS Transactions on Information Science and Applications*, vol. 2, no. 10, pp. 1541–1550, 2005.

[5] J. F. Sowa, *Knowledge Representation: Logical, Philosophical, and Computational Foundations*, Brooks Cole, Pacific Grove, Calif, USA, 2000..

[6] G. P. Zarri, "NKRL, a knowledge representation tool for encoding the "Meaning" of complex narrative texts," *Natural Language Engineering—Special Issue on Knowledge Representation for Natural Language Processing in Implemented Systems*, vol. 3, pp. 231–253, 1997.

[7] S. Oda, M. Oda, and M. Yokota, "Conceptual analysis and description of words for color and lightness for grounding them on sensory data," *Transactions of the Japanese Society for Artificial Intelligence*, vol. 16, no. 5, pp. 436–444, 2001.

[8] R. W. Langacker, *Concept, Image and Symbol, Mouton de Gruyter*, Berlin, Germany, 1991.

[9] G. A. Miller and P. N. Johnson-Laird, *Language and Perception*, Harvard University Press, 1976.

[10] M. Yokota, "Systematic formulation and computation of subjective spatiotemporal knowledge based on mental image directed semantic theory: toward a formal system for natural intelligence," in *Proceedings of the 6th International Workshop on Natural Language Processing and Cognitive Science (NLPCS '09)*, pp. 133–143, Milan, Italy, May 2009.

[11] M. Yokota, "Towards awareness computing under control by world knowledge grounded in sensory data," in *Proceedings of the IEEE International Conference on Systems, Man and Cybernetics (SMC '10)*, pp. 769–775, October 2010.

[12] B. M. Shariff, M. J. Egenhofer, and D. M. Mark, "Natural-language spatial relations between linear and areal objects: the topology and metric of English-language terms," *International Journal of Geographical Information Science*, vol. 12, no. 3, pp. 215–245, 1998.

[13] P. Roget, *Thesaurus of English Words and Phrases*, J.M. Dent & Sons Ltd, London, UK, 1975.

[14] R. Shepard and J. Metzler, "Mental rotation of three-dimensional objects," *Science*, vol. 171, no. 3972, pp. 701–703, 1971.

[15] M. Yokota, "Systematic analysis and synthesis of human subjective knowledge of space and time for intuitive human-robot interaction," in *Proceedings of the IEEE International Conference on Systems, Man, and Cybernetics (SMC '11)*, pp. 208–215, 2011.

[16] M. Yokota, "Towards artificial communication partners with a multiagent mind model based on mental image directed semantic theory," in *Humanoid Robots*, B. Choi, Ed., pp. 333–364, I-Tech Press, 2009.

[17] J. F. Allen, "Towards a general theory of action and time," *Artificial Intelligence*, vol. 23, no. 2, pp. 123–154, 1984.

[18] D. V. McDermott, "A temporal logic for reasoning about processes and plans," *Cognitive Science*, vol. 6, no. 2, pp. 101–155, 1982.

[19] Y. Shoham, "Time for actions: on the relationship between time, knowledge, and action," in *Proceedings of the International Joint Conference on Artificial Intelligence*, pp. 954–959, Detroit, Mich, USA, 1989.

[20] J. P. Eakins and M. E. Graham, "Content-based Image Retrieval: A report to the JISC Technology Applications Programme," Institute for Image Data Research, University of Northumbria at Newcastle, 1999.

[21] M. L. Kherfi, D. Ziou, and A. Bernardi, "Image retrieval from the World Wide Web: issues, techniques, and systems," *ACM Computing Surveys*, vol. 36, no. 1, pp. 35–67, 2004.

[22] M. Yokota, M. Shiraishi, and G. Capi, "Human-robot communication through a mind model based on the mental image directed semantic theory," in *Proceedings of the 10th International Symposium on Artificial Life and Robotics (AROB '05)*, pp. 695–698, Oita, Japan, 2005.

4

Controller Parameter Optimization for Nonlinear Systems Using Enhanced Bacteria Foraging Algorithm

V. Rajinikanth[1] and K. Latha[2]

[1] Department of Electronics and Instrumentation Engineering, St. Joseph's College of Engineering, Chennai 600 119, India
[2] Department of Instrumentation Engineering, MIT Campus, Anna University, Chennai 600 044, India

Correspondence should be addressed to V. Rajinikanth, rajinisjceeie@gmail.com

Academic Editor: Serafín Moral

An enhanced bacteria foraging optimization (EBFO) algorithm-based Proportional + integral + derivative (PID) controller tuning is proposed for a class of nonlinear process models. The EBFO algorithm is a modified form of standard BFO algorithm. A multiobjective performance index is considered to guide the EBFO algorithm for discovering the best possible value of controller parameters. The efficiency of the proposed scheme has been validated through a comparative study with classical BFO, adaptive BFO, PSO, and GA based controller tuning methods proposed in the literature. The proposed algorithm is tested in real time on a nonlinear spherical tank system. The real-time results show that, EBFO tuned PID controller gives a smooth response for setpoint tracking performance.

1. Introduction

In control literature, despite of significant developments in advanced process control schemes such as model predictive control (MPC), internal model control (IMC), and sliding mode control (SMC), PID controllers are still widely used in industrial control system where reference tracking and disturbance rejection are a major task.

The key merits of the PID controllers over the advanced control techniques are as follows: (i) available in a variety of structures such as series, parallel, and so forth; (ii) provides an optimal and robust performance for a variety of processes; (iii) supports online/offline tuning and retuning based on the performance requirement of the process under control (iv) simple structure and it can be easily implementable in analog or digital form; (v) along with the basic and the modified structures, it also supports the one degree of freedom (1DOF), 2DOF, and 3DOF controller structures.

Most of the real-time chemical process loops such as continuous stirred tank reactor (CSTR), biochemical reactor, spherical tank system, and conical tank system are nonlinear in nature. These nonlinear processes can be modelled as linear processes (stable or unstable process model with a delay time) around the operating region. The linear model is then efficiently controlled by employing a PID controller. The precision and performance of the PID controller mainly rely on three controller parameters such as proportional gain (K_p), integral gain (K_i), and derivative gain (K_d). In recent years, a number of tuning rules have been proposed for the PID controllers to enhance the performance of the process to be controlled. Maher and Samir [1] have discussed the robust stability criterion for a class of unstable systems under model uncertainty. Vijayan and Panda [2] have proposed a setpoint filter PID controller for a class of stable and unstable process models. Padmasree and Chidambaram [3] have provided a detailed review on the methods of controller tuning for a class of time delayed unstable system. Jhunjhunwala and Chidambaram [4] have examined an optimized PID controller tuning for nonlinear systems such as the biochemical reactor and the CSTR process, modelled as a time delayed unstable system around the operating region.

The classical PID tuning methods proposed by most of the researchers for the stable and unstable processes require an approximated first or second order transfer-function model with a time delay. The tuning procedure anticipated for one particular process model will not provide the fitting response for other process models. Hence, soft computing-based PID controller tuning is widely proposed by the researchers to design a robust PID controller. Chiha et al. [5] proposed a multiobjective ant colony optimization (ACO) algorithm-based PID controller tuning for a class of time delayed stable process models. Zamani et al. [6, 7] have discussed a multi objective particle swarm optimization (PSO) algorithm-based "H_∞" and fractional order PID controller design for stable systems. Chang and Shih [8] presented an improved PSO-based PID controller design for a nonlinear system. Hassan and Mobayen [9] have proposed genetic-algorithm (GA-), PSO- and ACO-based controller design for a rotary inverted pendulum. Kanth and Latha [10, 11] have presented a relative work with PSO-, improved PSO- and parallel PSO-based PID tuning for a class of unstable process models.

In this paper, bacteria foraging optimization- (BFO-) based PID tuning is proposed for a class of nonlinear process models. BFO algorithm is a nature inspired metaheuristic search technique, introduced by Passino [12] to design an adaptive controller for a tank liquid level control problem. It is a biologically inspired computation technique based on mimicking the foraging activities of *Escherichia coli* (*E. coli*) bacteria. In this algorithm, a collection of artificial bacteria cooperates to find the best possible solutions in the "*D*" dimensional search space during the optimization exploration. The previous research has reported the superiority of the BFO-based search for finding the optimum solution for a class of engineering problems.

Dasgupta et al. [13, 14] proposed an adaptive BFO (ABFO) algorithm to find optimal parameters for a variety of engineering optimization problems. Chen et al. [15, 16] proposed a cooperative BFO (CBFO) algorithm and ABFO algorithm. With a comparative study, they proved that the ABFO provides superior performance compared to PSO and GA. Das et al. [17, 18] provided the comprehensive analysis on the BFO algorithm. The discussion by Biswas et al. [19] provides the insight on the reproduction operator performance in BFO. A detailed study on the optimal controller parameter tuning for a class of process models are examined by Biswas et al. [20], Roy et al. [21], and Ghosh et al. [22]. Ali and Majhi [23] examined the BFO algorithm to tune the PID controller parameter for a class of stable process models. Korani et al. [24] presented a comparative study between the PSO, BFO, and hybrid-algorithm-tuned PID control for stable systems. Recently, Kanth and Latha [25] discussed about the BFO-tuned I-PD controller performance on a class of time delayed unstable process models.

In the present work, we propose an enhanced bacteria foraging optimization (EBFO) algorithm to identify optimised PID controller parameters for a class of stable and unstable process models by maintaining guaranteed accuracy in the optimized value. The need for multiobjective performance index in order to improve the exactness of the proposed controller is also discussed. The method is finally tested on a real time nonlinear spherical tank system.

Further, a detailed description of enhanced bacterial foraging optimization algorithm is provided in Section 2.

Section 3 presents the outline of the PID controller structure, problem formulation and the cost-function-based controller tuning. Section 4 discusses the simulated results on different nonlinear process models and the real-time test on a nonlinear spherical tank system. Section 5 deals about the conclusion of the present research work.

2. Bacteria Foraging Algorithm

Bacteria foraging optimization (BFO) algorithm is a new division of metaheuristic algorithm. It is a population-based optimization technique developed by inspiring the foraging manners of *E. coli* bacteria [12]. The basic operations of BFO algorithm is briefly discussed below.

Chemotaxis. During foraging operation (tracing, handling, and ingesting food), an *E. coli* bacterium moves towards the food location with the aid of swimming and tumbling by using flagella. Through swimming, it can move in a specified direction and during tumbling action, the bacteria can modify the direction of search. These two modes of operations are continuously executed to move in random paths to find adequate amount of positive nutrient gradient. These operations are performed in its whole lifetime.

Swarming. In this process, after the success in the direction of the best food position, the bacterium which has the knowledge about the optimum path to the food source will attempt to communicate to other bacteria by using an attraction signal. The signal communication between cells in *E. coli* bacteria is represented by the following equation:

$$J(\theta, D(j,k,l)) = \sum_{i=1}^{N} J_{cc}\big(\theta, \theta^i(j,k,l)\big) = A + B, \quad (1)$$

where

$$A = \sum_{i=1}^{N}\left[-d_{\text{attract}} \exp\left(-W_{\text{attract}} \sum_{m=1}^{D}\left(\theta_m - \theta^i{}_m\right)^2\right)\right],$$

$$B = \sum_{i=1}^{N}\left[h_{\text{repell}} \exp\left(-W_{\text{repell}} \sum_{m=1}^{D}\left(\theta_m - \theta^i{}_m\right)^2\right)\right], \quad (2)$$

where θ is the location of the global optimum bacterium till the jth chemotactic, kth reproduction, and lth elimination stage and "θ_m" is the mth parameter of global optimum bacteria.

Where $J(\theta, D(j,k,l))$ represents objective function assessment, "N" is the total number of bacterium, and "D" the total parameters to be optimised. The other parameters such as "d_{attract}" are the depth of attractant signal released by a bacteria and "W_{attract}" is the width of attractant signal. The signals "h_{repell}" and "W_{repell}" are the height and width of repellent signals between bacterium (attractant is the signal for food source and repellent is the signal for noxious reserve).

Reproduction. In swarming process, the bacteria build up as groups in the positive nutrient gradient and which may increase the bacterial concentration. After the congregation the bacteria are sorted in descending order based on its health values. The bacteria which have the least health will perish and the bacteria with the most health value will split into two and breed to maintain a constant population.

Elimination-Dispersal. Based on the environmental conditions such as change in temperature, noxious surroundings, and accessibility of food, the population of a bacteria may change either steadily or abruptly. During this stage, a group of the bacteria in a restricted region (local optima) will be eliminated or a group may be scattered (dispersed) into a new food location in the "*D*" dimensional search space. The dispersal possibly flattens the chemotaxis advancement. After dispersal, sometimes the bacteria may be placed near the good nutrient source and it may support the chemo-taxis, to identify the availability of other food sources. The above procedures are repeated until the optimized solutions are achieved.

2.1. Enhanced Bacteria Foraging Algorithm. The parameters of the basic BFO algorithms are defined in the following. D: the dimension of search space (the search boundary is $-100 < 0 < +100$), N: the total number of artificial *E. coli* bacteria, N_c: total number of chemotaxis steps, N_s: swim length during the search, N_{re}: total number of reproduction steps, N_{ed}: total number of elimination-dispersal events, N_r: number of reproduced bacteria, P_{ed}: the probability that each bacterium will be eliminated/dispersed, and n: the run length.

In the basic BFO algorithm, the fitness of each bacterium is determined from the average value of the entire chemotactic performance index before the reproduction operation. In the proposed EBFO algorithm, the bacterium with the maximum health is retained [12].

The health of the bacterium can be found by the following relation

$$J^i_{\text{health}} = \sum_{j=1}^{N_c+1} J(i, j, k, l), \tag{3}$$

where $i = 1, 2, \ldots, N$.

In the proposed algorithm, the retained bacterium is used to guide the reproduced bacteria towards the nutrient source. Due to this process, along with the accuracy in optimization, the iteration time can be reduced.

In the literature there is no apparent guide line to allocate the parameters for the BFO algorithm. In the proposed EBFO algorithm, we assigned the limitations for the algorithm parameters by considering the various stages of bacterium growth discussed in the book by El-Mansi and Bryce [26].

Stages of bacteria growth in a controlled environment are shown schematically in Figure 1.

   (i) *Lag phase:* Amendment of the cells to new environment take place and it is getting ready to begin reproduction.

   (ii) *Growth phase:* In this stage with the help of chemotaxis and swarming practice, the cells can reach the

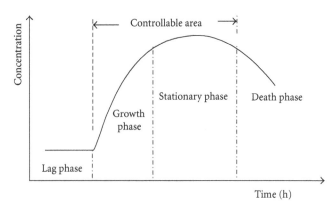

FIGURE 1: Stages of cell growth in an incubated environment.

location of food source. The growth rate is proportional to the cell concentration and the nutrient quantity. When the cell reaches the sufficient food location, the growth rate is rapid. When the cell reaches the maximum growth, it begins reproduction.

   (iii) *Stationary phase:* After growth and reproduction, the cell will reach a minimum biological space called stationary phase. Due to the lack of one or more nutrients, build up of toxic materials and organic acids generated during the growth phase, cell growth is restricted.

   (iv) *Death phase:* It is mainly due to the toxic by-products and depletion of nutrient supply. In this, a decrease in live cell concentration occurs. The cell with a minimum health is eliminated.

   The above process repeats until there exist a controlled environment such as constant temperature and pH.

In bacteria foraging algorithm, the total number of bacterium considered for the optimization practice plays a vital role in maintaining the optimization accuracy and algorithm convergence. The larger number of bacterium can offer an agreeable accuracy, but sometimes it may increase the computation time. In this paper, we performed a number of trials to fix the range of the bacteria group size. When the *E. coli* is placed in a controlled environment, it will reach the food source with the action of tumbling or swimming. The first half in the group swim towards the food and rest in the group tumbles. The bacterium which enters into the nutrient environment first, may grow earlier and starts the reproduction operation. Around 25% of cells may die due to lack of nutrients and build up toxic materials. The probability of bacterial elimination mainly depends on the bacteria at the noxious environment, initial population of the bacteria, and the bacterial with the reproduction process. The bacteria are living organism, which will act fast at toxic environment compared to the nutrient source. This process may help to fix the values for the attract and repel signal strength.

With the aid of the above information, the algorithm parameters are assigned as follows.

(i) The total number of *E. coli* bacteria = $10 < N < 30$ (even numbers).

(ii) The total number of chemotactic steps $(N_c) = N/2$.

(iii) Swim length during the search (N_s) = Total number of reproduction steps $(N_{re}) \approx N/3$.

(iv) The number of elimination-dispersal events $(N_{ed}) \approx N/4$.

(v) The total number of bacterial reproduction $(N_r) = N/2$.

(vi) The probability of the bacterial elimination/dispersal $(P_{ed}) = (N_{ed}/(N + N_r))$.

(vii) Total number of iterations during the search = N^2.

(viii) Swarming parameters can be assigned as follows:

$$d_{\text{attractant}} = W_{\text{attractant}} = \frac{N_s}{N},$$

$$h_{\text{repellant}} = W_{\text{repellant}} = \frac{N_c}{N}, \tag{4}$$

(ix) Initial positions for the bacterium (bacterium 1 to N) is assigned as follows

$$\text{PI(value1 : Dim1, Dim2, ... Dim} D)$$

$$= \text{SB for value1} * \text{rand}(N, \text{Dim1})$$

$$\text{PI(value2 : Dim1, Dim2, ... Dim} D)$$

$$= \text{SB for value 2} * \text{rand}(N, \text{Dim2}) \tag{5}$$

$$\vdots \qquad \vdots$$

$$\text{PI(value} D : \text{Dim1, Dim2, ... Dim} D)$$

$$= \text{SB for value} D * \text{rand}(N, \text{Dim3}),$$

where PI-Performance index which guides the algorithm, SB-Search boundary for the value, Dim = number of values to be optimized = total no of search dimension, rand = random number $(0 < \text{rand} < 1)$.

The main advantage of the proposed method is, the number of parameters to be assigned is very minimal (i.e., N, D, PI, and SB) compared to the basic BFO algorithm.

3. PID Controller Tuning

In process industries, PID controller is used to improve both the steady state as well as the transient response of a process plant. In a closed-loop control system, the controller continuously adjusts the final control element until the difference between reference input and process output is zero irrespective of the internal and/or external disturbance signal.

A universal closed-loop control system is depicted in Figure 2. The controller "$G_c(s)$" has to provide closed-loop

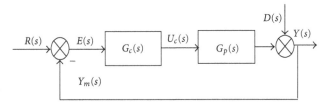

FIGURE 2: Block diagram of a closed loop control system.

stability, smooth reference tracking and load disturbance rejection [27].

Closed-loop response of the above system with setpoint "$R(s)$" and disturbance "$D(s)$" can be expressed as (3):

$$Y(s) = \left[\frac{G_p(s)G_c(s)}{1 + G_p(s)G_c(s)}\right]R(s) + \left[\frac{1}{1 + G_p(s)G_c(s)}\right]D(s). \tag{6}$$

The final steady state response of the system for the reference tracking and the disturbance rejection is presented, respectively, as the following:

$$Y_R(\infty) = \lim_{t \to \infty} sY_R(s) = \lim_{t \to \infty} sx\left[\frac{G_p(s)G_c(s)}{1 + G_p(s)G_c(s)}\right]\left(\frac{A}{s}\right) = A, \tag{7}$$

$$Y_D(\infty) = \lim_{t \to \infty} sx\left[\frac{1}{1 + G_p(s)G_c(s)}\right]\left(\frac{L}{s}\right) = 0, \tag{8}$$

where A = amplitude of reference signal; L = amplitude of disturbance signal.

To achieve a satisfactory $Y_R(\infty)$ and $Y_D(\infty)$, it is necessary to have optimally tuned values for K_p, K_i, and K_d. In this study, a noninteracting form of parallel PID controller is considered to to control the nonlinear system:

$$\text{Parallel PID structure} = K_p\left(1 + \frac{1}{\tau_i s} + \tau_d s\right)$$

$$= \left(K_p + \frac{K_i}{s} + K_d s\right), \tag{9}$$

where $\tau_i = K_p/K_i$, $\tau_d = K_d/K_p$.

3.1. Controller Tuning. The controller tuning process is employed to find the best possible values for K_p, K_i, and K_d. In order to achieve the superior accuracy during the optimization search, it is necessary to assign appropriate PI which guides the BFO algorithm. In recent years, the multiple objective performance index (MOPI) for PID controller optimization is widely proposed by most of the researchers [5–7, 25]. In Zamani et al., [6, 7], along with the error, additional values such as overshoot (M_p), settling time (t_s), steady state error (E_{ss}), rise time (t_r), gain margin (GM) and phase margin (PM) were considered in the performance criterion. Chiha et al. [5] considered M_p, t_s, t_r, IAE, ISE, ITAE, and ITSE.

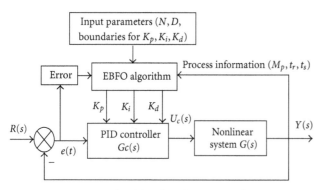

FIGURE 3: EBFO algorithm-based PID controller tuning.

The following performance criterion (9) with five parameters, such as ISE, IAE, M_p, t_r, and t_s are considered in this work:

$$J\left(K_p, K_i, K_d\right) = (w_1 \cdot \text{IAE}) + (w_2 \cdot \text{ISE}) \\ + \left(w_3 \cdot M_p\right) + (w_4 \cdot t_s) + (w_5 \cdot t_r), \quad (10)$$

where

$$\text{IAE} = \int_0^T |e(t)| dt = \int_0^{100} |r(t) - y(t)| dt,$$

$$\text{ISE} = \int_0^T e^2(t) dt = \int_0^{100} [r(t) - y(t)]^2 dt, \quad (11)$$

$$M_p = y(t) - r(t),$$

t_r = rise time (time required for $y(t)$ to reach 100% of its setpoint at the first instant), t_s = settling time—time required for $y(t)$ to reach an stay at $r(t)$ [i.e., $y(t) = r(t)$], and T = time considered for error calculation.

Where $w_1, w_2, \ldots, w_5$ are weighting functions used to set the priority of the MOPI parameters and the value of "w" varies from 0 to 10. The performance criterion $J(K_p, K_i, K_d)$ guides the EBFO algorithm to get appropriate values for the controller parameters.

3.2. Optimization Search. Prior to the optimization search, it is necessary to assign the parameters for EBSO and MOPI.

Figure 3 shows the basic block diagram of the EBFO-based PID controller tuning.

In this study, the following values are assigned.

(i) Dimension of the search space $(D) = 3$ (i.e., K_p, K_i, K_d).

(ii) The total number of *E. coli* bacteria = 10.

(iii) Boundaries for the three dimensional search space is assigned as

Value 1 = $-25\% < K_p < +50\%$ $\left(\text{i.e., } -2.5 < K_p < 5.0\right)$

Value 2 = $-20\% < K_i < +20\%$ (i.e., $-2.0 < K_i < 2.0$)

Value 3 = $-20\% < K_d < +30\%$ (i.e., $-2.0 < K_d < 3.0$)

(12)

(iv) The weighting function values are assigned as $w_1 = w_2 = w_3 = 10$, $w_4 = w_5 = 5$.

(v) Maximum simulation time is 100 sec.

(vi) The "t_r" is preferred as <25% of the maximum simulation time. The simulation time should be selected based on the process time delay.

(vii) The overshoot (M_p) range is selected as <100% of the reference signal.

(viii) The "t_s" is preferred as <50% of the maximum simulation time.

(ix) The reference signal is considered as unity (i.e., $R(s) = 1$).

(x) For each process example, five trials are carried out and the finest set of values among the trials is selected as the best optimized controller value.

3.3. Comparative Study. In order to evaluate the performance of the proposed EBFO algorithm, a comparative analysis is done with most successful soft computing methods such as PSO, BFO, adaptive BFO (ABFO), and GA.

PSO. The simulation is carried out by using the PSO algorithm attempted by Kanth and Latha [10, 11]. The following algorithm parameters are considered: dimension of search space is three (i.e., K_p, K_i, K_d); number of swarm and bird step is considered as 25; the cognitive (C_1) and global (C_2) search parameter is assigned the value of 2 and 1.5, respectively, the inertia weight "W" is set as 0.7.

BFO. For the basic BFO algorithm, the following values are considered: dimension of search space is three; number of bacteria is chosen as ten; number of chemotaxis step is set to five; number of reproduction steps and length of a swim is considered as four; number of elimination-dispersal events is two; number of bacteria reproduction is assigned as five; probability for elimination-dispersal has a value of 0.2 [10, 11, 25].

ABFO. The following values are considered for the ABFO algorith: dimension of search space is three; number of bacteria $(S) = 100$, number of chemotaxis step $(N_c) = 100$, $N_s = 12$, $N_{ed} = 4$, $N_{re} = 16$, $P_{ed} = 0.25$, $d_{\text{attractant}} = 0.1$, $W_{\text{attractant}} = 0.2$, $h_{\text{repellant}} = 0.1$, $W_{\text{repellant}} = 10$, and $\lambda = 400$ [13].

GA. In the GA-based search, the following parameters are assigned: population size is set to 20, generation size is chosen as 150, crossover probability is selected as 50%, and mutation probability is set as 0.2%. Roulette wheel based selection criterion is considered in this study.

*The MOPI proposed in this paper is utilised for all the evolutionary algorithms.

TABLE 1: PID controller values of EBFO algorithm and the performance index values for bioreactor model (five trials).

Trial	Iteration	K_p	K_i	K_d	IAE	ISE	M_p	t_r	t_s
1	51	−0.9330	−0.0171	−0.0628	8.828	77.93	0.721	1.97	62.5
2	57	−0.6289	−0.0672	−0.0386	2.537	6.439	0.718	2.39	27.6
3	67	−0.4418	−0.0503	−0.0714	3.390	11.49	0.775	2.95	30.3
4	72	−0.5928	−0.0730	−0.0288	2.336	5.456	0.759	2.48	18.1
5	59	−0.7117	−0.0391	−0.0433	4.359	19.00	0.638	2.3	38.2

4. Results and Discussions

Most of the real time chemical process systems exhibit multiple steady states due to nonlinear phenomena occurring in the systems. Around the operating region, such systems are adequately represented by a stable or unstable process model with a delay [4]. In order to show the efficiency of the EBFO tuned PID controller for the nonlinear system, approximated linear chemical (bioreactor and CSTR) process models are considered from the literature.

4.1. Process Model 1. The proposed PID controller is tested on a nonlinear bioreactor model discussed by Wayne-Bequette [28].

The following mathematical equations can describe a variety of industrial bioreactors. Equations (13)–(15) describes the balancing conditions and (16) depicts the specific growth rate.

Cell balance:

$$\frac{dX}{dt} = (\mu - D_s)X, \tag{13}$$

Substrate balance:

$$\frac{dS}{dt} = D_s\left(S_f - S\right) - \frac{\mu X}{Y}, \tag{14}$$

Product balance:

$$\frac{dP}{dt} = -D_s P + (\alpha\mu + \beta)X, \tag{15}$$

Monod kinetics:

$$\mu = \frac{\mu_{\max}S}{K_m + S + K_I S^2}, \tag{16}$$

For substrate inhibition model, the following parameters are considered [28]: $\mu_{\max} = 0.53\,\mathrm{hr}^{-1}$, $K_m = 0.12\,\mathrm{g/lit}$, $K_I = 0.4545\,\mathrm{lit/g}$, $Y = 0.4$. The steady state dilution rate is $D_s = 0.3\,\mathrm{h}^{-1}$ and the feed substrate concentration is $S_{fss} = 4.0\,\mathrm{g/lit}$. The nonlinear process has the three steady state operating points for a dilution rate of $0.3\,\mathrm{h}^{-1}$. Transfer function model can be obtained by applying linearization technique [4].

In this study a benchmark unstable bioreactor model is considered. The dilution rate is taken as the manipulated variable to control the cell mass concentration.

For the unstable operating point, the linearized model for the unstable bioreactor is

$$G_p(s) = \frac{-0.9951s - 0.2985}{s^2 + 0.1302s - 0.0509} = \frac{-5.8644}{5.89s - 1}. \tag{17}$$

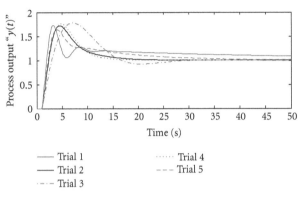

FIGURE 4: Servo response of bioreactor model with EBFO-based PID controller.

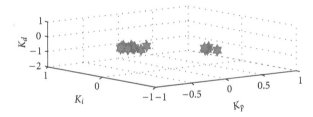

FIGURE 5: Final converged bacteria positions in three-dimensional space.

First part of (17) represents a second order model and the later part shows a reduced first order model. The delay time for both the model is considered as "1."

The EBFO-based PID controller tuning is proposed for the second order model as in Figure 2.

Five trials are performed during the optimization search. The convergence of the EBFO algorithm toward the global optimal solution of the controller parameters are presented in Table 1. Figure 4 depicts the qualitative comparison of the servo response for the trial values presented in Table 1. Among them, Trial 2 value shows the better result compared to other trial values. It also satisfies most of the performance criterion compared to other trial values (Table 1).

The position of the *E. coli* bacteria in the three dimensional search space for Trial 2 is depicted in Figure 5. In this search operation, the artificial bacterium finds the best possible controller parameters by minimizing the MOPI.

Figure 6 graphically represents the optimised K_p, K_i, and K_d values for Trial 2. The search value is converging at 57th iteration.

TABLE 2: Controller values and the performance comparison for bioreactor model.

Method	Iteration	K_p	K_i	K_d	IAE	ISE	M_p	t_r	t_s
GA	63	−0.9104	−0.0655	−0.0428	2.603	6.776	0.838	1.84	51.9
PSO	71	−0.4066	−0.0501	−0.1197	3.404	11.58	0.808	3.16	43.1
BFO	85	−0.5374	−0.0702	−0.0537	2.429	5.900	0.751	2.57	27.0
ABFO	66	−0.6113	−0.0714	−0.0518	2.388	5.704	0.720	2.40	28.3
EBFO	57	−0.6289	−0.0672	−0.0386	2.537	6.439	0.718	2.39	27.6

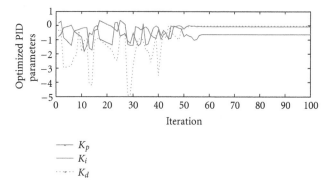

FIGURE 6: Final convergence of controller parameters for Trial 2.

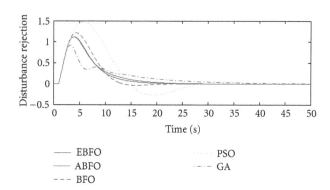

FIGURE 8: Disturbance rejection response of bioreactor model.

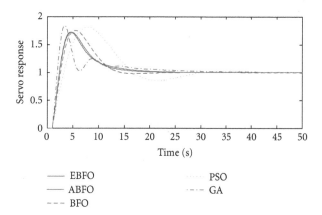

FIGURE 7: Servo response of bioreactor model with EBFO, ABFO, BFO, PSO, and GA tuned PID controller.

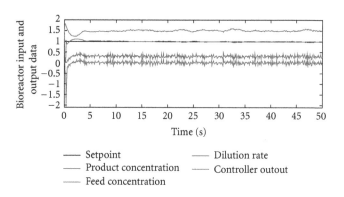

FIGURE 9: Variation of Biomass concentration and substrate concentration with respect to noise.

After finding the optimized controller value using EBSO algorithm; ABFO, classical BFO, PSO, and GA based PID controller tuning is attempted for the unstable bioreactor model. For each algorithm, five trials are performed and the best value among the trial is tabulated in Table 2. From Table 2, it is observed that the number of iteration of EBFO is smaller compared to other algorithms. The ISE and IAE value by the ABFO algorithm is lesser, but the other parameters such as M_p, t_r, and t_s are greater compared to EBFO algorithm.

From Table 2 and Figure 7 values show that, the overall performance of EBFO and ABFO are approximately similar. Disturbance rejection performance of the above methods are tested by applying a load disturbance of 50% (i.e., $D(s) = 0.5$). From Figure 8, the observation is that, the disturbance rejection performance of EBFO and ABFO are identical.

The performance of the EBFO tuned PID controller is tested on the nonlinear bioreactor model developed using the non linear equations (13)–(16). The objective is to maintain the concentration of biomass/product (S_{fs}) based on the setpoint, by adjusting the substrate/feed concentration (S_s). In order to test the robustness of the proposed controller, measurement noise (noise power of 0.001 with a sampling time of 0.1 sec) is introduced in the feedback loop. A feed dilution rate of 0.4 g/lit is considered in this study.

Figure 9 shows the variation of biomass concentration, substrate concentration, dilution rate and the controller output for the servo response. In this a setpoint of 0.995103 g/lit is considered for the biomass concentration. The response confirms that, the proposed scheme works well even in the noisy environment and helps to provide a smooth reference tracking performance.

TABLE 3: Controller values and the performance comparison for isothermal CSTR.

Method	Iteration	K_p	K_i	K_d	IAE	ISE	M_p	t_r	t_s
GA	138	1.1507	0.0074	4.9331	40.51	1641	0.741	42.2	423.7
PSO	144	1.2804	0.0207	8.0426	14.56	212.1	1.015	38.6	305.1
BFO	169	1.4538	0.0111	5.9842	27.01	729.5	0.905	37.7	351.4
ABFO	216	1.2660	0.0205	8.5283	14.68	215.5	1.034	38.9	284.8
EBFO	151	1.3882	0.0155	9.0343	19.42	377.0	0.843	37.2	177.3

4.2. Process Model 2. Isothermal Continuous Stirred Tank Reactor (CSTR) considered by Liou and Yu-Shu [29] has the following transfer function model:

$$\frac{dc}{dt} = \frac{nQ}{mV}\left(C_f - C\right) - \left[\frac{K_1 C}{(K_2 C + 1)^2}\right]. \tag{18}$$

From (18), it can be observed that, the differential equation which represents the concentration of the product with respect to time is nonlinear.

The parameter values of the CSTR are given by [3]: flow rate (Q) = 0.03333 lit/sec; volume (V) = 1 lit, K_1 = 10 lit/s; and K_2 = 10 lit/mol, $n = m = 0.75$. Linearizing the nonlinear model equation around the operating region with, concentration (C_f) = 3.288 mol/lit, gives two stable steady states at C = 1.7673 mol/lit and C = 0.01424 mol/lit. When C = 1.304 mol/lit, the CSTR provides an unstable steady state and it can be mathematically represented by the following unstable transfer function model (with a measurement delay of 20 sec):

$$G(s) = \frac{\Delta C(s)}{\Delta C_f(s)} = \frac{3.3226 \exp^{-20s}}{(99.69s - 1)}. \tag{19}$$

Equation (19) depicts a first order model and the controller setting for this model is proposed as discussed in Section 3.2 with the following values.

(i) The total number of *E. coli* bacteria = 20 (same value is assigned for the agents in BFO, PSO, and GA)

(ii) The numerator of the transfer function has a positive sign (i.e., +3.3266), since the lower boundary of the controller parameter search is assigned as zero. The three dimensional search space is assigned as follows:

Value 1 = $-0\% < K_p < +20\%$ $\left(\text{i.e., } 0 < K_p < 2.0\right)$

Value 2 = $-0\% < K_i < +10\%$ (i.e., $0 < K_i < 1.0$) (20)

Value 3 = $-0\% < K_d < +100\%$ (i.e., $0 < K_d < 10.0$)

The delay time of the process is 20 sec. Since the maximum simulation time is selected as 500 sec.

Five trials are performed using the evolutionary algorithms and the best value among the trial is tabulated in Table 3. Table 3 shows the optimized controller values and its performance measure for the isothermal CSTR model. Even though the iteration value of EBFO algorithm is large compared to the GA- and PSO-based methods, other

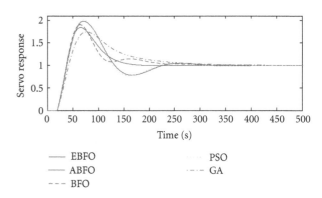

FIGURE 10: Servo response of CSTR model with EBFO, BFO, PSO, and GA tuned PID controller.

parameters such as ISE, IAE, t_r, and t_s are lesser than other algorithms. The ISE and IAE value by the ABFO algorith is smaller compared to GA, BFO, and EBFO. From Figure 10, the observation is that, the EBFO-based method provides significantly improved result compared with BFO, PSO, and GA.

4.3. Process Model 3. Continuous stirred tank reactor (CSTR) with nonideal mixing considered by Liou and Yu-Shu [29] is considered in this study. Linearizing the nonlinear model equation around the operating region with, concentration (C_f) = 3.288 mol/lit, C_e = 1.8 mol/lit and C = 1.304 mol/lit gives the following unstable transfer function model:

$$G(s) = \frac{\Delta C_e(s)}{\Delta C_f(s)} = \frac{2.21(1 + 11.133s)\exp^{-20s}}{(98.3s - 1)}. \tag{21}$$

The process model has one unstable pole and a stable zero. The time delay "θ" in the system is considered as 20 sec. The unstable system with a zero may produce a large overshoot or inverse response. Since during the optimization search, the boundary for the overshoot "M_p" is disconnected. For this process, the simulation study is performed as discussed in Section 3.2 with a simulation time of 500 sec.

Five trials are performed on this process model for each evolutionary algorithm and the best value among the trial is tabulated in Table 4. Figure 11 shows the servo response of the CSTR model with EBFO, ABFO, BFO, PSO, and GA tuned PID controller. Even though the overshoot is large compared to other methods; the overall performance of the present tuning method provides a better result with significantly reduced performance criterion values.

TABLE 4: Controller values and the performance comparison for process model 3.

Method	Iteration	K_p	K_i	K_d	IAE	ISE	M_p	t_r	t_s
GA	331	0.1970	0.0009	0.5109	41.32	1707	0.991	36.5	647.2
PSO	295	0.1270	0.0012	0.5338	31.08	965.9	0.869	43.7	406.1
BFO	324	0.1790	0.0019	0.3941	19.6	385.3	1.190	37.2	370.4
ABFO	360	0.1135	0.0014	0.5211	26.64	709.7	0.976	37.3	371.3
EBFO	319	0.2108	0.0025	0.8100	14.92	222.5	1.243	34.9	335.9

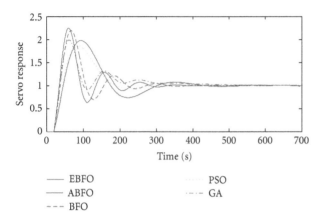

FIGURE 11: Servo response of process model 3.

Nonlinear process loop (spherical tank)

Specification

Tank diameter: 50 cmRotameter : 100–1000 lph (1.667–16.67 lpm)
I / P converter: ABB—modelTEIP 11.

Input: 4–20 mA and output: 3–15 psi

DPT : Rosemount make HARTenabled system, output: 4–20 mA
Control valve with smart positioner: current: 4–20 mA and
working pressure :19.9199.56 psi
Interfacing unit: VI-microsystems make MATLAB compatible,
VISA enabled, serial DAQ system

FIGURE 12: Real-time spherical tank setup and its specifications.

4.4. Real-Time Implementation. In this work, to evaluate the effectiveness of the proposed algorithm, a PID controlled nonlinear spherical tank system is considered. The spherical tank setup shown in Figure 12 is an image of a liquid storage structure widely used in oil and gas industries.

Modelling and control of nonlinear spherical tank system was widely addressed by the researchers. Faccin and Trierweiler [30] proposed a multimodel PID controller design for a spherical tank system. They also proposed a simple model identification technique using the first principle analysis. Madhavasarma and Sundaram [31] proposed a model-based controller tuning for the nonlinear spherical tank system. They developed an approximate stable first order plus dead time (FOPDT) model around the operating region and proposed an IMCPID controller. Nithya et al. [32] proposed a black box system identification technique and developed a FOPDT model. GA-tuned fuzzy logic controller (FLC) was proposed for the identified stable FOPDT model. Figure 12 shows the real time experimental setup of the spherical tank system and its specifications. The objective is to maintain the fluid level (h) by adjusting the inlet flow rate (F_{in}).

The first principle modelling equations for the tank is given below:

$$\frac{dV}{dt} = F_{in} - F_{out},$$

$$A\frac{dh}{dt} = F_{in} - F_{out}, \qquad (22)$$

$$\frac{dh}{dt} = \frac{F_{in} - \beta * \sqrt{h}}{\Pi * h * (D_t - h)},$$

where F_{in} = inlet flow rate, F_{out} = outlet flow rate, V = tank volume, A = area of tank, h = head, D_t = diameter of the tank based on the head, and β = outlet flow capacity coefficient.

The linearised transfer function of the system around the operating point can be developed by neglecting the wall thickness of the tank.

In this setup, a personal computer (PC) loaded with the MATLAB software allows the user to monitor and control the working process. The DAQ supports 4 analog input (voltge in the range of 1 to 5V or current in the range of 4 to 20 mA), 4 analog/digital input and 4 analog/digital output channels. A communication link between the process loop and the monitoring PC is established by the DAQ module through Universal Serial Bus (USB).

A level of 18 cm is considered as the operating point. To develop the transfer function around this operating

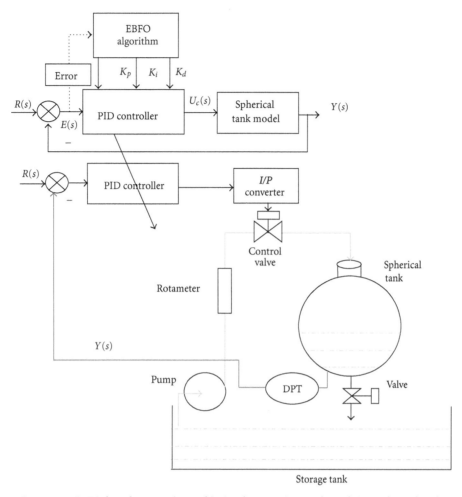

FIGURE 13: EBFO-based PID tuning and its implementation on the real time spherical tank.

point, open-loop step response test is performed with an inlet flow rate F_{in} = 9 lpm. At this operating region, 29.549% of tank is filled with the liquid (19.34 lit) and 70.451% is with the air, the model identified around this operating point using MATLAB software is gived in the following:

$$G_m(s) = \frac{3.6215e^{-\theta s}}{330.46s + 1} = \frac{3.6215e^{-11.7s}}{330.46s + 1}. \tag{23}$$

With the experimental result, the delay by the control valve and the DPT level transmitter is accounted as 11.7 sec.

Figure 13 shows the EBFO-based PID controller tuning procedure and its real time implementation on the spherical tank level control problem. The EBFO algorithm proposed in Section 3.2 is considered for the search. Initially the search is performed on the tank model using (23).

A simulation time of 500 sec is considered in the EBFO-based PID tuning procedure and the algorithm is converged at 57th iteration with the following values:

$$K_p = 7.2074, \qquad K_i = 1.1603, \qquad K_d = 2.0441. \tag{24}$$

Initially, the controller parameter optimization is searched with the process model, and later the identified PID values are transferred to the real time controller installed in the process loop through the monitoring and control program developed in MATLAB Simulink with ODE 45 solver. The Simulink program is directly interfaced with the real time process system through DAQ module. It is enabled with National Instruments VISA serial communication interface. The module supports ASCII data format with a sampling time of 0.1 sec and a baudrate of 38400. With this, Monitoring and control of the real-time process can be easily established with MATLAB software. In real time implementation, the maximum controller output is set as 90% in order to reduce the thrust on the control valve which allows the flow rate to the tank.

Figure 14 shows the variation of level based on the setpoint and the corresponding controller output during the real time study. The ISE and IAE values are obtained as 491.34 and 215.93, respectively, during the real time study.

From this study, it can be noted that the proposed EBFO algorithm presents a smooth servo response for the spherical tank level control problem and it can be easily implemented in real time using a MATLAB supported real time process loop.

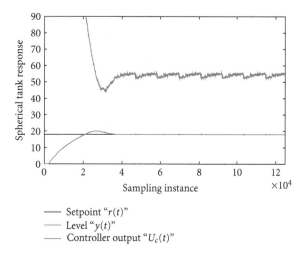

FIGURE 14: Response of spherical tank system for a setpoint of 18 cm (real-time data).

5. Conclusion

In this work, we proposed an enhanced bacterial foraging optimization (EBFO) algorithm to tune the parallel form of PID controller for a class of nonlinear process models. In order to minimize the algorithm complexity, guidelines are provided to select the BFO algorithm parameters. A comparative study is performed with the basic BFO-, ABFO-, PSO-, and GA-based PID controller tuning methods proposed in the literature. The study confirms that the EBFO-tuned PID controller provides improved overall performance compared to other algorithms considered for study. Finally the proposed algorithm is implemented in real time for a spherical tank level control problem. The real time result shows that, the EBFO-tuned PID controller gives a smooth response for reference tracking and maintains the level based on the reference signal.

References

[1] R. A. Maher and R. Samir, "Robust stability of a class of unstable systems under mixed uncertainty," *Journal of Control Science and Engineering*, vol. 2011, no. 970962, 8 pages, 2011.

[2] V. Vijayan and R. C. Panda, "Design of a simple setpoint filter for minimizing overshoot for low order processes," *ISA Transactions*, vol. 51, no. 2, pp. 271–276, 2012.

[3] R. Padma Sree and M. Chidambaram, *Control of Unstable Systems*, Narosa Publishing House, New Delhi, India, 2006.

[4] M. K. Jhunjhunwala and M. Chidambaram, "Pid controller tuning for unstable systems by optimization method," *Chemical Engineering Communications*, vol. 185, no. 1, pp. 91–113, 2001.

[5] I. Chiha, N. Liouane, and P. Borne, "Tuning PID controller using multiobjective ant colony optimization," *Applied Computational Intelligence and Soft Computing*, vol. 2012, Article ID 536326, 7 pages, 2012.

[6] M. Zamani, N. Sadati, and M. K. Ghartemani, "Design of an H∞, PID controller using particle swarm optimization," *International Journal of Control, Automation and Systems*, vol. 7, no. 2, pp. 273–280, 2009.

[7] M. Zamani, M. Karimi-Ghartemani, N. Sadati, and M. Parniani, "Design of a fractional order PID controller for an AVR using particle swarm optimization," *Control Engineering Practice*, vol. 17, no. 12, pp. 1380–1387, 2009.

[8] W. D. Chang and S. P. Shih, "PID controller design of nonlinear systems using an improved particle swarm optimization approach," *Communications in Nonlinear Science and Numerical Simulation*, vol. 15, no. 11, pp. 3632–3639, 2010.

[9] I. Zadeh Hassan and S. Mobayen, "Controller design for rotary inverted pendulum system using evolutionary algorithms," *Mathematical Problems in Engineering*, vol. 2011, Article ID 572424, 17 pages, 2011.

[10] V. Kanth and K. Latha, "Bacterial foraging optimization algorithm based pid controller tuning for time delayedunstable systems," *Mediterranean Journal of Measurement and Control*, vol. 7, no. 1, pp. 197–203, 2011.

[11] V. Kanth and K. Latha, "Optimization of PID controller parameters for unstable chemical systems using soft computing technique," *International Review of Chemical Engineering*, vol. 3, no. 3, pp. 350–358, 2011.

[12] K. M. Passino, "Biomimicry of bacterial foraging for distributed optimization and control," *IEEE Control Systems Magazine*, vol. 22, no. 3, pp. 52–67, 2002.

[13] S. Dasgupta, S. Das, A. Abraham, and A. Biswas, "Adaptive computational chemotaxis in bacterial foraging optimization: an analysis," *IEEE Transactions on Evolutionary Computation*, vol. 13, no. 4, pp. 919–941, 2009.

[14] S. Dasgupta, S. Das, A. Biswas, and A. Abraham, "Automatic circle detection on digital images with an adaptive bacterial foraging algorithm," *Soft Computing*, vol. 14, no. 11, pp. 1151–1164, 2010.

[15] H. Chen, Y. Zhu, and K. Hu, "Cooperative bacterial foraging optimization," *Discrete Dynamics in Nature and Society*, vol. 2009, Article ID 815247, 17 pages, 2009.

[16] H. Chen, Y. Zhu, and K. Hu, "Adaptive bacterial foraging optimization," *Abstract and Applied Analysis*, vol. 2011, Article ID 108269, 27 pages, 2011.

[17] S. Das, S. Dasgupta, A. Biswas, A. Abraham, and A. Konar, "On stability of the chemotactic dynamics in bacterial-foraging optimization algorithm," *IEEE Transactions on Systems, Man, and Cybernetics A*, vol. 39, no. 3, pp. 670–679, 2009.

[18] S. Das, A. Biswas, S. Dasgupta, and A. Abraham, "Bacterial foraging optimization algorithm: theoretical foundations, analysis, and applications," *Studies in Computational Intelligence*, vol. 203, pp. 23–55, 2009.

[19] A. Biswas, S. Das, A. Abraham, and S. Dasgupta, "Stability analysis of the reproduction operator in bacterial foraging optimization," *Theoretical Computer Science*, vol. 411, no. 21, pp. 2127–2139, 2010.

[20] A. Biswas, S. Das, A. Abraham, and S. Dasgupta, "Design of fractional-order PIλDμ controllers with an improved differential evolution," *Engineering Applications of Artificial Intelligence*, vol. 22, no. 2, pp. 343–350, 2009.

[21] G. G. Roy, P. Chakraborty, and S. Das, "Designing fractional-order PIλDμ controller using differential harmony search algorithm," *International Journal of Bio-Inspired Computation*, vol. 2, no. 5, pp. 303–309, 2010.

[22] A. Ghosh, S. Das, A. Chowdhury, and R. Giri, "An ecologically inspired direct search method for solving optimal control problems with Bézier parameterization," *Engineering Applications of Artificial Intelligence*, vol. 24, no. 7, pp. 1195–1203, 2011.

[23] A. Ali and S. Majhi, "Design of optimum PID controller by bacterial foraging strategy," in *Proceedings of IEEE International Conference on Industrial Technology (ICIT '06)*, pp. 601–605, December 2006.

[24] W. M. Korani, H. T. Dorrah, and H. M. Emara, "Bacterial foraging oriented by particle swarm optimization strategy for PID tuning," in *Proceedings of the 8th IEEE International Symposium on Computational Intelligence in Robotics and Automation (CIRA '09)*, pp. 445–450, December 2009.

[25] V. Kanth and K. Latha, "I-PD controller tuning for unstable system using bacterial foraging algorithm: a study based on various error criterion," *Applied computational Intelligence and Soft Computing*, vol. 2012, Article ID 329389, 10 pages, 2012.

[26] E. M. T El-Mansi and C. F. A. Bryce, *Fermentation Microbiology and Biotechnology*, Taylor and Francis, Indian reprint, 2003.

[27] M. A. Johnson and M. H. Moradi, *PID Control: New Identification and Design Methods*, Springer, London, UK, 2005.

[28] B. Wayne-Bequette, *Process Control—Modeling, Design and Simulation*, Prentice-Hall, New Delhi, India, 2003.

[29] C. T. Liou and C. Yu-Shu, "The effect of nonideal mixing on input multiplicity in a CSTR," *Chemical Engineering Science*, vol. 46, no. 8, pp. 2113–2116, 1991.

[30] F. Faccin and J. O. Trierweiler, "A novel toll for multi-model PID controller design," in *Proceedings of the 7th IFAC symposium on Dynamics and Control of Process Systems*, pp. 251–256, 2004.

[31] P. Madhavasarma and S. Sundaram, "Model based tuning of a non linear spherical tank process with time delay," *Instrumentation Science and Technology*, vol. 36, no. 4, pp. 420–431, 2008.

[32] S. Nithya, N. Sivakumaran, T. Balasubramanian, and N. Anantharaman, "Design of controller for nonlinear process using soft computing," *Instrumentation Science and Technology*, vol. 36, no. 4, pp. 437–450, 2008.

5

Smartphone Household Wireless Electroencephalogram Hat

Harold Szu,[1] **Charles Hsu,**[2] **Gyu Moon,**[3] **Takeshi Yamakawa,**[4]
Binh Q. Tran,[1] **Tzyy Ping Jung,**[5] **and Joseph Landa**[6]

[1] *Department of Biomedical Engineering, The Catholic University of America, Washington, DC 20064, USA*

[2] *Trident Systems Inc., Fairfax, VA 22030, USA*

[3] *Department of Electronic Engineering, Hallym University, Chuncheon, Gangwon-do 200-702, Republic of Korea*

[4] *Fuzzy Logic System Institute, Semiconductor Center, Kitakyushu Science and Research Park, Kitakyushu 808-0135, Fukuoka, Japan*

[5] *Swartz Center, University of California, San Diego, CA 92093, USA*

[6] *Briartek Inc., Alexandria, VA 22301, USA*

Correspondence should be addressed to Harold Szu; szuharoldh@gmail.com

Academic Editor: Soo-Young Lee

Rudimentary *brain machine interface* has existed for the gaming industry. Here, we propose a wireless, real-time, and smartphone-based electroencephalogram (EEG) system for homecare applications. The system uses high-density dry electrodes and compressive sensing strategies to overcome conflicting requirements between spatial electrode density, temporal resolution, and spatiotemporal throughput rate. *Spatial sparseness* is addressed by close proximity between active electrodes and desired source locations and using an adaptive selection of N active among $10N$ passive electrodes to form m-organized random linear combinations of readouts, $m \ll N \ll 10N$. *Temporal sparseness* is addressed via parallel frame differences in hardware. During the design phase, we took tethered laboratory EEG dataset and applied fuzzy logic to compute (a) spatiotemporal average of larger magnitude EEG data centers in 0.3 second intervals and (b) inside brainwave sources by Independent Component Analysis blind deconvolution without knowing the impulse response function. Our main contributions are the fidelity of quality wireless EEG data compared to original tethered data and the speed of compressive image recovery. We have compared our recovery of ill-posed inverse data against results using Block Sparse Code. Future work includes development of strategies to filter unwanted artifact from high-density EEGs (i.e., facial muscle-related events and wireless environmental electromagnetic interferences).

1. Introduction

A noninvasive electrical response exists near the scalp from neuron ionic transmission among neural network and may be measured via electroencephalography (EEG). Wang and colleagues of UCSD [1, 2] have demonstrated the efficacy of an untethered, wireless brain machine interface (BMI) system using 20 dry electrodes embedded into a head cap. The wireless EEG head cap system has a built-in bandwidth filter for eliminating environmental noise, for example, 60 Hz household utility line and also for pattern noise. Additionally, this pattern noise filter naturally represents a neuron threshold logic which can be used for assessment of cognitive function and for diagnosis.

Figure 1 shows various observed EEG state, representative EEG patterns, typical frequency ranges, correlation to different activities, and state of mind/levels of engagement. There is a simple rule of thumb about the mnemonics of brainwaves in terms of "D, T, A, B" phonetic equivalence with "deep tap." "Deep tap" separates apart D = delta (0–4 Hz); T = theta (4–7 Hz); A = alpha (8–12 Hz); B = beta (13–30 Hz) at about 4 Hz or more intervals. In classical neuropsychological studies, the central nervous system (CNS) is involved in the information processing of massively parallel and distributive associative memory stored at the hippocampus. This gives rise to an event-related potential (ERP) at latency greater than 300 milliseconds, or 0.3 second delay, often referred to as P300 brainwave component.

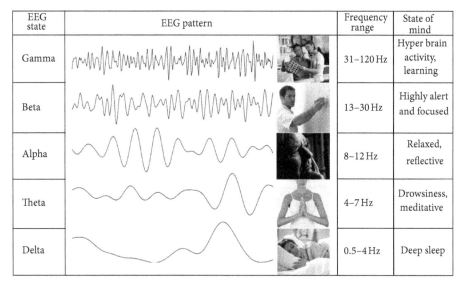

EEG state	EEG pattern		Frequency range	State of mind
Gamma			31–120 Hz	Hyper brain activity, learning
Beta			13–30 Hz	Highly alert and focused
Alpha			8–12 Hz	Relaxed, reflective
Theta			4–7 Hz	Drowsiness, meditative
Delta			0.5–4 Hz	Deep sleep

FIGURE 1: Typical EEG brainwavepatterns during various activities and cognitive states.

Compressive sensing (CS) techniques for dealing with sparse problem sets have been developed by Candès et al. [3, 4] and Donoho [5] (CRT&D) in 2007. Making a sparse m-linear combination, $m \approx 1.3k \ll N$, CRT&D proved a *restricted isometry property* theorem that permits an equivalent L_1-sparse source condition for a noisy LMS L_2-similarity. They adopt a purely random compressive sensing matrix $[\Phi]_{m,N}$ of the size of m-rows and N-columns and then solve by postprocessing a linear programming algorithm to invert an underdetermined linear m-combination of "N" data in a sparse Wavelet Transform representation $[\Psi]_{N,k}$. We wish to modify their mathematical general case to a special design of $[\Phi]_{m,N}$. We apply another well-known Independent Component Analysis (ICA) strategy whereby solving both the unknown mixing matrix $[ICA]_{m,k}$ and the unknown source $\vec{s}$ by means of *blind source separation* (BSS). Using this technique, we can specially design an organized sparse sensing matrix $[\Phi_s]_{m,N}$ to increase SNR to take advantage of the proximity effect by physically placing sensing elements at source locations [5]. We can then further enhance the degree of sparseness by video temporal frame differencing at the electrode sensor domain.

Compressive sensing (CS) is different from JPEG or JPEG2000 postprocessing compression. In a similar fashion to how a focal plane array CCD outputs from pixels sensors with m linear combinations of all N sensor data ($m \ll N$ underdetermined), the advantage of a true medical CS value is that it can be obtained more quickly and at a less exposure (i.e., radiation) to patients. This ill-posed inversion is mathematically possible, because CRT&D proved a CS theorem that the linear combinations readouts coefficients form a purely random bipolar analog CS sampling matrix $[\Phi]$ that is pseudoorthogonal among m rows, where $m \cong 1.3k$ corresponding to the intrinsic sparse degree-of-freedom of the information. In other words, small analog coefficients will be zeroed out, or the locations of N data will not send any X-ray radiation through the patients in the first place. Besides

optical imaging, no one has previously demonstrated CS in the X-ray domain.

The overall goal of this work, shown in Figure 2, is to develop an easy-to-use wireless, portable smartphone-based EEG system for at-home measures of cognitive function with the same accuracy and resolution of in-clinic measures of brain function.

2. Strategy of Generating Sparseness

To be successful in applying CS techniques, the sparse data acquisition strategy deserves a special attention. Usually, data acquisition intrinsically restricts how the sensor-material interaction generates spatiotemporal sampling. This elementary chemical-physics interaction is not flexible and cannot be easily manipulated into another representation where the intrinsic degree of freedom manifests clearly into a numerical quantization value. Without detailed knowledge of sensor-data interaction, the tricks of revealing itself as sparse information content are limited as follows. We consider first the mathematical transform to concentrate the spatiotemporal information and therefore reduce the apparent sparseness. Then, one considers how to embed the mathematics into sensor circuitry hardware, if possible.

(1) Event Correlation Domain. If the data is dense, the correlation of data might not be. After a proper threshold, the correlation, for example, motion target indicator (MTI), is sparse.

(2) Frequency Transform Domain. The histogram could be quantized differently into sparse resolution. Fourier transform frequency domain of a band-limited function requires the Gerchberg-Saxon-Papoulis super-resolution iteration algorithm in order to recover a postcompression algorithm. This is needed to shift to the sensor domain so as to manifest its data sparseness for CS implementation.

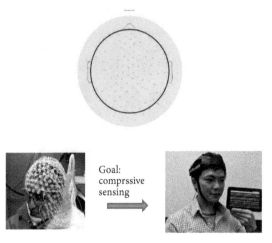

Goal: comprssive sensing

FIGURE 2: Proposed system for wireless wearable, cap-based high spatial density EEG intended for at-home use (right) to replace clinic-based, tethered EEG system (left).

(3) Time-Frequency Joint Representation (TFJR). Optimum concentration of information can be demonstrated using TFJR, Short-Time Fourier Transform, Wigner Distribution Function (frequency charge weighted convolution), and Woodward Ambiguity Function (Doppler shifted correlation).

(4) Frame Differencing Change Detection (FDCD). Often an oversampled video allows for redundancy reduction by a simple frame differencing.

(5) Sensor-Sensing Proximity Effect (SSPE) and Blind Source Separation (BSS). See the following theorem (Section 3).

We generate both spatial and temporal degrees of sparseness in EEG separately in (i) and (ii) as follows: (i) *spatial sparseness*: by *enhancing intrinsic* SNR by the closeness proximity between active electrodes and the desired EEG source locations, using an adaptive software-controlled selection of N active, among $10N$ passive, electrodes to form m-organized random linear combinations of readouts, $m \ll N \ll 10N$; (ii) *temporal sparseness*: massively parallel frame difference by means of *on-board-computing on each electrode* by sampling and hold low-power mixed-signal difference circuitry.

For example, during the design phase, we took the tethered laboratory EEG data set (see Figure 3), applying fuzzy logic to compute (a) spatiotemporal average of larger magnitude of EEG data centers in 0.3 second (i.e., Event Related Potential P300 brainwave) and (b) inside brainwave sources by Independent Component Analysis (ICA) blind deconvolution, without the need of knowing the impulse response function mixing matrix. Consequently, we can choose those active linear-combination read-out electrodes by software selection, as if we had tailored a nonuniform set of electrode distribution at exactly fuzzy-centered locations of sources for enhancing SNR and therefore the degree of sparseness by a simple band-passing threshold.

Point to left frame 1 in 0.003906 s

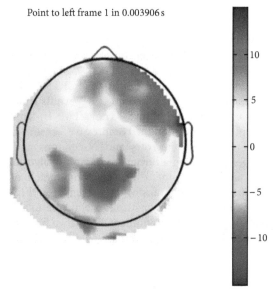

FIGURE 3: Mapping of spatiotemporal brainwave dynamics in high-density tethered lab measurement.

3. Theorem: Enhance the Sparseness by ICA

Given a CRT&D-defined purely random CS $[\Phi]_{m,N}$, we can permute column vectors maintaining the pseudoorthogonality and yet produce an organized CS $[\Phi_s]_{m,N}$ according to sensor-sensing proximity effect as follows:

$$\text{Input } R^N: \vec{X} = \sum_{n=1}^{N} s_n \Psi_n^T \cong \sum_{n_k=1}^{k} s_{n_k} \Psi_{n_k}^T = [\Psi]_{N,k} \vec{s},$$

$$\text{Output } R^m: \vec{Y} = \sum_{m=1}^{M} x_m \Phi_m^T = [\Phi]_{m,N} \vec{X},$$

$$\text{ICA } R^m: \vec{Y} = [\Phi]_{m,N}[\Psi]_{N,k}\vec{s} = [ICA]_{m,k}\vec{s},$$

$$[\Phi_s]_{m,N} \cong [ICA]_{m,k}[\Psi]_{N,k}^{-1}.$$

$$(1)$$

In Figures 4 and 5, we illustrated the difference between CRT&D CS versus our video CS. The difference may be rooted in the method of producing information concentration. Unlike previous applications that concentrated on generating a single-frame sparseness, we applied the video change detection to produce a naturally sparseness. While CRT&D generated the information concentration by some favored transform (FFT or DWT) domain, we worked on a spatiotemporal information processing using the change detection by difference frames. Two resulting sampling matrices may be shown to be equivalent in the sense that a full row or column permutations will not alter the original matrix determinant, and thus we can permute the nonzero value pixels of CRT&D template in Figure 4 to the significant change pixels' location, for example, smiling face. This is to illustrate the potential rank equivalence between CRT&D purely random matrix and our organized pseudorandom matrix. In our video CS approach, we constructed directly the sampling pixels through frame differences, without the aforementioned detouring. The benefit of our organized sparseness may be measured by a good quality of video sending through a narrow bandwidth of smart phone in Figure 6.

4. Hardware and Software Approach

Our improvement is mainly due to aforementioned enhancing SNR for the manifest of intrinsic sparseness using the physical sensor-sensing proximity mechanism. Secondly, we apply the temporal oversampling video nature to reduce the sparseness between frames furthermore by reducing the redundancy using the neighborhood frame differencing. Hardware implementation is illustrated by Simulation Program with Integrated Circuit Emphasis SPICE as shown in Figure 6.

In Figure 6, semiconductors have 3 ports: anode, cathode, and a gate. The gate has two ports, left and right lower corners, denoted by V_1 and V_2. Gate potentials are taken sequentially from an electric potential detector for the prior and subsequent potential intensities. The difference in the output current, I_{out}, located at the right-hand side middle portion is obtained by locally and adaptively modifying the time span between detectors V_1 and V_2 according to current EEG potential and its early EEG potential.

5. Modeling and Simulation

We can iteratively recover the compressive sensing image data, because we have enhanced SNR intrinsically by a proper placement of electrodes close to desired brainwave sources reducing the apparent degree of sparseness by threshold. The apparent sparseness is further reduced by a smart video data change acquisition strategy in the sensor electrode domain. For *spatial sparseness*, we concentrated the measurement electrodes at known desired positions of brainwave sources, reducing further the contact impedance of each electrode using a gecko-like directional nano-grip conducting surface. Toward *temporal sparseness*, we note that the originally CRT&D CS algorithm has m pseudoorthogonal

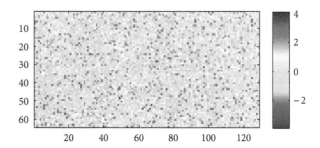

FIGURE 4: CRT&D 2 : 1 ratio compressive sensing coefficients generated by uniformly random bipolar analog values for linear combination of measured data value $N = 128$ and $m = 64$.

linear combinations forming the sparse sensing matrix [Φ] of the size $m \times N$, where $m \ll N$. We moved those larger L_1 norm column vectors of [Φ] as wholes to desired brainwave sources, overlaid with nonuniform designed locations of electrodes. In short, by rearranging the column vector as a whole, we did not disturb the inner products among any two rows of [Φ]. The degree of sparseness can be increased serendipitously if electrodes are properly placed at desired brainwave sources. Then, the physics and the geometry of our nonuniform sampling can concentrate the desired brainwave measurement, naturally generating the source and the weighted-measurement proximity effect, so that the larger SNR is coincided with the larger weight coefficient of [Φ_S]. This procedure completed our theory of organized sensing matri [Φ_S] [6].

Figures 7 and 8 show representative data using the proposed CS algorithm (column 2) for measurement of spatiotemporal brainwave dynamics as compared to clinic-based EEG measures (column 1). The differences between the original and CS images are shown in the 3rd column of Figures 7 and 8.

6. Conclusion

An at-home EEG system capable of real-time monitoring has several potential health monitoring applications, particularly for aging populations who desire to age-in-place as well as those living with acute health conditions. Utilization of EEG for detecting convulsive [7–9] and nonconvulsive [10, 11] epilepsy is well developed and documented in the literature with sensitivities between 80%–90%. Nonconvulsive seizures may mimic EEG patterns seen in encephalopathy's, that is, diminished states of consciousness. Real-time EEG monitoring during sleep may provide valuable information on alterations in sleep patterns, which has been demonstrated to be effective in detecting and predicting anxiety, depression, and early dementia in the elderly [12–15]. Anxiety and depression have been directly correlated to numerous deleterious chronic health conditions such as cardiovascular disease, stroke, sleep disorders, and diabetes to name a few. In many cases, medications prescribed in response to these conditions may cause the onset of depression in patients. Having a mechanism to detect and predict onset of anxiety and depression would be a powerful out-of-clinic tool.

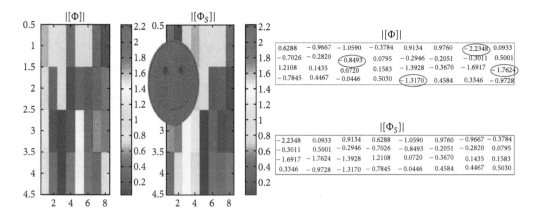

FIGURE 5: Illustration of whole column-wise permutations to move the larger column vector of l_1 norm to a specific location, for example, the left top corner, where the brainwave sources are known to be located.

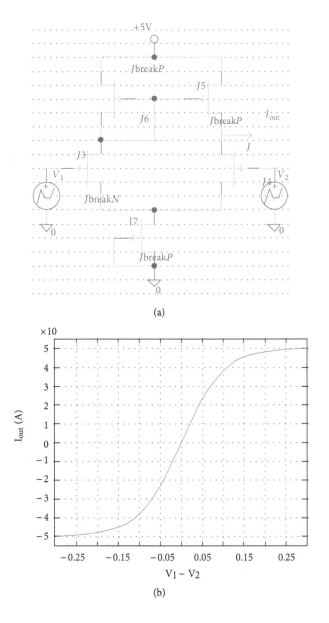

(a)

(b)

FIGURE 6: SPICE implementation of the working CS strategy.

However, further research efforts are required to enhance specificity and sensitivity of EEG for these applications as drowsiness and response to medications have been shown to directly affect EEG patterns. A potential application for at-home EEG monitoring includes assessment of head injuries and postconcussion syndrome. As these conditions affect the alertness of individuals, there is evidence that head injuries affect alpha wave patterns of the EEG in the range of 8–10 Hz [16–18].

While many of the previously discussed studies have demonstrated the potential for EEG to detect and assess cognitive impairments, most have been conducted under controlled research conditions in the clinic. Extensions of these findings to the home require further investigation as environmental conditions are likely to affect EEG data collected. The impact of alertness/drowsiness is a confounding factor that requires further study as well as psychotropic medications that may be prescribed to consumers. Further developments in automated EEG analyses and data reduction techniques, as well as event recording for future analysis, are required to manage the vast amounts of data collected from the proposed system.

Scalp EEG (i.e., EEG from electrodes over the skin and hair through electrically conductive paste) is often affected by a variety of unwanted artifact such as (i) EMG, EOG, and so forth, (ii) biologically-related signal distortion by the skull bone and skin, and (iii) environmental noise and electromagnetic interference (i.e., 60 Hz powerline, computers, and some other electric equipment). Thus, the scalp EEG is often unstable and unreliable, even in a shielded space, which leads to misidentification of the position and volume of the epileptogenic focus and other cognitive measures. Ideally, we wish to improve our strategies and proposed system to more accurately measure electrocorticography (ECoG). Future improvements will focus on a CS module of high-density dry electrodes with nano-grid surface, thereby reducing contact impedance of the original inconvenient EEG measuring wet electrodes. Two spatiotemporal analog filters at electrode level will be implemented to eliminate both the unstable motion-generated EMG and *wireless environmental electromagnetic interference* (we-EMI). Such

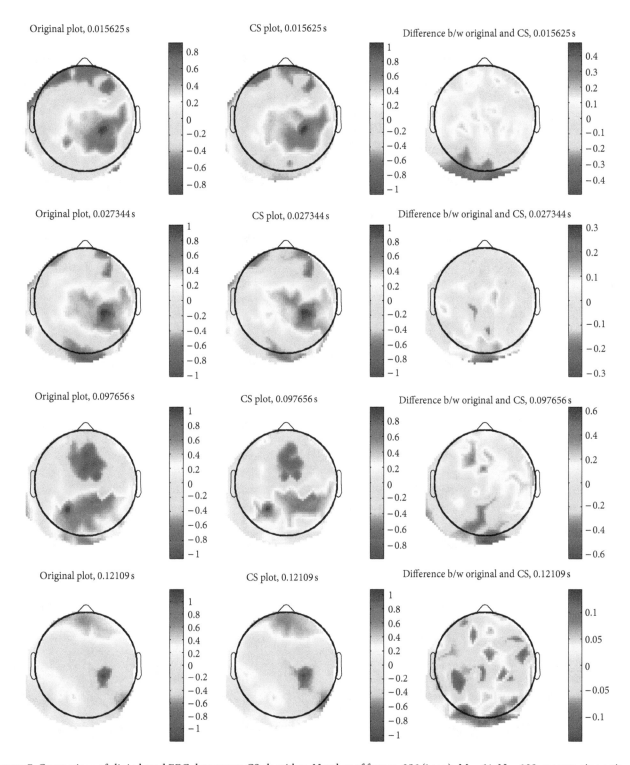

FIGURE 7: Comparison of clinic-based EEG data versus CS algorithm. Number of frames: 256 (1 sec.), $M = 64$, $N = 128$, compression ratio = 2 : 1.

an approach can clean up EEG data for accurate pinpointing the center of epilepsy as proven by Thatcher et al. [17]. This cleaned up version will be useful for a home-based patient monitoring system for epileptic seizures and other cognitive measures.

In this paper, we have jointly addressed the possibility of real-time in situ EEG measurement using CS firmware technology intended for out-of-clinic applications. However, to complete the design of video EEG, additional challenges remain such as (i) need for fuzzy logic-based strategy for optimal, nonuniform placement of electrodes that generates stronger SNR for natural sparseness, (ii) a lower-power mixed-signal processor at each electrode (denoise, A/D, etc.), and (iii) new advanced system design using an

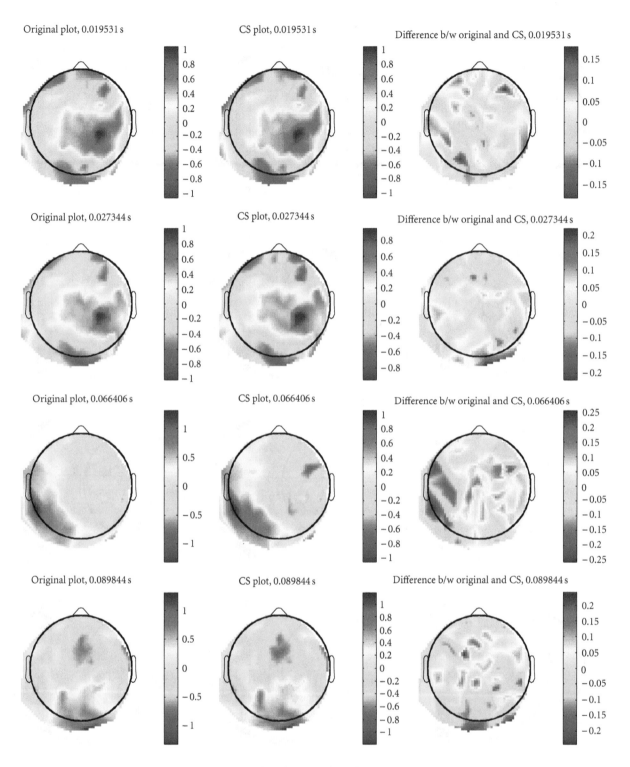

FIGURE 8: Comparison of clinic-based EEG data versus CS algorithm. Number of frames: 256 (1 sec.), $M = 32$, $N = 128$, compression ratio = $4:1$.

ultra-high-density distribution of 500 electrodes adaptively on-off switch of 128 locally. Additional technological challenges, include electromagnetic interference affecting wireless transmission, spatiotemporal delays, and computational speed required by real-time in situ processing.

Acknowledgments

Original data was taken by a traditional tethered EEG head mount, sponsored by ONR and provided by Dr. Yijun Wang of Swartz Center of UCSD. T. Yamakawa wishes to acknowledge a partial support (Project no. 20001008) of de-EMG and de-EMI EEG data called ECoG data for pinpointing the epileptic center entitled "Identification of Epileptogenic Focus by Employing Softcomputing and Establishment of Minimally Invasive and Definitive Surgery" from June 2008 to March 2012 [17].

References

[1] Y. Wang and T. P. Jung, "A collaborative brain-computer interface for improving human performance," *PLoS ONE*, vol. 6, no. 5, article e20422, 2011.

[2] Y. T. Wang, Y. Wang, and T. P. Jung, "A cell-phone-based brain-computer interface for communication in daily life," *Journal of Neural Engineering*, vol. 8, no. 2, Article ID 025018, 2011.

[3] E. J. Candès, J. Romberg, and T. Tao, "Robust uncertainty principles: exact signal reconstruction from highly incomplete frequency information," *IEEE Transactions on Information Theory*, vol. 52, no. 2, pp. 489–509, 2006.

[4] E. J. Candes and T. Tao, "Near-optimal signal recovery from random projections: universal encoding strategies?" *IEEE Transactions on Information Theory*, vol. 52, no. 12, pp. 5406–5425, 2006.

[5] D. L. Donoho, "Compressed sensing," *IEEE Transactions on Information Theory*, vol. 52, no. 4, pp. 1289–1306, 2006.

[6] H. Szu, C. Hsu, J. Jenkins, J. Willey, and J. Landa, "Capturing significant events with neural networks," *Neural Networks Journal*, vol. 29-30, pp. 1–7, 2012.

[7] F. Pauri, F. Pierelli, G. E. Chatrian, and W. W. Erdly, "Long-term EEG-video-audio monitoring: computer detection of focal EEG seizure patterns," *Electroencephalography and Clinical Neurophysiology*, vol. 82, no. 1, pp. 1–9, 1992.

[8] A. J. Gabor and M. Seyal, "Automated interictal EEG spike detection using artificial neural networks," *Electroencephalography and Clinical Neurophysiology*, vol. 83, no. 5, pp. 271–280, 1992.

[9] H. Qu and J. Gotman, "A seizure warning system for long-term epilepsy monitoring," *Neurology*, vol. 45, no. 12, pp. 2250–2254, 1995.

[10] G. Bauer, F. Aichner, and U. Mayr, "Nonconvulsive status epilepticus followed generalized tonic-clonic seizures," *European Neurology*, vol. 21, no. 6, pp. 411–419, 1982.

[11] H. Doose, "Nonconvulsive status epilepticus in childhood: clinical aspects and classfication," *Advances in Neurology*, vol. 34, pp. 115–125, 1984.

[12] C. F. Reynolds, D. J. Kupfer, P. R. Houck et al., "Reliable discrimination of elderly depressed and demented patients by electroencephalographic sleep data," *Archives of General Psychiatry*, vol. 45, no. 3, pp. 258–264, 1988.

[13] G. C. Blackhart, J. A. Minnix, and J. P. Kline, "Can EEG asymmetry patterns predict future development of anxiety and depression? A preliminary study," *Biological Psychology*, vol. 72, no. 1, pp. 46–50, 2006.

[14] G. Morabito, A. Bramanti, D. Labate, F. La Foresta, and F. C. Morabito, "Early detection of Alzheimer's onset with Permutation Entropy analysis of EEG," *NATO*, vol. 1, pp. 30–32, 2011.

[15] C. Bandt and B. Pompe, "Permutation entropy: a natural complexity measure for time series," *Physical Review Letters*, vol. 88, no. 17, Article ID 174102, 2002.

[16] M. T. Tebano, M. Cameroni, G. Gallozzi et al., "EEG spectral analysis after minor head injury in man," *Electroencephalography and Clinical Neurophysiology*, vol. 70, no. 2, pp. 185–189, 1988.

[17] R. W. . Thatcher, R. A. Walker, I. Gerson, and F. H. Geilser, "EEG discriminant analysis of mild head trauma," *Electroencephalography and Clinical Neurophysiology*, vol. 73, pp. 94–106, 1989.

[18] R. W. Thatcher, D. S. Cantor, R. McAlaster, F. Geisler, and P. Krause, "Comprehensive predictions of outcome in closed head-injured patients. The development of prognostic equations," *Annals of the New York Academy of Sciences*, vol. 620, pp. 82–101, 1991.

Four Machine Learning Algorithms for Biometrics Fusion: A Comparative Study

I. G. Damousis and S. Argyropoulos

Informatics and Telematics Institute, Centre for Research and Technology Hellas, 57001 Thessaloniki, Greece

Correspondence should be addressed to I. G. Damousis, damousis@gmail.com

Academic Editor: Cheng-Jian Lin

We examine the efficiency of four machine learning algorithms for the fusion of several biometrics modalities to create a multimodal biometrics security system. The algorithms examined are Gaussian Mixture Models (GMMs), Artificial Neural Networks (ANNs), Fuzzy Expert Systems (FESs), and Support Vector Machines (SVMs). The fusion of biometrics leads to security systems that exhibit higher recognition rates and lower false alarms compared to unimodal biometric security systems. Supervised learning was carried out using a number of patterns from a well-known benchmark biometrics database, and the validation/testing took place with patterns from the same database which were not included in the training dataset. The comparison of the algorithms reveals that the biometrics fusion system is superior to the original unimodal systems and also other fusion schemes found in the literature.

1. Introduction

Identity verification has many real-life applications such as access control and economic or other transactions. Biometrics measure the unique physical or behavioural characteristics of an individual as a means to recognize or authenticate their identity. Common physical biometrics include fingerprints, hand or palm geometry, and retina, iris, or facial characteristics. On the other hand, behavioural characteristics include signature, voice (which also has a physical component), keystroke pattern, and gait. Although some technologies have gained more acceptance than others, it is beyond doubt that the field of access control and biometrics as a whole shows great potential for use in end user segments, such as airports, stadiums, defence installations, but also the industry and corporate workplaces where security and privacy are required.

Biometrics may be used for identity establishment. A new measurement that purports to belong to a particular entity is compared against the data stored in relation to that entity. If the measurements match, the assertion that the person is whom they say they are is regarded as being authenticated. Some building access schemes work in this way, with the

system comparing the new measure against the company's employee database. Also authentication of the identity of a person is frequently used in order to grand access to premises or data.

Since authentication takes place instantaneously and usually only once, identity fraud is possible. An attacker can bypass the biometrics authentication system and continue undisturbed. A cracked or stolen biometric system presents a difficult problem. Unlike passwords or smart cards, which can be changed or reissued, absent serious medical intervention, a fingerprint or iris is forever. Once an attacker has successfully forged those characteristics, the end user must be excluded from the system entirely, raising the possibility of enormous security risks and/or reimplementation costs. Static physical characteristics can be digitally duplicated, for example, the face could be copied using a photograph, a voice-print using a voice recording, and the fingerprint using various forging methods. In addition static biometrics could be intolerant of changes in physiology such as daily voice changes or appearance changes.

Unimodal biometric systems have to contend with a variety of problems such as noisy data, intraclass variations, restricted degrees of freedom, non-universality, spoof

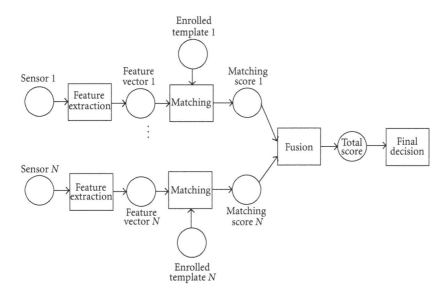

FIGURE 1: Fusion at the matching score level.

attacks, and unacceptable error rates. Some of these limitations can be addressed by deploying multimodal biometric systems [1, 2] that integrate the evidence presented by multiple sources of information. Indeed, the development of systems that integrate two or more biometrics is emerging as a trend. Such systems, known as multimodal biometric systems, are expected to be more reliable due to the presence of multiple, (fairly) independent pieces of evidence. These systems are able to meet the stringent performance requirements imposed by various applications. They address the problem of nonuniversality, since multiple traits ensure sufficient population coverage. They also deter spoofing since it would be difficult for an impostor to spoof multiple biometric traits of a genuine user simultaneously. Furthermore, they can facilitate a challenge response type of mechanism by requesting the user to present a random subset of biometric traits thereby ensuring that a "live" user is indeed present at the point of data acquisition.

In the present paper we present the development and evaluation of four machine learning algorithms for the fusion of the similarity scores of several biometric experts to form a multimodal biometrics system, aiming to raise significantly the recognition accuracy and reduce the false acceptance and false rejection rates. The supervised algorithms are trained using samples from a well known biometrics database and then validated using samples from the same database that are different from the training ones. The aim is to compare the developed algorithms with existing techniques and also find the most efficient one out of the four, in order to use it for the fusion of novel biometrics within project HUMABIO [3].

2. Supervised Fusion Algorithms

Fusion at matching score level is the most common approach of fusion in multimodal biometric systems [2]. This fact is mainly due to the easy accessibility and availability of the matching scores in many biometric modules. The input for a fusion algorithm at matching score level is the (dis-) similarity score provided by a biometric module (Figure 1). There are different approaches of merging scores at the matching score level. In this approach, output scores of the individual matching algorithms constitute the components of a multidimensional vector for example, a 3D vector is created if scores from a face, gait, and voice matching module are available. The resulting multi-dimensional vector is then classified using a classification algorithm such as Support Vector Machines (SVM), Fuzzy Expert systems (FES), neural networks, and so forth, to solve the two class classification problem of classifying the output vector into either "impostor" (unauthorized users) or "genuine" (authorized users, or *clients*) class. One advantage of the approach is the fact that scores may be inhomogeneous such as a mix of similarities and distances possibly located in different intervals. Thus, no pre-processing is required for classification fusion.

In supervised learning, the learning algorithm is provided a training set of patterns (or inputs) with associated labels (or outputs). Usually, the patterns are in the form of attribute vectors and once the attribute vectors are available, machine-learning methods can be applied, ranging from simple Boolean operators, to Bayesian classification and more sophisticated methods. The performance of a fusion algorithm relies on the tuning of the system. This tuning usually consists in a group of hyper-parameters that can be set manually (such as type of kernel in SVMs, number of chromosomes in Genetic Algorithms (GA), etc.) and another group that is set during the training phase. The training is used so that the algorithm can estimate (learn) the client and impostor spaces and is crucial for the performance of the fusion system.

In this study four state of the art fusion techniques were utilized, namely Support Vector Machines, Fuzzy Expert Systems, Gaussian Mixture Models and Artificial Neural

Networks. Each of these techniques follows a different philosophy for the fusion of the unimodal biometric inputs in order to produce an overall estimation of whether the person is a client or an impostor.

2.1. Support Vector Machine.

A typical SVM implementation was developed [4]. A radial basis kernel function was used to map the input data to a higher dimensional space, in which they were linearly separable [5]. The radial basis kernel (RBF) was selected in order to handle probable nonlinearities between the input vectors and their corresponding class. It also has less hyperparameters than the polynomial kernel thus making training easier.

After the selection of the kernel, the process followed consists of identifying the best pair of C and γ, that is, the pair with the best cross-validation accuracy. Following the guidelines found in [6], the training set was divided into equal sized subsets and one subset was the validation dataset using the classifier that was trained on the remaining subsets. The process was repeated sequentially until all subsets acted a validation dataset. The selection of C and γ was done via grid search, that is, trying exponentially growing sequences of C and γ [7]. The penalty parameters for each of the two classes ("Genuine", "Impostor") was done via complete enumeration trials.

The final trained SVM model was then used with the optimal C, γ pair in order to check the classifier performance on the test dataset which is comprised of "unknown" patterns that were not used for the SVM training.

2.2. Fuzzy Expert System.

A TSK FES [8] was developed as described in [9]. The FES's premise space consisted of three inputs ($NPI = 3$). Each premise input was segmented by three trapezoid membership functions described by the following equation:

$$\mu_i^j\left(x_{p,i}\right) = \max\left(\min\left(\frac{x_{p,i} - a_{i,j}}{b_{i,j} - a_{i,j}}, 1, \frac{d_{i,j} - x_{p,i}}{d_{i,j} - c_{i,j}}\right), 0\right), \quad (1)$$

where the parameters $a_{i,j}$ and $d_{i,j}$ locate the "feet" of the "jth" trapezoid of the "ith" premise input and the parameters $b_{i,j}$ and $c_{i,j}$ locate the "shoulders".

This segmentation leads to the creation of 27 three-dimensional fuzzy rules (Figure 2).

The firing strength of the rule $R(j)$, representing the degree to which $R(j)$ is excited by a particular premise input vector $\overline{X}_p$, is determined by

$$\mu_j\left(\overline{X}_p\right) = \prod_{i=1}^{NPI}\mu_i^j\left(x_{p,i}\right). \quad (2)$$

The premise inputs were selected via extensive experimentation from the available biometric experts (shown in Table 1). Each fuzzy rule produces an output which is a linear function of the unimodal classifiers' scores $x_{c,i}$ shown in

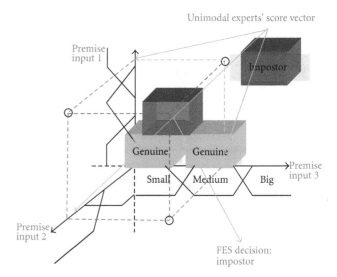

FIGURE 2: Three membership functions with linguistic expressions "low", "medium", "high" (score) are used for the partitioning of three premise inputs, leading to the formation of 27 fuzzy rules.

TABLE 1: EER of the unimodal experts in the XM2VTS database.

Expert	EER (%)
1 (Face)	1.83
2 (Face)	4.13
3 (Face)	1.78
4 (Face)	3.50
5 (Face)	6.50
6 (Voice)	1.09
7 (Voice)	6.50
8 (Voice)	4.50

Table 1 so as to include all of the available information from the unimodal biometric experts:

$$y_j = F\left(\overline{X}_c\right) = \lambda_0^j + \sum_{i=1}^{NI}\lambda_i^j x_{c,i} + \sum_{k=1}^{NI}\lambda_k^j\frac{1}{x_{c,i}}, \quad (3)$$

where NI is the number of unimodal classifiers.

The FES estimation of the client's authenticity is a synthesis (weighted average) of the 27 fuzzy rule outputs:

$$y = \frac{\sum_{j=1}^{NR}\mu_j\left(\overline{X}_p\right) \cdot F_j\left(\overline{X}_c\right)}{\sum_{j=1}^{NR}\mu_j\left(\overline{X}_p\right)}. \quad (4)$$

This estimation is compared to a threshold T and if it is higher than the FES classifies the pattern as genuine transaction while if it is lower it classifies it as impostor.

The parameters λ of the fuzzy rules' linear output functions (3), the parameters of the trapezoid membership functions (1) that define the position of the fuzzy rules in the premise space (or in other words the segmentation of the premise inputs via the shape and positioning of the membership functions), and also the decision threshold T are optimized by a real coded [9] genetic algorithm [10].

The GA fitness function was selected so as to minimize the false acceptance of impostors and maximize correct authentication rate through the evolution of the GA:

$$\text{Fitness function} = \frac{\text{correct\_out}}{\text{error\_out} + \text{false\_normal} + 1}, \quad (5)$$

where correct_out is the accumulated distance of the fuzzy output from the decision threshold in case of correct authentication (genuine or impostor), error_out is accumulated distance of the fuzzy output from the threshold in case of incorrect authentication for all training patterns, and false_normal is the number of falsely accepted impostor individuals.

In that way the solutions that have minimum false acceptance occurrences have higher fitness value. The same stands for solutions (chromosomes) that produce outputs that have larger distance from the threshold T in correct authentications (more robust solutions) and smaller distance from the threshold in case of erroneous authentications (thus driving wrong solutions towards the threshold and rectifying them).

2.3. Gaussian Mixture Model. Bayesian classification and decision making is based on probability theory and the principle of choosing the most probable or the lowest risk (expected cost) option. The Gaussian distribution is usually quite good approximation for a class model shape in a suitably selected feature space. In a Gaussian distribution lies an assumption that the class model is truly a model of one basic class. However, if the actual model is multimodal, this model cannot capture coherently the underlying distribution. Gaussian Mixture Model (GMM) is a mixture of several Gaussian distributions and can therefore represent different subclasses within a class [11]. The probability density function is defined as a weighted sum of Gaussians:

$$P(x; \theta) = \sum_{c=1}^{C} \alpha_c N(x; \mu_c, \Sigma_c), \quad (6)$$

where α_c is the weight of component c, $0 \leq \alpha_c \leq 1$ and

$$\sum_{c=1}^{C} \alpha_c = 1. \quad (7)$$

The parameter list $\theta = \{\alpha_1, \mu_1, \Sigma_1, \ldots, \alpha_c, \mu_c, \Sigma_c\}$ defines a particular Gaussian mixture probability density function. Estimation of the Gaussian mixture parameters for one class can be considered as unsupervised learning of the case where the samples are generated by individual components of the mixture distribution and without the knowledge of which sample was generated by which component.

A GMM was developed, which comprised of four mixture components. The weights of the components were estimated after extensive experimentation.

2.4. Artificial Neural Network. The fourth algorithm was a three-layer feed-forward neural network (NN) [12]. The layers consist of N input neurons, Y hidden neurons, and one output neuron where N is equal to the number of unimodal biometric experts (from Table 1, $N = 8$) and Y is set through experimentation equal to ten. The neurons are fully interconnected and a bias is applied on each neuron. The transfer function is selected to be sigmoid so as to address nonlinearities of the input data set. For the training of the weights, the typical back propagation method was used. The optimum number of training iterations and training parameters was set heuristically. Convergence was achieved after 500 iterations.

3. Benchmark Database

The developed fusion schemes were tested on the publicly available XM2VTS face and speech database [13, 14]. The XM2VTS database contains facial and speech data from 295 subjects, recorded during four sessions taken at one-month intervals. It includes similarity scores from five face experts and three speech experts. The protocol consists of two sets: the development (training) set and the evaluation (validation) set. The development set, which is used for training, contains scores from three multimodal recordings for each of 200 client users and eight transactions from each of the 25 impostors. The evaluation set, which is used for testing the system, contains scores from two multimodal recordings of the (same) 200 client users and eight transactions for each of the 70 (new) impostors. The impostors in the evaluation set are different from the impostors in the development. Thus, the development set contains 600 (200 × 3) client transactions and 40000 (25 × 200 × 8) impostor transactions whereas the evaluation set contains 400 (200 × 2) client transactions and 112000 (70 × 200 × 8) impostor transactions.

Two metrics are computed: the False Acceptance Rate (FAR) and the False Rejection Rate (FRR) defined as

$$\text{FAR} = \frac{\text{number of accepted impostors}}{\text{number of impostor transactions}},$$

$$\text{FRR} = \frac{\text{number of rejected clients}}{\text{number of client transactions}}. \quad (8)$$

The Half Total Error Rate (HTER) is also reported which is defined as

$$\text{HTER} = \frac{\text{FAR} + \text{FRR}}{2}. \quad (9)$$

The Equal Error Rate (EER) is computed as the point where FRR = FAR; in practice, FRR and FAR are not continuous functions and a crossover point might not exist. In this case, the interval [EER*lo*, EER*hi*] should be reported. Also, another useful tool for the evaluation of the performance of a biometric system is the Rate Operating Characteristic (ROC) curve, which is produced by plotting FAR versus FRR.

The EERs of the unimodal experts for the XM2VTS database are shown in Table 1.

Figure 3 shows indicative FAR-FRR diagrams for two face and voice unimodal biometrics experts of the XM2VTS database. It can be seen from the threshold T range that the expert scores that characterize someone as impostor or genuine differ significantly. However, this does not pose a problem for the fusion algorithms.

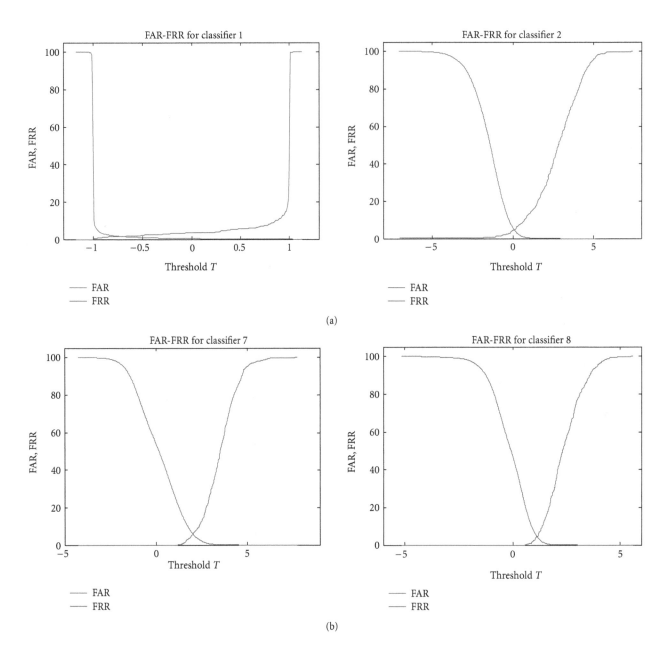

FIGURE 3: FAR-FRR diagrams and EER for (a) two face and (b) two voice biometrics experts of the XM2VTS database.

TABLE 2: Summary table of verification results of different fusion methods for the XM2VTS database.

Fusion method	Training set			Test set		
	FAR (%)	FRR (%)	HTER (%)	FAR (%)	FRR (%)	HTER (%)
SVM	0	0	0	0.0	0.5	**0.25**
FES	0	0.005	0.0025	0.15	0.75	**0.45**
NN	0.0025	0.33	0.17	0.0	1	**0.5**
GMM	0.0225	0.33	0.18	0.028	1	**0.51**
OR	12.63	0	6.31	19.46	0.0	**9.73**
AND	0.22	12.83	6.52	0.0	19.75	**9.87**

TABLE 3: Performance comparison of fusion schemes for the XM2VTS database.

Fusion scheme	HTER (%)
Product	3.50
Max	2.35
Min	1.13
Dempster-Shafer	0.76
Sum	0.75
Weighted sum	0.63
SVM	0.52
SumPro	0.31
Presented SVM	**0.25**

4. Test Results

4.1. Comparative Results. Table 2 summarizes the results of the investigated machine learning algorithms for multimodal fusion. More specifically, the classification of the XM2VTS patterns was performed using the SVM, GMM, FES, and NN fusion schemes. Furthermore, some simple combination rules (AND, OR) were also tested. The first conclusion we can reach from the results illustrated in the table is that all of the fusion schemes perform better than the best performing unimodal expert (i.e., expert 6 with EER 1.09%) and the classification absolute improvement using the SVM fusion method is 0.84% (SVM HTER = 0.25%, ~77% relative improvement over unimodal expert 6 classification error). This corroborates the statement that the effective combination of information coming from different experts can improve significantly the performance of a biometric system. Moreover, this table also confirms the superiority of the SVM fusion scheme over the other machine learning techniques. More specifically, the FAR and FRR using the SVM fusion classifier on the XM2VTS database are 0.0% and 0.5%, respectively. The superior performance of the SVM fusion classifier over the second best FES, which is 0.2%, is mainly attributed to the more efficient modelling of the feature space. Moreover, the SVM fusion expert performs very satisfactory when the number of the feature vectors (comprised of the matching scores in this case) is relatively large, as in the case of the XM2VTS database, where there are 8 unimodal experts.

4.2. Comparison with State-of-the-Art Methods. An experimental study was also conducted to compare the developed schemes with state-of-the-art fusion methods on the XM2VTS database. The same unimodal experts and the same protocol were employed so that any performance gain or decrease can be attributed only to the fusion algorithm. The following table illustrates the HTER values of various fusion schemes, as reported in [15].

The first conclusion from Table 3 is that the reported results are inferior compared to the results presented in the previous section. Specifically, the best result, in terms of HTER, is 0.31%, whereas the best result of the algorithms presented in this paper is 0.25%. Moreover, it can be seen that the accuracy achieved in [15] for SVM classification

is lower than the authentication accuracy produced by our implementation of the SVM fusion scheme. This could be attributed partly to the different implementation of the algorithm. The comparison results validate the superiority of the developed SVM scheme and indicate its appropriateness for the application scenarios examined within HUMABIO [16, 17].

5. Conclusions

Four machine learning algorithms were developed for the fusion of several biometric modalities in order to detect the most efficient one for use within the project HUMABIO. The algorithms were Gaussian Mixture Models, an Artificial Neural Network, a Fuzzy Expert System, and Support Vector Machines. The algorithms were trained and tested using a well-known biometric database which contains samples of face and speech and similarity scores of five face and three speech biometric experts. The fusion results were compared against existing fusion techniques and also against each other, showing that the fusion schemes presented in this paper produce better biometric accuracy from conventional methods. From the four algorithms, the most efficient one proved to be the support vector machines-based one offering significant performance enhancement over unimodal biometrics, over more traditionally combined multimodal biometrics, but also over the SoA.

Acknowledgments

This work was supported in part by the EC under Contract FP6-026990 HUMABIO [3, 16]. I. G. Damousis, when the research reported in this paper took place, was with the Informatics and Telematics Institute of the Centre for Research and Technology Hellas in Thessaloniki, Greece (e-mail: damousis@gmail.gr). S. Argyropoulos, when the research reported in this paper took place, was with the Informatics and Telematics Institute of the Centre for Research and Technology Hellas in Thessaloniki, Greece (e-mail: savvas@ieee.org).

References

[1] A. Ross and A. Jain, "Information fusion in biometrics," *Pattern Recognition Letters*, vol. 24, no. 13, pp. 2115–2125, 2003.

[2] A. K. Jain and A. Ross, "Multibiometric systems," *Communications of the ACM*, vol. 47, no. 1, pp. 34–40, 2004.

[3] I. G. Damousis, D. Tzovaras, and E. Bekiaris, "Unobtrusive multimodal biometric authentication: the HUMABIO project concept," *Eurasip Journal on Advances in Signal Processing*, vol. 2008, Article ID 265767, 11 pages, 2008.

[4] C. J. C. Burges, "A tutorial on support vector machines for pattern recognition," *Data Mining and Knowledge Discovery*, vol. 2, no. 2, pp. 121–167, 1998.

[5] N. Christianini and J. Shawe-Taylor, *An Introduction to Support Vector Machines and Other Kernel-based Learning Methods*, Cambridge University Press, 2000.

[6] C. W. Hsu, C. C. Chang, and C. J. Lin, "A practical guide to support vector classification," *Test*, vol. 1, no. 1, pp. 1–16, 2010.

[7] R. E. Fan, P. H. Chen, and C. J. Lin, "Working set selection using second order information for training support vector machines," *Journal of Machine Learning Research*, vol. 6, pp. 1889–1918, 2005.

[8] T. Takagi and M. Sugeno, "Fuzzy identification of systems and its applications to modeling and control," *IEEE Transactions on Systems, Man and Cybernetics*, vol. 15, no. 1, pp. 116–132, 1985.

[9] I. G. Damousis and D. Tzovaras, "Fuzzy fusion of eyelid activity indicators for hypovigilance-related accident prediction," *IEEE Transactions on Intelligent Transportation Systems*, vol. 9, no. 3, pp. 491–500, 2008.

[10] D. E. Goldberg, *Genetic Algorithms in Search, Optimization, and Machine Learning*, Addison-Wesley, New York, NY, USA, 1989.

[11] M. A. T. Figueiredo and A. K. Jain, "Unsupervised learning of finite mixture models," *IEEE Transactions on Pattern Analysis and Machine Intelligence*, vol. 24, no. 3, pp. 381–396, 2002.

[12] T. Masters, *Signal and Image Processing with Neural Networks*, John Wiley & Sons, 1994.

[13] N. Poh and S. Bengio, "A score-level fusion benchmark database for biometric authentication," in *Proceedings of the 5th International Conference on Audio, and Video-Based Biometric Person Authentication (AVBPA '05)*, vol. 3546 of *Lecture Notes in Computer Science*, pp. 1059–1070, July 2005.

[14] XM2VTS database, http://www.ee.surrey.ac.uk/CVSSP/xm2vtsdb/.

[15] L. Shoushan and Z. Chengqing, "Classifier combining rules under independence assumptions," in *Proceedings of the 7th international Conference on Multiple Classifier Systems (MCS '07)*, vol. 4472 of *lecture Notes in Computer Science*, pp. 322–332, 2007.

[16] HUMABIO project, http://www.humabio-eu.org/.

[17] A. Vatakis et al., "Deliverable 7.1 HUMABIO Pilot plans," 2008.

7

Exploiting Mobile Ad Hoc Networking and Knowledge Generation to Achieve Ambient Intelligence

Anna Lekova

Institute of System Engineering and Robotics, Bulgarian Academy of Sciences, Acad. G. Bonchev Street, Block 2, 1113 Sofia, Bulgaria

Correspondence should be addressed to Anna Lekova, alekova@icsr.bas.bg

Academic Editor: Tzung P. Hong

Ambient Intelligence (AmI) joins together the fields of ubiquitous computing and communications, context awareness, and intelligent user interfaces. Energy, fault-tolerance, and mobility are newly added dimensions of AmI. Within the context of AmI the concept of mobile ad hoc networks (MANETs) for "anytime and anywhere" is likely to play larger roles in the future in which people are surrounded and supported by small context-aware, cooperative, and nonobtrusive devices that will aid our everyday life. The connection between knowledge generation and communication ad hoc networking is symbiotic—knowledge generation utilizes ad hoc networking to perform their communication needs, and MANETs will utilize the knowledge generation to enhance their network services. The contribution of the present study is a distributed evolving fuzzy modeling framework (EFMF) to observe and categorize relationships and activities in the user and application level and based on that social context to take intelligent decisions about MANETs service management. EFMF employs unsupervised online one-pass fuzzy clustering method to recognize nodes' mobility context from social scenario traces and ubiquitously learn "friends" and "strangers" indirectly and anonymously.

1. Introduction

Ambient intelligence (AmI) is emerging as a new research discipline joining the fields of ubiquitous computing and communications, context-awareness, and intelligent user interfaces. The paradigm is also known as "pervasive computing", "things that think", "ubiquitous computing", and so forth. Energy, fault-tolerance, and mobility are newly added dimensions of the AmI [1]. AmI places people and social contexts at the centre, while the information and communication technologies as well as network context go to the background. The new AmI paradigm is made possible by the convergence of low-cost sensors, embedded processors, and wireless ad hoc networks in new generation industrial digital products and services. Mobile ad hoc networks (MANETs) are multihop wireless networks without fixed infrastructure, formed by mobile nodes. The connection between knowledge generation and mobile ad hoc networks will be symbiotic—knowledge generation will utilize the wireless ad hoc networking to perform their communication needs, and MANETs will utilize knowledge generation to enhance their network services. Current mobile devices, which go together with us anywhere and at anytime, are the most convenient tools to help us in ubiquitous computing, that is, to intermediate between us and our surroundings in an unobtrusive fashion. In other terms, the data processing and communication go to the background and must adjust to the user's personality. Some of the decisions related to communication have to be completely made at run time by learning the users' mobility patterns based on personal actions, roles, and social networks. The routing services need local neighbor view over time (who are friends and who are strangers) and which friends can be a source of support to convey messages. The presented routing heuristic takes the idea of today social networks. Our society is divided into groups of interest, and in groups of moving people and vehicles, entities with similar mobility patterns tend to cluster together and form support groups with certain mobility and social characteristics. Members belonging to one group interact in several ways with members within that group, and the mobility patterns of specific groups are often predictable [2]. Moreover, the social factor impacts the effectiveness of a particular MANET, that is, whether users will allow their phones to participate in this kind of networks. We assume that users from specific social networks are supposed to accept that power for the batteries of their own phones will be drawn, and their phones will convey messages between third parties without any benefit for them.

MANETs concept for "anytime and anywhere" is supposed to support network services independent on the application scenarios. Context is any information that can be used to characterize the network environment. Context awareness is the ability of the system to infer contextual knowledge in order to recognize nodes' situations. Dynamism in MANETs and major concerns, such as unpredictable bandwidth and topology changes, make questionable the usage of analytical modeling. At the same time, data-driven artificial intelligence (AI) approaches are capable of modeling nonlinear relationships, adapting and managing uncertainties by learning from empirical data without human participation. By "learning in MANETs", the researchers most often understand how a node constantly updates its view of the local network and, given the same inputs, the node may respond differently later than it did earlier. Usually, learning mechanisms use interaction with the neighboring nodes to extract information about the local topology and broadcast learning parameters in data packets or in control packets. Much of the focus of machine learning in MANETs has been on supervised learning (SL) and reinforcement learning (RL). In both approaches, the learner receives feedback from the environment about the appropriateness of its response as an output or reward. However, active broadcast of learning parameters or feedbacks could easily congest the network and degrade throughput when network topology changes frequently. SL main drawback is the need to know exactly what the learner should do a priory, which cannot meet MANETs unpredictable topology changes. RL main drawbacks are assumptions for finite set of state actions in learner's environment and its slow convergence speed. At the same time, unsupervised learning (UL) is based on the similarities and differences among data without a feedback from the environment. UL represents the input data in a more efficient way and the system context is the outcome of some cognitive process, for example, data mining. Therefore, we apply an unsupervised approach to learn context from data in a passive (nonintrusive) mode without a priory knowledge and focus our study on context-awareness for routing services. Thus, embedded intelligence in MANETs is supposed to support network services independently on application scenarios by managing uncertainties and inferring contextual knowledge by learning from empirical data without human participation. The contribution of the present study is ubiquitous computing by distributed evolving fuzzy modeling framework (EFMF) for dynamic context-awareness of mobility for routing services. EFMF determines the paths that data packets take across MANETs based on relationships and activities of mobile applications and users that carry mobile devices. The EFMF acts in the routing layer and observes and categorize the "social context" in the layers above to take intelligent routing decisions. EFMF employs unsupervised online one-pass fuzzy clustering method to derive contextual knowledge from social scenario traces and ubiquitously learn "friends" and "strangers" indirectly and anonymously by observing

and analyzing fluctuations in local mobility context. The heuristic "care of myself by leaning on friends for support" is applied in a local scope (direct communication in one hop) for packets transmission, while the heuristic "the friends of my friends are my friends too"—in a global scope.

2. Problem Definition and Our Solutions

In this section, we present the framework for evolving fuzzy modeling, as well as what type of data mining technique we use for knowledge discovery. We introduce in brief a metric using the concept of binary-coded trend in fluctuations for context that we later use to analyze the network connections and service reliability.

In the present work, we studied multicast routing services for group-oriented application in disaster area (DA) scenario. The maneuver, took place in May 2005 in Cologne, Germany, has been simulated [3]. Communication is a challenge for all MANETs protocols, since nodes have heterogeneous area-based movements, pass by obstacles, and join/leave subareas. For instance, in the disaster area (DA) scenario, people or vehicles behavior changes over time and "neighbor relations" are not random, since particular group of rescue agents reacts in a similar way. Events act as motivations for mobile nodes to react and move according to the high-level context of their roles. The average density of nodes increases in response to the events due to gathering around the "incident location". Roles aid the learning of mobility, node density, and traffic patterns. For instance, ambulance teams are immobile when rescue patients in the casualties' treatment areas and oscillate for a certain time before reaching the next treatment area. Police and firefighters approach the "incident location", while patients flee it. Neighbors with similar roles have similar mobility and are supposed to remain connected for a certain time. Therefore, we can lean on these nodes for support in local communication (in vicinity) for information propagation. As a consequence, if a node logs scenario traces in vicinity over time and categorize them using a relevant clustering algorithm it might learn its behavior dynamically and its local network view over time. "Friends" are all nodes that show up similar mobility behavior. To comply to MANETs concerns, clustering should be a passive, fast, and one-pass algorithm.

First, we observed and analyzed MANETs DA scenario traces in structural, special, and temporal characteristics and according to metrics for context, described below, we further analyze the network connections and service reliability. We concluded that (1) the nodes in a local talk group are positioned inside one area and throughput is high since the number of hops, the packets are transmitted, is small (a lot of one-hop connections); (2) higher density of nodes in DA subareas [3] near the "incident location" and entry/exit points might cause packet collisions and calls for reducing the flood of control packets; (3) reaction to events is repetitive over time. It is our belief that if we utilize hidden knowledge and dependencies from high-level context of DA scenario, we will increase the intelligence of service protocols' algorithms. Thus, we tailor the evolving fuzzy modeling, proposed by Lekova in [4], to enhance low-level services in mobile ad hoc networking by observing and categorizing social activities in user and application level.

Key factors for reliable performance of services in MANETs are protocols' adaptation to mobility and traffic patterns. The problem complexity and the lack of knowledge about the functional dependence of the movement patterns and node density over time to future mobility and density impose the necessity to perform clustering analysis to extract knowledge from data and search a model determined by IF-THEN fuzzy rule base. Fuzzy logic [5] is applied because there are uncertainties associated with estimating node mobility and link crash, as well as handling missing data as result of missing data observation when nodes enter and exit subareas. Fuzzy clustering is a well-known technique for unsupervised learning when data are not labeled and clusters we are searching for are not well defined and possess smooth boundaries. Moreover, the fuzzy mathematical model allows extending control factors into consideration to accomplish multicriteria evaluation. As a consequence, we designed unsupervised evolving fuzzy method in order to categorize node context and to adapt services to the current scenario for improving the network performance in nonobtrusive way.

We exploit the concept of binary-coded trend in fluctuations for mobility (BTFM) that is applied to manage the routing services. BTFM describes the dynamic nature of movement context. By exchanging it among neighbors, the mobility in a local scope could be analyzed. We studied ordered sequence of scenario traces in consecutive data periods, since we are interested in the trace dynamism. One of the reasons for not using any statistical metrics is that all samples in n consecutive time steps that show equal *mean* and *standard deviation* have different trend in fluctuations. Additional benefit of using BTFM is that it is computationally less intensive than the standard deviation. Thus, we use base-2 number system to code with "1" the state of moving and with "0"—immobility and obtain a digit in a binary format. BTFM decimal equivalent is denoted as decimal-coded trend in fluctuations for mobility (DTFM). It facilitates BTFM broadcasting and categorizing of movement context. For instance, if after eight steps the BTFM for an "ambulance agent" is 11011000, the corresponding DTFM is 216. All nodes in vicinity with DTFM = 216 are indexed as friends, other—as strangers. The key idea of the proposed by us heuristics "lean on my friends for support" is to enhance destination-initiated mesh-based multicast protocol, such as CAMP [6], by increasing the life time of routing after ensuring stable routes by carefully chosen forwarders for the next time period. We select the most reliable nodes (friends) that will stay connected in n consecutive time steps. These nodes show similar mobility patterns as the destination nodes in the next n-hop scope. The value of DTFM is carried and broadcasted by the *join query* message in the ODMRP protocol. After converting the DTFM into binary-number system, bitwise operation "AND" for BTFM of the node with BTFM of the destination node in the *join query* is performed to decide which node is a "friend" to forward data packets.

3. Overview of Evolving Fuzzy Modeling Framework

In this section, the evolving fuzzy modeling framework and LEFCM algorithm are described and explained by an example in 2D space.

The fuzzy modeling task demands in an adaptive, lifetime, and distributed way to partition the input data space in order to identify the rules and determine of the model parameters according to a fuzzy rule of inference. Evolving fuzzy clustering and reasoning on each node are performed to ensure a system to evolve its structure and functionality gradually from a continuous input data stream. Evolving clustering approaches do not need the number of clusters to be prespecified. Their algorithms are one-pass than batch-mode, fast, and do not keep any information of passed examples; therefore, they are applicable for mobile applications not wasting resources during the run of MANETs. LEFCM is a distance-based and computationally less intensive algorithm. The data space to be clustered consists of DTFM and *mean* of the actual values of deviation in coordinates for n consecutive time steps, which each mobile node extracts from its movement traces (relative coordinates). After quantifying DTFM, the trend in fluctuations for mobility over time is derived to predict the upcoming reliability and according to relevant heuristic, specific to the implemented routing protocol, the routing services are managed.

Figure 1 represents the corresponding clustering partition for a node located near the "incident site". Data are given by dots and cluster centers—by stars. The repetitive categories of node movement patterns have three feature values—the *mean* and the trend in a node movement for the past n steps, and the trend in a node movement for the next n steps. The model for prediction is determined by fuzzy rules that are given by representative values of the cluster-centered coordinates. On each node, the membership degree to ith cluster for the input data vector x^k is matched online, where k is an index related to the time instant. The crisp output values for mobility—O^{k+n} is returned by fuzzy reasoning model. The specifics of the used metric, that is, conversion of numbers in base-2 arithmetic into base-10, and the difference of how the numbers in these two numeric systems are comparable to each other, causes a big value for the *mean threshold* [4], such as *0.8*, to be assigned. This results in a model with more rules but more correct estimation.

3.1. Overview of the Lightweight Evolving Fuzzy Clustering Method. In the online clustering process, the given data set consists of input vectors (examples) $X = \{x_1,\ldots, x_p\}$ which are p points in q-*dimensional* space, $x \in R^q$. Examples come from a data stream one by one, and the algorithm starts with an empty set of clusters. When a new cluster C^k is created (k is an index related to the time instant), the current input vector is assigned to be a cluster center (Cc) and its cluster radius (Ru) is initially set to zero. Then, this cluster is updated or new cluster is created depending on a threshold value (D_{thr}) that affects the number of clusters. The maximum distance from any cluster center to the examples that belong to this cluster is not greater than the threshold

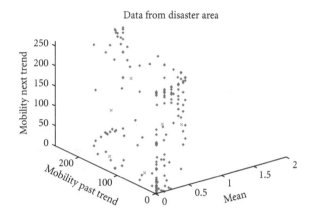

FIGURE 1: Clustering of data from DA scenario.

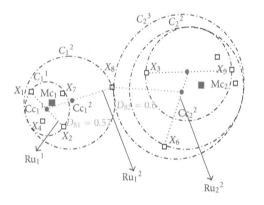

$D_{\text{thr}} = S/2$

$Md_{\text{thr}} = 0.4$

X_8

$Md = 0.47$

$DMc_1 = 0.5$

$DMc_2 = 0.41$

FIGURE 2: A brief clustering process using LEFCM with input vectors x_1 to x_8 in a 2D space. x_1 causes the LEFCM to create a new cluster C_1^0 with center Cc_1^0 and radius $Ru_1^0 = 0$; x_2 update cluster $C_1^0 \rightarrow C_1^1$ with center Cc_1^1; x_3: create a new cluster Cc_2^2; x_4 and x_7— do nothing; x_5 and x_6 update cluster $C_2^1 \rightarrow C_2^2$; x_8 update cluster $C_1^1 \rightarrow C_1^2$ with center Cc_1^2.

value D_{thr}. Therefore, D_{thr} affects the number of clusters by updating existing clusters changing their centers' positions and increasing their radii or creating new clusters. Estimating the number of clusters online means online optimization of threshold value D_{thr}. We incorporate the fuzzy membership degrees and distance to *reference center* for each cluster into the clustering process (solid squares denote reference centers for the two clusters in Figure 2). Input vector is bound to each cluster by means of a *membership degree* (*Md*), which is a number between 0 and 1, and makes clustering more accurate in case of overlapping clusters. A novel multidimensional membership function equation (1)

is proposed for obtaining the degree of membership between data and centers of clusters:

$$Md_{ij} = 1 - \frac{\left(\left\| x_i - Cc_{j\,\min} \right\|\right)^{(2/(m-1))}}{\sum_{j=1}^n \left(\left\| x_i - Cc_j \right\|\right)^{(2/(m-1))}}, \quad x \in R^q, \quad (1)$$

where $\| x_i - Cc_j \| = 1$, when $\| x_i - Cc_j \| > 1$, $m \in [1, \infty)$ is the weighted exponent coefficient which determines how much clusters may overlap. We set m to be equal to 2, since in the fuzzy clustering literature, a value of $m = 2$ is the commonly used value.

A *reference center* (the arithmetic mean) $\overline{Mc}_j$ for each cluster j, described by its center coordinates in q space $\overline{Mc}_j$.

$$\overline{Mc}_j = \frac{\sum_{i=1}^{cp} x_i}{cp}, \quad (2)$$

where $x \in R^q$ and cp is the number of the input data in cluster j.

When the current input vector x_i comes, the distances between this new input and *mean center for each cluster* $DMc_{ij} = \| x_i - \overline{Mc}_j \|$, $i = 1, \dots, p$, is calculated. We introduce two new thresholds: (1) Md threshold (Md_{thr}) in the range [0.4–0.6]; (2) mean threshold (M_{thr}) in the range [0.5–0.7]. We establish that for $Md_{\text{thr}} = 0.5$ and $M_{\text{thr}} = 0.6$ we obtain optimal (or at least feasible) cluster centers and radii. These numbers are used in Figure 2. When DMc_{ij} is less or equal to M_{thr}, we can increase the radius of this cluster, otherwise we make new cluster. In other words, a cluster will not be updated any more if DMc_{ij} is bigger than the acceptable tolerance to the mean center. When data are not well partitioned in the input space, that is, sparse data exist, the M_{thr} should be bigger. The increasing of Md_{thr} to 0.6 or decreasing M_{thr} to 0.5 results in more clusters.

The LEFCM algorithm is described as follows.

Step 1. Set up a small value for D_{thr}, that is, 0.1. *Normalize the input vector* in [0-1] using (3):

$$x_{i\_\text{norm}} = \frac{x_i - x_{\min}}{x_{\max} - x_{\min}}, \quad (3)$$

where the range of x_i is $[x_{\min} - x_{\max}]$ and $x \in R^q$.

Create the first cluster C_1^0 by taking the position of the first example from the input stream as the first cluster center Cc_1^0, then setting a value for its cluster radius $Ru_1^0 = 0$. Add the value of x_i to $\overline{Mc}_j$ and set up the number for inputs in this cluster to 1.

Step 2. If all examples of the data stream have been processed, the algorithm is finished. Else, the current input example, x_i, is taken and the distances between this example and all of the n already created cluster centers Cc_j, $D_{ij} = \| x_i - Cc_j \|$, $j = 1, \dots, n$, are calculated.

Step 3. If there is any distance value, $D_{ij} = \| x_i - Cc_j \|$ equal to, or less than, at least one of the radii, Ru_j, it means that the current example belongs to a cluster C_m with the minimum distance $D_{im} = \| x_i - Cc_m \| = \min(\| x_i - Cc_j \|)$ subjected to the constraint $D_{ij} < Ru_j$, $j = 1, \dots, n$.

Add the value of x_i to $\overline{Mc}_j$ and increase the number of inputs in cluster j by one.

In this case, neither a new cluster is created nor any existing cluster is updated, and the algorithm returns to Step 2.

Step 4. Else, find cluster C_a^k (with center Cc_a^k and cluster radius Ru_a^k) from all existing cluster centers through calculating the values $S_{ij}^k = D_{ij} + Ru_j^k$, $j = 1, \ldots, n$, and then choosing the cluster center Cc_a^k with the minimum value S_{ia}^k:

$$S_{ij}^k = D_{ij} + Ru_j^k = \min\left(S_{ij}^k\right), \quad j = 1, \ldots, n. \quad (4)$$

Step 5. Calculate Md according to (1).

Step 6. Calculate the distances between the new input and *mean center* for each cluster—$\overline{Mc}_j$, $DMc_{ij} = \|x_i - \overline{Mc}_j\|$, $i = 1, \ldots, p$.

Step 7. If Md is greater than Md_{thr} and $DMc_{ij} \leq M_{thr}$, then $D_{thr} = S_{im}/2$. This means that the input example is very close to that cluster and its *mean center* and D_{thr} is set up to produce cluster updating instead of new cluster creation.

Step 8. If S_{ia} is greater than $2 \times D_{thr}$, the example does not belong to any existing clusters. A new cluster is created in the same way as described in Step 1, and the algorithm returns to Step 2.

Step 9. If S_{ia}^k is not greater than $2 \times D_{thr}$, the cluster C_a^k is updated by moving its center, Cc_a^k, and increasing the value of its radius, Ru_a^k. The updated new radius Ru_a^{k+1} is set to be equal to $S_{ia}/2$, and the new center is located at the point on the line connecting the x_i and Cc_a^k, and the distance from the new center Cc_a^{k+1} to the point x_i is equal to Ru_a^{k+1}. Add the value of x_i to $\overline{Mc}_j$ and increment the number of inputs in cluster j. The algorithm returns to Step 2.

Let us explain the clustering process by a 2D example shown on Figure 2. The input vectors x_1 causes the LEFCM to create a new cluster C_1^0 with center Cc_1^0 and radius $Ru_1^0 = 0$ according to Step 1. Correspondingly, x_2 updates cluster $C_1^0 \rightarrow C_1^1$ with center Cc_1^1. x_3 creates a new cluster Cc_2^0; x_4 and x_7—do nothing; x_5 and x_6 update cluster $C_2^1 \rightarrow C_2^2$. When x_8 comes, if $D_{thr} = 0.1$ x_8 will create a new cluster, if $D_{thr} = 0.6$, two clusters are candidates to be updated—cluster $C_1^1 \rightarrow C_1^2$ or cluster $C_2^2 \rightarrow C_2^3$—since the distances to the first and second clusters are almost equal ($D_{81} = 0.57$ and $D_{82} = 0.6$). Applying the LEFCM algorithm, where the threshold D_{thr} is tuning online, the degree of membership between data and centers of clusters as well as reference centers are evaluated. According to Step 6, $\overline{DMc}_1 = 0.5$ and $\overline{DMc}_2 = 0.41$. According to Steps 7 and 9, cluster C_1^1 has to be updated to C_1^2 with center Cc_1^2 and radius Ru_1^2.

4. Related Work

In this section, the related works are briefly described. They present general models for monitoring and estimating the quality of links among nodes in MANETs.

Related works for efficient routing management based on quality of links are in the research community. Prediction of stable routes could be based on simple heuristics [7]; "graph theory" algorithms [8]; AI techniques: fuzzy-logic approaches [9–12]; multicriteria decision making, other theories [13, 14]. The mentioned algorithms rely on frequently update and broadcasting the information about ad hoc topological parameters acquired from the underlying routing protocols, such as number of neighbors, rate of changing the neighbors, receiving power of consecutive packets, and GPS location information. Routing table of each node or control packets are extended with new fields about this extra information, which increase the burden of these data structures and the overhead, since extra information is disseminated. In contrast, we summarize and predict mobility context as one digit, which is easy to be disseminated or compared to these of neighbors.

Only few studies learn node mobile motion behavior. A classification of the existing mobility prediction methods can be found in [15]. Authors determine a mobility prediction process as the future location of a mobile node. Their prediction scheme applies the evidence theory of Dempster-Shafer in order to predict the future position of the mobile node by evaluating itself on relevant criteria. In [7], authors propose a mobility prediction scheme based on GPS tracking to help select stable routes and to perform rerouting in anticipation of topology changes. In [16], mobile nodes learn using a hidden Markov model to predict the future state of host's movement. Fuzzy applicability to express the matching degree among neighboring nodes is used in [17]. In [13], the authors introduce an adaptive mobility prediction that uses learning automation to estimate the coefficients of a simple adaptive filter to predict the future distance of two neighboring nodes. Distributed bioinspired routing algorithms explore the network and learn good routes, using variations of reinforcement learning (RL). These algorithms are adaptive to MANETs topology dynamism and changes in link costs; however, they inherent the above-mentioned RL drawbacks. GA-ODMRP [18] optimizes the route selection using particle swarm optimization. PIDIS [19] exploit swarm intelligence to keep track of the changing topology by a combination of positive/negative reinforcement and amplification of local network fluctuations.

Only few studies deal with social network routing [2, 20]. In [20], the authors use "social similarity" to destination node for information propagation in wireless networks. To the best of our knowledge, our framework is more inherit, generalized, and involves more abstract social level. It can be used for enhancing the service protocol algorithms for sending data packet from source to destination in an unsupervised and passive mode. It is reactive to environmental events in a role-based mode after deriving knowledge from the user and application high-level context.

5. Conclusions

The main and novel contribution of this paper is the distributed evolving fuzzy modeling framework (EFMF) to observe and categorize relationships and activities in the user and application level and based on that social context to take intelligent decisions about ambient intelligence mobile ad hoc networks (MANETs) service management. Especially, the EFMF employs unsupervised online one-pass fuzzy clustering method to recognize nodes mobility context from social scenario traces and ubiquitously learn "friends" and "strangers" indirectly and anonymously. The proposed evolving fuzzy modeling framework (EFMF) is applied for mobility context-awareness and routing services; however, EFMF is flexible and can be extended to learn ubiquitously traffic patterns over time or to aid security services—misbehaving nodes can be detected and reported to the upper layer and other nodes. The selfish or malicious nodes can be discovered by their social reaction to environmental events in a diverse role-based mode. The other nodes can isolate the misbehaving nodes, resulting in MANETs composed of only well-behaving nodes.

References

[1] M. Lindwer, D. Marculescu, T. Basten et al., "Ambient intelligence visions and achievements: linking abstract ideas to real-world concepts," in *Proceedings of the Design Automation & Test in Europe (DATE '03)*, pp. 10–15, 2003.

[2] Y. Chen, A. Medina, and P. Basu, Mobility Modeling for MANETs: Generation and Understanding of Mobility Traces, ITA, 2009, https://www.usukita.org/files/paper_mobmodel_chen_09.pdf.

[3] N. Aschenbruck, C. de Waal, and P. Martini, "Distribution of nodes in disaster area scenarios and its impact on topology control strategies," in *Proceedings of the IEEE International Conference on Computer Communications (IEEE INFOCOM '08)*, pp. 1–6, Phoenix, Ariz, USA, April 2008.

[4] A. Lekova, "Evolving fuzzy modeling for MANETs using lightweight online unsupervised learning," *International Journal of Wireless Information Networks*, vol. 17, no. 1-2, pp. 34–41, 2010.

[5] L. A. Zadeh, "Fuzzy sets," *Information and Control*, vol. 8, no. 3, pp. 338–353, 1965.

[6] E. L. Madruga and J. J. Garcia-Luna-Aceves, "Scalable multicasting: the core-assisted mesh protocol," *Mobile Networks and Applications*, vol. 6, no. 2, pp. 151–165, 2001.

[7] W. Su, S. J. Lee, and M. Gerla, "Mobility prediction in wireless networks," in *Proceedings of the 21st Century Military Communications Conference Proceedings (IEEE MILCOM '00)*, pp. 491–495, October 2000.

[8] S. Merugu, M. Ammar, and E. Zegura, "Routing in space and time in networks with predictable mobility," Tech. Rep. GIT-CC-04-7, Georgia Institute of Technology, 2004.

[9] R. Hu, Z. Hu, and H. Ma, "A reliable routing algorithm based on fuzzy applicability of F sets in MANET," in *Proceedings of the 11th Pacific Rim International Symposium on Dependable Computing (PRDC '05)*, pp. 245–249, December 2005.

[10] S. Roychoudhury, P. Dutta, and B. Maiti, "Enhancing efficiency towards handling mobility uncertainty in mobile ad-hoc network (MANET)," in *Proceedings of the 11th International Conference on Information Technology (ICIT '08)*, pp. 159–164, December 2008.

[11] B. L. Su, M. S. Wang, and Y. M. Huang, "Fuzzy logic weighted multi-criteria of dynamic route lifetime for reliable multicast routing in ad hoc networks," *Expert Systems with Applications*, vol. 35, no. 1-2, pp. 476–484, 2008.

[12] C. Wang, S. Chen, X. Yang, and Y. Gao, "Fuzzy logic-based dynamic routing management policies for mobile ad hoc networks," in *Proceedings of the Workshop on High Performance Switching and Routing (HPSR '05)*, pp. 341–345, May 2005.

[13] S. M. Mousavi, H. R. Rabiee, M. Moshref, and A. Dabirmoghaddam, "Model based adaptive mobility prediction in mobile ad-hoc networks," in *Proceedings of the International Conference on Wireless Communications, Networking and Mobile Computing (WiCOM '07)*, pp. 1713–1716, September 2007.

[14] N. Samaan and A. Karmouch, "A Mobility prediction architecture based on contextual knowledge and spatial conceptual maps," *IEEE Transactions on Mobile Computing*, vol. 4, no. 6, pp. 537–551, 2005.

[15] L. Dekar and H. Kheddouci, "A cluster based mobility prediction scheme for ad hoc networks," *Ad Hoc Networks*, vol. 6, no. 2, pp. 168–194, 2008.

[16] J. Francois, G. Leduc, and S. Martin, "Learning movement patterns in mobile networks: a generic approach," in *Proceedings of the European Wireless*, pp. 128–134, Barcelona, Spain, 2004.

[17] B. Rong, G. Amoussou, Z. Dziong, M. Kadoch, and A. K. Elhakeem, "Mobility prediction aided dynamic multicast routing in MANET," in *Proceedings of the IEEE/Sarnoff Symposium on Advances in Wired and Wireless Communication*, pp. 21–24, April 2005.

[18] E. Baburaj and V. Vasudevan, "An intelligent mesh based multicast routing algorithm for MANETs using particle swarm optimization," *International Journal of Computer Science and Network Security*, vol. 8, no. 5, pp. 214–218, 2008.

[19] C. C. Shen and S. Rajagopalan, "Poster: protocol-independent packet delivery improvement service for mobile ad hoc networks," in *Proceedings of the IEEE International Conference on Mobile Ad-Hoc and Sensor Systems*, pp. 582–584, October 2004.

[20] E. M. Daly and M. Haahr, "Social network analysis for routing in disconnected delay-tolerant MANETs," in *Proceedings of the 8th ACM International Symposium on Mobile Ad Hoc Networking and Computing (MobiHoc '07)*, pp. 32–40, September 2007.

8

A Real-Time Angle- and Illumination-Aware Face Recognition System Based on Artificial Neural Network

Hisateru Kato, Goutam Chakraborty, and Basabi Chakraborty

Faculty of Software and Information Science, Iwate Prefectural University, Iwate, Takizawamura 020-0193, Japan

Correspondence should be addressed to Hisateru Kato, nd4y2518@docomo.ne.jp

Academic Editor: Cheng-Hsiung Hsieh

Automatic authentication systems, using biometric technology, are becoming increasingly important with the increased need for person verification in our daily life. A few years back, fingerprint verification was done only in criminal investigations. Now fingerprints and face images are widely used in bank tellers, airports, and building entrances. Face images are easy to obtain, but successful recognition depends on proper orientation and illumination of the image, compared to the one taken at registration time. Facial features heavily change with illumination and orientation angle, leading to increased false rejection as well as false acceptance. Registering face images for all possible angles and illumination is impossible. In this work, we proposed a memory efficient way to register (store) multiple angle and changing illumination face image data, and a computationally efficient authentication technique, using multilayer perceptron (MLP). Though MLP is trained using a few registered images with different orientation, due to generalization property of MLP, interpolation of features for intermediate orientation angles was possible. The algorithm is further extended to include illumination robust authentication system. Results of extensive experiments verify the effectiveness of the proposed algorithm.

1. Introduction

The need for personal identification has grown enormously in the last two decades. Previously, biometric identification using fingerprints or face images was restricted to criminal prosecution only. A few experts could serve the demand. With increased terrorist activities, stricter security requirements for entering buildings, and other related applications, need for automatic biometric machine-authentication systems is getting more and more important.

Recognizing people from face (face image) is the most natural and widely used method we human do always and effortlessly. Due to ease of collection without disturbing the subject, it is one of the most popular ways of automatic machine authentication. An excellent survey of face-recognition algorithms is available in [1].

In automatic face recognition, the first step is to identify the boundary of the face and separate it from the photographed image. Next, recognition algorithms extract feature vectors from the input (probe) image. These features are then compared with the set of such features stored in the database. The database (gallery image) contains same set of features already extracted and stored during registration phase for all persons required to be authenticated.

There are two classes of algorithms to extract features from the image—model based and appearance based. Model-based algorithms use explicit 2D or 3D models of the face. In model-based algorithms, geometrical features like relative positions of important facial components, for example, eyes, nose, mouth, and so forth, and their shapes are used as features. These features are robust to lighting conditions but weak for change in the orientation of the face. We use a subset of such features as "Angle-feature" in our previous work [2]. In appearance-based methods pattern of the light and shade distribution in the facial image is used to derive features. Being computationally simpler, appearance-based paradigm is more popular. One of the significant works is the eigenface approach [3] by Turk and Pentland. We also used appearance-based algorithms to extract facial features.

Though automated face recognition by computers for frontal face images taken under controlled lighting conditions is more or less successful, recognition in uncontrolled environment is an extremely complex and difficult task. Lots of researchers are trying to develop unconstrained face recognition system [4], specially for pose and illumination invariant face recognition [5], for a wide variety of real-time applications.

For most of the biometric applications, we need to authenticate a particular person in *real time* from his/her *quickly taken* face image. The face image has to be already registered in the system. For proper verification, the input image (probe image) should exactly match the registered image (gallery image) of that particular person (to avoid false rejection of the genuine person) and not with anyone else's face image (to avoid false acceptance). The algorithm has to be efficient to work in real time. The task becomes difficult because the quickly taken probe image may differ in illumination and pose (and therefore features) from the image of the individual registered in the data base.

Even though the person is same, the automatic authentication system may fail due to angle orientation, ambient lighting, age, make-up, glasses, expression of the face, and so forth which are different from the stored gallery image of the individual. It is said that about 75% of the authentication failure is due to the fact that angle of orientation of the probe face image is different from the stored image. It is impossible and very inefficient to store the images (i.e., image features) of an individual taken at all possible angles and at different illuminations in the gallery. But we need that information for correct recognition. In this work, we focus on angle-aware face recognition, and then the proposed algorithm is extended to include ambient light-aware face recognition. In the proposed angle- and illumination-aware face recognition, we store the available (training) information in a trained Artificial Neural Network. Retrieval of the features for any intermediate angle and illumination from the trained ANN is very efficient. The algorithm can be used in real time. We experimented with a benchmark database. Our system could achieve excellent results both for false-acceptance rate (FAR) as well as for false-rejection rate (FRR).

In the next section we briefly discuss related works on orientation and illumination robust face recognition. In Section 3 we represent our proposed idea for angle-aware face recognition and its extension to illumination-aware recognition which is followed by Section 4 containing simulation experiments and results. Section 5 contains conclusion and discussion.

2. Related Works on Angle and Illumination Invariant Face Recognition

According to FERET and FRVT [6] test reports, performance of face recognition systems drops significantly when large pose variations are present in the input images. Though the registration image is a frontal face image, the probe image is more often than not a perfect frontal image. Angle-aware face recognition is a major research issue. Approaches to address

the pose variation problem are mainly classified into three categories.

(1) Single-view approach in which invariant features or 3D model based methods are used to produce a canonical frontal view from various poses. In [7] a Gabor wavelet-based feature extraction method is proposed which is robust to small angle variations. This approach did not receive much attention due to high computational cost.

(2) Multiview face recognition is an extension of appearance-based frontal image recognition. Here, gallery images of every subject at many different poses are needed. Earlier works on pose invariant appearance based on multiview algorithms are reported in [8–10]. Most algorithms in this category require several images of each subject in the data base and consequently require much more computation for searching and memory for storage.

(3) Class-based hybrid methods in which multiview training images are available during training but only one gallery image per person is available for recognition. The popular eigenface approach [3] has been extended in [11] in order to achieve pose invariance. In [12] a robust face recognition scheme based on graph matching has been proposed.

More recent methods to address pose and illumination are proposed in [2, 13–21].

The simplest approach is to look for a feature which is invariant to variation of pose. But, till now such a feature is not found. Reference [7] works only for very small range of angle variation, and the algorithm is too heavy to be used real time. Geometrical features are very weak to angle variation. Variation of image-pattern-based features due to angle variation exceeds variation of features across individuals, jeopardizing the recognition process and would lead to high FAR and FRR. Prince and Elder [22] presented a heuristic algorithm to construct a single feature which does not vary with pose. Murase and Nayer [23] have used principle components of many views to visualize the change due to pose variation. Graham and Allison [24] sampled input sequences of varying pose to form eigensignature when projected into an eigenspace. A good review of these approaches can be found in [5, 25].

3. Angle- and Illumination-Aware Face Recognition

Our approach is to store multiple pose image features in a single trained MLP, so that both storage and searching for intermediate angles are efficient. We do not overload the database by adding features for the same face at different angles. We train an artificial neural network to store them all as a function of the orientation angle. Due to good generalization property of MLP, it can give feature values at intermediate angles and very efficiently too. Through experiments, we realized that geometrical features are fragile to angle variation. We used a subset of geometrical features

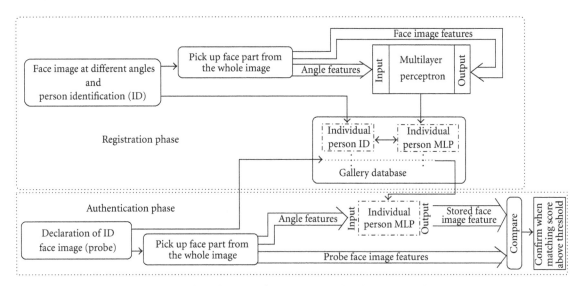

FIGURE 1: Block diagram of registration and authentication phase.

to express the pose angle. The following important aspects were investigated while selecting the efficient angle features:

(1) low computational complexity to extract the angle feature, so that the algorithm can run real time

(2) the pose-angle feature contains enough information about the angle

(3) the feature values vary smoothly with angle variation, so that MLP can be trained easily and with little error.

The two main contributions regarding pose invariant face authentication, over our previous work [17], are to automatize the angle-feature extraction from the face image and enrich the angle feature vector with more relevant features. We also verified that artificial neural network could achieve good generalization for intermediate angles of orientation, for which data were not available during training phase. A brief description of the whole algorithm, with an emphasis on the new contribution, is presented in this section.

Figure 1 shows the block diagram of the proposed angle invariant face recognition system. The system consists of two phases, registration phase and recognition phase. In registration phase, a set of face images are taken from equal distance but at different angles.

If the number of cameras is n, we get n training samples to train the individual person's MLP at the time of registration. From all the n photographs, taken by n cameras, first the training data is created to train that individual's MLP. The input vector of the training data is the angle feature vector, and the output vector is the image feature. Procedures to extract angle features and image features are explained in Sections 3.1 and 3.2, respectively.

A person's identification (ID) and the corresponding trained MLP (using her/his face image angle feature and image feature) are stored as a pair. Such ID-MLP pair forms gallery image "DATA BASE." In the recognition phase, the individual's face image (probe image) is presented

with her/his ID. From gallery "DATA BASE" of MLPs, the particular trained MLP for the claimed ID is retrieved. Angle features from the image are extracted and used as input to that person's MLP retrieved from the data-base. Image-feature from the probe image and that obtained as output from the MLP are compared. If the distance between two feature vectors are below some predefined threshold, the decision is accept, otherwise reject. The implicit assumption here in that the MLP would be able to deliver correct image feature for any intermediate face orientation due to its good interpolation (generalization) property.

In the following section, we will discuss how angle features are extracted from the face image. We will also show what angle features are finally selected for our system and why.

3.1. Angle Feature Extraction. Angle feature should contain the information of the orientation angle of the face image. Geometrical features of a face image, which uses distances between important parts of the face and angle between connecting lines, are capable of expressing the orientation of the face image. We used cues from those approaches of feature extraction. In our previous work [17], we used three points, the left and right eye locations and the middle of mouth. The distances between them and the slope of the lines connecting them are used as elements of the feature vector. The distance between the two eyes decreases as the orientation angle increases. Similarly, the slope of the line connecting eyes and the mouth changes as the face turns towards right or left. The results obtained using these six elements of angle-feature vector gave reasonably good results. But, in our previous work, the three points from the face image were manually identified, and feature vectors were manually evaluated from all face images under investigation. In total we used 10 facial images, each for 21 different angles. Therefore, 210 angle feature vectors were hand calculated.

In the present work, we wrote algorithm to automatically identify the important points on the face. This facilitated

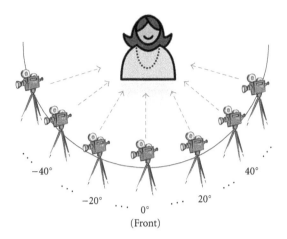

FIGURE 2: Collection of several face images taken from equal distance but at different angles.

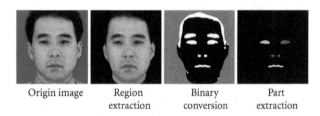

Origin image   Region   Binary   Part
                extraction   conversion   extraction

FIGURE 3: Images after different filtering steps.

working with a larger data set. Moreover, after filtering, we could always identify the eyebrows, eyes, nostrils, and mouth. All possible identifying points can be listed as two end points of left eyebrow, two end points of right eyebrow, two end points of left eye, two end points of right eye, nostril (sometimes two), and two end points of mouth. This is clear from the picture after binary conversion (the best result obtained with a threshold of 0.75), as shown in Figure 3. We used the database with oriental faces only. A lot of angle vector elements can be identified whose values change as the angle changes. We tried different combinations taking care that the procedure is simple and efficient.

The important parts from the face image are separated as follows. At first minimum value filter is used. The minimum value filter emphasizes the part where the image is dark, because important parts on face are darker than that of surrounding skin. Through experiments, we ensured that this technique is effective to identify locations of eyebrows, eyes, nostrils, and mouth. After using the minimum value filter, binarization is performed to clearly identify important parts of the face. In addition to our targeted important parts of the face, hair also is filtered out. First the hair part is detected. Though it is an important element too to profile the face image, we do not use it. We delete the hair part and the background. We then identify eyebrows, eyes, nose, and mouth, with heuristic algorithm using knowledge of their relative positions. As we do not use eyebrows to create the angle-feature vector, eyebrows are also deleted after identification. Once both eyes, nose and mouth are located on the face image, we generate the angle features.

TABLE 1: Distance components of angle feature.

Description	Symbol
Distance between LE and RE	D_1
Distance between LE and N	D_2
Distance between RE and N	D_3
Distance between LE and M	D_4
Distance between RE and M	D_5

TABLE 2: Gradient components of angle feature.

Description	Symbol
Gradient of line joining LE and N	m_1
Gradient of line joining LE and M	m_2
Gradient of line joining RE and N	m_3
Gradient of line joining RE and M	m_4

First we will give the details of the elements of angle-feature vector and then explain the rationality of choosing them. The angle feature vector is

$$\text{AF} = (W_1, W_2, W_3, D_1, D_2, D_3, D_4, D_5, m_1, m_2, m_3, m_4). \tag{1}$$

It consists of 12 elements. W_1, W_2, and W_3 are the widths of the left eye, the right eye, and the mouth. Following that, we find the center for left eye, right eye, nostrils, and mouth. Let us denote the coordinates of these four points of left eye (LE) as (x_1, y_1), right eye (RE) as (x_2, y_2), mouth (M) as (x_3, y_3), and nose (N) as (x_4, y_4). We have six distances taking any two points from the above four points. Except the distance between N and M, all other distances change with face angle orientation. We use the five distances shown in Table 1 as components of angle feature vector. The remaining four features are the gradient of lines described in Table 2.

All these features are easy to calculate and change more or less smoothly with angle variation. We did not include the distance between mouth and nose, the gradient of the line joining mouth and nose, and the line joining the two eyes. This is because these parameters do not change with angle change.

In order to ensure how our angle feature vector changes with change in the orientation of the face image, we plotted the Euclidean distance between angle vectors against the angle of orientation. It is shown in Figure 4(a). We have not discussed about the face-image feature yet. But in Figure 4(b), we have shown the Euclidean distance between face image feature vectors as the orientation angle changes.

The plots were for all training samples. It shows the smooth changes, though nonlinear but monotonic. From this plot, we can ensure that our angle feature is suitably chosen, and an MLP could be trained in a small number of epochs. Of course, during registration period, this training will be done off-line, and a longer training time is permissible. At the time of authentication, the MLP will give out the face image feature, from the input angle feature, instantly. That will ensure real-time application.

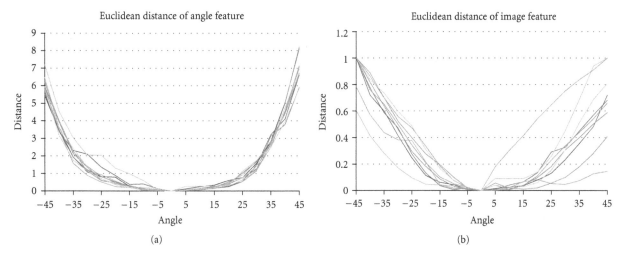

FIGURE 4: Euclidean distance of (a) angle feature and (b) image feature.

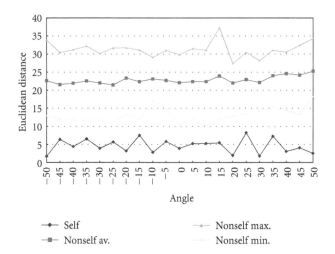

FIGURE 5: The results of distances between self and non-self-face image features at different angles of orientation.

In summary, compared to our previous work, we have improved our angle feature extraction technique not only by automating it but also by adding six more elements in the angle-feature vector to capture the angle of orientation information more faithfully. This also enables us to work with larger data set of face images.

3.2. Image Feature Extraction.
The image feature captures the characteristic of the entire image, the spatial distribution of the pixel values. The most widely used method is eigenface, first proposed byTurk and pentland in [3]. It is based on principal component analysis. First few principal components are used as features, and every face image is expressed as a vector with values of the few principal components. We used the same technique to create image feature vector.

In our experiments 8 principal components, which carry 99% of the image information, were used. We further extended our experiments using independent components on image feature. As independent component feature of the image gave better results, in this paper we will only present those results.

3.3. Neural Network for Mapping Angle Feature to Image Feature.
Multilayer neural network, trained with error backpropagation, is used as a mapping function—to map an individual's face orientation angle to his/her face image features for that particular angle. As angle feature vector consists of 12 elements, the MLP has 12 input nodes plus one bias node. We use a single hidden layer with 15 hidden nodes. Experiments were tried with different number of hidden nodes. The training is fast and quickly converges to very low MSE. Even with hidden nodes 10, it is possible to get low error after training, but we need more numbers of training epochs. The number of output nodes is eight, equal to the number of image features by using independent component analysis.

As already mentioned, we have separate MLP for every individual. For every registered individual, we have face images taken with orientation angle from −50 degrees to +50 degrees, at an interval of 5 degrees. In total, we have 21 image data for any individual. Out of the available 21 data, we use those taken at orientation −50, −40, −30, −20, −10, 0, +10, +20, +30, +40, and +50, that is, in total 11, for training the MLP. The rest 10 images, taken at angles −45, −35, −25, and so forth, were used for testing the trained MLP. Figure 5 shows the result after averaging over all images against a single self-image. A very good generalization is obtained. We can notice that at testing points the error is a little more than the points where it is trained. Yet, the distance between self and non-self-images is quite large, ensuring low values for both FAR as well as FRR, when threshold is properly chosen.

3.4. Robust Systems to Illumination Variation.
In this work we also proposed an extension of our system to include correction for illumination variation. Two alternative systems are proposed shown in Figures 6 and 7. In System I, only one MLP is used as in the case of angle invariant system. The only difference is that one input to the MLP

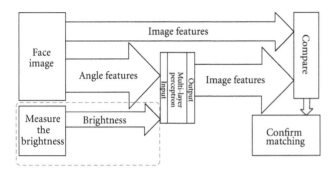

FIGURE 6: Block diagram of System I.

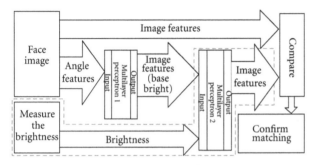

FIGURE 7: Block diagram of System II.

is added to include image brightness information. The rest of the algorithm remains the same. In System II, two MLPs were used. Both of them were trained separately. The first MLP (MLP1) output the image feature using angle feature as input. While training this, we train with image using base brightness, that is, 0% darkness. When darker images are input to this MLP, the output image features will be incorrect. The second MLP (MLP2) takes the output of MLP1 and brightness information. It is trained to give correct image feature for the darker image. Finally, the output of MLP2 is compared to image feature of the probe face image to take the authentication decision.

4. Simulation Experiments and Results

As already mentioned, the system consists of two stages—learning of MLP, that is, the registration phase, and using the learned MLP in the authentication stage.

4.1. Registration Phase. When person "A" is to be registered, face photograph of person "A" is taken using multiple cameras set at different angles, as shown in Figure 2. We use the database [26] from Softopia, Japan. The database has images taken at an interval of 5 degrees. For registration, we use face image data at intervals of 10 degrees, from −50 degrees to +50 degrees. The registration system is shown in Figure 8. First, the image is converted to grey-scale image, face part is cut out, and the angle and independent component features of the face image are extracted. The angle feature is used as input to the MLP and the image features as teacher signal. From the database, 11 of such data are used for training. The training is converged within 5000 epochs, with very low mean square error.

4.2. Authentication Phase. In authentication phase, the person announces his/her identification and let the image be taken. The angle is arbitrary, depending on how the person poses in front of the camera. We assume this angle to be within −50 to +50 degrees. The mapping task of MLP is to interpolate. The layout of the authentication system is shown in Figure 9. From the camera image, the face part is cut out. The angle features are extracted and input to the MLP trained for the person, as retrieved from the database according to identification declaration. The image feature taken from the image and that obtained as output of the MLP are compared. The Euclidean distance is calculated. If the distance is below a threshold value, the person is accepted, and otherwise rejected. The Euclidean distance is calculated by (2) as follows:

$$R = \sqrt{\sum_{i=1}^{m}(NN_i - IN_i)^2}. \qquad (2)$$

Here, $IN = \langle IN_1, IN_2, IN_3, IN_4, IN_5, IN_6, IN_7, IN_8 \rangle$ is image feature vector from input image. $NN = \langle NN_1, NN_2, NN_3, NN_4, NN_5, NN_6, NN_7, NN_8 \rangle$ is the image vector from MLP output. Judgment of the proper threshold value is important. If the threshold is too low, false accept rate (FAR) will increase. On the other hand, if the threshold is set too high, false reject rate (FRR) will be high. Depending on the application, the threshold is fixed. For a heavily secured place, where false acceptance is not tolerable at the cost of a few misjudgment in face rejection, the threshold is kept high. In general, the threshold is kept at a value where FAR is equal to FRR.

4.3. Experimental Setup and Results. Compared to our previous work, in the present work the angle feature vector has changed, from 6 elements to 12 elements. The image feature vector is also changed from PCA to ICA, the number of elements remaining the same 8. As the number of input nodes is increased, we increased the hidden nodes to 16 for faster training. We used face image data, taken in same illumination condition, with orientation angle from −50 degrees to +50 degrees, taken at intervals of 5 degrees. Image data at intervals 10 degrees was used for training, and the intermediate is for testing. In total, face image of 15 individuals was used. Experiments were performed by varying the threshold in steps.

Experimental results, for the angle variation from −50 degrees to +50 degrees, are summarized in Figure 10. Average FAR and FRR for all the images were calculated and plotted in this figure. The value of FAR and FRR at proper threshold is improved from our previous work about 20% to 10%, that is, an overall improvement of 10% in recognition rate over the whole range of angle variation. We attribute this to our improved angle feature vector. It is also important to note that the optimum threshold value is now increased from 9 to 12, and the slope around that threshold is lower. In the previous work, as shifting of threshold value greatly changed FAR and FRR, it is difficult to select proper threshold, as it would be different for different individuals. The new result

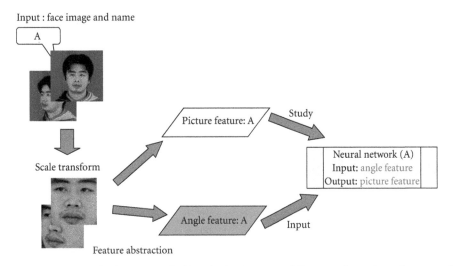

FIGURE 8: Registration phase which consists of taking the face image at different angles and use them to train an MLP.

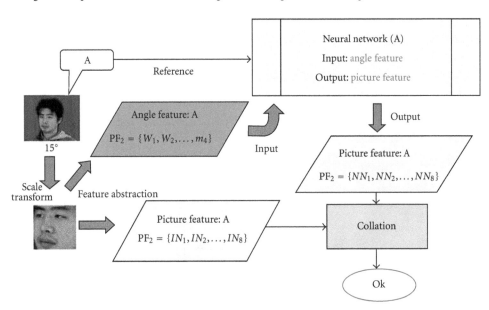

FIGURE 9: Description of the authentication phase.

shows that FAR and FRR do not change much when the threshold is changed.

4.4. Experiments with Changing Illumination.

The image feature changes also with illumination condition. We did a preliminary experiment to investigate the image feature change with brightness and on the basis of our investigation proposed the robust systems for illumination variation presented in the earlier section.

To investigate the pattern of change, we varied the brightness of face image by steps of 4% (of the original brightness) to a level up to −80% of the original value. Here, maximum value of the brightness is considered to be 0%. The image features at different illumination levels are compared, in terms of Euclidean distance, with respect to the brightest image, that is, 0%. The results are summarized in

Figure 11. Though the variation of image feature is different for different images, the nature is same.

As shown, the Euclidean distances are larger with the decrease of brightness values. The nature of variation is easy to be learned by ANN. From this, we conclude that, we can extend the proposed system to be able to perform well in case of illumination variation too.

4.5. Experiments with Extended System and Results.

We compared our results for System I and System II. We use brightness of different image features at intervals of 4%, from −80% to 0%. The image features are the same. ICA features are used in Section 4.

All the experimental results are summarized in Figure 12 and Table 3. Figure 12 shows the average value of misidentification with variation of both orientation angle and brightness. Least misidentification remains almost unchanged

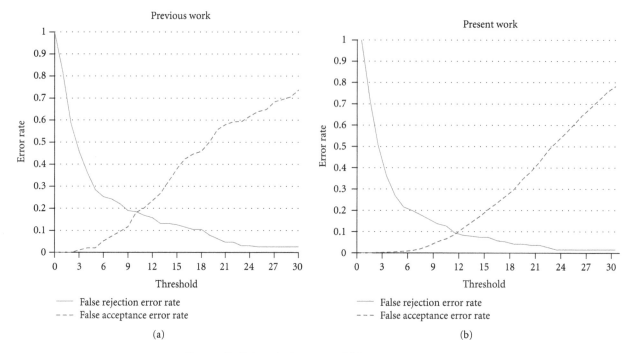

FIGURE 10: False rejection rate and false acceptance rate.

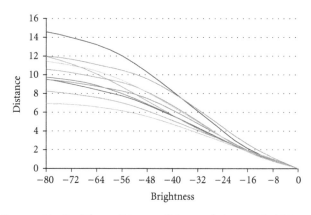

FIGURE 11: Euclidean distance of image feature as brightness changes.

TABLE 3: Misidentification at different brightness levels.

	Only angle	System I	System II
0%	0.090	0.182	0.127
−20%	0.114	0.205	0.114
−40%	0.287	0.199	0.172

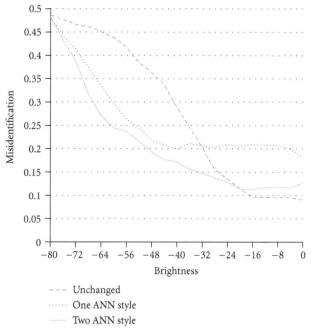

FIGURE 12: Error rate due to changes in brightness.

when brightness is reduced from 0% to 20%. It shows that when illumination is strong, there is no need to correct the original system. Misidentification using System I and System II is much less compared to the original system when the image is dark. To train System II, it takes more time and memory. But System II gives much better result. It is also found that System II's performance is consistent, and correct authentication rate steadily improves as image brightness decreases more and more.

5. Conclusion

In this work we have proposed an efficient technique for angle-aware face recognition and extended the same technique to take care of the effect of illumination variation. Though there are lots of works on angle invariant and illumination invariant face recognition proposed in the literature so far, there is a very few work in which same framework is used for taking care of both the problems simultaneously. Our proposed system can take care of angle variation from -50 degrees to $+50$ degrees and at the same time 40 sets and different image feature set. The results are now reliable to work with larger data set. We used only one data set and currently are engaged in using other data sets for simulation experiments.

In this work, we considered the change in angle orientation in the horizontal plane, but orientation in the vertical plane may also vary and affect face recognition. We would like to extend our work to take care of the change in orientation in the vertical plane. Further experiments to work with more bench mark data sets are also our future target.

References

[1] W. Zhao, R. Chellappa, P. J. Phillips, and A. Rosenfeld, "Face recognition: a literature survey," *ACM Computing Surveys*, vol. 35, no. 4, pp. 399–458, 2003.

[2] B. Chakraborty, "A novel ANN based approach for angle invariant face verification," in *Proceedings of the IEEE Symposium on Computational Intelligence in Image and Signal Processing (CIISP '07)*, pp. 72–76, April 2007.

[3] M. A. Turk and A. P. Pentland, "Face recognition using eigen faces," in *Proceedings of the IEEE Computer Society Conference on Computer Vision and Pattern Recognition (CVPR '91)*, pp. 586–591, June 1991.

[4] S. K. Zhou, R. Chellappa, and W. Zhao, *Unconstrained Face Recognition*, Springer, 2006.

[5] R. Gross, S. Baker, I. Matthews, and T. Kanade, "Face recognition scross pose and illumination," in *Handbook of Face Recognition*, S. Z. Li and A. K. Jain, Eds., Springer, 2004.

[6] P. J. Phillips et al., "Face recognition vendor test 2002: evaluation report," NISTIR 6965, 2003, http://www.frvt.org/.

[7] T. Maurer and C. von der Malsburg, "Single-view based recognition of faces rotated in depth," in *Proceedings of the International Workshop on Automatic Face and Gesture Recognition*, pp. 248–253, 1995.

[8] D. Beymer, "Face recognition under varying pose," Technical Report 1461, MIT AI Laboratory, Cambridge, Mass, USA, 1995.

[9] S. Ullman and R. Basri, "Recognition by linear combinations of models," *IEEE Transactions on Pattern Analysis and Machine Intelligence*, vol. 13, no. 10, pp. 992–1006, 1991.

[10] A. S. Georghiades, P. N. Belhumeur, and D. J. Kriegman, "From few to many: illumination cone models for face recognition under variable lighting and pose," *IEEE Transactions on Pattern Analysis and Machine Intelligence*, vol. 23, no. 6, pp. 643–660, 2001.

[11] A. Pentland, B. Moghaddam, and T. Starner, "View-based and modular eigenspaces for face recognition," in *Proceedings of the IEEE Computer Society Conference on Computer Vision and Pattern Recognition (CVPR '94)*, pp. 84–91, June 1994.

[12] L. Wiskott, J. M. Fellous, N. Krüger, and C. D. Von Malsburg, "Face recognition by elastic bunch graph matching," *IEEE Transactions on Pattern Analysis and Machine Intelligence*, vol. 19, no. 7, pp. 775–779, 1997.

[13] R. Gross, I. Matthews, and S. Baker, "Eigen Light-Fields and Face Recognition across Pose," in *Proceedings of the 5th International Conference on Automatic Face and Gesture Recognition*, 2002.

[14] T. Kanade and A. Yamada, "Multi-Subregion based probabilistic approach toward pose invariant face recognition," in *Proceedings of the IEEE International Symposium on Computational Intelligence in Robotics and Automation (CIRA '3)*, pp. 954–959, 2003.

[15] R. Gross, I. Matthews, and S. Baker, "Appearance-based face recognition and light-fields," *IEEE Transactions on Pattern Analysis and Machine Intelligence*, vol. 26, no. 4, pp. 449–465, 2004.

[16] S. K. Zhou and R. Chellappa, "Image-based face recognition under illumination and pose variations," *Journal of the Optical Society of America A*, vol. 22, no. 2, pp. 217–229, 2005.

[17] G. Chakraborty, B. Chakraborty, J. C. Patra, and C. Pornavalai, "An MLP-based face authentication technique robust to orientation," in *Proceedings of the International Joint Conference on Neural Networks (IJCNN '09)*, pp. 481–488, Atlanta, Ga, USA, June 2009.

[18] J. Shermina and V. Vasudevan, "An efficient face recognition system based on the hybridization of invariant pose and illumination process," *European Journal of Scientific Research*, vol. 64, no. 2, pp. 225–243, 2011.

[19] H. F. Liau and D. Isa, "New illumination compensation method for face recognition," *International Journal of Computer and Network Security*, vol. 2, no. 3, pp. 5–12, 2010.

[20] J. Shermina, "Impact of locally linear regression and fisher linear discriminant analysis in pose invariant face recognition," *International Journal of Computer Science and Network Security*, vol. 10, no. 10, 2010.

[21] J. Shermina, "Illumination invariant face recognition using discrete cosine transform and principal component analysis," in *Proceedings of the International Conference on Emerging Trends in Electrical and Computer Technology (ICETECT '11)*, pp. 826–830, March 2011.

[22] S. J. D. Prince and J. H. Elder, "Creating invariance to "nuisance parameters" in face recognition," in *2005 IEEE Computer Society Conference on Computer Vision and Pattern Recognition (CVPR '05)*, pp. 446–453, June 2005.

[23] H. Murase and S. K. Nayar, "Visual learning and recognition of 3-d objects from appearance," *International Journal of Computer Vision*, vol. 14, no. 1, pp. 5–24, 1995.

[24] D. Graham and N. Allison, "Face recognition from unfamiliar views: subspace methods and pose dependency," in *Proceedings of the International Conference of Automatic Face and Gesture Recognition*, pp. 348–353, 1998.

[25] W. Zhao and R. Chellappa, "A guided tour of face processing," in *Face Processing*, Zhaoo and Chellappa, Eds., Academic Press, 2006.

[26] http://www.softopia.or.jp/rd/facedb/top.html.

9

I-PD Controller Tuning for Unstable System Using Bacterial Foraging Algorithm: A Study Based on Various Error Criterion

V. Rajinikanth[1] and K. Latha[2]

[1] Department of Electronics and Instrumentation Engineering, St Joseph's College of Engineering, Chennai 600 119, India
[2] Division of Avionics, Department of Aerospace Engineering, MIT Campus, Anna University, Chennai 600 044, India

Correspondence should be addressed to V. Rajinikanth, rajinisjceeie@gmail.com

Academic Editor: Sebastian Ventura

This paper proposes a novel method to tune the I-PD controller structure for the time-delayed unstable process (TDUP) using Bacterial Foraging Optimization (BFO) algorithm. The tuning process is focussed to search the optimal controller parameters (K_p, K_i, K_d) by minimising the multiple objective performance criterion. A comparative study on various cost functions like Integral of Squared Error (ISE), Integral of Absolute Error (IAE), Integral of Time-weighted Squared Error (ITSE), and Integral of Time weighted Absolute Error (ITAE) have been attempted for a class of TDUP. A simulation study for BFO-based I-PD tuning has been done to validate the performance of the proposed method. The results show that the tuning approach is a model independent approach and provides enhanced performance for the setpoint tracking with improved time domain specifications.

1. Introduction

Proportional + Integral + Derivative (PID) controllers are widely used in various industrial applications in which set-point tracking and disturbance rejection are necessary. This controller provides an optimal and robust performance for a wide range of operating conditions for stable, unstable and nonlinear processes. Based on the controller configuration (position of P, I, and D), the PID is classified as ideal PID, series PID, and parallel PID.

Since an ideal PID controller has practical difficulties due to its unrealizable nature, it is largely considered in academic studies. Parallel PID controllers are widely used in industries due to its easy accomplishment in analog or digital form. The major drawbacks of the basic parallel PID controllers are the effects of proportional and derivative kick. In order to minimize these effects, modified forms of parallel controller structures such as ID-P and I-PD are widely considered [1].

Time Delayed Unstable Processes (TDUP) considered in this work are widely observed in chemical process industries (exothermic stirred reactors with back mixing, pump with liquid storage tank, combined feed/effluent heat exchanger with adiabatic exothermic reaction, bioreactor, polymerization reactor, jacketed CSTR) [2]. Fine tuning of controller parameters for these systems is highly difficult than in open loop stable systems since (i) unstable processes are hard to stabilize due to unstable poles, (ii) the controller gains are limited by a minimum and maximum value based on the process time delay (ratio of process time delay to process time constant, that is, d/τ ratio). The increase in time delay "d" in the process narrows down the limiting value and it restricts the performance of the closed loop system under control, (iii) unusual overshoot and/or inverse response due to the presence of zeros in the process model.

In control literature, many efforts have been attempted to design optimal and robust controllers for TDUP. Panda has proposed a synthesis method to design an Internal Model Controller-based PID (IMC-PID) controller for a class of time-delayed unstable process [2]. Padhy and Majhi have proposed a PI-PD controller design for unstable systems based on the phase and gain margin criteria [3]. Marchetti et al. have considered a relay-based identification and PID controller tuning [4]. Liu et al. have developed an analytical two-degree freedom setpoint tracking control scheme [5]. Shamsuzzoha and Lee have proposed a control scheme for enhanced disturbance rejection [6]. Chen et al. have discussed a setpoint weighted-PID controller tuning for time-delayed unstable system. It has been reported that, based on the setpoint weighting parameter, a simple PID-PD controller can be used to achieve basic and modified PID structures [7]. Apart from the above methods, a review on the methods of controller tuning for a class of time-delayed unstable system could be found in the book by Padma Sree and Chidambaram [8]. Most of these approaches require an approximated first or second-order transfer-function model with a time delay. In real time, the approximated model parameter may be changing or subject to uncertainty. The model-based controller tuning also requires complex computations to identify the controller parameters. To overcome this, it is necessary to use soft computing-based model independent controller tuning methods.

In recent years, evolutionary approach-based controller autotuning methods has attracted the control engineers and the researchers due to it is nonmodel-based approach, simplicity, high computational efficiency, easy implementation, and stable convergence [9–13]. In this paper, the I-PD controller tuning is proposed for unstable system using the Bacteria Foraging Optimization (BFO) algorithm introduced by Passino [14]. It is a biologically inspired computation technique based on mimicking the foraging activities of *Escherichia coli (E. coli)* bacteria, and it is successfully used in various engineering applications. The literature gives the application details of BFO in PID controller tuning for a class of stable systems [15, 16]. Hybridization-based optimization techniques, such as Genetic Algorithm (GA) [17, 18] and Particle Swarm Optimization (PSO) [19–21] have also been used in PID controller tuning. The above methods are proposed for stable systems only. For stable systems, the overshoot and the error value will be very small and it supports the PID controller tuning efficiently. For unstable systems, the controller parameter tuning seems to be difficult task and is limited due to "d/τ" ratio. Since the basic PID controller will not provide the optimised parameter and this may require a modified PID structure such as I-PD.

Recently, the author has attempted BFO-based PID and I-PD tuning for a class of TDUP [22]. In this work, ISE minimization (single-objective function) is highly prioritized as a performance measure and it monitors the BFO until the controller parameters converge to a minimized value. From the work it has demonstrated that a BFO-based PID controller tuning can be performed for the unstable system when the "d/τ" ratio is below 0.2. PID-based tuning results large overshoot which tends to increase the ISE value, when the d/τ ratio is greater than 0.2. This phenomenon disrupts the convergence of BFO algorithm. In order to overcome the problem, an I-PD structure is employed to obtained better results. They have also presented a comparative study with the Particle-Swarm-Optimization-(PSO-) based controller tuning and classical controller tuning methods with a simulation study. The BFO-based controller tuning approach shows improved performance of the process in terms of

time domain specification, error minimization, disturbance rejection, setpoint, and multiple setpoint tracking than the PSO and classical tuning methods.

In this work, a multiple-objective function-based BFO algorithm has been proposed for the controller parameter tuning for TDUP. Further, an attempt has been made by considering a TDUP with a zero. A comparative study on various cost functions such as ISE, IAE, ITSE, and ITAE, has been attempted. To evaluate the performance of the proposed method, a simulation study is carried out using a class of unstable system models.

The remaining part of the paper is organized as follows: an overview of bacterial foraging optimization algorithm is provided in Section 2, Section 3 presents the problem formulation and the cost function-based design of I-PD controller. Section 4 discusses the simulated results on different process models followed by the conclusion of the present research work in Section 5.

2. Bacteria Foraging Optimization Algorithm

Bacteria Foraging Optimization (BFO) algorithm is a new class of biologically inspired stochastic global search technique based on mimicking the foraging (methods for locating, handling, and ingesting food) behavior of *E. coli* bacteria. During foraging, a bacterium can exhibit two different actions: tumbling or swimming. The tumble action modifies the orientation of the bacterium. During swimming (chemotactic step), the bacterium will move in its current direction. Chemotactic movement is continued until a bacterium goes in the direction of positive-nutrient gradient. After a certain number of complete swims, the best half of the population undergoes reproduction, eliminating the rest of the population. In order to escape local optima, an elimination-dispersion event is carried out where some bacteria are liquidated at random with a very small probability and the new replacements are initialized at random locations of the search space [14, 16, 19]. Figure 1 shows the flow chart of the BFO algorithm.

The working principle for the bacterial foraging optimization algorithm can be defined as shown in Figure 1.

3. I-PD Controller Tuning Procedure

3.1. Problem Formulation. In process industries, PID controller is used to improve both the steady state as well as the transient response of the plant. Consider the closed loop control system as shown in Figure 2, where $G_p(s)$ is the process under control and $G_c(s)$ is the controller. The main objective of this system is to make $Y(s) = R(s)$. In this system, the controller continuously adjusts the value of "$U_c(s)$" until the error "$E(s)$" is zero irrespective of the disturbance signal "$D(s)$."

For practical applications, the term "$G_c(s)$" can be replaced by a simple PID controller or a modified structure PID controller.

(i) Let, $G_c(s)$ has the noninteracting (K_p, K_i, K_d works independently on error signal) form of parallel PID structure as shown in Figure 3.

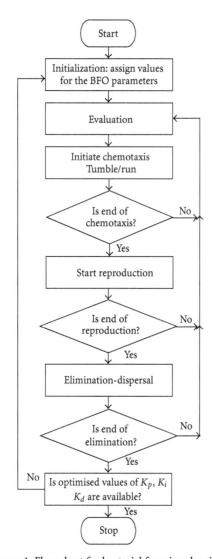

FIGURE 1: Flow chart for bacterial foraging algorithm.

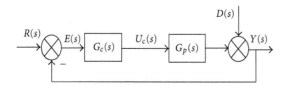

FIGURE 2: Block diagram of the closed loop control system.

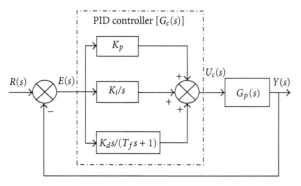

FIGURE 3: Structure of parallel PID control system.

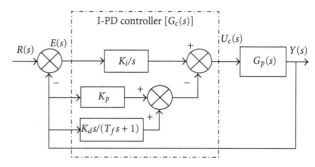

FIGURE 4: Structure of parallel I-PD control system.

Mathematical representation of parallel form of PID controller is given in (1):

$$G_c(s) = \left(K_p + \frac{K_i}{s} + \frac{K_d s}{T_f s + 1} \right), \qquad (1)$$

where T_f if the filter time constant. $T_f = T_d/N$; $T_d =$ Derivative controller time constant (K_d/K_p); $N =$ derivative filter constant. For this study it is assigned as 10.

The output signal from the controller is

$$U_c(s) = K_p e(t) + K_i \int_0^T e(t)dt + \left(\frac{K_d}{T_f s + 1} \right) \frac{de(t)}{dt}. \qquad (2)$$

In this structure, a step change in the reference input "$R(s)$" will cause an immediate spiky change in the control signal "$U_c(s)$." This abrupt change in the controller output is represented as the proportional and/or derivative kick. These kick effects rapidly change the command signal to the actuator which controls the entire operation of the plant $(G_p(s))$ [1]. To overcome this drawback, a modified controller structure knows as I-PD is considered in this study.

(ii) The noninteracting form of I-PD controller structure is shown in Figure 4.

The output signal from the I-PD controller is

$$U_c(s) = K_i \int_0^T e(t)dt - \left[K_p y(t) + K_d \frac{dy(t)}{dt} \right]. \qquad (3)$$

In this structure, the integral term (K_i) responds on error signal "$e(t)$." An abrupt change in the reference input "$R(s)$" will not affect the proportional (K_p) and derivative (K_d) terms, since these two terms works on the process output "$y(t)$." The I-PD is a modified form of a parallel PID structure and is always preferred in industries, where a smooth set point tracking is required.

3.2. Cost Function. A generalized closed loop response of a system is shown in Figure 5. For closed loop systems, the main objective of the controller is to make the peak overshoot (M_p), settling time (t_s) and final steady state error (E_{ss}), as small as possible. During the optimization search, along with the cost function it is necessary to assign the essential values for M_p, t_s and E_{ss}.

(i) "M_p" is the difference between the reference input "$R(s)$" and the maximum process output "$Y(s)$."

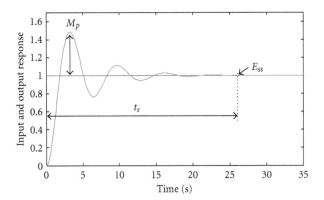

Figure 5: Closed loop response of the system.

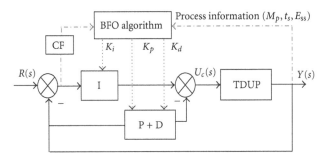

Figure 6: BFO-based I-PD controller tuning.

(ii) "t_s" is the time required for the process output to reach a final steady state value.

(iii) "E_{ss}" is the value of error "$e(t)$" when time "t" tends to infinity.

The Cost Function (CF) guides the algorithm to search the optimised controller parameters. Equation (4) shows the normally considered CF to evaluate the performance of the closed loop system:

$$\text{IAE} = \int_0^T |e(t)|dt = \int_0^T |r(t) - y(t)|dt,$$

$$\text{ISE} = \int_0^T e^2(t)dt = \int_0^T [r(t) - y(t)]^2 dt,$$

$$\text{ITAE} = \int_0^T t|e(t)|dt = \int_0^T t|r(t) - y(t)|dt, \qquad (4)$$

$$\text{ITSE} = \int_0^T te^2(t)dt = \int_0^T t[r(t) - y(t)]^2 dt,$$

where $e(t)$ = error, $r(t)$ = reference input (set point), and $y(t)$ = process output.

The performance criterion in the proposed method is expressed as,

$$J_1\left(K_p, K_i, K_d\right) = (w_1 \cdot \text{CF}) + \left(w_2 \cdot M_p\right) \\ + (w_3 \cdot t_s) + (w_4 \cdot E_{ss}), \qquad (5)$$

where $w_1 \cdots w_4$ are weighting functions for the performance index (range is from 0-1), CF is the error criterion from the error detector, and M_p, t_s, and E_{ss} are additional performance index obtained from the process output.

The performance criterion presented in (5) is a multiobjective criterion and has four terms accompanied by a weighting factor "w," and it should be set based on the priority level. If the parameter "$J_1(K_p, K_i, K_d)$" does not converge with an optimal value during the entire search, then the exploration is reinitialized with "w_1" alone by making other weights as zero.

3.3. Design of I-PD Controller Using BFO. The controller tuning process is to find the optimal values for K_p, K_i, and K_d from the search space that minimizes the objective function (5). Figure 6 illustrates the basic block diagram for I-PD controller tuning using BFO algorithm. In this, the performance criterion "$J_1(K_p, K_i, K_d)$" guides the optimization algorithm to get appropriate value for the controller parameters.

Prior to the optimization search, it is necessary to assign the following algorithm parameters.

Dimension of search space is three; number of bacteria is chosen as ten; number of chemotaxis step is set to five; number of reproduction steps and length of a swim is considered as four; number of elimination-dispersal events is two; number of bacteria reproduction is assigned as five; probability for elimination dispersal has a value of 0.2.

In the literature, there is no guide line to allot the tuning parameters for the BFO algorithm.

In this study, before proceeding with the BFO-based I-PD controller tuning, the following values are assigned.

(i) The three dimensional search space is defined as:

K_p: min -60% to max $+60\%$;
K_i: min -30% to max $+30\%$;
K_d: min -30% to max $+30\%$.

If the search does not converge with an optimal K_p, K_i, K_d values, increase the search range by 10% and begin a new search.

(ii) The maximum overshoot (M_p) range is selected as 50% of the reference signal. The overshoot in the process output is limited by inserting a rate and limiter block between the controller and the TDUP.

(iii) The steady state error (E_{ss}) in the process output is assigned as zero.

(iv) There is no guideline to specify the values for CF and settling time (t_s). The "t_s" is preferred as 25% of the maximum simulation time. The simulation time should be selected based on the process time delay (d).

(v) For each process example, five trials with a particular CF are carried out and the finest set of values among the trials are selected as the optimized controller parameter set.

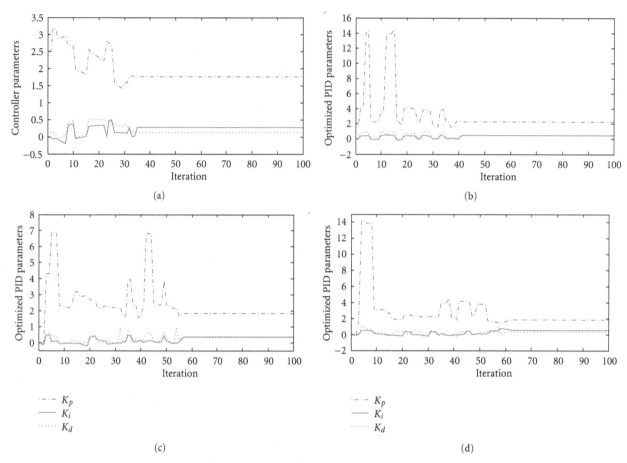

FIGURE 7: Final convergence of controller parameters with (a) ISE-, (b) IAE-, (c) ITAE-, and (d) ITSE-guided BFO algorithm.

TABLE 1: Optimised controller values.

Method	Iteration number	K_p	K_i	K_d
ISE I-PD	35	1.7726	0.2809	0.1339
IAE I-PD	41	2.2530	0.4752	0.4628
ITAE I-PD	57	1.8399	0.3722	0.3194
ITSE I-PD	62	1.8874	0.5199	0.3836

(vi) A unity reference signal is considered for all the process models, (that is, $R(s) = 1$).

4. Results and Discussions

To study the closed loop performance of the TDUP with BFO tuned I-PD controller, mathematical model of the processes from literature are considered.

Example 1. The first order system with the following transfer function model is considered:

$$G_p(s) = \frac{e^{-ds}}{\tau s - 1} = \frac{e^{-0.4s}}{s - 1}. \tag{6}$$

This process has an unstable pole with process time constant $(\tau) = 1$ and time delay $(d) = 0.4$. For the above process "d/τ" is 0.4.

The BFO-based I-PD controller tuning is proposed for the system as in Figure 6. The final convergence of the controller parameters are shown in Figure 7 and the optimised K_p, K_i, K_d values are tabulated in Table 1. The result shows that the ISE-based tuning has less number of iteration compared to other methods.

The process model (6) is initially tested with the parallel PID controller (Figure 3) with the optimal values given in Table 1. From Figure 8(a), it is noted that the overshoot observed in the process output is very large and the controller output illustrates a large spike as in Figure 8(b).

An enlarged view of the controller output "$U_c(s)$" is presented in Figure 9. When the process is excited with a reference signal, the controller will produce proportional and derivative kick initially. When the output reaches the final steady state value, the abrupt change in the controller signal vanishes slowly, and finally it reaches a smooth stable value. The initial part of the controller output is the cause for the process overshoot "M_p."

The given process model is then proceeded with an I-PD controller (Figure 4) with Table 1 parameters. Figures 10(a) and 10(b) show the process and controller outputs respectively. The present method provides enhanced performance compared to the basic PID controller.

The regulatory response is then studied with a load disturbance of 0.1 (10% of setpoint) introduced at 30 sec.

TABLE 2: Performance comparisons for Example 1 with I-PD controller.

Method	Reference tracking								Disturbance rejection			
	ISE	IAE	ITAE	ITSE	$t_r(s)$	M_p	$t_s(s)$	E_{ss}	ISE	IAE	ITAE	ITSE
ISE I-PD	1.959	2.750	4.989	3.582	4.50	0	8.20	0	2.051	3.234	20.36	19.62
IAE I-PD	1.813	2.637	4.687	3.225	4.60	0	8.25	0	1.872	3.938	46.79	37.85
ITAE I-PD	1.793	2.441	3.889	2.923	3.65	0.0323	9.55	0	1.926	3.151	19.44	17.03
ITSE I-PD	1.565	2.230	3.675	2.681	2.85	0.1039	8.25	0	1.700	2.935	17.92	15.92

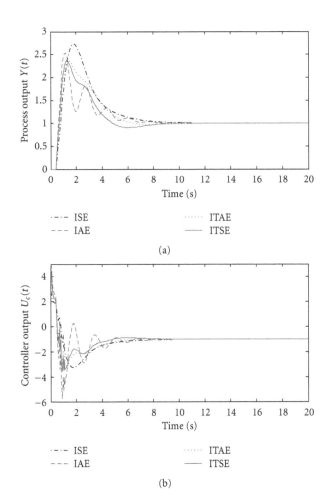

(a)

(b)

FIGURE 8: PID controller performance for Example 1, (a) process output, (b) controller output.

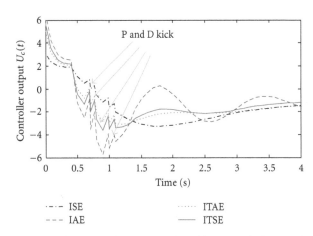

FIGURE 9: The effect of proportional and derivative kick in $U_c(t)$.

Table 2 presents the performance of the I-PD controller for setpoint tracking and load disturbance rejection. The overshoot produced by the ITSE tuned controller (ITSE I-PD) has a large overshoot compared to other methods. But the final error by this method is modest compared with the ISE, IAE, and ITSE.

Example 2. The second order TDUP with the following transfer function is considered. It has one unstable pole and a stable pole:

$$G_p(s) = \frac{\exp^{-s}}{(2s - 1)(0.5s + 1)}. \tag{7}$$

For this process delay time (d) is unity. The PID-tuning scheme previously proposed for the above model is presented in the literature [7].

For this model, the BFO-based I-PD is proposed with a bacteria size of 18 and the other values as given in Section 3.3. The time delay (d) for the system is 1, hence the simulation time is fixed as 200 sec. The trials are executed with each CF and the optimal values are tabulated in Table 3. ISE-based method offers the optimal values with less convergence time than IAE, ITAE, and ITSE.

Figure 12 and Table 4 depict the reference tracking performance of the process model with I-PD structure. The overshoot produced by the ISE (ISE I-PD) is large. The response by the IAE is more oscillatory since the settling time of the system is large. The final steady state error by all the methods are zero. ITAE-based I-PD has a lesser overshoot.

TABLE 3: Optimised K_p, K_i, and K_d values for Example 2.

Method	Iteration number	K_p	K_i	K_d
ISE I-PD	174	1.3394	0.0479	0.6195
IAE I-PD	189	1.9037	0.1173	0.9032
ITAE I-PD	238	1.5518	0.0968	0.8471
ITSE I-PD	251	1.5892	0.1204	0.8949

From Figure 11, it is observed that the I-PD controller tuned with ISE, ITAE, and ITSE offers a stable response. The IAE tuned controller provides an oscillatory response for load disturbance rejection.

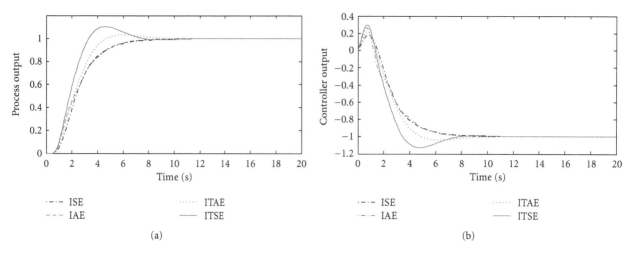

FIGURE 10: I-PD controller performance, (a) process output, (b) controller output.

TABLE 4: Performance evaluation for Example 2.

Method	Reference tracking							
	ISE	IAE	ITAE	ITSE	$t_r(s)$	M_p	$t_s(s)$	E_{ss}
ISE I-PD	5.775	7.485	33.73	24.71	11.1	0.0343	27.9	0
IAE I-PD	4.852	7.706	47.50	39.42	13.7	0.0003	40.2	0
ITAE I-PD	4.541	5.702	18.62	17.55	8.59	0.0002	19.1	0
ITSE I-PD	4.184	5.239	10.00	9.681	7.33	0.0009	18.5	0

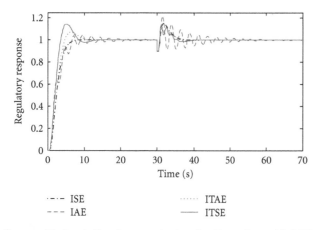

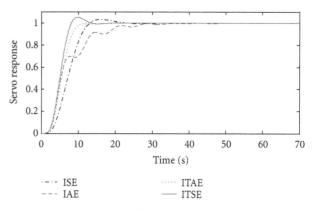

FIGURE 12: Servo response for Example 2 with I-PD controller.

FIGURE 11: Load disturbance rejection for Example 1 with I-PD controller.

TABLE 5: Optimised controller parameters.

Method	Iteration number	K_p	K_i	K_d
ISE I-PD	153	1.5309	0.0349	1.1747
IAE I-PD	169	1.7045	0.0596	2.1298
ITAE I-PD	378	1.8996	0.0807	1.5813
ITSE I-PD	391	2.0109	0.1052	1.8934

The overall response of ITAE-based tuning outperforms the remaining methods considered in this study.

The robustness of the I-PD controller is analysed by changing the delay time of the process model. The controller

values by ISE are employed to test the controller performance.

(i) −50% change is applied in the delay ($d = 0.5$ sec). The process model is as in (8):

$$G_p(s) = \frac{\exp^{-0.5s}}{(2s-1)(0.5s+1)}. \qquad (8)$$

The above model has been studied by the researchers and classically tuned controller settings are existing in the literature [2, 8].

(ii) +25% change in the delay ($d = 1.25$) is tested with the I-PD and PID structures and the results are presented in Figures 13 and 14, respectively.

TABLE 6: Reference tracking performance.

Method				Reference tracking				
	ISE	IAE	ITAE	ITSE	$t_r(s)$	M_p	$t_s(s)$	E_{ss}
ISE I-PD	11.70	15.42	147.9	162.8	23.2	0.0134	67.8	0
IAE I-PD	9.899	13.48	118.1	137.5	19.0	0.0189	62.5	0
ITAE I-PD	8.591	11.58	95.06	124.9	15.9	0.0121	68.8	0
ITSE I-PD	7.841	10.85	87.12	115.2	14.0	0.0184	75.5	0

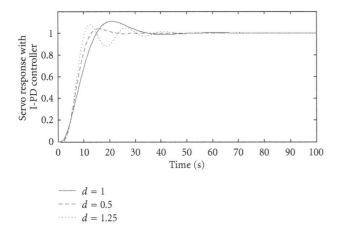

—— $d = 1$
--- $d = 0.5$
······ $d = 1.25$

FIGURE 13: BFO-based I-PD controller tuning.

TABLE 7: Optimised parameters for CSTR model.

Method	Iteration number	K_p	K_i	K_d
ISE I-PD	439	1.913	0.0412	0.1094
IAE I-PD	493	2.4571	0.0509	0.2109
ITAE I-PD	526	1.8662	0.0258	0.2168
ITSE I-PD	558	1.6984	0.0195	0.1107

From Figures 13 and 14, the increase in the time delay may increase the overshoot of the system. When the time delay is large, the system condition will move from stable state to unstable state. From the result, it is noted that the proposed BFO-based tuning provides the optimal controller parameters and it works well for the system with a time delay uncertainty.

Example 3. A third order unstable process with delay studied by Chen et al. [7] is considered. The model has one unstable pole and two stable poles:

$$G_p(s) = \frac{\exp^{-0.5s}}{(5s-1)(0.5s+1)(2s+1)}. \qquad (9)$$

The BFO-tuned controller gains and the final iteration numbers are provided in Table 5. The ISE-based controller parameter search value is converging at 153rd iteration.

Figure 15 and Table 6 show the servo response of the process for unity step input ($R(s) = 1$). The overshoots produced by these methods are negligible. The BFO-tuned I-PD controller provides an enhanced reference tracking with improved time domain specifications.

Example 4. Continuous Stirred Tank Reactor (CSTR) with nonideal mixing considered by Liou and Yu-Shu [23] has the transfer function model:

$$\frac{dC}{dt} = \frac{nQ}{mV}\left(C_f - C\right) - \left[\frac{K_1 C}{(K_2 C + 1)^2}\right],$$
$$nC + (1 - n)C_f = C_e, \qquad (10)$$
$$\text{at } t = 0, \quad C = C_0.$$

In this process the nonideal mixing is described by Cholette's model. The values of the operating conditions are given by flow rate (Q) = 0.03333 lit/sec; volume (V) = 1 lit, K_1 = 10 lit/s; K_2 = 10 lit/mol, $n = m = 0.75$; concentration (C_f) = 3.288 mol/lit; C_e = 1.8 mol/lit. Measurement delay is 20 sec. Linearization of the model equation around the operating condition "$C = 1.304$ mol/lit" gives the following unstable transfer function model:

$$G_p(s) = \frac{\Delta C_e(s)}{\Delta C_f(s)} = \frac{2.21(1 + 11.133s)\exp^{-20s}}{(98.3s - 1)}. \qquad (11)$$

The process model has one unstable pole and a stable zero (numerator "s" value). The unstable system with a zero may produce a large overshoot or inverse response. The time delay "d" for the system is 20 sec.

The optimization search is initiated with the following algorithm parameters.

Number of bacteria is chosen as 25; number of chemotactic steps is set to ten; number of reproduction steps and length of a swim is considered as ten; number of elimination-dispersal events is five; number of bacteria reproduction is assigned as ten; probability for elimination dispersal has a value of 0.3.

In the performance criterion (5), the overshoot "M_p" is removed by assigning the weighting function value with a zero ($w_2 = 0$). During the simulation study, the overshoot in the process output is controlled with a rate and the limiter unit. For this process, the simulation time is chosen as 500 s.

The BFO I-PD parameters converge at 439th iteration for ISE and 558th iteration for ITSE. The controller gains and the performance measure are presented in Tables 7 and 8, respectively. The servo response of the process model with unit step input is illustrated in Figure 16. The ITSE I-PD controller provides a smooth performance for reference

TABLE 8: Performance index for the CSTR model.

Method	Reference tracking							
	ISE	IAE	ITAE	ITSE	$t_r(s)$	M_p	$t_s(s)$	E_{ss}
ISE I-PD	137.8	279.3	82112.9	67391.4	59.4	0.1409	287	0
IAE I-PD	135.3	275.2	81416.4	66942.7	53.7	0.0681	396	0
ITAE I-PD	113.3	253.0	80461.3	59448.0	94.7	0.0431	380	0
ITSE I-PD	106.9	244.2	79848.5	57489.3	111.3	0.0407	320	0

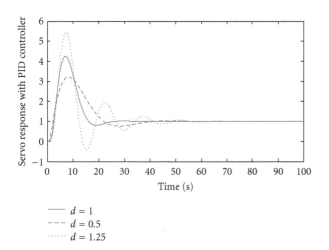

—— $d = 1$
--- $d = 0.5$
······ $d = 1.25$

FIGURE 14: BFO-based PID controller tuning.

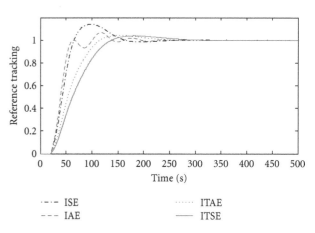

-·-· ISE ······ ITAE
--- IAE —— ITSE

FIGURE 16: Reference tracking performance of CSTR model.

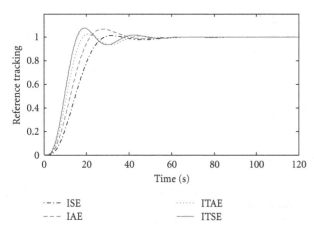

-·-· ISE ······ ITAE
--- IAE —— ITSE

FIGURE 15: Servo response for Example 3 with BFO-based I-PD controller.

tracking and it outperforms the performance by other methods analysed in this study.

5. Conclusion

In this work, an attempt has been made for tuning an I-PD controller structure for a class of unstable process models using Bacterial Foraging Optimization (BFO) algorithm with minimizing the multiple objective performance criterion. A comparative study with Integral of Squared Error (ISE), Integral of Absolute Error (IAE), Integral of Time weighted Squared Error (ITSE), and Integral of Time weighted Absolute Error (ITAE) have been discussed. The ISE based method provides the optimized value with a small iteration time than the IAE, ITAE, and ITSE. Hence, ISE-based controller tuning can be employed for unstable systems to obtain optimal controller settings compared to other methods. The I-PD structure provides an enhanced setpoint tracking performance with minimal cost function. It also provides improved time domain specifications and robust performance for the system with time delay uncertainty.

Nomenclature

$R(s)$: Reference/input signal for the closed loop system
$Y(s)$: Process output
$U_c(s)$: Controller output
$E(s)$: Error signal = $R(s) - Y(s)$
$D(s)$: External disturbance
$r(t)$: Laplace inverse of $R(s)$ that is, $L^{-1}[R(s)]$
$y(t)$: $L^{-1}[Y(s)]$
$e(t)$: $L^{-1}[E(s)] = r(t) - y(t)$
K_p: Proportional gain
K_i: Integral gain
K_d: Derivative gain
t_r: Rise time
t_s: Settling time
M_p: Over shoot
E_{ss}: Steady state error
K_1, K_2: CSTR constants.
n, m: Constants

Subscripts

d: Derivative
i: Integral
p: Proportional
f: Feed.

References

[1] M. A. Johnson and M. H. Moradi, *PID Control: New Identification and Design Methods*, chapter 2, Springer, London, UK, 2005.

[2] R. C. Panda, "Synthesis of PID controller for unstable and integrating processes," *Chemical Engineering Science*, vol. 64, no. 12, pp. 2807–2816, 2009.

[3] P. K. Padhy and S. Majhi, "Relay based PI-PD design for stable and unstable FOPDT processes," *Computers & Chemical Engineering*, vol. 30, no. 5, pp. 790–796, 2006.

[4] G. Marchetti, C. Scali, and D. R. Lewin, "Identification and control of open-loop unstable processes by relay methods," *Automatica*, vol. 37, no. 12, pp. 2049–2055, 2001.

[5] T. Liu, W. Zhang, and D. Gu, "Analytical design of two-degree-of-freedom control scheme for open-loop unstable processes with time delay," *Journal of Process Control*, vol. 15, no. 5, pp. 559–572, 2005.

[6] M. Shamsuzzoha and M. Lee, "Enhanced disturbance rejection for open-loop unstable process with time delay," *ISA Transactions*, vol. 48, no. 2, pp. 237–244, 2009.

[7] C. C. Chen, H. P. Huang, and H. J. Liaw, "Set-point weighted PID controller tuning for time-delayed unstable processes," *Industrial and Engineering Chemistry Research*, vol. 47, no. 18, pp. 6983–6990, 2008.

[8] R. Padma Sree and M. Chidambaram, *Control of Unstable Systems*, Narosa Publishing House, New Delhi, India, 2006.

[9] M. Zamani, N. Sadati, and M. K. Ghartemani, "Design of an $H\infty$, PID controller using particle swarm optimization," *International Journal of Control, Automation and Systems*, vol. 7, no. 2, pp. 273–280, 2009.

[10] M. Zamani, M. Karimi-Ghartemani, N. Sadati, and M. Parniani, "Design of a fractional order PID controller for an AVR using particle swarm optimization," *Control Engineering Practice*, vol. 17, no. 12, pp. 1380–1387, 2009.

[11] D. H. Kim and J. H. Cho, "A biologically inspired intelligent PID controller tuning for AVR systems," *International Journal of Control, Automation and Systems*, vol. 4, no. 5, pp. 624–636, 2006.

[12] U. S. Banu and G. Uma, "Fuzzy gain scheduled continuous stirred tank reactor with particle swarm optimization based PID control minimizing integral square error," *Instrumentation Science and Technology*, vol. 36, no. 4, pp. 394–409, 2008.

[13] Y.-B. Wang, X. Peng, and B. Z. Wei, "A new particle swarm optimization based auto-tuning of PID controller," in *Proceedings of the 7th International Conference on Machine Learning and Cybernetics*, pp. 1818–1823, Kunming, China, July 2008.

[14] K. M. Passino, "Biomimicry of bacterial foraging for distributed optimization and control," *IEEE Control Systems Magazine*, vol. 22, no. 3, pp. 52–67, 2002.

[15] T. Jain and M. J. Nigam, "Optimization of PD-PI controller using swarm intelligence," *International Journal of Computational Cognition*, vol. 6, no. 4, pp. 55–59, 2008.

[16] A. Ali and S. Majhi, "Design of optimum PID controller by bacterial foraging strategy," in *Proceedings of the IEEE International Conference on Industrial Technology (ICIT '06)*, pp. 601–605, Mumbai, Indian, December 2006.

[17] D. H. Kim, "Hybrid GA-BF based intelligent PID controller tuning for AVR system," *Applied Soft Computing Journal*, vol. 11, no. 1, pp. 11–22, 2011.

[18] D. H. Kim, A. Abraham, and J. H. Cho, "A hybrid genetic algorithm and bacterial foraging approach for global optimization," *Information Sciences*, vol. 177, no. 18, pp. 3918–3937, 2007.

[19] A. Biswas, S. Dasgupta, S. Das, and A. Abraham, "Synergy of PSO and bacterial foraging optimization—a comparative study on numerical benchmarks," in *Advances in Soft Computing*, vol. 44 of *Innovations in Hybrid Intelligent Systems*, pp. 255–263, 2007.

[20] S. V. R. S. Gollapudi, S. S. Pattnaik, O. P. Bajpai, S. Devi, and K. M. Bakwad, "Velocity modulated bacterial foraging optimization technique (VMBFO)," *Applied Soft Computing Journal*, vol. 11, no. 1, pp. 154–165, 2011.

[21] W. M. Korani, H. T. Dorrah, and H. M. Emara, "Bacterial foraging oriented by particle swarm optimization strategy for PID tuning," in *Proceedings of the 8th IEEE International Conference on Computational Intelligence in Robotics and Automation (CIRA '09)*, pp. 445–450, Daejeon, Korea, December 2009.

[22] V. Rajinikanth and K. Latha, "Bacterial foraging optimization algorithm based pid controller tuning for time delayedunstable systems," *The Mediterranean Journal of Measurement and Control*, vol. 7, no. 1, pp. 197–203, 2011.

[23] C. T. Liou and C. Yu-Shu, "The effect of nonideal mixing on input multiplicity in a CSTR," *Chemical Engineering Science*, vol. 46, no. 8, pp. 2113–2116, 1991.

10

Using Multicore Technologies to Speed Up Complex Simulations of Population Evolution

Mauricio Guevara-Souza and Edgar E. Vallejo

ITESM-CEM, Carretera a Lago de Guadalupe km 3.5, Col. Margarita Maza de Juarez, 52956 Atizapan de Zaragoza, MEX, Mexico

Correspondence should be addressed to Mauricio Guevara-Souza; a00456476@itesm.mx

Academic Editor: Cheng-Jian Lin

We explore with the use of multicore processing technologies for conducting simulations on population replacement of disease vectors. In our model, a native population of simulated vectors is inoculated with a small exogenous population of vectors that have been infected with the *Wolbachia* bacteria, which confers immunity to the disease. We conducted a series of computational simulations to study the conditions required by the invading population to take over the native population. Given the computational burden of this study, we decided to take advantage of modern multicore processor technologies for reducing the time required for the simulations. Overall, the results seem promising both in terms of the application and the use of multicore technologies.

1. Introduction

We are part of a research program whose main purpose is to develop computational tools and models that are useful to gain insights on population dynamics of disease vectors and its potential application to develop new strategies to control vector borne diseases such as malaria and dengue [1].

The introduction of transgenic vectors that are refractory to the disease into wild native populations to achieve the replacement of disease carrying populations is a promising strategy for disease control but so far has only been explored to a limited extent [2, 3].

One possible alternative that seems promising is the introduction of mosquitoes infected with the *Wolbachia* bacteria into wild populations for dengue or malaria disease control. The bacteria produces a variety of fitness and reproduction altering mechanisms that contribute to the establishment of immune populations [4].

Wolbachia pipientis is a bacteria that infects a wide variety of invertebrate taxa. It is estimated that approximately 20% of the insects are all infected with this bacteria [5].

The bacteria can spread rapidly over an uninfected population due to the cytoplasmic incompatibility that it induces in its hosts [6, 7].

This mechanisms cause the progeny of a female that is not infected with *Wolbachia* and a male that is infected to die. If the female is infected, the offspring will survive and will be infected with *Wolbachia* no matter the infection status of the male (see Figure 1).

Moreover, it has been shown that *Wolbachia* provides some virus resistance to their hosts and thus contribute to overcoming loss of fitness. For all this, this mechanism results in the rapid invasion of the host population.

Theoretical models on the dynamics of *Wolbachia* infection have been developed in the past [8]. In principle, these models should be able to explain the dynamics of the infection in native populations. However, theoretical population dynamics models often require strong assumptions, such as unbounded population sizes, probability calculations that are difficult in practice, among others. In this context, computational simulations have proven to be useful for confirming the validity of the theory in practical scenarios. We believe that successful experimental work should rely crucially on sound theoretical work validated by thorough computer simulations.

Based on this premise, we have been developing and testing computer simulation models for several years for

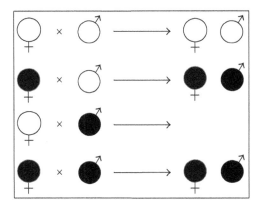

FIGURE 1: Cytoplasmatic incompatibility induced by *Wolbachia* infection.

a variety of gene drive mechanisms such as transposable elements and the maternal effect dominant embryonic arrest (MEDEA) in order to cast a prediction about the effectiveness of such population replacement strategies for disease control [9, 10].

We are confident that these mechanisms hold much promise in the effective replacement of wild populations in a way that does not affect the food chain or other important variables of the ecosystem. The environment is in such a subtle balance that any external intervention can break the equilibrium with severe consequences.

In this paper, we present a series of experiments of wild population replacement using vectors infected with the *Wolbachia* bacteria. A variety of scenarios are explored using different parameters for each one. The main objective of the simulations has been to determine the conditions required by *Wolbachia* infection to take over the entire native population.

Given the computational intensive simulations required for this study, we used several computer technologies both sequential and parallel to contrast all of them in terms of efficiency in the usage of computer resources.

We believe this kind of benchmark would be valuable for scientists that are not versed in computer technologies to help them choose the most appropriate technology for their studies.

Towards this end, we also explored to what extent we can speed up the simulations by using a variety of multicore technologies, including OpenMP and Java Threads. It is important to point out that we programmed the four simulators as close as possible using the same design and coding standards to be fair in the comparisons between technologies.

In terms of the application, the experimental results presented here provided valuable insights related to the conditions required by population replacement to occur, including the size of the native and the invading populations, among others.

As mentioned above, these results presented here are very preliminary and we only used the simulator to examine whether multicore technologies are applicable to real problems but we want to focus on the benchmark between technologies and not on the results of the computational model.

In terms of the technologies employed for this study, we found that Java threads is a more capable technology for reducing the time required by the simulations and also since it is a computer language that is relatively easy to learn, the time needed to build the software is significantly less.

The organization of the paper is as follows. In Section 2 we describe very briefly some theory about programming languages and programming paradigms for those who are not up to date in the matter. Section 3 describes the computer model we use in our research program. In Section 4, we present the preliminary results obtained with the simulator and the performance benchmark of the different technologies. Section 5 presents our conclusions, both about the experiments performed with the simulator and the performance benchmark.

2. Background

2.1. Computer Technologies

2.1.1. Compiled Programming Languages versus Interpreted. According to their implementation, there are two main categories to classify programming languages: compiled and interpreted. With compiled languages, the code entered by the programmer is reduced to a series of machine language instructions that are stored in an executable file. On the other hand, with interpreted languages, the code is saved in the same language the programmer introduced it or as an alternative it is stored in an intermediate language to be interpreted by a virtual machine.

It is believed that compiled programs run faster than interpreted ones because interpreted programs have to be translated to machine instructions at runtime, but there is a tradeoff: interpreted languages are more flexible. To give an example, interpreted programs can add or modify functions and variables at runtime, compiled programs can not. Another advantage of interpreted languages is that they are usually easier to learn and debug.

Nowadays, the preferred languages in scientific computing are the compiled ones. This preference is due to the belief that compiled languages are more efficient and make a better memory usage. However, with the advance of virtual machine technologies, the efficiency gap has been narrowing.

In this work we made experiments with two different programming languages: one compiled and one interpreted. The languages we used are C++ and Java; both of them are widely used.

2.1.2. Serial versus Parallel Processing. When computers first made their appearance, and until recently, serial processing was the dominant paradigm. The instructions in the computer were processed mainly in a first in first out manner with some hierarchies between the instructions to get sure critical operations were performed before less critical ones.

When CPUs turned fast enough, multitasking operating systems were developed. This multitasking is only an illusion, actually only one task was performed at a time. The processor switched tasks so fast that the user could not notice the switching between tasks. In serial processing, there is only one path for instruction execution and data flow between processes.

One advantage of serial processing is that the results of a program are very predictable and usually is easier to build a serial program. Computer hardware nowadays is becoming cheaper and more powerful very rapidly. Some years ago, personal computers were very limited in primary memory and processor power, but today, anyone can get a computer that is more powerful than the supercomputers thirty years ago at an affordable price.

It is common that personal computers are equipped with more than one processor and each processor with more than one core. This opened the door to a different computing paradigm called parallel processing.

Parallel processing is the use of more than one CPU or core to execute a program, generally by using threads. Ideally, parallel processing helps the program to execute faster because more hardware is allocated to execute the instructions but this is not always the case.

To take advantage of multiple processing units, the program has to be designed in such a way that several instructions can be executed at once and it is important to state that not every program can be broken into code segments that can be processed in parallel.

The main disadvantage of parallel processing is the complexity of the programs, they are harder to write and debug. Another disadvantage is the power consumption and hardware required, not suitable for mobile devices for the time being.

In this work we wrote the same program in a sequential and parallel programming. For the sequential programs we used Java and C++, for the parallel programs we used Java threads and C++ with OpenMP library, respectively.

2.1.3. Java Virtual Machine. The Java virtual machine (JVM) is responsible of executing the intermediate language of Java, called Java bytecode. The JVM also provides an environment in which the program can be executed providing some utilities like error handling. The main advantage of using the JVM is the portability of the programs written in Java. The same code can be executed in any computer or device that has a JVM enabled.

The JVM provides hardware access protection. Every Java program has assigned a maximum amount of memory it can use. The amount of memory is configured in the JVM parameters. If the program uses more memory than the established, the JVM throws an exception and then kills the process. This protection mechanism is implemented to protect the computer's memory for being corrupted by a malicious program or programming error.

In the mid 90s when Java made its appearance, the main complaints were about the performance of the programs. They were very slow compared with the popular languages at that time like C or C++. In general, scientists still have this idea but at present the JVM has had significant improvements in that aspect, closing the gap in efficiency between compiled languages and Java.

Moreover, since every JVM is made according to the operating system and the hardware, nowadays JVM are designed to fully exploit the computer resources available, feature that a traditional compiled language like C++ does not have. As an example of this, JVM can recognize the pieces of code that are more processor consuming and compile them into machine language to increase efficiency, while the rest of the program is kept in Java bytecodes [11].

2.1.4. Java Threads. Java Threads are incorporated in the core of the language so there is no need for additional libraries to use them. The concept of threads is easy to grasp. In simple terms, a thread is another path in execution through program code so more than one instruction can be executed simultaneously. There are some programs that need to execute several processes at a time, so threads can be very useful in these situations.

All Java programs start with one thread that is the main one. In the body of the program, several new threads can be instantiated and used, each thread with its own call stack. Programming with threads introduces new challenges, especially if they share some memory that needs to be read or written by more than one thread at a time. Several mechanisms are available to prevent shared memory corruption, concurrency problems or deadlock, but thread management is out of the scope of this work.

In summary, threads can be a very valuable tool to speed up and increase efficiency of Java programs but they have to be used with caution, the tradeoff is efficiency against complexity in the design and coding [12].

2.1.5. OpenMP. OpenMP is a third party library that can be used with C, C++, or Fortran programming languages. It is extensively used in scientific and commercial computing. OpenMP application programming interface (API) uses the well-known fork-join model to allow parallel execution in a program that otherwise would be entirely sequential. With OpenMP, multiple threads of execution can perform different task using the directives available in the library. The directives are designed to use all the cores available in the computer.

One advantage of using OpenMP is the capacity of correctly execute the same program both in a sequential or parallel manner. However, there are some programs that would execute correctly as a parallel program but not as a sequential one. Furthermore, when there are mathematical calculations involved, the same program running with different number of threads can yield different results due to the associations of numbers.

As in Java threads, the program starts with a single thread of execution called the initial thread. This thread executes the instructions sequentially until it reaches a region enclosed by a parallel directive. When this happens, the thread creates a team of threads to execute the instructions enclosed inside the parallel directive. The number of threads can be specified in the OpenMP directive. At the end of the parallel block, the team of threads joins to one thread and the execution of the program continues sequentially [13, 14].

3. Materials and Methods

The computer model proposed for this work is a set of mosquito populations connected via migration. Each population evolves independently from each other. We simulated the *Wolbachia* mechanism during reproduction to observe if it is possible for a transgenic mosquito population to replace a native one with the help of *Wolbachia* infection.

To conduct the simulations, two variations of the computer model were used. The difference between them is merely computational. The first one runs in a sequential way while the other one uses multicore technologies to evolve each population on parallel using all the cores available. The simulated biological processes the populations suffer are identical in both variations.

3.1. Mosquito Representation. Each mosquito of the population is represented by a set of attributes that model the most important features of a living being in nature. The first characteristic of the mosquito is the chromosome that is represented by an array of letters. All letters belong to the DNA alphabet (A, G, C, T).

The length of the chromosome was kept small to save computational resources and since *Wolbachia* infection is bacterial and not a DNA modification, the length of the chromosome does not affect the results of the simulations.

The second feature we included in the model is the sex. This distinction between individuals is very important since we want to emulate the reproduction process as closely to the nature as possible. As expected, the sex attribute can assume only two values: male and female.

Another important characteristic is the location of the individuals in the population. For this purpose we used a couple of variables. Location is important specially in the reproduction stage and population structure.

To simulate the *Wolbachia* infection process we used a boolean flag that indicates whether the individual was infected or not.

Finally, we kept track of the fitness of the individual. This value always fell in a range of 0 to 100. It is one of the most important characteristics of an individual. A high fitness value increases the chances of an individual to produce offspring and it also controls the number of offspring that it can produce.

3.2. Population Structure. The individuals are organized in a two-dimensional toroidal square grid that is used to simulate their natural habitat. The position of each individual is important for reproduction because we restricted the females to only mate with males that are located inside a fixed neighborhood (see Figure 2).

The composition of the population is approximately half males and half females but since the sex of the individual is generated randomly at the moment of breeding, this composition can vary from generation to generation.

We decided to use this population structure to get closer to how the reproduction takes place in natural populations where the location of the individuals is not random, it relies

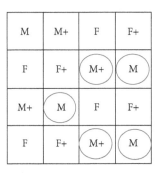

FIGURE 2: Population structure. Red circles indicate the possible mates of the female in the center of the neighborhood. Individuals with the plus sign are infected with *Wolbachia* bacteria.

heavily in the location of the individuals. In many populations it is known that the best adapted individuals tend to get together in the center of the population and the less favored ones are relegated to remote locations.

3.3. Wolbachia Infection. In this work, the *Wolbachia* infection manifests in the individuals as cytoplasmic incompatibility. The infection process is carried out at the beginning of the simulation. Different percentages of infected mosquitoes are introduced in all the populations and we tracked how many mosquitoes are infected with *Wolbachia* at the end of each generation. Then, we calculate the percentage of infection of every population. In our experiments as in nature, the *Wolbachia* infection does not involve a penalty in the fitness.

3.4. Mating Restriction. In ideal populations, reproductions take place with random mating. In nature, very few or none populations reproduce like that. There are a lot of circumstances that make random mating impossible. In our model, we use geographic restriction in order to make the reproduction more alike as wild populations reproduce.

3.5. Genetic Operators

3.5.1. Selection. The selection of suitable parents is done using tournament selection but with two significant restrictions. The first important restriction is the sex of the individuals. The first parent we selected is the female. After selecting the female, the next step is to find a suitable male.

The second constraint comes in at this point. We used a neighborhood restriction so only the males that are inside the neighborhood can be selected as the female mate. We used tournament selection for choosing both the female and male.

3.5.2. Crossover. In our model, we used a single point crossover to generate the chromosome of the offspring. Before performing the crossover, we checked the *Wolbachia* status of the parents. As described in the *Wolbachia* section, if the female is not infected with *Wolbachia* and the male is, the cytoplasmic incompatibility would kill all the offspring so there is no need to generate the chromosome of the offspring.

If the offspring is feasible, the crossover operation takes place with a probability of 100%.

After the crossover is done, the *Wolbachia* flag is updated in the offspring according to the parents infection status. We believe that always carrying out the crossover operation is closer to how reproduction takes place in nature since the offspring always inherits genetic material from both parents.

3.5.3. Mutation. In our experiments we used uniform mutation in all cases. Since the chromosome of the individual is not binary but contains letters, we had to apply little modifications to the mutation process. For every letter in the chromosome we generated a random number and if it surpassed a threshold the letter was mutated. For every letter that has to be mutated, we used another random generated number. Based on that number we picked another letter of the DNA alphabet to replace it with uniform probability distribution.

3.5.4. Migration. Migration is the movement of some individuals of one population to another one. In nature, this mechanism is important because it introduces some genetic diversity to the populations. In our model, before each new generation is generated, we gather a percentage of individuals of one population and move them to another population to mimic the migration process.

The newcomers participate in the reproduction process, introducing new genetic material and in some cases more probabilities of *Wolbachia* infection.

4. Results and Discussion

4.1. Population Replacement Driven by Wolbachia Infection. Genetic engineering has made great strides in the last few years. It is thought that a transgenic mosquito can be engineered in order to replace the malaria carrying alleles with inoffensive ones. If this is true, founding the more feasible scenarios and mechanisms that can lead to the replacement of a wild population would be very valuable. The goal of this experiment is to found possible scenarios to replace a wild mosquito population with another population infected with *Wolbachia*.

To determine the parameters for the experiments we divided them to two groups. The first group are parameters that were fixed in all the experiments. We decided to keep these parameters unchanged because we think they do not have an important impact in the outcome of the experiments, so varying them would not affect the results in a definitive manner.

These parameters and its values are shown in Table 1. The values stated in this table were used for all experiments.

The second group of parameters were determined using the widely used statistical method known as Latin hypercube sampling (LHS) [15]. LHS is used in computer simulations because it generates a distribution of plausible collection of parameter values from a multidimensional distribution. These parameters were chosen among others because we think they are the most important ones. Additionally, in

TABLE 1: Fixed parameters.

Parameter	Value
Chromosome length	20 bases
Generations	100
Mutation probability	1%
Migration	3%
Tournament size	3
Maximum offspring	10
Neighborhood size	30
Crossover probability	100%

TABLE 2: Variable parameters.

Parameter	Value
Population size	2,500–250,000
Number of populations	2–4
Percentage of infection	1%–5%

experiments with real mosquitoes, we can have some control over them.

These parameters are shown in Table 2 and are represented as a range, not as a simple value like the other parameters.

We made exhaustive experiments combining the values of the different parameters in order to cover as much scenarios as possible. Due to the large number of combinations of parameters, we obtained a lot of data that we analyzed and synthesized so we are only presenting the results that we considered the most important.

In all cases, several runs with the same parameters were made, and the results presented are an average of all the runs. We are separating the results of our experiments in three parts. We considered each of the parts is important to understand the effect of the different parameters in the infection process.

4.1.1. Population Size Effect. In this scenario we wanted to observe the effect of the population size in the fixation of the *Wolbachia* infection. The results of the experiment are shown in Figure 3.

As can be seen in Figure 3, as populations become larger, the infection expedites its infection. In large populations, the infection spreads through all the individuals in only 80 generations. In contrast, in small populations the infection remains near zero. We think this behavior is produced by the influence of genetic drift.

It is important to denote that a very small percentage of infection were used for this experiment. The results suggest that it is more probable to infect a large population using a small infection percentage than to try to infect a small population even with a larger percentage of infection.

4.1.2. Percentage of Infection. In this result, we show how the percentage of infection affects the speed of the infection process. In this case we are using a medium sized population

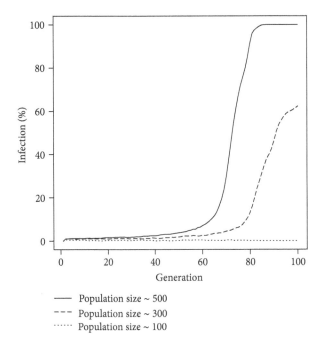

FIGURE 3: Effect of population size.

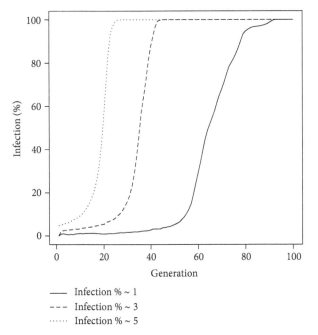

FIGURE 4: Percentage of infection.

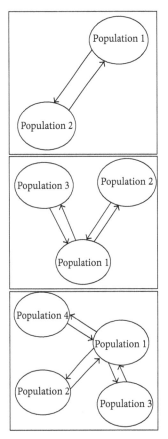

FIGURE 5: Simulation Environments.

4.1.3. Number of Populations. In this experiment, we wanted to observe if the number of populations can affect the infection process. We are comparing the results obtained with two, three, and four populations connected via migration (see Figure 5). In this case, there is one central population and one, two, or three subpopulations. The migration is between the central population to the subpopulation and vice versa. There is no migration between subpopulations.

The results of this experiment are shown in Figure 6.

The figure shows that the number of populations does not have a direct impact in the infection process. If the number of population increases, there is a small perturbation due to the migration process but is not important enough to consider the number of population a crucial parameter. Conversely, we would like to explore in the future if inoculating just one population would be sufficient for propagating the *Wolbachia* infection to the entire neighbor populations.

4.2. Computer Technologies Benchmark. The goal of this experiment is to benchmark different computer technologies to observe the efficiency of each of them when executing the exact same computer program. For this experiment, we are using a compiled language and a semi-interpreted language, both of them with a sequential program and a parallel one. We are considering Java a semi-interpreted language because in a strict sense it is compiled to bytecodes, but those bytecodes have to be interpreted by the JVM.

of about 90,000 individuals to observe the effect of different percentages of infection.

The results of this experiment are shown in Figure 4.

There are no surprises in the results obtained in this experiment. In all cases, the infection spread in the entire population, but the spread is faster with a higher percentage of infection. The valuable information obtained with this experiment is that even with a very small percentage of infection, if the population is large enough, the replacement of the native population is feasible.

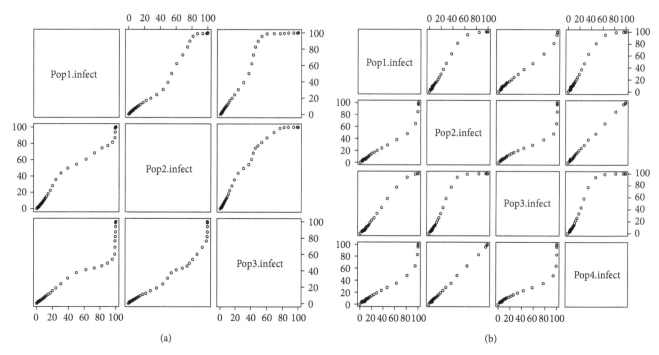

FIGURE 6: Number of populations.

TABLE 3: Simulation parameters.

Parameter	Value
Chromosome length	20 bases
Generations	100
Mutation probability	1%
Migration	1%
Tournament size	3
Maximum offspring	5
Infection percentage	1%
Neighborhood size	30
Crossover probability	100%

We used two scenarios. The first one with two populations and the second one with four populations. We used three different population sizes, all of them structured as a two-dimensional square grid. The parameters for the simulation are specified in Table 3 and were the same for all the simulations in this experiment.

We choose these parameters in order to keep the simulations as close as possible as how the populations and the individuals behave in nature. The only parameter that is out of tune is the length of the individual's chromosome. In nature, the chromosome is about thousands of bases but we considered that using such a large chromosome would result in a waste of memory.

The computer used to run the experiments has an Intel Core i5 dual core processor capable of executing four tasks at a time using hyper threading. The machine has four Gigabytes of random access memory (RAM), but the JVM is configured to use at most one Gigabyte of memory for every experiment.

To track the time that each of the experiments took to complete we used two measurements. The first one was the clock of the integrated development environment (IDE). The second one was a clock inside each program that started when the first instruction was executed and ended when all the computation was finished. Both of them yielded the exact same time in milliseconds.

To perform a benchmark like this, it is important to isolate the program as much as possible. When the experiments were running, none of the other programs was executed by the computer. Also, the computer was disconnected from the internet to prevent the unintentional downloading of internet content like operating system updates.

Additionally, we killed all the user and system processes that could bias the result, but we could not kill all the processes due to operating system restrictions. The results of the experiments are shown in Table 4.

For every scenario, 30 runs were performed. The values of the table are the average of all the runs. The values are expressed as a percentage and reflect the speed up of every technology against the slowest one, in this case C++.

As can be seen in Table 4, Java Threads were very superior compared to the other three technologies in all experiments.

Java and OpenMP yielded similar results in overall, in some experiments Java obtained a better speed up but in the rest OpenMP was better.

C++ was far behind all other technologies. Considering that C++ is a compiled language and in general it is considered a very efficient language, the results of these experiments are surprising.

Java Threads speed-up was very constant in all experiments. It does not matter the size of the population or the number of them, the results were almost the same.

On the other hand, OpenMP apparently started to close the gap against Java Threads as the number and size of the populations were increased. Maybe for a simulation with a

TABLE 4: Simulation results. The slowest technology has a score of 0. The other three technologies have a percentage according to how faster they were compared with the slowest one.

	Two populations			Four populations		
	50×50	100×100	200×200	50×50	100×100	200×200
C++	0	0	0	0	0	0
Java	14.7%	43.1%	36.6%	54.9%	41.7%	34.8%
OpenMP	24.1%	33.1%	38.1%	41.9%	46%	48.6%
Java threads	63.7%	61.6%	60.7%	65.6%	66.1%	61.7%

very large number of populations or with populations with millions of individuals, OpenMP would be the more efficient technology.

In nature, the size of *Anopheles gambiae* mosquito populations rarely is above the 40,000 individuals. Using this premise, Java Threads would be the technology of choice to simulate populations of *Anopheles gambiae* mosquitoes.

Another reason to chose Java or Java Threads among C++ or OpenMP is the complexity of the design and coding of the programs. Programming with Java technologies is far easier than C++ due to the automatic management of memory, the more extensive and useful API and the more robust IDEs available in the open source community.

5. Conclusion

The work presented here showed that computer modeling and simulations simplify the study of population-based phenomena. Particularly, we showed that computational simulations could provide important insights on the conditions required to implement population replacement strategy for controlling vector borne diseases such as malaria and dengue.

The determination of such conditions experimentally would be extremely onerous in practice. Furthermore, we believe that computational simulations are capable of modeling reasonably well evolutionary and genetic aspects of population biology, such as genetic drift and cytoplasmic incompatibility, among others.

The availability of such computer simulation tools is rapidly coming to be crucial as several research groups have already started the actual release of *Wolbachia*-infected mosquitoes. Countries such as China, Australia, Indonesia, Vietnam, Brazil, among others, have joined to the Eliminate Dengue Program, which aims to control dengue by *Wolbachia* induced population replacement. Information about the field release of *Wolbachia*-infected mosquitoes for dengue fever control can be found at (http://www.eliminatedengue.com/).

In addition, we demonstrated that using modern multicore technologies can be extremely useful for reducing the time required for conducting population based simulations, both the experimentation and the programming of the simulator. In effect, simulations on population biology are highly parallelizable in general, so these applications and modern hight throughput computing technologies will be a very good fit.

We also found that computer technologies are advancing so rapidly, that most preconceptions (such as the superiority of compiled versus interpreted programming languages) are no longer valid, at least for a particular set of problems.

References

[1] M. Guevara-Souza and E. E. Vallejo, "Computer simulation on disease vector population replacement driven by the maternal effect dominant embryonic arrest(medea)," in *Software Tools and Algorithms for Biological Systems*, pp. 335–344, Springer, 2011.

[2] J. M. Marshall and C. E. Taylor, "Malaria control with transgenic mosquitoes," *PLoS Medicine*, vol. 6, no. 2, Article ID e1000020, 2009.

[3] A. A. Hoffmann, B. L. Montgomery, J. Popovici et al., "Successful establishment of *Wolbachia* in Aedes populations to suppress dengue transmission," *Nature*, vol. 476, no. 7361, pp. 454–459, 2011.

[4] C. J. McMeniman, R. V. Lane, B. N. Cass et al., "Stable introduction of a life-shortening *Wolbachia* infection into the mosquito Aedes aegypti," *Science*, vol. 323, no. 5910, pp. 141–144, 2009.

[5] P. R. Crain, J. W. Mains, E. Suh, Y. Huang, P. H. Crowley, and S. L. Dobson, "*Wolbachia* infections that reduce immature insect survival: predicted impacts on population replacement," *BMC Evolutionary Biology*, vol. 11, no. 1, article 290, 2011.

[6] S. L. Dobson, C. W. Fox, and F. M. Jiggins, "The effect of *Wolbachia*-induced cytoplasmic incompatibility on host population size in natural and manipulated systems," *Proceedings of the Royal Society B*, vol. 269, no. 1490, pp. 437–445, 2002.

[7] D. C. Presgraves, "A genetic test of the mechanism of *Wolbachia*-induced cytoplasmic incompatibility in *Drosophila*," *Genetics*, vol. 154, no. 2, pp. 771–776, 2000.

[8] V. A. A. Jansen, M. Turelli, and H. C. J. Godfray, "Stochastic spread of *Wolbachia*," *Proceedings of the Royal Society B*, vol. 275, no. 1652, pp. 2769–2776, 2008.

[9] M. Guevara and E. E. Vallejo, "A computer simulation model of gene replacement in vector populations," in *Proceedings of the 8th IEEE International Conference on BioInformatics and BioEngineering (BIBE '08)*, pp. 1–6, IEEE, October 2008.

[10] M. Guevara and E. E. Vallejo, "Computer simulation on the maternal effect dominant embryonic arrest (MEDEA) for disease vector population replacement," in *Proceedings of the 11th Annual Genetic and Evolutionary Computation Conference (GECCO '09)*, pp. 1787–1788, July 2009.

[11] C. Horstman and G. Cornell, *Core Java*, Sun Microsystems Press, San Diego, Calif, USA, 2007.

[12] B. Goetz, *Java Concurrency in Practice*, Addison-Wesley, New York, NY, USA, 2006 .

[13] B. Chapman, *Using OpenMP: Portable Shared Memory Parallel Programming*, MIT Press, Boston, Mass, USA, 2008.

[14] W. Savitch, *Problem Solving with C++*, Addison-Wesley, New York, NY, USA, 2011.

[15] T. Santner, B. Williams, and W. Notz, *The Design and Analysis of Computer Experiments*, Springer Series in Statistics, Springer, 2003.

11

Data and Feature Reduction in Fuzzy Modeling through Particle Swarm Optimization

S. Sakinah S. Ahmad[1] and Witold Pedrycz[1, 2]

[1] *Department of Electrical and Computer Engineering, University of Alberta, Edmonton, Canada T6G 2G7*
[2] *Systems Research Institute, Polish Academy of Sciences, 01-447 Warsaw, Poland*

Correspondence should be addressed to S. Sakinah S. Ahmad, sh_sakinah@yahoo.com

Academic Editor: Miin-Shen Yang

The study is concerned with data and feature reduction in fuzzy modeling. As these reduction activities are advantageous to fuzzy models in terms of both the effectiveness of their construction and the interpretation of the resulting models, their realization deserves particular attention. The formation of a subset of meaningful features and a subset of essential instances is discussed in the context of fuzzy-rule-based models. In contrast to the existing studies, which are focused predominantly on feature selection (namely, a reduction of the input space), a position advocated here is that a reduction has to involve both data and features to become efficient to the design of fuzzy model. The reduction problem is combinatorial in its nature and, as such, calls for the use of advanced optimization techniques. In this study, we use a technique of particle swarm optimization (PSO) as an optimization vehicle of forming a subset of features and data (instances) to design a fuzzy model. Given the dimensionality of the problem (as the search space involves both features and instances), we discuss a cooperative version of the PSO along with a clustering mechanism of forming a partition of the overall search space. Finally, a series of numeric experiments using several machine learning data sets is presented.

1. Introduction

In fuzzy modeling, the two main approaches for generating the rules rely on knowledge acquisition from human experts and knowledge discovery from data [1, 2]. In recent years, knowledge discovery from data or data-driven fuzzy modeling has become more important [2–4]. In many cases, the ability to develop models efficiently is hampered by the dimensionality of the input space as well as the number of data. If we are concerned with rule-based models, the high-dimensionality of the feature space along with the topology of the rules gives rise to the curse of dimensionality [1, 4]. The number of rules increases exponentially and is equal to P^n, where n is the number of features and P stands for the number of fuzzy sets defined for each feature.

The factors that contribute most to the accuracy of the data-driven fuzzy modeling are associated with the size of the input space and the decomposition of the input data. A Large number of data points or instances in a continuous input-output domain exhibit a significant impact on fuzzy models. It is well known that more training data will not always lead to a better performance for data-driven models. Large amount of training data have important implications on the modeling capabilities. Since the number of fuzzy sets determines the family of realizable approximation functions, larger datasets present the possibility of over-fitting the training data [1, 4]. Thus, the effectiveness of the fuzzy models relies on the quality of the training data. In addition, the main drawback is the fuzzy models' relative inefficiency as the size of the data increases, regarding both the number of data points in the data set and the number of features. Moreover, one of the most widely used approaches in fuzzy modeling is the fuzzy C-means (FCM) algorithm for constructing the antecedents of the rules associated with curse of dimensionality [5, 6].

The dimensionality problem can be addressed by reducing the constructed fuzzy rules. The reduction method plays two important roles: it increases the effectiveness of

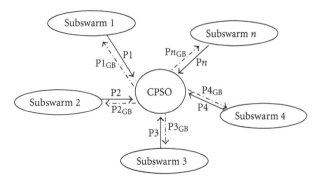

FIGURE 1: The schematic diagram of information sharing in CPSO.

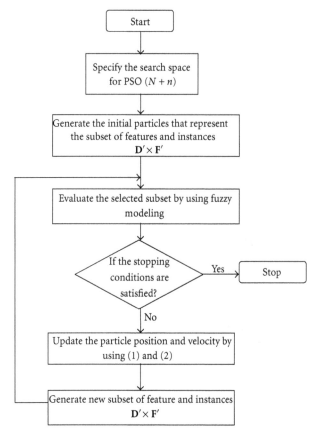

FIGURE 2: The scheme of the proposed data and reduction for fuzzy modeling.

the learning algorithm, since the learning algorithm will concentrate only on the most useful subset of data, and it also improves the computational efficiency as the learning algorithm involves only a subset of data smaller than the original dataset [7]. This reduction can be realized by removing the redundant fuzzy rules by exploiting a concept of fuzzy similarity [3, 7, 8]. Evolutionary algorithms have also been used for building compact fuzzy rules [9–12]. An evolutionary algorithm is used to tune the structure and the rules' parameter of the fuzzy systems [13, 14]. However, in numerous cases, some variables are not crucial to the realization of the fuzzy model. A suitable way to

overcome this problem is to implement feature selection before constructing the fuzzy models. Therefore, during the last decade, feature selection methods in conjunction with constructing fuzzy models for reducing the curse of dimensionality were developed [15–22]. This process reduces the fuzzy rule search space and increases the accuracy of the model.

As mentioned above, forming the best input data as the training set to construct the fuzzy modeling is also important. However, as far as we know there is no research that has been done to simultaneously select the best subset of features and input data for constructing the fuzzy model. Most of the research is focused on reducing the fuzzy rules, and the process of simplifying the system is done once the design has been completed. Here we propose a method that reduces the complexity of the system starting from the design stage. however, the process of constructing the antecedent and the consequent parts of the fuzzy model is realized using the best subset of input data.

In this paper, a comprehensive framework is proposed to construct fuzzy models from the subset of numerical input-output data. First, we develop a data-driven fuzzy modeling framework for a high-dimensional large dataset, which is capable of generating a rule-based automatically from numerical data. Second, we integrate the concept of feature selection and data selection together in the unified form to further refine (reduce) the fuzzy models. In this regard, the PSO technique is applied in order to search for the best subset of data. In order to increase the effectiveness of the PSO techniques, we introduce a new cooperative PSO method based on the information granulation approach. Third, we develop a flexible setup to cope with the optimization of variables and data to be used in the design of the fuzzy model. The proposed approach allows the user to choose the predetermined fraction of variables and data that can be used to construct the fuzzy models.

This paper is organized as follows. We briefly elaborate on the selected approaches to data and feature space reduction in Section 2, and then in Section 3, we recall the main algorithmic features of PSO and its cooperative version, CPSO, which is of interest in problems of high-dimensionality. The proposed fuzzy modeling framework along with its main algorithmic developments is presented in Section 4. Experimental studies are presented in Section 5, and conclusions are provided in Section 6.

2. Selected Approaches to Data and Space Reduction

In general, reduction processes involve feature selection (FS), instances (data) selection (IS), and a combination of these two reduction processes: feature and Instances selection (FIS). Feature selection is a subject of the main reduction pursuits. The goal of FS, which is commonly encountered in problems of system modeling and pattern recognition, is to select the best subset of features so that the model formed in this new feature (input) space exhibits the highest accuracy (classification rate) being simultaneously associated with the

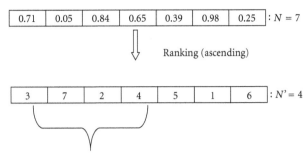

Subset of selected instances $(3, 7, 2, 4)$

FIGURE 3: From a particle in $[0, 1]^{N+n}$ search space to a subset of instances and features.

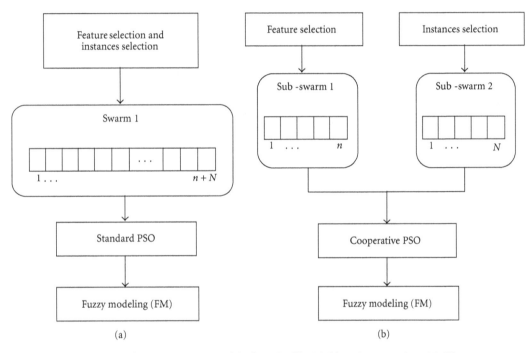

FIGURE 4: The particle scheme of the "standard" PSO (a) and cooperative PSO (b).

increased transparency of the resulting construct [23]. The process aims to discard irrelevant and/or redundant features [24]. In general, the FS algorithms can be classified into three main categories: filters, wrappers, and embedded methods. The filter method selection criterion is independent of the learning algorithm. In contrast to the wrapper method, the selection criterion is dependent on the learning algorithm and uses its performance index as the evaluation criterion. The embedded method incorporates feature selection as part of the training process. The reader can refer to [23–25] for more details.

Instances selection (IS), another category of reduction approaches, is concerned with the selection of the relevant data (instances) reflective of the knowledge pertinent to the problem at hand [26, 27]. The three main functions forming the essence of IS include enabling, focusing and cleaning [26].

In this study, as stated earlier, instead of approaching feature selection and instances selection separately, we focus on the integration of feature selection and instances selection in the construction of the fuzzy models. Both processes are applied simultaneously to the initial dataset, in order to obtain a suitable subset of feature and data to construct the parameters for the fuzzy model. In the literature, some methods for integrating feature and instances selection are more focused on a class of classification problems [28, 29].

The ideas of feature and data reduction as well as hybrid approaches have been discussed in the realm of fuzzy modeling. Table 1 offers a snapshot at the diversity of the existing approaches and the advantages gained by completing the reduction processes.

3. Particle Swarm Optimization and Its Cooperative Version

Population-based algorithms provide interesting solutions since any constructive method can be used to generate the initial population, and any local search technique can

TABLE 1: A summary of selected studies in data and feature reduction in fuzzy modeling.

Reference	Feature reduction technique	Dataset, fuzzy model and data	Original data used in modeling		Number of selected features	Number of resulting rules
			Number of instances	Number of features		
Gaweda et al. [15]	The use of sensitivity analysis Determination of essential features	Box-Jenkins gas furnace	296	10	3	2
Hadjili and Wertz [16]	Deviation criterion (DC): to measure the change in fuzzy partition. Removal of features that do not significantly change the fuzzy partition	Nonlinear systems in noisy environment	250	3	1	4
		Nonlinear dynamical system excited by a sinusoidal signal	800	10	6	8
		Run-out cooling table in a hot strip mill	1000	17	5	12
Zarandi et al. [18]	Heuristic method to select features	Nonlinear System used in [3]	50	4	2	4
		Supplier chance management dataset	300	9	5	5
Du and Zhang [19]	Evolutionary optimization	Box-Jenkins gas furnace	296	10	3	4
		MR damper identification	5000	11	6	10
Ghazavi and Liao [20]	(1) Mutual correlation methods, (2) gene selection criteria (3) the relief algorithm	Wisconsin breast cancer	569	30	3	250 (3)
		PIMA Indian diabetes	768	8	3	125 (3)
		Welding flaw identification	399	25	3	—
Zhang et al. [21]	Iterative search margin based algorithm (Simba)	Wisconsin breast cancer	699	9	5	3
		Wine	178	13	4	5
		Iris	150	4	3	3
		Ionosphere	351	34	10	4

TABLE 2: Description of data used in the experiments.

Data set	Abbreviation	Number of features	Number of data	Sparsity ration, κ
Air pollution PM10	PM10	7	500	71.43
Boston housing	Housing	13	506	38.92
Body fat	Body fat	14	252	18.00
Parkinson's telemonitoring	Parkinson	17	5875	345.59
Computer activity	Computer	21	8192	390.09

be used to improve each solution in the population [30]. In addition, population-based methods have the advantage of being able to combine good solutions in order to obtain potentially better ones. Most of the population-based algorithm approaches in FS and IS are based on GAs. Some recent studies [28, 29, 31] have employed population-based optimization techniques to carry out search for the best subset of variables and data for solving the application problems, but all of them were carried out to solve the classification problem. Therefore, in this study, we use population-based technique for selecting the best subset of feature and data for the regression problem. Here, we implement particle swarm optimization (PSO) techniques to intelligently search for the best subset of features and data (instances).

PSO, developed by Kennedy and Eberhart, inspired by the collective behavior of birds or fish [32], is a population-based algorithm where each individual, referred to as a particle, represents a candidate solution. Each particle proceeds through the search space at a given velocity v that

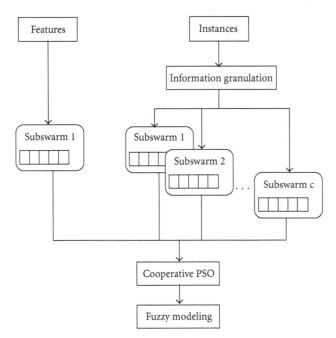

FIGURE 5: The particle scheme of cooperative PSO with more subswarms.

TABLE 3: The values of the parameters used in the experiments; CPSO[1]: swarms located in the feature space. CPSO[2]: swarms located in the instance (data) space.

Optimization method	Subswarms	Generation	Particles
PSO	1	50	300
CPSO[1]	2	50	100
CPSO[2]	4	30	50

is dynamically modified according to its own experience and results in its local best (lb) performance. It is also affected by others particles flying experience resulting in the best value, global best (gb). The underlying expression for the update of the velocity in successive generations reads as follows:

$$v_i\,(t+1) = w \cdot v_i(t) + c_1 \cdot r_{1,i}(t)[\text{lb}_i(t) - x_i(t)]$$

$$+ c_2 \cdot r_{2,i}(t)[\text{gb}_i(t) - x_i(t)], \tag{1}$$

$$x_i(t+1) = x_i(t) + v_i(t+1),$$

where $i = 1, 2, \ldots, N + n$ (the search space is equal to the sum of the dimensionalities of the feature space and the size of the data). The inertia weight (w) is confined to the range $[0, 1]$; its values can decrease over time. The cognitive factor c_1 and social factor c_2 determine the relative impact coming from the particle's own experience and the local best and global best. r_1 and r_2 are numbers drawn from a uniform distribution over the unit interval that brings some component of randomness to the search process.

In this research, we employed the PSO-based method to handle two optimization tasks, namely, (1) selection of the optimal subset of features and (2) selection of the optimal subset of instances based on the concept of information

granularity. In order to reduce the computational complexity of using the standard PSO, we employed cooperative PSO method to simultaneously solve the two optimization tasks. The motivation behind the use of cooperative PSO, as advocated in [33], is to deal effectively with the dimensionality of the search space, which becomes a serious concern when a large number of data with a large dimensionality are involved. This curse of dimensionality is a significant impediment negatively impacting the effectiveness of standard PSO. The essence of the cooperative version of PSO is essentially a parallel search for optimal subset of features and its optimal subset of instances. The cooperative strategy is achieved by dividing the candidate solution vector into components, called subswarm, where each subswarm represents a small part of the overall optimization processes. By doing this, we implement the concept of divide and conquer to solve the optimization problem, so that the process will become more efficient and fast.

The mechanism of information sharing of CPSO is shown in Figure 1. The cooperative search between one subswarm and other is achieved by sharing the information of the global best position (P_{GB}) across all subswarm. Here the algorithm has the advantage of taking two steps forward because the candidate solution comes from the best position for all subswarm except only for the current subswarms being evaluated. Therefore, the algorithm will not spend too much time optimizing the features or instances that have little effect to the overall solution. The rate at which each swarm converges to the solution is significantly higher than the rate of convergence of the standard PSO.

The essence of the cooperative version of PSO is to split the data into several groups so that each group is handled by a separate PSO. The main design question involves splitting the variables into groups. A sound guideline is to keep the related (associated) variables within the same group. Obviously, such relationships are not known in advance. Several possible methods are available for addressing this issue in more detail in the context of the problem at hand.

(a) As we are concerned with a collection of features and data (instances), a natural way to split the variables would be to form two groups ($K = 2$), one for the features (n) and another one for the instances (N). This split would be legitimate if the dimensionality of both subsets was quite similar.

(b) In some situations, one of the subsets (either the data or the features) might be significantly larger than the other one. We often encounter a large number of data, but in some situations, a large number of features might be present (for instance, in microarray data analysis). This particular collection of data or features is then split into K groups. Clustering such items is a viable algorithmic approach. Running K-means or fuzzy C-means produces clusters (group) of variables that are used in the individual PSO.

(c) In case both subsets are large, the clustering is realized both for the features and data, and the resulting, structure (partition) is used to run cooperative PSO.

TABLE 4: Results for housing data; the number of clusters is set to 4, $c = 4$; κ is the ratio of the number of selected data versus the number of selected features.

Feature	Data = 10% (# of data = 51)		Data = 20% (# of data = 101)		Data = 30% (# of data = 152)		Data = 40% (# of data = 202)		Data = 50% (# of data = 253)		Data = 60% (# of data = 304)		Data = 70% (# of data = 354)		Data = 80% (# of data = 405)		Data = 90% (# of data = 455)		Data = 100% (# of data = 506)	
	κ	RMSE	κ	RMSE	κ	RMSE	κ	RMSE	κ	RMSE	κ	RMSE	κ	RMSE	κ	RMSE	κ	RMSE	κ	RMSE
10%	51.0	6.341 ± 0.253	101.0	6.262 ± 0.171	152.0	5.777 ± 0.207	202.0	6.227 ± 0.351	253.0	6.389 ± 0.063	304	6.483 ± 0.214	354.0	6.610 ± 0.211	405.0	6.387 ± 0.026	455.0	6.655 ± 0.061	506	7.437 ± 0
20%	17.0	6.664 ± 0.233	33.7	5.389 ± 0.253	50.7	5.191 ± 0.185	67.3	4.884 ± 0.118	84.3	4.805 ± 0.047	101	4.882 ± 0.080	118.0	4.906 ± 0.040	135.0	5.011 ± 0.077	151.7	5.149 ± 0.071	169	5.039 ± 0.096
30%	12.8	6.127 ± 0.245	25.3	5.468 ± 0.290	38.0	4.853 ± 0.183	50.5	4.574 ± 0.078	63.3	4.619 ± 0.294	76	4.45 ± 0.092	88.5	4.398 ± 0.035	101.3	4.56 ± 0.053	113.8	4.536 ± 0.026	127	4.578 ± 0.01
40%	10.2	6.321 ± 0.518	20.2	5.122 ± 0.245	30.4	4.626 ± 0.075	40.4	4.362 ± 0.190	50.6	4.172 ± 0.123	60.8	4.06 ± 0.099	70.8	4.126 ± 0.105	81.0	4.18 ± 0.177	91.0	4.343 ± 0.026	101	4.233 ± 0.079
50%	7.3	7.126 ± 0.835	14.4	5.046 ± 0.312	21.7	4.574 ± 0.206	28.9	4.018 ± 0.109	36.1	3.916 ± 0.224	43.4	3.927 ± 0.089	50.6	4.009 ± 0.093	57.9	4.085 ± 0.132	65.0	4.077 ± 0.092	72.3	4.005 ± 0.082
60%	6.4	8.133 ± 0.782	12.6	5.120 ± 0.189	19.0	4.504 ± 0.207	25.3	4.052 ± 0.196	31.6	3.912 ± 0.120	38	3.935 ± 0.129	44.3	3.934 ± 0.035	50.6	3.923 ± 0.117	56.9	3.931 ± 0.102	63.3	3.803 ± 0.088
70%	5.7	9.379 ± 0.984	11.2	5.003 ± 0.232	16.9	4.345 ± 0.134	22.4	3.949 ± 0.125	28.1	3.721 ± 0.071	33.8	3.722 ± 0.065	39.3	3.722 ± 0.066	45.0	3.787 ± 0.046	50.6	3.799 ± 0.041	56.2	3.668 ± 0.043
80%	5.1	10.57 ± 2.251	10.1	5.107 ± 0.262	15.2	4.232 ± 0.173	20.2	3.67 ± 0.093	25.3	3.617 ± 0.108	30.4	3.659 ± 0.128	35.4	3.568 ± 0.064	40.5	3.567 ± 0.086	45.5	3.645 ± 0.065	50.6	3.526 ± 0.049
90%	4.3	24.05 ± 7.681	8.4	5.324 ± 0.207	12.7	4.173 ± 0.181	16.8	3.809 ± 0.080	21.1	3.652 ± 0.050	25.3	3.569 ± 0.028	29.5	3.555 ± 0.017	33.8	3.533 ± 0.016	37.9	3.541 ± 0.015	42.2	3.550 ± 0
100%	3.9	44.39 ± 17.65	7.8	5.409 ± 0.201	11.7	4.082 ± 0.047	15.5	3.781 ± 0.055	19.5	3.687 ± 0.038	23.4	3.654 ± 0.015	27.2	3.631 ± 0.021	31.2	3.615 ± 0.011	35.0	3.605 ± 0.015	38.9	4.023 ± 0

TABLE 5: Results for PM10 dataset; $c = 3$.

Feature	Data = 10% (# of data = 50)		Data = 20% (# of data = 100)		Data = 30% (# of data = 150)		Data = 40% (# of data = 200)		Data = 50% (# of data = 250)		Data = 60% (# of data = 300)		Data = 70% (# of data = 350)		Data = 80% (# of data = 400)		Data = 90% (# of data = 450)		Data = 100% (# of data = 500)	
	κ	RMSE	κ	RMSE	κ	RMSE	κ	RMSE	κ	RMSE	κ	RMSE	κ	RMSE	κ	RMSE	κ	RMSE	κ	RMSE
10%	50.0	0.931 ± 0.036	100.0	0.979 ± 0.018	150.0	0.983 ± 0.006	200.0	0.985 ± 0.010	250.0	0.998 ± 0.021	300.0	1.036 ± 0.022	350.0	1.071 ± 0.016	400.0	1.088 ± 0.002	450.0	1.099 ± 0.003	500.0	1.116 ± 0
20%	50.0	0.896 ± 0.034	100.0	0.98 ± 0.013	150.0	0.987 ± 0.009	200.0	0.994 ± 0.008	250.0	1.004 ± 0.018	300.0	1.025 ± 0.032	350.0	1.075 ± 0.009	400.0	1.090 ± 0.003	450.0	1.098 ± 0.003	500.0	1.116 ± 0
30%	25.0	0.825 ± 0.087	50.0	0.902 ± 0.04	75.0	0.918 ± 0.007	100.0	0.916 ± 0.003	125.0	0.918 ± 0.010	150.0	0.920 ± 0.005	175.0	0.922 ± 0.003	200.0	0.937 ± 0.001	225.0	0.948 ± 0.005	250.0	0.964 ± 0
40%	16.7	0.829 ± 0.023	33.3	0.877 ± 0.007	50.0	0.877 ± 0.010	66.7	0.862 ± 0.009	83.3	0.865 ± 0.004	100.0	0.869 ± 0.008	116.7	0.887 ± 0.004	133.3	0.892 ± 0.006	150.0	0.902 ± 0.002	166.7	0.915 ± 0
50%	12.5	0.802 ± 0.029	25.0	0.816 ± 0.008	37.5	0.822 ± 0.012	50.0	0.826 ± 0.028	62.5	0.843 ± 0.024	75.0	0.870 ± 0.023	87.5	0.891 ± 0.022	100.0	0.906 ± 0.004	112.5	0.905 ± 0.002	125.0	0.925 ± 0
60%	12.5	0.804 ± 0.027	25.0	0.818 ± 0.013	37.5	0.825 ± 0.014	50.0	0.834 ± 0.016	62.5	0.841 ± 0.006	75.0	0.879 ± 0.012	87.5	0.898 ± 0.006	100.0	0.897 ± 0.006	112.5	0.907 ± 0.002	125.0	0.925 ± 0
70%	10.0	0.783 ± 0.030	20.0	0.781 ± 0.031	30.0	0.804 ± 0.017	40.0	0.782 ± 0.039	50.0	0.806 ± 0.014	60.0	0.832 ± 0.016	70.0	0.851 ± 0.010	80.0	0.856 ± 0.004	90.0	0.864 ± 0.003	100.0	0.900 ± 0
80%	8.3	0.768 ± 0.024	16.7	0.769 ± 0.007	25.0	0.776 ± 0.017	33.3	0.768 ± 0.024	41.7	0.796 ± 0.010	50.0	0.805 ± 0.016	58.3	0.826 ± 0.013	66.7	0.839 ± 0.007	75.0	0.847 ± 0.001	83.3	0.878 ± 0
90%	8.3	0.774 ± 0.026	16.7	0.771 ± 0.017	25.0	0.767 ± 0.014	33.3	0.796 ± 0.010	41.7	0.777 ± 0.019	50.0	0.815 ± 0.017	58.3	0.820 ± 0.014	66.7	0.843 ± 0.001	75.0	0.851 ± 0.003	83.3	0.878 ± 0
100%	7.1	0.786 ± 0.012	14.3	0.758 ± 0.017	21.4	0.764 ± 0.007	28.6	0.765 ± 0.015	35.7	0.772 ± 0.016	42.9	0.795 ± 0.004	50.0	0.808 ± 0.010	57.1	0.818 ± 0.005	64.3	0.824 ± 0.003	71.4	0.883 ± 0

TABLE 6: Results for Parkinson's data; $c = 3$.

Feature	Data = 10% (# of data = 346)		Data = 20% (# of data = 691)		Data = 30% (# of data = 1037)		Data = 40% (# of data = 1382)		Data = 50% (# of data =1728)		Data = 60% (# of data = 2074)		Data = 70% (# of data =2419)		Data = 80% (# of data = 2765)	
	κ	RMSE	κ	RMSE	κ	RMSE	κ	RMSE	κ	RMSE	κ	RMSE	κ	RMSE	κ	RMSE
10%	346	6.388 ± 0.182	691	6.221 ± 0.064	1037	6.393 ± 0.140	1382	6.495 ± 0.106	1728	6.644 ± 0.137	2074	6.644 ± 0.137	2419	6.515 ± 0.006	2765	6.406 ± 0.005
20%	173	6.183 ± 0.110	346	5.857 ± 0.031	519	5.932 ± 0.023	691	5.972 ± 0.008	864	6.247 ± 0.137	1037	6.247 ± 0.137	1210	6.066 ± 0.018	1382	5.970 ± 0.002
30%	115	6.152 ± 0.151	230	5.799 ± 0.061	346	5.703 ± 0.067	461	5.708 ± 0.045	576	6.077 ± 0.048	691	6.077 ± 0.048	806	5.964 ± 0.276	922	5.740 ± 0.089
40%	86	6.328 ± 0.456	173	5.900 ± 0.087	259	5.886 ± 0.342	346	6.175 ± 0.358	432	6.461 ± 0.261	518	6.461 ± 0.261	605	6.299 ± 0.563	691	6.308 ± 0.677
50%	69	6.991 ± 0.525	138	7.585 ± 0.755	207	6.448 ± 0.580	276	7.493 ± 0.303	346	8.057 ± 0.037	415	8.057 ± 0.037	484	8.160 ± 0.018	553	8.110 ± 0.012
60%	58	8.357 ± 0.164	115	8.088 ± 0.028	173	8.069 ± 0.078	230	7.960 ± 0.021	288	8.104 ± 0.021	346	8.104 ± 0.021	403	8.147 ± 0.017	461	8.101 ± 0.002
70%	49	8.401 ± 0.068	99	8.074 ± 0.064	148	8.087 ± 0.015	197	8.008 ± 0.011	247	8.123 ± 0.009	296	8.123 ± 0.009	346	8.158 ± 0.011	395	8.107 ± 0.007
80%	43	8.419 ± 0.091	86	8.257 ± 0.048	130	8.187 ± 0.017	173	8.092 ± 0.020	216	8.177 ± 0.008	259	8.177 ± 0.008	302	8.194 ± 0.008	346	8.138 ± 0.005
90%	38	8.500 ± 0.106	77	8.258 ± 0.024	115	8.199 ± 0.017	154	8.139 ± 0.013	192	8.200 ± 0.009	230	8.200 ± 0.009	269	8.217 ± 0.004	307	8.157 ± 0.006
100%	35	8.560 ± 0.026	69	8.249 ± 0.033	104	8.262 ± 0.013	138	8.223 ± 0.007	173	8.239 ± 0.006	207	8.239 ± 0.006	242	8.235 ± 0.002	276	8.223 ± 0.001

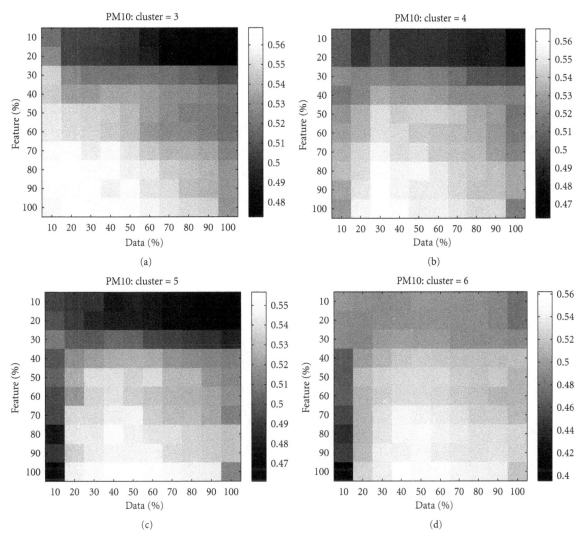

FIGURE 6: Heat map for PM 10 data for c varying in-between 3 to 6.

Algorithm 1 presents the Cooperative PSO pseudocode implementing the optimization process [33]. Firstly, the PSO is divided into m subspaces, called subswarms. In our case the first subswarm represents the features search space and the rest are for instances search space. $P_j(x_i)$ refers to the position of particle i of subswarms j. The global best for each subswarm defined as $P_{j(GB)}$, and the local best is defined as $P_{j(LB_i)}$. The cooperation between the subswarms employed in the function $\mathbf{C}(j, k)$, which returns m-dimensional vector formed by concatenating all the global best vector across all subswarms, except for the current position j. Here the jth component is called k and represent the position of any particle from subswarm P_j.

4. PSO-Integrated Feature and Data Reduction in Fuzzy-Rule-Based Models

As the problem of feature data reduction is inherently combinatorial nature, PSO provides an interesting and computationally viable optimization alternative. In the following subsections, we start with a general optimization setting and then discuss the PSO realization of the search process (here, a crucial design phase is a formation of the search space with a suitable encoding mechanism). Although the proposed methodology is of general nature, we concentrate on rule-based models, which are commonly present in fuzzy modeling, to help offer a detailed view of the overall design process.

4.1. An Overall Reduction Process. As is usual in system modeling, we consider a supervised learning scenario ion which we encounter in a finite set of training data $(\mathbf{x}_k, t_k)$, $k = 1, 2, \ldots, N$. By stressing the nature of the data and their dimensionality, the data space along with n-dimensional feature vectors can be viewed as a Cartesian product of the data and features $\mathbf{D} \times \mathbf{F}$. The essence of the reduction is to arrive at the Cartesian product of the reduced data and feature spaces, $\mathbf{D}' \times \mathbf{F}'$, where, $\mathbf{D}' \in \mathbf{D}$ and $\mathbf{F}' \in \mathbf{F}$. The cardinality of the reduced spaces is equal to N' and n', where $N' < N$ and $n' < n$.

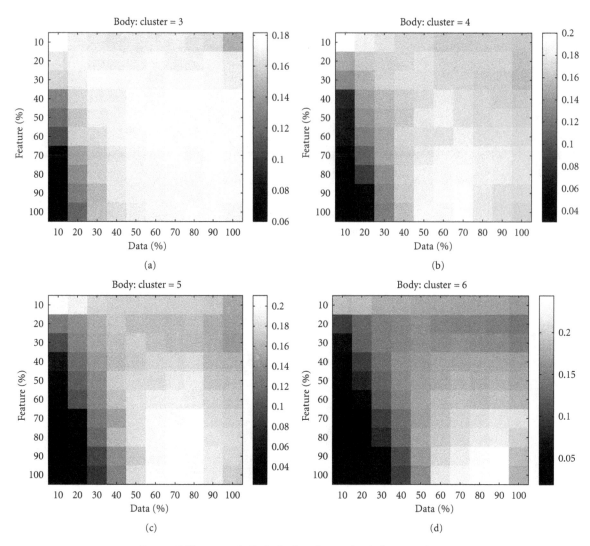

FIGURE 7: Heat map for Body fat data for varying in-between 3 to 6.

The overall scheme of the reduction process outlining a role of the PSO-guided reduction is illustrated in Figure 2. The scheme can be divided into two important parts and can be described as follows.

(a) Reduction process via PSO: a reduction process tackles both feature reduction and data reduction simultaneously. PSO algorithm is used to search for the best feature and data for constructing the fuzzy model. Here, the size of the selected features (n') and data (N') is provided in advance by the user. After the PSO meets the maximum generation, the process is stopped, and the last best subset of features and data is the best subset of data for constructing the fuzzy model.

(b) Evaluation process: the fuzzy C-means algorithm is used to convert the numerical data into the information granules. Here, the information granularity process deals only with the subset of the data and features ($\mathbf{D}' \times \mathbf{F}'$). Next, the consequent parameter $\mathbf{a}$ constructed from the fuzzy models is use to evaluate

the performance of the selected data and features. At this stage we access the performance of the constructed fuzzy model in terms of their capability to fit the model by using the all instances in the original data set.

As it becomes apparent, the original space $\mathbf{D} \times \mathbf{F}$ is reduced, and in this Cartesian product a fuzzy model, denoted by FM, is designed in the usual way (we elaborate on the form of the fuzzy model in the subsequent section). Its design is guided by a certain objective function Q expressed over all elements of original instances. The quality of the reduced space is assessed by quantifying the performance of the fuzzy model operating over the original, non-reduced space. The same performance index as used in the construction of the fuzzy model in the reduced space is used to describe the quality of the fuzzy model:

$$Q = \sqrt{\frac{1}{N} \sum_{\mathbf{x}_k \in \mathbf{D} \times \mathbf{F}'} (\mathrm{FM}(\mathbf{x}_k) - t_k)^2}. \qquad (2)$$

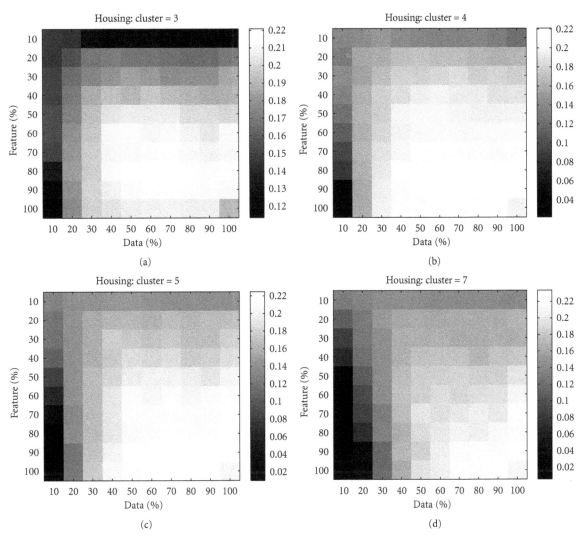

FIGURE 8: Heat map for housing data for c = 3, 4, 5, and 7.

Note that the summation shown above is taken over all the elements forming the data space **D**. By taking another look at the overall reduction scheme, it is worth noting that the reduction is realized as in the wrapper mode, in which we use a fuzzy model to evaluate the quality of the reduction mechanism.

4.2. The PSO-Based Representation of the Search Space.

The reduction of the data and feature spaces involves a selection of a subset of the data and a subset of the features. Therefore, the problem is combinatorial in its nature. PSO is used here to form a subset of integers which are indexes of the data or features to be used in the formation of $\mathbf{D}' \times \mathbf{F}'$. For instance, $\mathbf{D}'$ is represented as a set of indexes $\{i_1, i_2, \ldots, i_{N'}\}$ being a subset of integers $\{1, 2, \ldots, N\}$. From the perspective of the PSO, the particle is formed as a string of real numbers in $[0, 1]$ of the length of $N + n$; effectively, the search space is a hypercube $[0, 1]^{N+n}$. The first substring of length N represents the data; the second one (having n entries) is used

to optimize the subset of features. The particle is decoded as follows. Each substring is processed (decoded) separately. The real number entries are ranked. The result is a list of integers viewed as the indexes of the data. The first N' entries out of the N-position substring are selected to form $\mathbf{D}'$. The same process is applied to the substring representing the set of features. An overall decoding scheme is illustrated in Figure 3.

The information given by the PSO is used to represent the subset of features and data to construct the data-driven fuzzy models. Then, the numerical data are represented in terms of a collection of information granules (a fuzzy sets) produced through some clustering (fuzzy clustering). The information about the granules (clusters) is then used to construct the fuzzy models.

In the cooperative PSO, the formation of the search space is realized in a more sophisticated way. The cooperative facet involves mainly exchanging information about the best positions found by the different subswarms. Here, we present a new cooperative PSO (CPSO) algorithm for the

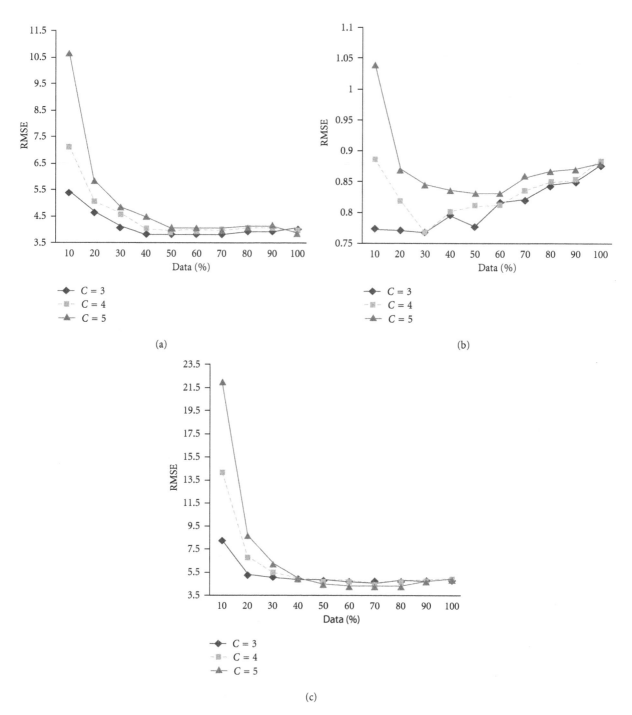

FIGURE 9: The values of RMSE versus the percentage of data for selected number clusters: (a) housing data, (b) PM10 data, and (c) body fat data.

data and feature reduction process. The selection of the number of cooperating swarms is important because it will affect the performance of the cooperative PSO model. Subswarm 1 represents the features' column and subswarm 2 represents the instances' row of the particular data set. Figure 4 illustrates the main difference between standard PSO and cooperative PSO. The standard PSO contains one swarm with a large dimension of search space. In contrast, for the cooperative PSO, we divide the search space into

two subswarms: subswarm 1 for feature representation and subswarm 2 for instances representation. All the subswarms share the same basic particles definition illustrated in Figure 4.

In general, the dimensionality for the data (instances) selection is higher than that of the feature selection. In order to reduce the impact of the curse of dimensionality, we decompose the data into several groups by using the information granulation approach. In this paper, we used

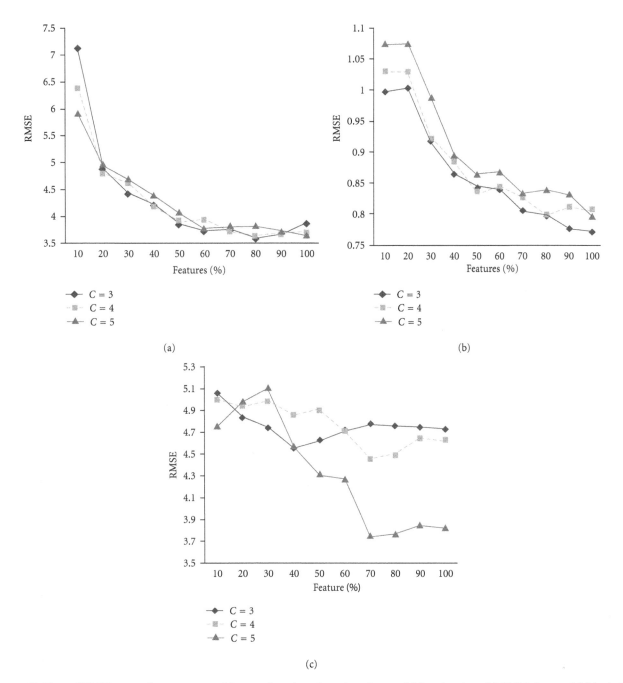

FIGURE 10: Plots of RMSE versus the percentage of features for selected number clusters: (a) housing data, (b) PM10 data, and (c) body Fat data.

the fuzzy C-means (FCMs) to construct the information granules. Therefore, the number of decomposition groups is actually the number of the clusters (c) used in the FCM. For example, if we want to decompose the data into three groups, we use the number of clusters equal to three. As a result, instead of having only two subswarms, we introduce more subswarms that represent different groups of data.

Figure 5 presents the process of constructing the subswarms for cooperative PSO by decomposing the instances into several subswarms. As mentioned earlier, we apply the concept of information granulation to decompose the data group. In order to identify the selected data in each de-

composed group, we use the information granules (membership degrees) values to identify the index of the instances in each group. Here, we employ a winner-takes-all scheme to determine a single group for each granule, that is, the index of the instances in each of the decomposition group related to the information granule that gets the highest degrees of activation. We denote the set of data associated with the ith granules by $X(i_0)$:

$$X(i_0) = \left\{ x_k \in X \mid U_{i0k} = \max_i U_{ik} \right\}$$

$$\text{for } 1 \leq k \leq M, \ 1 \leq i \leq c,$$

(3)

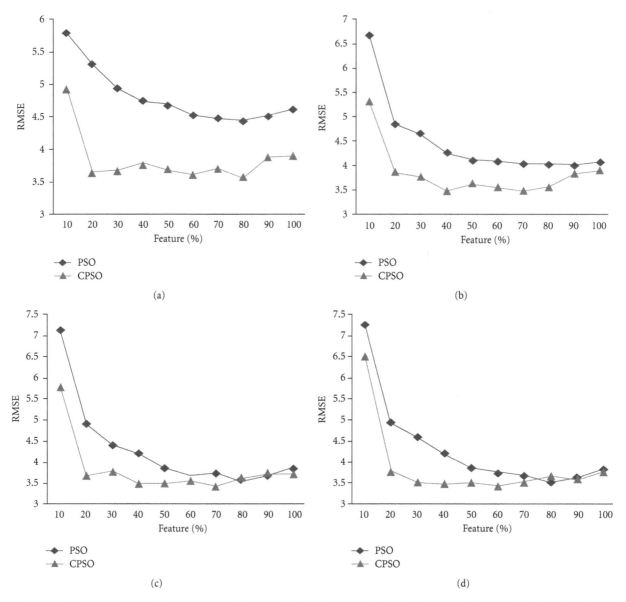

FIGURE 11: Values of RMSE versus the percentage of features selected when running PSO and CPSO—the use of the housing dataset: (a) 20% of selected data, (b) 30% of selected data, (c) 50% of selected data, and (d) 70% of selected data.

where $X(i_0)$ is the decomposition groups, U_{ik} is the information granules for each data, x_k is the data (instances), M and c are the number of data and the level of information granulation, respectively.

4.3. A Category of Fuzzy-Rule-Based Models. To make an overall presentation more focused, we consider a class of fuzzy-rule-based models governed by the collection of "c" rules:

$$\text{if } \mathbf{x} \text{ is } A_i \quad \text{then} \quad y = f_i(\mathbf{x}, \mathbf{a}_i), \tag{4}$$

where $i = 1, 2, \ldots, c$ (c is the number of clusters), A_i are the information granules formed in the input space, and f_i is a local linear function with some parameters $\mathbf{a}_i$ associated with the corresponding information granule. The information granules A_i are constructed by means

of fuzzy clustering, namely, fuzzy C-means (FCMs). The corresponding membership functions A_i are thus described as

$$A_i(x) = \frac{1}{\sum_{j=1}^{c} \left(\|\mathbf{x} - \mathbf{v}_i\| / \|\mathbf{x} - \mathbf{v}_j\| \right)^{2(m-1)}}, \tag{5}$$

where $\mathbf{v}_i$, $i = 1, 2, \ldots, c$ are the prototypes formed through clustering, and m, $m > 1$ is a fuzzification coefficient.

5. Experimental Studies

In this section, we report our results from a set of experiments, using several machine learning data sets (see http://www.ics.uci.edu/~mlearn/MLRepository.html and http://lib.stat.cmu.edu/datasets/). The main objective of these

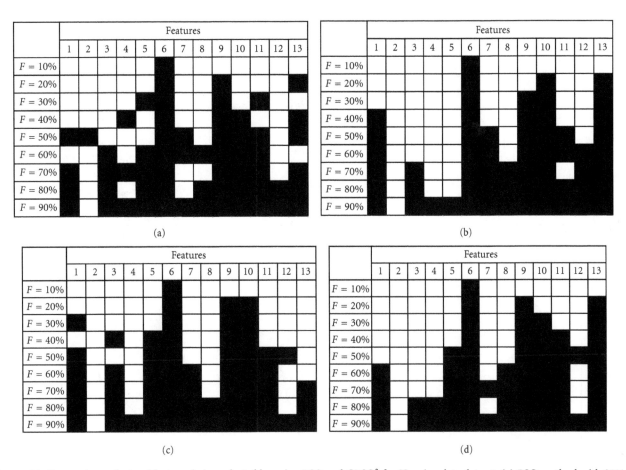

FIGURE 12: Comparison of sets of features being selected by using PSO and CPSO² for Housing data dataset: (a) PSO method with 30% of selected data, (b) CPSO² method with 30% of selected data, (c) PSO method with 70% of selected data, and (d) CPSO² method with 70% of selected data.

TABLE 7: The optimal % of features and data for different clusters.

Data set and number of clusters	% of features	% of data
Pima with $C = 3$	70	40
Pima with $C = 4$	100	20
Pima with $C = 5$	100	20
Pima with $C = 6$	100	40
Pima with $C = 7$	100	80
Housing with $C = 3$	80	70
Housing with $C = 4$	80	50
Housing with $C = 5$	80	100
Housing with $C = 6$	80	80
Housing with $C = 7$	90	100
Body Fat with $C = 3$	30	30
Body Fat with $C = 4$	100	70
Body Fat with $C = 5$	90	70
Body Fat with $C = 6$	90	90
Parkinson with $C = 3$	30	30

of features and instances, and arrive at some general conclusions. A concise summary of the data sets used in the experiment is presented in Table 2. All the data concern continuous output.

5.1. Parameter Setup. The values of the PSO and CPSO parameters were set using the standard form as follows. The values of the inertia weight, w, were linearly from 1 to 0 over the course of optimization. The values of the cognitive factor, c_1, and social factor c_2, were set to 0.5 and 1.5, respectively. In Table 3, we also list the numeric values of the parameters of the PSO and CPSO environment. As to the size of the population and the number of generations, we used a larger population and a larger number of generations in the generic version of the PSO than in the CPSO because of the larger search space this algorithm operates in.

The number of subswarms used in the optimization method is also shown in Table 3. The PSO method comprises only a single swarm whose individuals concatenate features and instances. In contrast, for the CPSO, we divided the search space into several subswarms that can cooperate with each other and where the individuals in the subswarms are used to represent a portion of the search space. The CPSO[1] contains two subswarms that cover the data and

experiments is to show the abilities of the proposed approach, quantify the performance of the selected subsets

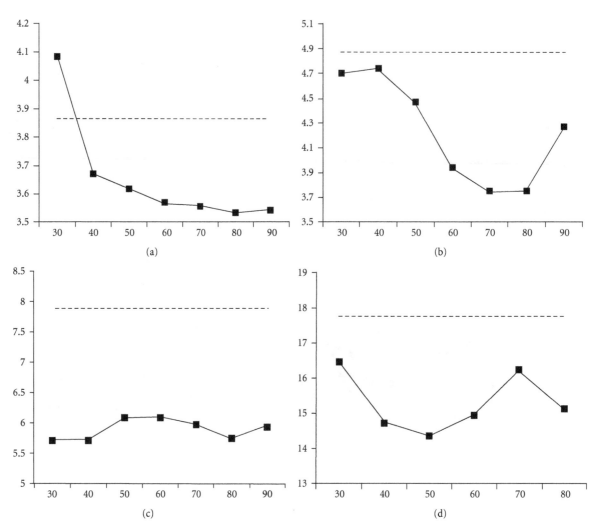

FIGURE 13: Comparison of RMSE by using proposed method (straight line) and standard fuzzy model (dotted line): (a) Housing dataset with $c = 4$, (b) body fat dataset with $c = 5$, (c) Parkinson's dataset with $c = 3$, and (d) computer dataset with $c = 3$.

TABLE 8: Best subsets of features for PM10 data.

F	Subset of features						
	$D = 30\%$	$D = 40\%$	$D = 50\%$	$D = 60\%$	$D = 70\%$	$D = 80\%$	$D = 90\%$
10%	1	1	1	1	1	1	1
20%	1	1	1	1	1	1	1
30%	1, 7	1, 7	1, 7	1, 7	1, 6	1, 6	1, 6
40%	1, 6, 7	1, 6, 7	1, 6, 7	1, 6, 7	1, 6, 7	1, 6, 7	1, 6, 7
50%	1, 2, 6, 7	1, 2, 6, 7	1, 2, 6, 7	1, 2, 6, 7	1, 2, 6, 7	1, 2, 6, 7	1, 2, 6, 7
60%	1, 2, 6, 7	1, 2, 6, 7	1, 2, 6, 7	1, 2, 6, 7	1, 2, 6, 7	1, 2, 6, 7	1, 2, 6, 7
70%	1, 2, 3, 6, 7	1, 2, 3, 6, 7	1, 2, 3, 6, 7	1, 2, 3, 6, 7	1, 2, 3, 6, 7	1, 2, 4, 6, 7	1, 2, 4, 6, 7
80%	1, 2, 3, 4, 6, 7	1, 2, 3, 5, 6, 7	1, 2, 3, 4, 6, 7	1, 2, 3, 4, 6, 7	1, 2, 3, 4, 6, 7	1, 2, 3, 4, 6, 7	1, 2, 3, 4, 6, 7
90%	1, 2, 3, 4, 6, 7	1, 2, 3, 4, 6, 7	1, 2, 3, 4, 6, 7	1, 2, 3, 5, 4, 7	1, 2, 3, 4, 5, 7	1, 2, 3, 4, 6, 7	1, 2, 3, 5, 4, 7

features, respectively. In CPSO^2, we used three subswarms to represent data point; in the data used here, the number of data is larger than the number of features, so a better balance of the dimensionality of the spaces is achieved. The data (instances) search space is divided into three subswarms, and the decomposition process is realized by running fuzzy clustering (each cluster forms a subswarm). In the table we used a smaller size of generation compared to particles size. This is because in [34] Shi and Eberhart mentioned that the population size does not exhibit any significant impact on

TABLE 9: Best subsets of features for body fat data.

F	Subset of features			
	$D = 50\%$	$D = 60\%$	$D = 70\%$	$D = 80\%$
10%	1	1	1	1
20%	1, 6, 7	1, 3, 7	1, 3, 7	1, 3, 7
30%	1, 6, 7, 9	1, 7, 8, 9	1, 3, 7, 9	1, 3, 7, 9
40%	1, 6, 7, 8, 9, 12	1, 3, 4, 7, 8, 9	1, 3, 6, 7, 8, 9	1, 7, 8, 9, 11, 12
50%	1, 2, 6, 7, 8, 12, 14	1, 4, 8, 9, 11, 12, 14	1, 3, 7, 8, 9, 12, 14	1, 3, 4, 5, 7, 8, 12
60%	1, 2, 6, 7, 8, 11, 12, 14	1, 3, 4, 7, 8, 9, 11, 14	1, 3, 5, 7, 9, 11, 12, 14	1, 3, 5, 7, 8, 11, 12, 14
70%	1, 3, 4, 5, 6, 8, 9, 11, 12, 14	1, 3, 4, 5, 7, 8, 9, 11, 12, 14	1, 3, 4, 5, 7, 8, 9, 11, 12, 14	1, 3, 4, 5, 7, 8, 9, 11, 12, 14
80%	1, 3, 4, 5, 6, 7, 8, 9, 10, 12, 14	1, 3, 4, 5, 6, 7, 8, 9, 10, 12, 14	1, 3, 4, 5, 6, 7, 8, 9, 11, 12, 14	1, 3, 4, 5, 6, 7, 8, 9, 11, 12, 14
90%	1, 2, 3, 4, 5, 6, 8, 9, 10, 11, 12, 13, 14	1, 3, 4, 5, 6, 7, 8, 9, 10, 11, 12, 13, 14	1, 3, 4, 5, 6, 7, 8, 9, 10, 11, 12, 13, 14	1, 23, 4, 5, 6, 7, 8, 9, 10, 11, 12, 14

TABLE 10: Best subsets of features for housing data.

F	Subset of features				
	$D = 10\%$	$D = 30\%$	$D = 50\%$	$D = 70\%$	$D = 90\%$
10%	12	6	6	12	12
20%	5, 12, 13	6, 9, 13	6, 9, 10	6, 9, 10	6, 9, 10
30%	6, 7, 9, 13	5, 6, 9, 11	4, 6, 9, 13	1, 6, 9, 10	2, 3, 12, 13
40%	1, 3, 6, 10, 13	4, 6, 9, 10, 13	6, 9, 10, 12, 13	3, 5, 6, 9, 10	1, 4, 6, 9, 10
50%	3, 6, 7, 8, 9, 10, 11	1, 2, 6, 9, 10, 11, 13	1, 3, 5, 6, 8, 9, 11	1, 5, 6, 9, 10, 11, 12	1, 6, 9, 10, 11, 12, 13
60%	3, 5, 6, 7, 8, 9, 12, 13	3, 5, 6, 7, 8, 9, 10, 11	1, 3, 5, 6, 7, 9, 10, 11	1, 3, 5, 6, 7, 9, 10, 11	1, 3, 6, 7, 8, 9, 11, 13
70%	3, 5, 6, 7, 8, 9, 10, 12, 13	1, 3, 4, 5, 6, 9, 10, 11, 13	1, 3, 5, 6, 7, 9, 10, 11, 13	1, 3, 5, 6, 7, 9, 10, 11, 13	1, 3, 6, 7, 8, 9, 10, 11, 13
80%	1, 3, 4, 5, 6, 8, 9, 10, 11, 13	1, 3, 5, 6, 8, 9, 10, 11, 12, 13	1, 3, 5, 6, 7, 8, 9, 10, 11, 13	1, 3, 5, 6, 7, 8, 9, 10, 11, 13	1, 3, 5, 6, 7, 8, 9, 10, 11, 13
90%	1, 2, 3, 4, 5, 6, 7, 8, 10, 11, 12, 13	1, 3, 4, 5, 6, 7, 8, 9, 10, 11, 12, 13	1, 3, 4, 5, 6, 7, 8, 9, 10, 11, 12, 13	1, 3, 4, 5, 6, 7, 8, 9, 10, 11, 12, 13	1, 3, 4, 5, 6, 7, 8, 9, 10, 11, 12, 13

Initialize m one-dimensional PSO: P_j, $j \in [1, \ldots, m]$
Create
$\mathbf{C}(j, k) = [P_{1(BG)}, P_{2(BG)}, \ldots, P_{j-1(BG)}, k, P_{j+1(BG)}, \ldots, P_{m(BG)}]$
While stop criteria not met **do**
    for each subswarm $j \in [1, \ldots, m]$ **do**
        for each particle $i \in [1, \ldots, s]$ **do**
            if fitness($\mathbf{C}(j, P_j(x_i))$) > fitness($\mathbf{C}(j, P_{j(LB_i)})$)
                then $P_{j(LB_i)} = P_j(x_i)$
            if fitness($\mathbf{C}(j, P_{j(LB_i)})$) > fitness($\mathbf{C}(j, P_{j(BG)})$)
                then $P_{j(BG)} = P_{j(lb_i)}$
        end for
        for each P_j **do**
            $v_{i,j}(t+1) = w \cdot v_{i,j}(t) + c_1 \cdot r_{1,i}(t)[P_{LB_{i,j}}(t) - x_{i,j}(t)]$
                $+ c_2 \cdot r_{2,i}(t)[P_{BG_{i,j}}(t) - x_{i,j}(t)]$
            $x_{i,j}(t+1) = x_{i,j}(t) + v_{i,j}(t+1)$

ALGORITHM 1: Pseudocode for cooperative PSO.

TABLE 11: Standard deviations for PSO and CPSO (housing and PM10 data sets).

Housing ($D = 50\%$)		PM10 ($D = 50\%$)	
PSO	CPSO	PSO	CPSO
0.066	0.072	0.021	**0.007**
0.192	**0.015**	0.018	**0.009**
0.199	**0.039**	0.010	**0.007**
0.11	**0.093**	0.004	**0.007**
0.115	**0.079**	0.024	**0.008**
0.091	**0.071**	0.006	**0.009**
0.058	0.094	0.014	**0.010**
0.044	0.064	0.010	**0.007**
0.053	**0.042**	0.019	**0.009**
0.021	0.042	0.016	**0.009**

the performance of the PSO method. However, the size of particles is high given the size of the search space. Here we require more particles to capture the large search space of instances selection for using the standard PSO. As a result we can find the best solution faster than using a smaller particles size. On the other hand, the number of particle is decreased when we implement the CPSO method. This is because the original large search space is divided into several groups, and the processes of searching the best subset are done in parallel.

5.2. Results of the Experiments.

In the experiments, we looked at the performance—an average root mean squared error (RMSE)—obtained for the selected combinations of the number of features and data (instances). The results obtained for the Housing data, PM10 data, and Parkinson's data for $c = 4$ and $c = 3$ clusters are summarized in Tables 4, 5, and 6, respectively. The experiments were repeated 10 times, and the reported results are the average RMSE values. We also report the values of the standard deviation of the performance index to offer a better insight into the variability of the performance. It is noticeable that the standard deviation is reduced with the increase of the data involved and the decrease of the dimensionality of the feature space.

The visualization of the results in the form of a series of heat maps, see Figures 6, 7, and 8, helps us arrive at a number of qualitative observations as well as to look at some quantitative relationships. In most cases, the performance index remains relatively low in some regions of the heat map. This finding demonstrates that the available data come with some evident redundancy, which exhibits a negative impact on the designed model. For the PM10 data, there is a significantly reduced performance of the model when, for a low percentage of data, the number of features starts growing. This effect is present for different numbers of clusters. The same tendency is noticeable for the other data sets. There is a sound explanation to this phenomenon: simply, the structure formed by fuzzy clustering does not fully reflect the dependencies in the data (due to the effect of the sparsity of the data), and this problem, in turn, results

in the deteriorating performance of the fuzzy model. In this case, one would be better off to consider a suitable reduced set of features. In all cases experimented with, we noted an optimal combination of features and data that led to the best performance of the model. Table 7 summarizes the optimal combinations of features and data.

The relationships between the percentage of data used and the resulting RMSE values are displayed in Figures 9 and 10. Some interesting tendencies are worth noting. A critical number of data are required to form a fuzzy model. Increasing the number of data does not produce any improvement as the curves plotted on Figures 9(a), 9(c), and 9(a) achieve a plateau or even some increase of the RMSE is noticeable.

Considering a fixed percentage of the data used, we look at the nature of the feature sets. Tables 8, 9 and 10 displays the best feature for PM10 data, Body fat data, and Housing data, respectively. Overall, the selected subsets of features are almost the same for different numbers of the clusters being used. Furthermore, we observe that in most cases, the reduced feature spaces exhibit an interesting "nesting" property, meaning that the extended feature space constructed subsumes the one formed previously. For example, for the Housing data, we obtain the following subsets of features:

$$\{\text{feature 6}\} \subset \{\text{feature 6, feature 9, feature 13}\}$$
$$\subset \{\text{feature 6, feature 9, feature 10, feature 13}\}. \tag{6}$$

Here, the corresponding features are as follows: 6: average number of rooms per dwelling, 9: index of accessibility to radial highways, 13: percentage of lower status population, and 10: full-value property-tax rate per \$10,000. This combination is quite convincing.

For the PM10 data, we arrive at a series of nested collections of features:

$$\{\text{feature 1}\} \subset \{\text{feature 1, feature 7}\}$$
$$\subset \{\text{feature 1, feature 6, feature 7}\} \tag{7}$$
$$\subset \{\text{feature 1, feature 2, feature 6, feature 7}\},$$

where the corresponding features include: 1: the concentration of PM10 (particles), 7: hour of experiment per day, 6: wind direction, and 2: the number of cars per hour.

Turning to the comparative analysis of performance of the swarm optimization methods, we summarize the obtained results in Figure 11. For all data, the CPSO performed better than the standard PSO. Although both algorithms show the same tendency when the percentage of feature is 100% however, the RMSE produced by the CPSO is lower than the one obtained when running the PSO. Furthermore, the CPSO algorithm is more stable than the standard PSO. In most cases, the standard deviations of error produced by the CPSO are smaller than the results obtained for the standard PSO (see Table 11).

Figure 12 shows the subsets of the features selected for different percentages of the features used in construction of the fuzzy model. The CPSO algorithm is more consistent while selecting the increasing number of features. For

TABLE 12: Percentage of improvement of the RMSE obtained when using CPSO over the results formed by the PSO; Housing data set.

F	D = 10%	D = 20%	D = 30%	D = 40%	D = 50%	D = 60%	D = 70%	D = 80%	D = 90%
10%	13	15	20	26	19	18	10	19	11
20%	31	31	20	24	25	16	24	23	17
30%	33	26	19	20	14	15	24	18	21
40%	28	21	19	14	17	17	17	18	19
50%	34	21	12	7	9	9	9	12	8
60%	23	21	13	7	4	7	8	9	7
70%	19	17	14	4	9	6	4	8	8
80%	33	19	12	4	2	3	3	8	9
90%	22	14	4	5	2	1	2	2	1
100%	17	4	4	7	3	1	1	1	1

TABLE 13: The comparison of RMSE obtained when using standard PSO, CPSO, and standard fuzzy model with holdout method for housing data with $C = 3$.

% of data	Standard PSO		Cooperative PSO[1]		Holdout method	
	% of feature	MSE	% of feature	MSE	% of feature	MSE
30	90	4.015	40	3.473	100	17.593
40	80	3.699	70	3.464	100	10.803
50	80	3.573	70	3.414	100	9.907
60	80	3.556	70	3.435	100	8.507
70	80	3.527	60	3.413	100	8.312
80	80	3.654	90	3.449	100	8.164
90	80	3.679	90	3.615	100	7.641

TABLE 14: The comparison of RMSE obtained when using standard PSO, CPSO, and standard fuzzy model with holdout method for body fat data with $C = 3$.

% of data	Standard PSO		Cooperative PSO[1]		Holdout method	
	% of feature	MSE	% of feature	MSE	% of feature	MSE
30	30	4.677	30	4.6847	100	11.586
40	30	4.717	30	4.5409	100	8.291
50	40	4.617	30	4.5136	100	7.548
60	50	4.636	40	4.4289	100	7.073
70	40	4.548	40	4.4234	100	6.658
80	40	4.553	40	4.4233	100	6.239
90	40	4.582	40	4.3771	100	6.102

TABLE 15: The comparison of RMSE obtained when using standard PSO, CPSO, and standard fuzzy model with holdout method for PM10 data with $C = 3$.

% of data	Standard PSO		Cooperative PSO[1]		Holdout method	
	% of feature	MSE	% of feature	MSE	% of feature	MSE
30	100	0.764	80	0.7338	100	2.100
40	100	0.765	80	0.7432	100	2.018
50	90	0.777	90	0.7790	100	2.030
60	80	0.805	80	0.7769	100	1.986
70	90	0.820	80	0.8052	100	2.001
80	80	0.839	90	0.8206	100	1.983
90	70	0.847	90	0.8417	100	1.976

TABLE 16: The comparison of RMSE obtained when using CPSO and standard fuzzy model with holdout method for computer data with $C = 3$.

% of data	Cooperative PSO		Holdout method	
	% of feature	MSE	% of feature	MSE
30	40	16.446	100	17.453
40	30	14.712	100	17.524
50	30	14.350	100	17.680
60	40	14.935	100	17.837
70	40	16.237	100	17.918
80	40	15.122	100	18.351

example, features 6 and 13 were selected when using both 30% and 70% of data. In contrast to the selection made with the PSO algorithm, the subset of the features selected here is not as stable, especially when using only 30% of data.

Table 12 presents the percentage of the improvement when using the CPSO algorithm compared to the PSO algorithm. Note that in this percentage we included all different combinations of the features' percentages and the data percentages being used. The percentage of the improvement is higher when dealing with a smaller percentage of features and data. For example, the percentage of improvement is 34% for 10% of the instances and 50% of the features selected while the percentage of improvement is less than 10% for 60% of instances and features used. These results occurred because the PSO method has to deal with a large search space for selecting a small subset of features and instances. In contrast to the search space for CPSO, the large search space is decomposed into multiple subswarms that reduce the dimensionality of the original search space.

Tables 13, 14, 15, and 16 show the comparison of RMSE when using the proposed method and the standard fuzzy modeling method. Here the standard fuzzy model is constructed without using any feature and instances selection and the holdout method is used to select the data based on the percentage given. The experiment for using the standard fuzzy modeling is repeated for 50 times. If we analyze the tables, we can observe that our proposed method outperforms the standard method of constructing the fuzzy model from the dataset. This can be seen clearly when using the CPSO method to search for the best subset of feature and instances. For example, in Table 13 if we use the CPSO method, the RMSE for using 70% of data is 3.413, whereas the RMSE for the standard method is 8.312. The same tendency occurs for all datasets used here.

Figure 13 shows the comparison plot between the proposed method and the "standard" fuzzy modeling. In most of the cases, the proposed method showed better performance.

It becomes clear that one is able to reduce the input data in terms of the number features and instances. Moreover, the flexibility of choosing the reduction level helps the user focus on the most essential subsets of data and features (variables). The knowledge acquired about the best subset of data can be used for future data collection. In addition, the user can put

more effort analyzing only the best subset of data that give more impact to the overall prediction.

6. Conclusions

In this paper, we proposed a simple framework for constructing fuzzy modeling from high-dimensional and large data. This framework has several advantages that make it better suited than other frameworks for sharing various real-life problems. Firstly, the simultaneous feature and instances selection is easily adapted to construct the structure of the fuzzy model. Secondly, the best selected subset of data obtained with this framework is capable of representing the original large data set. Thirdly, we construct an optimal (or suboptimal) collection of features and data based on the PSO. In addition, a cooperative PSO is developed in order to overcome the limitation of using standard PSO when dealing with a high-dimensional search space. The size of the selected features and data used to construct the fuzzy model can be adjusted based upon the feedback provided in terms of the performance of the model constructed for the currently accepted.

The effectiveness of the framework was validated by using four well-known regression data sets. The experiment results showed that the proposed fuzzy modeling framework is able to handle high dimensionality and a large data set simultaneously. Moreover, the curse of dimensionality problem in fuzzy modeling was substantially reduced.

In the future work one could concentrate on improving the cooperative PSO by fine-tuning the parameters of the method such as, for example, the cognitive and social parameter.

Acknowledgments

Support from the Ministry of Higher Education (MOHE) Malaysia and Universiti Teknikal Malaysia Melaka (UTeM) is gratefully acknowledged.

References

[1] W. Pedrycz and F. Gomide, *Fuzzy Systems Engineering*, John Wiley & Sons, Hoboken, NJ, USA, 2007.

[2] G. Castellano, C. Castiello, A. M. Fanelli, and C. Mencar, "Knowledge discovery by a neuro-fuzzy modeling framework," *Fuzzy Sets and Systems*, vol. 149, no. 1, pp. 187–207, 2005.

[3] Y. Jin, "Fuzzy modeling of high-dimensional systems: complexity reduction and interpretability improvement," *IEEE Transactions on Fuzzy Systems*, vol. 8, no. 2, pp. 212–221, 2000.

[4] Q. Zhang and M. Mahfouf, "A hierarchical Mamdani-type fuzzy modelling approach with new training data selection and multi-objective optimisation mechanisms: a special application for the prediction of mechanical properties of alloy steels," *Applied Soft Computing Journal*, vol. 11, no. 2, pp. 2419–2443, 2011.

[5] G. E. Tsekouras, "On the use of the weighted fuzzy c-means in fuzzy modeling," *Advances in Engineering Software*, vol. 36, no. 5, pp. 287–300, 2005.

[6] A. G. Di Nuovo, M. Palesi, and V. Catania, "Multi-objective evolutionary fuzzy clustering for high-dimensional problems," in *Proceedings of the IEEE International Conference on Fuzzy Systems*, pp. 1–6, July 2007.

[7] M. Setnes, R. Babuška, U. Kaymak, and H. R. Van Nauta Lemke, "Similarity measures in fuzzy rule base simplification," *IEEE Transactions on Systems, Man, and Cybernetics B*, vol. 28, no. 3, pp. 376–386, 1998.

[8] M. Y. Chen and D. A. Linkens, "Rule-base self-generation and simplification for data-driven fuzzy models," *Fuzzy Sets and Systems*, vol. 142, no. 2, pp. 243–265, 2004.

[9] H. Wang, S. Kwong, Y. Jin, W. Wei, and K. F. Man, "Multi-objective hierarchical genetic algorithm for interpretable fuzzy rule-based knowledge extraction," *Fuzzy Sets and Systems*, vol. 149, no. 1, pp. 149–186, 2005.

[10] F. J. Berlanga, A. J. Rivera, M. J. del Jesus, and F. Herrera, "GP-COACH: genetic Programming-based learning of COmpact and ACcurate fuzzy rule-based classification systems for High-dimensional problems," *Information Sciences*, vol. 180, no. 8, pp. 1183–1200, 2010.

[11] J. Alcalá-Fdéz, R. Alcalá, and F. Herrera, "A fuzzy associative classification system with genetic rule selection for high-dimensional problems," in *Proceedings of the 4th International Workshop on Genetic and Evolutionary Fuzzy Systems (GEFS '10)*, pp. 33–38, March 2010.

[12] Y. Chen, B. Yang, A. Abraham, and L. Peng, "Automatic design of hierarchical Takagi-Sugeno type fuzzy systems using evolutionary algorithms," *IEEE Transactions on Fuzzy Systems*, vol. 15, no. 3, pp. 385–397, 2007.

[13] M. R. Delgado, F. V. Zuben, and F. Gomide, "Coevolutionary genetic fuzzy systems: a hierarchical collaborative approach," *Fuzzy Sets and Systems*, vol. 141, no. 1, pp. 89–106, 2004.

[14] N. Xiong and L. Litz, "Reduction of fuzzy control rules by means of premise learning—method and case study," *Fuzzy Sets and Systems*, vol. 132, no. 2, pp. 217–231, 2002.

[15] A. E. Gaweda, J. M. Zurada, and R. Setiono, "Input selection in data-driven fuzzy modeling," in *Proceedings of the 10th IEEE International Conference on Fuzzy Systems*, vol. 3, pp. 1251–1254, December 2001.

[16] M. L. Hadjili and V. Wertz, "Takagi-Sugeno fuzzy modeling incorporating input variables selection," *IEEE Transactions on Fuzzy Systems*, vol. 10, no. 6, pp. 728–742, 2002.

[17] R. Šindelář and R. Babuška, "Input selection for nonlinear regression models," *IEEE Transactions on Fuzzy Systems*, vol. 12, no. 5, pp. 688–696, 2004.

[18] M. H. F. Zarandi, I. B. Türkşen, and B. Rezaee, "A systematic approach to fuzzy modeling for rule generation from numerical data," in *Proceedings of the Annual Meeting of the North American Fuzzy Information Processing Society (NAFIPS '04)*, pp. 768–773, June 2004.

[19] H. Du and N. Zhang, "Application of evolving Takagi-Sugeno fuzzy model to nonlinear system identification," *Applied Soft Computing Journal*, vol. 8, no. 1, pp. 676–686, 2008.

[20] S. N. Ghazavi and T. W. Liao, "Medical data mining by fuzzy modeling with selected features," *Artificial Intelligence in Medicine*, vol. 43, no. 3, pp. 195–206, 2008.

[21] Y. Zhang, X. B. Wu, Z. Y. Xing, and W. L. Hu, "On generating interpretable and precise fuzzy systems based on Pareto multi-objective cooperative co-evolutionary algorithm," *Applied Soft Computing Journal*, vol. 11, no. 1, pp. 1284–1294, 2011.

[22] F. Wan, H. Shang, L. X. Wang, and Y. X. Sun, "How to determine the minimum number of fuzzy rules to achieve given accuracy: a computational geometric approach to SISO

case," *Fuzzy Sets and Systems*, vol. 150, no. 2, pp. 199–209, 2005.

[23] I. Guyon and A. Elisseeff, "An introduction to variable and feature selection," *Journal of Machine Learning Research*, vol. 3, pp. 1157–1182, 2003.

[24] H. Liu and L. Yu, "Toward integrating feature selection algorithms for classification and clustering," *IEEE Transactions on Knowledge and Data Engineering*, vol. 17, no. 4, pp. 491–502, 2005.

[25] H. Liu and H. Motoda, *Computational Methods of Feature Selection*, Chapman & Hall/CRC, Boca Raton, Fla USA, 2008.

[26] J. A. Olvera-López, J. A. Carrasco-Ochoa, J. F. Martínez-Trinidad, and J. Kittler, "A review of instance selection methods," *Artificial Intelligence Review*, vol. 34, no. 2, pp. 133–143, 2010.

[27] H. Liu and H. Motoda, *Instance Selection and Construction for Data Mining*, Kluwer Academic Publishers, Boston, Mass USA, 2001.

[28] H. Ishibuchi, T. Nakashima, and M. Nii, "Genetic-Algorithm-Based instance and feature selection," in *Instance Selection and Construction for Data Mining*, H. Lui and H. Motoda, Eds., pp. 95–112, Kluwer Academic Publishers, Boston, Mass, USA, 2001.

[29] J. Derrac, S. García, and F. Herrera, "IFS-CoCo: instance and feature selection based on cooperative coevolution with nearest neighbor rule," *Pattern Recognition*, vol. 43, no. 6, pp. 2082–2105, 2010.

[30] A. Hertz and D. Kobler, "Framework for the description of evolutionary algorithms," *European Journal of Operational Research*, vol. 126, no. 1, pp. 1–12, 2000.

[31] J. R. Cano, F. Herrera, and M. Lozano, "Using evolutionary algorithms as instance selection for data reduction in KDD: an experimental study," *IEEE Transactions on Evolutionary Computation*, vol. 7, no. 6, pp. 561–575, 2003.

[32] J. Kennedy and R. Eberhart, "Particle swarm optimization," in *Proceedings of the IEEE International Conference on Neural Networks*, pp. 1942–1948, Perth, Australia, December 1995.

[33] F. van den Bergh and A. P. Engelbrecht, "A cooperative approach to particle swarm optimization," *IEEE Transactions on Evolutionary Computation*, vol. 8, no. 3, pp. 225–239, 2004.

[34] Y. Shi and R. C. Eberhart, "Empirical study of particle Swarm Optimization," *Congress on Evolutionary Computing*, vol. 3, pp. 1945–1950, 1999.

12

Multilevel Cognitive Machine-Learning-Based Concept for Artificial Awareness: Application to Humanoid Robot Awareness Using Visual Saliency

Kurosh Madani, Dominik M. Ramik, and Cristophe Sabourin

Images, Signals and Intelligence Systems Laboratory (LISSI/EA 3956) and Senart-FB Institute of Technology, University Paris-EST Créteil (UPEC), Bât.A, avenue Pierre Point, 77127 Lieusaint, France

Correspondence should be addressed to Kurosh Madani, madani@u-pec.fr

Academic Editor: Qiangfu Zhao

As part of "intelligence," the "awareness" is the state or ability to perceive, feel, or be mindful of events, objects, or sensory patterns: in other words, to be conscious of the surrounding environment and its interactions. Inspired by early-ages human skills developments and especially by early-ages awareness maturation, the present paper accosts the robots intelligence from a different slant directing the attention to combining both "cognitive" and "perceptual" abilities. Within such a slant, the machine (robot) shrewdness is constructed on the basis of a multilevel cognitive concept attempting to handle complex artificial behaviors. The intended complex behavior is the autonomous discovering of objects by robot exploring an unknown environment: in other words, proffering the robot autonomy and awareness in and about unknown backdrop.

1. Introduction and Problem Stating

The term "cognition" refers to the ability for the processing of information applying knowledge. If the word "cognition" has been and continues to be used within quite a large number of different contexts, in the field of computer science, it often intends artificial intellectual activities and processes relating "machine learning" and accomplishment of knowledge-based "intelligent" artificial functions. However, the cognitive process of "knowledge construction" (and in more general way "intelligence") requires "awareness" about the surrounding environment and, thus, the ability to perceive information from it in order to interact with the surrounding milieu. So, if "cognition" and "perception" remain inseparable ingredients toward machines intelligence and thus toward machines (robots', etc.) autonomy, the "awareness" skill is a key spot in reaching the above-mentioned autonomy.

Concerning most of the works relating modern robotics, and especially humanoid robots, it is pertinent to note that they either have concerned the design of controllers controlling different devices of such machines [1, 2] or have focused the navigation aspects of such robots [3–5]. In the same way, the major part of the work dealing with human-like, or in more general terms intelligent, behavior, has connected abstract tasks, as those relating reasoning inference, interactive deduction mechanisms, and so forth. [6–10]. Inspired by early-ages human skills developments [11–15] and especially human early-ages walking [16–19], the present work accosts the robots intelligence from a different slant directing the attention to emergence of "machine awareness" from both "cognitive" and "perceptual" traits. It is important to note that neither the presented work nor its related issues (concepts, architectures, techniques, or algorithms) pretend being "artificial versions" of the complex natural (e.g., biological, psychological, etc.) mechanisms discovered, pointed out, or described by the above-referenced authors or by numerous other scientists working within the aforementioned areas whose works are not referenced in this paper. In [20] Andersen wrote concerning artificial neural networks: "*It is not absolutely necessary to believe that neural network models have anything to do with the nervous*

Multilevel Cognitive Machine-Learning-Based Concept for Artificial Awareness: Application to Humanoid
Robot Awareness Using Visual Saliency

109

system, but it helps. Because, if they do, we are able to use a large body of ideas, experiments, and facts from cognitive science and neuroscience to design, construct, and test networks. Otherwise, we would have to suggest functions and mechanism for intelligent behavior without any examples of successful operation." In the same way, those natural mechanisms help us to look for plausible analogies between our down-to-earth models and those complex cognitive mechanisms.

Combining cognitive and perceptual abilities, the machine (robot) shrewdness is constructed on the basis of two kinds of functions: "unconscious cognitive functions" (UCFs) and "conscious cognitive functions" (CCFs). We identify UCFs as activities belonging to the "instinctive" cognition level handling reflexive abilities. Beside this, we distinguish CCFs as functions belonging to the "intentional" cognition level handling thought-out abilities. The two above-mentioned kinds of functions have been used as basis of a multilevel cognitive concept attempting to handle complex artificial behaviors [21]. The intended complex behavior is the autonomous discovering of objects by robot exploring an unknown environment. The present paper will not itemize the motion-related aspect that has been widely presented, analyzed, discussed and validated (on different examples) in [21]. It will focus on perceptual skill and awareness emergence. Regarding perceptual skill, it is developed on the basis of artificial vision and "salient" object detection. The paper will center this foremost skill and show how the intentional cognitive level of the above-mentioned concept could be used to proffer a kind of artificial awareness skill. The concept has been applied in design of "motion-perception-" based control architecture of a humanoid robot. The designed control architecture takes advantage of visual intention allowing the robot some kind of artificial awareness regarding its surrounding environment.

The paper is organized in five sections. The next section briefly introduces the multilevel cognitive concept. Section 3 describes the general structure of a cognitive function and depicts the suggested motion-perception control strategy. Section 4 presents the visual intention bloc. Validation results, obtained from implementation on a real humanoid-like robot, are reported in this section. Finally, the last section concludes the paper.

2. Brief Overview of Multilevel Cognitive Concept

Within the frame of this concept, we consider a process (mainly a complex process) as a multimodel structure where involved components (models), constructed as a result of machine learning (ML), handle two categories of operational levels: reflexive and intentional [21]. This means that ML and related techniques play a central role in this concept and the issued architectures. According to what has been mentioned in the introductory section, two kinds of functions, so-called UCFs and CCFs, build up functional elements ruling the complex task or the complex behavior. Figure 1 illustrates the bloc diagram of the proposed cognitive conception. As it is noticeable from this figure, within the proposed concept,

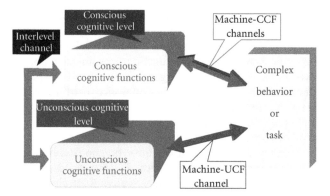

FIGURE 1: Robot coordinates described by a triplet as $P(x, y, \theta)$.

the overall architecture is obtained by building up cognitive layers (levels) corresponding to different skills fashioning the complex task. It is pertinent to remind that, as well as UCFs, CCFs enclose a number of "elementary functions" (EFs). Within such a scheme, a cognitive layer may fulfil a skill either independently of other layers (typically, the case of unconscious cognitive levels) or using one or several talents developed by other layers (characteristically, the case of conscious cognitive levels) [21].

The first key advantage of conceptualizing the problem within such an incline is to detach the modelling of robots complex artificial behaviours from the type of robot. In other words, models built within such conceptualizing could be used for modelling the same kind of complex behaviours for different kinds of robots. An example of analogy (similarity) with natural cognitive mechanisms could be found in early-ages human walking development. In fact, in its global achievement, the early-ages human abilities development does not depend on the kind of "baby." The second chief benefit of such a concept is that the issued artificial structures are based on "machine learning" paradigms (artificial neural networks, fuzzy logic, reinforcement learning, etc.), taking advantage of "learning" capacity and "generalization" propensity of such approaches. This offers a precious potential to deal with high dimensionality, nonlinearity, and empirical (non-analytical) proprioceptive or exteroceptive information.

3. From Cognitive Function to Motion-Perception Architecture

As it has been mentioned above, a cognitive function (either UCF or CCF) is constructed by a number of EFs. EF is defined as a function (learning-based or conventional) realizing an operational aptitude composing (necessary for) the skill accomplished by the concerned cognitive function. An EF is composed of "elementary components" (ECs). An EC is the lowest level component (module, transfer function, etc.) realizing some elementary aptitude contributing in EF operational aptitude. Two kinds of ECs could be defined (identified): the first corresponding to elementary action that we call "action elementary component" (AEC) and the second corresponding to elementary decision that we call "decision elementary component" (DEC). An EF may include one or both kinds of the above-defined EC. In the same way, a cognitive function may include one or several ECs. Figure 2 gives the general structure of a cognitive function. However, it is pertinent to notice that there is any restriction to the fact that when it may be necessary, an EC could play the role of an EF. In the same way, when necessary, a cognitive function could include only one EF.

Supposing that a given cognitive function (either conscious or unconscious) includes K ($K \in N$, where N represents the "natural numbers ensemble) elementary functions, considering the kth EF (with $k \in N$ and $k \leq K$) composing this cognitive function, we define the following notations.

Ψ_k is the input of kth EF: $\Psi_k = [\psi_1, \ldots, \psi_j, \ldots, \psi_M]^T$, where ψ_j represents the input component of the jth EC of this EF, $j \leq M$, and M the total number of elementary components composing this EF.

O_k is the output of kth EF.

o_j is the output of the jth EC of the kth EF, with $j \leq M$, and M the total number of elementary components composing the kth EF.

$F_k(\cdot)$ is the skill performed by the kth EF.

$f_j^A(\cdot)$ is the function (transformation, etc.) performed by jth AEC.

$f^D(\cdot)$ is the decision (matching, rule, etc.) performed by DEC.

Within the above-defined notation, the output of kth EF is formalized as shown in (1) with o_j given by (2). In a general case, the output of an EC may also depend on some internal (specific) parameters particular to that EC [21]:

$$O_k = F_k(\Psi_k) = f^D\left(\Psi_k, o_1, \ldots, o_j, \ldots, o_M\right),$$
$$o_j = f_j^A\left(\psi_j\right). \tag{1}$$

Based on the aforementioned cognitive concept, the control scheme of a robot could be considered within the frame of "motion-perception-" (MP-) based architecture. Consequently, as well as the robot motions its perception of the environment is obtained combining UCF and CCF. Robot sway is achieved combining unconscious and conscious cognitive motion functions (UCMFs and CCMFs, resp.). In the same way, essentially based on vision, robot perceptual ability is constructed combining unconscious and conscious cognitive visual functions (UCVFs and CCVFs, resp.). Figure 3 shows such an MP-based robot cognitive control scheme. It is pertinent to notice that the proposed control scheme takes advantage of some universality, conceptualizing the build-up of both robot motion and perception abilities independently of the type of robot. It is also relevant to emphasize that the proposed cognitive

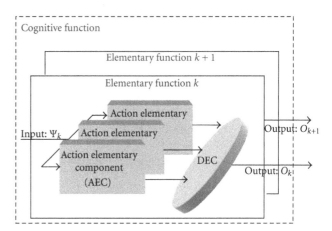

FIGURE 2: General bloc diagram of a cognitive function.

scheme links the behavior control construction to perception constructing the robot action from and with perceptual data and interaction with the context. This slant of view lays the robot way of doing (e.g., robot knowledge construction) to the human way of learning and knowledge construction: humans or animals learn and construct the knowledge by interacting with the environment. In other words, these natural intelligent beings operate using "awareness" about the surrounding environment in which they live.

If the question of how humans learn, represent, and recognize objects under a wide variety of viewing conditions is still a great challenge to both neurophysiology and cognitive researchers [22], a number of works relating the human early-ages cognitive walking ability construction process highlighting a number of key mechanisms. As shows clinical experiments (as those shown by [23]), one them is the strong linkage between visual and motor mechanisms. This corroborates the pertinence of the suggested cognitive MP-based scheme. Beside this, [24, 25] show that apart of shaping (e.g., recognizing objects and associating shapes with them), we (human) see the world by bringing our attention to visually important objects first. This means that the visual attention mechanism plays also one of the key roles in human infants learning of the encountered objects. Thus, it appears appropriate to draw inspiration from studies on human infants visual learning in constructing robots awareness on the basis of learning by visual revelation.

Making an intelligent system perceive the environment in which it evolves and construct the knowledge by learning unknown objects present in that environment makes a clear need appear relating the ability to select from the overwhelming flow of sensory information only the pertinent ones. This foremost ability is known as "visual saliency," sometimes called in the literature "visual attention," unpredictability, or surprise. It is described as a perceptual quality that makes a part of an image stand out relative to the rest of the image and to capture attention of observer [26]. It may be generalized that it is the saliency (in terms of motion, colors, etc.) that lets the pertinent information "stand out" from the context [27]. We argue that in this context visual saliency may be helpful to enable unsupervised extraction and subsequent learning of

Multilevel Cognitive Machine-Learning-Based Concept for Artificial Awareness: Application to Humanoid
Robot Awareness Using Visual Saliency

111

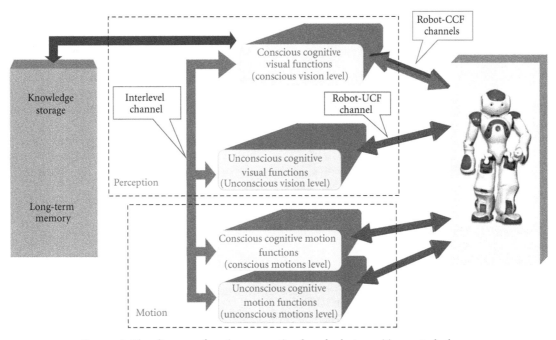

FIGURE 3: Bloc diagram of motion-perception-based robot cognitive control scheme.

a previously unknown object by a machine, in other words, proffering to the machine (robot) the awareness about its environment.

Referring to the perception bloc of Figure 3, the visual perception is composed of an unconscious visual level including UCVF and one conscious visual level containing CCVF. Unconscious visual level handles reflexive visual tasks, namely, the preprocessing of acquired images, the salient objects detection, and the detected salient objects storage. If the preprocessing could appear as an independent UCVF, it also may be an EF of one of UCVFs composing the unconscious visual level. In this second way of organizing the unconscious visual level, the UCVF including the preprocessing task will deliver the preprocessing results (as those relating image segmentation, different extracted features, etc.) as well to other UCVFs composing the unconscious level as to those CCVFs of conscious level which need the aforementioned results, using the interlevel channel. Conscious visual level conducts intentional visual tasks, namely, the objects learning (including learning detected salient objects), the knowledge construction by carrying out an intentional storage (in unconscious visual level) of new detected salient objects, the detected salient objects recognition in robot surrounding environment (those already known and the visual target (recognized salient object) tracking) allowing the robot self-orientation and motion toward a desired recognized salient object. Consequently, the conscious level communicates (e.g., delivers the outputs of concerned CCVF) with unconscious level (e.g., to the concerned UCVF) as well as with unconscious motion and conscious motion levels (e.g., with the bloc in MP-based robot cognitive control scheme in charge of robot motions).

4. From Salient Objects Detection to Visual Awareness

This section is devoted to description of two principle cognitive visual functions. The first subsection will detail the main UCVF, called "salient vision," which allows robot to self-discover (automatically detect) pertinent objects within the surrounding environment. While, the second subsection will spell out one of the core CCVFs, called "visual intention," which proffers the robot artificial visual intention ability and allows it to construct the knowledge about the surrounding environment proffering the robot the awareness regarding its surrounding environment.

Before describing the above-mentioned functions, it is pertinent to note that a recurrent operation in extracting visually salient objects (from images) is image segmentation. Generally speaking, one can use any available image segmentation technique. However, the quality of segmentation may be weighty for an accurate extraction of salient objects in images. In fact, most of the usual segmentation techniques (used beside standard image salient object extraction techniques) using manual or automatic thresholding remain limited because they do not respect the original image features. That is why we made use of the algorithm proposed recently by [28]. It is based on K-means clustering of color space with an adaptive selection of K and a spatial filter removing meaningless segments. The used algorithm is very fast (tens of milliseconds for a 320×240 pixels image on a standard PC) and it claims to have results close to human perception. The execution speed is a major condition in effective implementation in robotics applications reinforcing our choice for this already available algorithm, which keeps upright between execution speed and achieved segmentation quality.

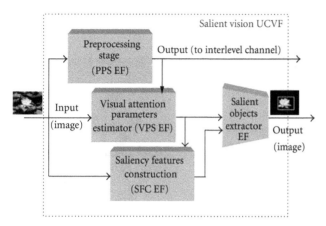

FIGURE 4: Bloc-diagram of Salient Vision UCVF, handling the automated detection of salient objects.

4.1. Salient Vision UCVF and Salient Objects Detection.

The bloc diagram detailing the structure of "salient vision" UCVF is given in Figure 4. As it is visible from this figure, the "salient vision" UCVF includes also the preprocessing stage (defined as one of its constituting EFs), meaning that this UCVC handles the image segmentation and common image features' extraction tasks, delivering the issued results to other UCVFs as well as to conscious visual level. Beside this EF, it includes three other EF: the "visual Attention parameters estimator" (VAPE) EF, the "salient features construction" (SFC) EF, and the "salient objects extraction" (SOE) EF. This last EF plays the role of a decision-like elementary component, implemented as an independent EF.

4.1.1. Visual Attention Parameters Estimation Elementary Function.

The visual attention parameter estimation (VAPE) elementary function determines what could be assimilated to some kind of "visual attention degree." Computed on the basis of preprocessing bloc issued results and controlling local salient features, visual attention parameter p constructs a top-down control of the attention and of the sensitivity of the feature in scale space. High value of p (resulting in a large sliding window size) with respect to the image size will make the local saliency feature more sensitive to large objects. In the same way, low values of p allow focusing the visual attention on smaller objects and details. The value of visual attention parameter p can be hard-set to a fixed value based on a heuristic according to [29]. However, as different images usually present salient objects in different scales, this way of doing will limit the performance of the system. Thus, a new automated cognitive estimation of the parameter p has been designed. The estimation is based, on the one hand, on calculation (inspired from the work presented in [30]) of the histogram of segment sizes from the input image, and on the other hand, on using of an artificial neural network (ANN). The ANN receives (as input) the feature vector issued from the above-mentioned histogram and provides the sliding window value. The weights of the neural network are adapted in training stage using a genetic algorithm.

To obtain the aforementioned histogram, the input image is segmented into n segments $(S_1, S_2, \ldots, S_n)$. For each

one of the found segments S_i (where $S_i \in \{S_1, S_2, \ldots, S_n\}$), its size $|S_i|$ (measured in number of pixels) is divided by the overall image size $|I|$. An absolute histogram H_{SA} of segment sizes is constructed according to (2), avoiding leading to a too sparse histogram. This ensures that the first histogram bin contains the number of segments with area larger than $1/10$ of the image size, the second contains segments from $1/10$ to $1/100$ of the image size, and so forth. For practical reasons we use a 4-bin histogram. Then, this absolute histogram leads to a relative histogram H_{SR} computed according to relation (3):

$$H_{\mathrm{SA}}(i) = \sum_{j=1}^{n} \begin{cases} 1 & \text{if } 10^{i-1} \leq \dfrac{|S_i|}{|I|} \leq 10^i, \\ 0 & \text{otherwise,} \end{cases} \tag{2}$$

$$H_{\mathrm{SR}}(i) = \frac{H_{\mathrm{SA}}(i)}{\sum_j H_{\mathrm{SA}}(j)}. \tag{3}$$

The core of the proposed visual attention parameter estimator is a fully connected three-layer feed-forward MLP-like ANN, with a sigmoidal activation function, including 4 input nodes, 3 hidden neurons, and 1 output neuron. The four input nodes are connected each to its respective bin from the H_{SR} histogram. The value of the output node, belonging to the continuous interval $[0, 1]$, could be interpreted as the ratio of the estimated sliding window size p and the long side size of the image. The ANN is trained making use of a genetic algorithm described in [31]. Each organism in the population consists of a genome representing an array of floating point numbers whose length corresponds with the number of weights in MLP. To calculate the fitness of each organism, the MLP weights are set according to its current genome. Once visual attention parameter p is available (according to the MLP output) saliency is computed over the image and salient objects are extracted. The result is compared with ground truth and the precision, the recall and the F-ratio (representing the overall quality of the extraction) are calculated (according to [32] and using the measures proposed in the same work to evaluate quantitatively the salient object extraction). The F-ratio is then used as the measure of fitness. In each generation, the elitism rule is used to explicitly preserve the best solution found so far. Organisms are mutated with 5% of probability. As learning data set, we use 10% of the MSRA-B data set (described in [32]). The remaining 90% of the above-indicated data set has been used for validation.

4.1.2. Salient Features Construction Elementary Function.

The salient features construction (SFC) elementary function performs two kinds of features (both used for salient objects detection). The first kind is global saliency features and the second local saliency features. Global saliency features capture global properties of image in terms of distribution of colors. The global saliency is obtained combining "intensity saliency" and the "chromatic saliency." Intensity saliency $M_l(x)$, given by relation (4), is defined as Euclidean distance of intensity I to the mean of the entire image. Index l stands

Multilevel Cognitive Machine-Learning-Based Concept for Artificial Awareness: Application to Humanoid
Robot Awareness Using Visual Saliency

113

FIGURE 5: Examples of global and local saliency features: original image (a), global saliency map (b), local saliency map (c), and final saliency map.

for intensity channel of the image, and $I_{\mu l}$ is the average intensity of the channel. In the same way, chromatic saliency, given by relation (6), is defined as Euclidean distance of azimuth and zenith components intensities (e.g., azimuth ϕ and zenith θ, resp.) to their means ($I_{\mu\phi}$ and $I_{\mu\theta}$ resp.) in the entire image. Term (x) denotes coordinates of a given pixel on the image:

$$M_l(x) = \left\| I_{\mu l} - I_l(x) \right\|,$$
$$M_{\phi\theta}(x) = \sqrt{\left(I_{\mu\phi} - I_\phi(x)\right)^2 + \left(I_{\mu\theta} - I_\theta(x)\right)^2}. \qquad (4)$$

The global saliency map $M(x)$, given by relation (5) is a hybrid result of combination of maps resulted from (1) according to logistic sigmoid blending function. Blending of the two saliency maps together is driven by a function of color saturation C of each pixel. It is calculated from RGB color model for each pixel as pseudonorm, given by $C = \text{Max}[R, G, B] - \text{Min}[R, G, B]$. When C is low, importance is given to intensity saliency. When C is high, chromatic saliency is emphasized:

$$M(x) = \frac{1}{1 - e^{-C}} M_{\phi\theta}(x) + \left(1 - \frac{1}{1 + e^{-C}}\right) M_l(x). \qquad (5)$$

The global saliency (and related features) captures the visual saliency with respect to the colors. However, in real cases, the object visual saliency may also consist in its particular shape or texture, distinct to its surroundings, either beside or rather than simply in its color. To capture this aspect of visual saliency, a local feature over the image is determined. Inspired from a similar kind of feature introduced in [32], the local saliency has been defined as a centre-surround difference of histograms. The idea relating the local saliency is to go through the entire image and to compare the content of a sliding window with its surroundings to determine how similar the two are. If

similarity is low, it may be a sign of a salient region within the sliding window.

To formalize this idea leading local saliency features, let us have a sliding window P of size p, centered over pixel (x). Define a (centre) histogram H_C of pixel intensities inside it. Then, let us define a (surround) histogram H_S as histogram of intensities in a window Q surrounding P in a manner that the area of $(Q - P) = p^2$. The centre-surround feature $d(x)$ is then given as (6) over all histogram bins (i):

$$d(x) = \sum_i \frac{|H_C(i) - H_S(i)|}{p^2}. \qquad (6)$$

Resulting from computation of the $d(x)$ throughout all the l, ϕ, and θ channels, the centre-surround saliency $D(x)$ on a given position (x) is defined according to (7). Similarly to (5), a logistic sigmoid blending function has been used to combine chromaticity and intensity in order to improve the performance of this feature on images with mixed achromatic and chromatic content. However, here the color saturation C refers to average saturation of the content of the sliding window P:

$$D(x) = \frac{1}{1 - e^{-C}} d_l(x) + \left(1 - \frac{1}{1 + e^{-C}}\right) \text{Max}\left(d_\phi(x), d_\theta(x)\right). \qquad (7)$$

4.1.3. Salient Objects Extraction Elementary Function. Salient objects extraction (SOE) elementary function acts as the last step of saliency map calculation and salient objects detection. The extracted global and local salient features (e.g., $M(x)$ and $D(x)$, resp.) are combined using (8), resulting in final saliency map $M_{\text{final}}(x)$, which is then smoothed by Gaussian filter. The upper part of the condition in (8) describes a particular case, where a part of image consists of a color that is not considered salient (i.e., pixels with low $M(x)$ measure) but which is distinct from the surroundings by virtue of its shape.

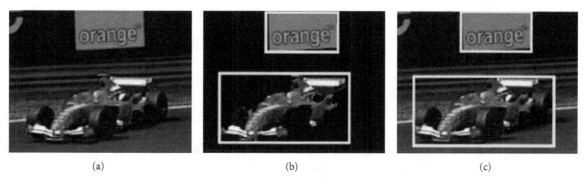

FIGURE 6: Examples of salient object detection: input image (a), detected salient objects (b), and ground truth salient objects (c).

FIGURE 7: Effect of the visual attention parameter p: input image (a), detected salient objects with high values of p (b) and small values of p (c).

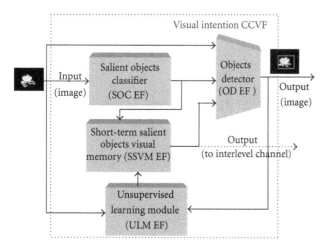

FIGURE 8: Bloc diagram of visional intention CCVF.

The final saliency map samples are shown on the column d of Figure 5:

$$M_{\text{final}}(x) = \begin{cases} D(x) & \text{if } M(x) < D(x), \\ \sqrt{M(x)D(x)} & \text{otherwise.} \end{cases} \quad (8)$$

Accordingly to segmentation and detection algorithms described in [30, 33], the segmentation splits an image into a set of chromatically coherent regions. Objects present on the scene are composed of one or multiple such segments. For visually salient objects, the segments forming them should cover areas of saliency map with high overall saliency, while visually unimportant objects and background should have this measure comparatively low. Conformably to [33], input image is thus segmented into connected subsets of pixels or segments $(S_1, S_2, \ldots, S_n)$. For each one of the found segments S_i (where $S_i \in \{S_1, S_2, \ldots, S_n\}$), its average saliency $\overline{S_i}$ and variance (of saliency values) $\text{Var}(S_i)$ are computed over the final saliency map $M_{\text{final}}(x)$. All the pixel values $p(x, y) \in S_i p(z, y)$ of the segment are then set following (9), where $\tau_{\overline{S_i}}$ and τ_{Var} are thresholds for average saliency and its variance, respectively. The result is a binary map containing a set of connected components $C = \{C_1, C_2, \ldots, C_n\}$ formed by adjacent segments S_i evaluated by (9) as binary value "1". To remove noise, a membership condition is imposed that any $C_i \in C$ has its area larger than a given threshold. Finally, the binary map is projected on the original image leading to a result that is part (areas) of the original image containing its salient objects. References [33, 34] give different values for the aforementioned parameters and thresholds:

$$p(x, y) = \begin{cases} 1 & \text{if } \overline{S_i} > \tau_{\overline{S_i}}, \ \text{Var}(S_i) > \tau_{\text{Var}}, \\ 0 & \text{otherwise.} \end{cases} \quad (9)$$

Figure 5 shows examples of global and local saliency features extracted from two images. In the first image the global salient feature (upper image of column b) is enough to track salient objects, while for the second, where the salient object (leopard) is partially available, chromatic saliency is not enough to extract the object. Figures 6 and 7 show examples

Multilevel Cognitive Machine-Learning-Based Concept for Artificial Awareness: Application to Humanoid
Robot Awareness Using Visual Saliency

115

FIGURE 9: NAO robot camera issued images (upper images) and corresponding salient objects found and segmented by NAO (lower images).

FIGURE 10: Results relative to a set of objects detection by robot.

of salient object detection as well as effect of the visual attention parameter p on extracted salient regions, respectively.

4.2. Visual Intention CCVF. As it has previously been stated, composed of conscious cognitive visual functions (CCVFs), the conscious visual level conducts intentional visual tasks. One of the core functions of this level is "visual intention" CCVF, proffering the robot some kind of "artificial visual intention ability" and allowing the machine to construct its first knowledge about the surrounding environment. Figure 8 gives the bloc diagram of visional intention CCVF. As it could be seen from this figure, this CCVF is composed of four elementary functions: "short-term salient objects visual memory" (SSVM) EF, "unsupervised learning module" (ULM) EF, "salient objects classifier" (SOC) EF, and "object detector" (OD) EF.

The main task of short-term salient objects visual memory (SSVM) EF is to provide already known objects and store currently recognized or detected salient objects. It could also be seen as the first knowledge construction of surrounding environment because it contains the clusters of salient objects resulting from unsupervised learning. Its content (e.g., stored salient objects or groups of salient objects) could supply the main knowledge base (a long-term memory). That is why its output is also connected to interlevel channel.

The role of unsupervised learning (performed by ULM EF) is to cluster the detected (new) salient objects. The learning process is carried out on line. When an agent (e.g., robot) takes images while it encounters a new object, if the objects are recognized to be salient (e.g., extracted) they are grouped incrementally while new images are acquired.

The action flow of the learning process is given below. In the first time, the algorithm classifies each found fragment, and, in a second time, the learning process is updated (online learning)

```
acquire image
extract fragments by salient object
detector
for each fragment F
  if(F is classified into one group)
    populate the group by F
  if(F is classified into multiple
groups)
    populate by F the closest group by
Euclidian distance of features
    if(F is not classified to any group)
      create a new group and place F
inside
select the most populated group G
use fragments from G as learning samples
for object detection algorithm
```

The salient objects classifier is a combination of four weak classifiers $\{w_1, w_2, w_3, w_4\}$, each classifying a fragment as belonging or not belonging to a certain class. F denotes the currently processed fragment, and G denotes an instance of the group in question. The first classifier w_1, defined by (10), separates fragments with too different areas. In experiments $t_{area} = 10$. The w_2, defined by (11), separates fragments whose aspects are too different to belong to the same object.

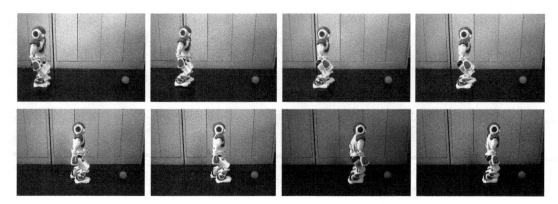

FIGURE 11: Results relative to an intentional object tracking: the robot tracks a red ball moving toward it.

In experiments, t_{aspect} has been set to 0.3. The classifier w_3, defined by (12), separates fragments with clearly different chromaticity. It works over 2D normalized histograms of ϕ and θ component denoted by $G_{\phi\theta}$ and $F_{\phi\theta}$, respectively, with L bins, calculating their intersection. We use $L = 32$ to avoid too sparse histogram and $t_{\phi\theta}$ equal to 0.35. Finally, w_4 (defined by (13)) separates fragments whose texture is too different. We use the measure of texture uniformity calculated over the l channel of fragment. $p(z_i)$, where $i \in \{0, 1, 2, \ldots, L - 1\}$, is a normalized histogram of l channel of the fragment, and L is the number of histogram bins. In experiments, 32 histogram bins have been used to avoid too sparse histogram and value $t_{\text{uniformity}}$ of 0.02. A fragment belongs to a class if $\prod_{i=1}^{n} w_i = 1$:

$$w_1 = \begin{cases} 1 & \text{if } c_{w1} < t_{\text{area}}, \\ 0 & \text{otherwise}, \end{cases} \quad c_{w1} = \frac{\max(G_{\text{area}}, F_{\text{area}})}{\min(G_{\text{area}}, F_{\text{area}})}, \quad (10)$$

$$w_2 = \begin{cases} 1 & \text{if } c_{w2} < t_{\text{aspect}}, \\ 0 & \text{otherwise}, \end{cases}$$

$$c_{w2} = \left\| \log\left(\frac{G_{\text{width}}}{G_{\text{hight}}}\right) - \log\left(\frac{F_{\text{width}}}{F_{\text{hight}}}\right) \right\|, \quad (11)$$

$$w_3 = \begin{cases} 1 & \text{if } c_{w3} < t_{\phi\theta}, \\ 0 & \text{otherwise}, \end{cases} \text{ with}$$

$$c_{w3} = \frac{\sum_{j=1}^{L-1} \sum_{k=1}^{L-1} \min\left(G_{\phi\theta}(j, k) - F_{\phi\theta}(j, k)\right)}{L^2}, \quad (12)$$

$$w_4 = \begin{cases} 1 & \text{if } c_{w4} < t_{\text{uniformity}}, \\ 0 & \text{otherwise}, \end{cases}$$

$$c_{w4} = \left\| \sum_{j=0}^{L-1} p_G^2(z_j) - \sum_{k=0}^{L-1} p_F^2(z_k) \right\|. \quad (13)$$

4.3. Implementation on Real Robot and Experimental Validation. The above-described concept has been implemented on NAO robot, which includes vision devices and a number of onboard preimplemented motion skills. It also includes a number of basic standard functions that have not been used. For experimental verification, the robot has been introduced in a real environment with different common objects (representing different surface, shapes, and properties). Several objects were exposed in robots field of view, presented in a number of contexts different from those used in the learning phase. The number of images acquired for each object varied between 100 and 600 for learning sequences and between 50 and 300 for testing sequences, with multiple objects occurring on the same scene. During the learning process, the success rate of 96% has been achieved concerning pertinent learned objects (e.g., those identified by the robot as salient and then learned), that is, only 4% of image fragments were associated with wrong groups. During the testing process, objects were correctly extracted reaching 82% success rate.

To demonstrate real-time abilities of the system, the NAO robot was required to find some learned objects in its environment and then to track them. It is pertinent to emphasize that those objects have been learned in different environment. A sample of results of those experiments is shown in Figures 9 to 12. Figures 9 and 10 show results relating robot ability to detect and extract salient objects from its surrounding environment. It is pertinent to notice the multiple salient objects detection ability of the implemented strategy representing different shapes and various natures. Figure 11 shows the expected robot ability to detect and to follow a simple object in real environment, validating the correct operation of unconscious and intentional cognitive levels transitions in accomplishing the required task. Finally, Figure 12 shows the robot ability to detect, isolate, and follow a previously detected and learned salient object in a complex surrounding environment. The video of this experiment could be seen using the link indicated in the legend of this figure. It is pertinent to emphasize the fact that the object (a "book" in the experiment shown by the Figure 12) has been detected and learned in different conditions (as one could see this from the above-indicated video). Thus, this experiment shows the emergence of a kind of robot "artificial awareness" about the surrounding environment validating the presented cognitive multilevel concept and issued "perception-motion" architecture.

Multilevel Cognitive Machine-Learning-Based Concept for Artificial Awareness: Application to Humanoid Robot Awareness Using Visual Saliency

117

FIGURE 12: Tracking a previously learned moving object (upper images: video http://www.youtube.com/watch?v=xxz3wm3L1pE). The upper right corner of each image shows robot camera picture.

5. Conclusion

By supplanting the modeling of robots complex behavior from the "control theory" backdrop to the "cognitive machine learning" backcloth, the proposed machine-learning-based multilevel cognitive motion-perception concept attempts to offer a unified model of robot autonomous evolution, slotting in two kinds of cognitive levels: "unconscious" and "conscious" cognitive levels, answerable of its reflexive and intentional visual and motor skills, respectively.

The first key advantage of conceptualizing the problem within such incline is to detach the build-up of robot perception and motion from the type of machine (robot). The second chief benefit of the concept is that the issued structure is "machine-learning-" based foundation taking advantage from "learning" capacity and "generalization" propensity of such models.

The "visual intention" built-in CCVF proffers the robot artificial visual intention ability and allows it to construct the knowledge about the surrounding environment. This intentional cognitive function holds out the robot awareness regarding its surrounding environment. The extracted knowledge is first stored in (and recalled from) short-term memory. It could then be stored in a long-term memory proffering the robot some kind of learning issued knowledge about previously (already) explored environments or already known objects in a new environment. Beside this appealing ability, the unconscious visual level realizing the salient objects detection plays a key role in the so-called "artificial awareness" emergence. In fact, the ability of automatic detection of pertinent items in surrounding environment proffers the robot some kind of "unconscious awareness" about potentially significant objects in the surrounding environment. The importance of this key skill appears not only in emergence of "intentional awareness" but also in construction of new knowledge (versus the already learned items) upgrading the robot (or machine's) awareness regarding its surrounding environment.

References

[1] E. R. Westervelt, G. Buche, and J. W. Grizzle, "Experimental validation of a framework for the design of controllers that induce stable walking in planar bipeds," *International Journal of Robotics Research*, vol. 23, no. 6, pp. 559–582, 2004.

[2] J. H. Park and O. Kwon, "Reflex control of biped robot locomotion on a slippery surface," in *Proceedings of the IEEE International Conference on Robotics and Automation (ICRA '01)*, pp. 4134–4139, May 2001.

[3] J. Chestnutt and J. J. Kuffner, "A tiered planning strategy for biped navigation," in *Proceedings of the 4th IEEE-RAS International Conference on Humanoid Robots (Humanoids '04)*, vol. 1, pp. 422–436, November 2004.

[4] Q. Huang, K. Yokoi, S. Kajita et al., "Planning walking patterns for a biped robot," *IEEE Transactions on Robotics and Automation*, vol. 17, no. 3, pp. 280–289, 2001.

[5] K. Sabe, M. Fukuchi, J. S. Gutmann, T. Ohashi, K. Kawamoto, and T. Yoshigahara, "Obstacle avoidance and path planning for humanoid robots using stereo vision," in *Proceedings of the IEEE International Conference on Robotics and Automation (ICRA '4)*, pp. 592–597, May 2004.

[6] R. Holmes, *Acts of War: The Behavior of Men in Battle*, The Free Press, New York, NY, USA, 1st American edition, 1985.

[7] M. Tambe, W. L. Johnson, R. M. Jones et al., "Intelligent agents for interactive simulation environments," *AI Magazine*, vol. 16, no. 1, pp. 15–40, 1995.

[8] P. Langley, "An abstract computational model of learning selective sensing skills," in *Proceedings of the 18th Conference of the Cognitive Science Society*, pp. 385–390, 1996.

[9] C. Bauckhage, C. Thurau, and G. Sagerer, "Learning human-like opponent behavior for interactive computer games," *Lecture Notes in Computer Science*, vol. 2781, pp. 148–155, 2003.

[10] V. Potkonjak, D. Kostic, S. Tzafestas, M. Popovic, M. Lazarevic, and G. Djordjevic, "Human-like behavior of robot arms: general considerations and the handwriting task—part II: the robot arm in handwriting," *Robotics and Computer-Integrated Manufacturing*, vol. 17, no. 4, pp. 317–327, 2001.

[11] J. Edlund, J. Gustafson, M. Heldner, and A. Hjalmarsson, "Towards human-like spoken dialogue systems," *Speech Communication*, vol. 50, no. 8-9, pp. 630–645, 2008.

[12] A. Lubin, N. Poirel, S. Rossi, A. Pineau, and O. Houdé, "Math in actions: actor mode reveals the true arithmetic abilities of french-speaking 2-year-olds in a magic task," *Journal of Experimental Child Psychology*, vol. 103, no. 3, pp. 376–385, 2009.

[13] F. A. Campbell, E. P. Pungello, S. Miller-Johnson, M. Burchinal, and C. T. Ramey, "The development of cognitive and academic abilities: growth curves from an early childhood educational experiment," *Developmental Psychology*, vol. 37, no. 2, pp. 231–242, 2001.

[14] G. Leroux, M. Joliot, S. Dubal, B. Mazoyer, N. Tzourio-Mazoyer, and O. Houdé, "Cognitive inhibition of number/length interference in a Piaget-like task in young adults: evidence from ERPs and fMRI," *Human Brain Mapping*, vol. 27, no. 6, pp. 498–509, 2006.

[15] A. Lubin, N. Poirel, S. Rossi, C. Lanoë, A. Pineau, and O. Houdé, "Pedagogical effect of action on arithmetic performances in Wynn-like tasks solved by 2-year-olds," *Experimental Psychology*, vol. 57, no. 6, pp. 405–411, 2010.

[16] O. C. S. Cassell, M. Hubble, M. A. P. Milling, and W. A. Dickson, "Baby walkers—still a major cause of infant burns," *Burns*, vol. 23, no. 5, pp. 451–453, 1997.

[17] M. Crouchman, "The effects of babywalkers on early locomotor development," *Developmental Medicine and Child Neurology*, vol. 28, no. 6, pp. 757–761, 1986.

[18] A. Siegel and R. Burton, "Effects of babywalkers on early locomotor development in human infants," *Developmental & Behavioral Pediatrics*, vol. 20, pp. 355–361, 1999.

[19] I. B. Kauffman and M. Ridenour, "Influence of an infant walker on onset and quality of walking pattern of locomotion: an electromyographic investigation," *Perceptual and Motor Skills*, vol. 45, no. 3, pp. 1323–1329, 1977.

[20] J. A. Andersen, *An Introduction to Neural Network*, MIT Press, Cambridge, Mass, USA, 1995.

[21] K. Madani and C. Sabourin, "Multi-level cognitive machine-learning based concept for human-like "artificial" walking: application to autonomous stroll of humanoid robots," *Neurocomputing*, vol. 74, no. 8, pp. 1213–1228, 2011.

[22] H. Bülthoff, C. Wallraven, and M. Giese, "Perceptual robotic," in *Handbook of Robotics*, B. Siciliano and O. Khatib, Eds., Springer, 2007.

[23] http://www.universcience-vod.fr/media/577/la-marche-des-bebes.html.

[24] P. Zukow-Goldring and M. A. Arbib, "Affordances, effectivities, and assisted imitation: caregivers and the directing of attention," *Neurocomputing*, vol. 70, no. 13–15, pp. 2181–2193, 2007.

[25] R. J. Brand, D. A. Baldwin, and L. A. Ashburn, "Evidence for "motionese": modifications in mothers' infant-directed action," *Developmental Science*, vol. 5, no. 1, pp. 72–83, 2002.

[26] R. Achanta, S. Hemami, E. Estrada, and S. Susstrunk, "Frequency-tuned salient region detection," in *Proceedings of the IEEE International Conference on Computer Vision and Pattern Recognition (CVPR '09)*, 2009.

[27] J. M. Wolfe and T. S. Horowitz, "What attributes guide the deployment of visual attention and how do they do it?" *Nature Reviews Neuroscience*, vol. 5, no. 6, pp. 495–501, 2004.

[28] T. W. Chen, Y. L. Chen, and S. Y. Chien, "Fast image segmentation based on K-means clustering with histograms in HSV color space," in *Proceedings of the IEEE 10th Workshop on Multimedia Signal Processing (MMSP '08)*, pp. 322–325, October 2008.

[29] X. Hou and L. Zhang, "Saliency detection: a spectral residual approach," in *Proceedings of the IEEE Conference on Computer Vision and Pattern Recognition (CVPR'07)*, vol. 2, pp. 1–8, June 2007.

[30] R. Moreno, M. Graña, D. M. Ramik, and K. Madani, "Image segmentation by spherical coordinates," in *Proceedings of the 11th International Conference on Pattern Recognition and Information Processing (PRIP '11)*, pp. 112–115, 2011.

[31] J. H. Holland, *Adaptation in Natural anti Artificial Systems: An introductory Analysis with Applications to Biology, Control and Artificial Intelligence*, MIT Press, 1992.

[32] T. Liu, Z. Yuan, J. Sun et al., "Learning to detect a salient object," *IEEE Transactions on Pattern Analysis and Machine Intelligence*, vol. 33, no. 2, pp. 353–367, 2011.

[33] D. M. Ramík, C. Sabourin, and K. Madani, "Hybrid salient object extraction approach with automatic estimation of visual attention scale," in *Proceedings of the 7th International Conference on Signal Image Technology & Internet-Based Systems (IEEE—SITIS '11)*, pp. 438–445, 2011.

[34] D. M. Ramík, C. Sabourin, and K. Madani, "A cognitive approach for robots' vision using unsupervised learning and visual saliency," in *Advances in Computational Intelligence*, vol. 6691 of *LNCS*, pp. 65–72, Springer, 2011.

13

Neural Behavior Chain Learning of Mobile Robot Actions

Lejla Banjanovic-Mehmedovic,[1] **Dzenisan Golic,**[2]
Fahrudin Mehmedovic,[3] **and Jasna Havic**[4]

[1] Faculty of Electrical Engineering, University of Tuzla, 75000 Tuzla, Bosnia and Herzegovina
[2] Infonet, 75000 Tuzla, Bosnia and Herzegovina
[3] ABB, 75000 Tuzla, Bosnia and Herzegovina
[4] General Secretariat Council of Ministers of B&H, 71000 Sarajevo, Bosnia and Herzegovina

Correspondence should be addressed to Lejla Banjanovic-Mehmedovic, lejla.mehmedovic@untz.ba

Academic Editor: R. Saravanan

This paper presents a visual/motor behavior learning approach, based on neural networks. We propose Behavior Chain Model (BCM) in order to create a way of behavior learning. Our behavior-based system evolution task is a mobile robot detecting a target and driving/acting towards it. First, the mapping relations between the image feature domain of the object and the robot action domain are derived. Second, a multilayer neural network for offline learning of the mapping relations is used. This learning structure through neural network training process represents a connection between the visual perceptions and motor sequence of actions in order to grip a target. Last, using behavior learning through a noticed action chain, we can predict mobile robot behavior for a variety of similar tasks in similar environment. Prediction results suggest that the methodology is adequate and could be recognized as an idea for designing different mobile robot behaviour assistance.

1. Introduction

The robotics research covers a wide range of application scenarios, from industrial or service robots up to robotic assistance for disabled or elderly people. Robots in industry, mining, agriculture, space exploration, and health sciences are just a few examples of challenging applications where human attributes such as cognition, perception, and intelligence can play an important role. Inducing perception and cognition, and thence the intelligentsia into robotics machines is the main aim in constructing a robot, able to "think" and operate in uncertain and unstructured conditions.

To successfully realize the instruction capability (e.g., object manipulation, haptically guided teleoperation, robot surgery manipulation, etc.), a robot must extract relevant input/output control signals from the manipulation system task in order to learn the control sequences necessary for task execution [1]. The concept of the visual-motor mapping, which describes the relationship between visually perceived features and the motor signals necessary to act, is very popular in robotics [2]. There are many visual-motor mappings, defined between cameras and a robot. Since the large variation of visual inputs makes it nearly impossible to represent explicitly the sequence of actions, such knowledge must be obtained from a set of machine learning technique examples [3]. A robot fulfils appropriate purposes using its learning and prediction skills.

Predictive strategy in robotics may be implemented in the following ways [4, 5].

(i) Model-based reinforcement learning. The environment model is learnt, in addition to reinforcement values.

(ii) Schema mechanism. A model is represented by rules and learnt bottom-up by generating more specialized rules where necessary.

(iii) The expectancy model. Reinforcement is only propagated once a desired state is generated by a behavioral module and the propagation is accomplished using dynamic programming techniques, applied to the learnt predictive model and sign list.

(iv) Anticipatory learning classifier systems. Similar to the schema mechanism and expectancy model, they contain an explicit prediction component. The predictive model consists of a set of rules (classifiers) which are endowed with an "effect" part, to predict the next situation the agent will encounter if the action specified by the rules is executed. These systems are able for generalization over the sensory input.

(v) Artificial neural network (ANN). The agent controller sends outputs to the actuators, based on sensory inputs. Learning to control the agent consists of learning to associate the good set of outputs to any set of inputs that the agent may experience. The most common way to perform such learning is through using the back-propagation algorithm.

The learning trajectory in the context of programming by demonstration through reinforcement learning is presented under [6]. A visual servobehavior for a real mobile robot, learned through a trial and error method and by using reinforcement learning, is demonstrated under [7].

Different forms of visual-based learning are presented in [8], in each of which the visual perception is tightly coupled with actuator effects, so as to learn an adequate behavior. Learning several behaviors, such as obstacle avoidance or target pursuit through motion sketch, are some of the examples.

The paper [9] deals with the visually guided grasping of unmodeled objects for robots which exhibit an experience-based adaptive behavior. The features are computed from the object image and the kinematics of a hand. Real experimental data on a humanoid robot is employed by a classification strategy, based on the k-nearest neighbor estimation rule, to predict the reliability of a grasp configuration.

In [10], results are presented from experiments with a visually guided four wheeled mobile robot carrying out perceptual judgment based on visual-motor anticipation to exhibit the ability to understand a spatial arrangement of obstacles in its behavioral meaning. The robot learns a forward model by moving randomly within arrangements of obstacles and observing the changing visual input. For perceptual judgment, the robot stands still, observes a single image, and internally simulates the changing images, given a sequence of movement commands (wheel speeds), as specified by a certain movement plan. With this simulation, the robot judges the distance to a frontal obstacle and recognizes, in the arrangement of obstacles, either a dead end or passage. Images are predicted using a set of multilayer perceptrons, where each pixel is computed by a three-layer perceptron.

The perception-action scheme for visually guided manipulation that includes mechanisms for visual predictions and detecting unexpected events by comparisons between the anticipated feedback and incoming feedback is proposed under [11]. Anticipated visual perceptions are based on motor commands and the associated proprioception of the robotic manipulator. If the system prediction is correct, full processing of the sensory input is not needed at this stage. Only when expected perceptions do not match the incoming sensory data, a full perceptual processing is activated.

Artificial neural networks (ANN), as universal approximators, are capable of modeling complex mappings between the inputs and outputs of a system up to an arbitrary precision. The ALVINN example illustrates the power of standard feed-forward networks, as well as their limitations. The control network solved a difficult pattern recognition task, which required complex image preprocessing, the use of line extraction algorithms, and so forth, if programmed by a human designer. However, due to its use of a feed-forward network, the ALVINN is a reactive system. This means that it has no notion of the temporal aspects of its task and will always react to its visual input in the same fashion, regardless of the current context [12].

The situation, however, changes fundamentally, as soon as the artificial neural networks are used as robot controllers; that is, the network could, by means of the robot body (sensors and effectors), interact with the physical objects in its environment, independent of an observer's interpretation or mediation. In [13], the recurrent control networks (RNN) have analyzed and shown that they utilize their internal state (i.e., the hidden unit activation values) to carry out behavioral sequences corresponding to particular motion strategies instead of merely reacting to the current input. The RNNs play a central role in such approaches to the study of cognitive representation. This is because they account for the (long-term) representation of learning experience in the connection weights, as well as the (short-term) representation of the controlled agent's current context or immediate past in the form of internal feedback. But, every task solved by a higher-order RNN could also be solved by some first-order net [14].

The various forms of the neurologically inspired RNN networks were referred to in literature in recent years. For example, a continuous recurrent neural network (CTRNN) was implemented in a humanoid robot for object-manipulation tasks [15]. The proposed network is designed to learn and to regenerate trained visual-proprioceptive sensation sequences, which we assume to correspond to a similar activity in the parietal cortex. Its feature is learning spatial-temporal structures in a continuous time and space domain. The latest biological observations of the brain served as an inspiration for developing Multiple Timescales Recurrent Neural Networks (MTRNN) [16]. The initial testing of the MTRNN model is on iCub humanoid robot, which is able to replicate sequences of manipulating the object.

The most important factor of robot assistance by the behavior sequence learning is the design of interface between neural network and sensors/actuators. Although an ANN could theoretically adapt to different representations of sensor/actuator interfaces, it was necessary to find an interface with low cognitive complexity for the ANN [17].

This paper presents the behavior description, which emphasizes the repetition of numbering in a sequence of actions, noticed as Behavior Chain Learning. In our research, using the characteristics of neural networks, the system learns the necessary set of actions for movement of a mobile

FIGURE 1: Experimental mobile robot with gripped target.

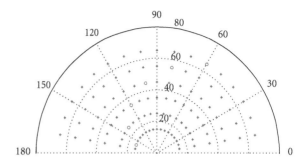

+ Ball position (training data)
+ Ball position (training data)
○ Ball position (prediction data)

FIGURE 2: Initial target position for experimantal setup.

robot in order to access the object in space of observation. On the basis of such trained and tested network, the prediction set of robotic actions for new scenarios of object recognition is constructed. The learned motions can be applied in similar circumstances. Our approach is easily scalable for other applications.

2. Robot Behavior Setting

Our approach focuses on a behavioral system that learns to correlate visual information with motor commands in order to guide a robot towards a target. We chose this task setting, because this approach can be useful for any form of visual/motor coordination, so the task specification can be reformulated as a variety of behavioral responses.

Figure 1 shows an experimental mobile robot platform Boe-Bot by Parallax, with CMUcam1 AppMod vision system for tracking color task.

This camera can detect stationary and moving objects. CMUcam1 is an SX28 microcontroller, interfaced with OV6620 Omnivision CMOS camera on a chip. The mobile robot has a gripper, whose length is 12 cm, and it serves him to grip the ball. The gripper length specifies that it must stop at a distance of 9–13 cm in front of the target.

The robot is in the center of environment and the ball could be at any position in front of robot with respective angle in scope (0–180°). An interaction between the visual perception and motor behavior (a sequence of actions) is obtained through the real-time visual 2D tracking routines.

Figure 2 shows all ball positions, for which the sequences of actions are experimentally determined.

The robot is able to find the ball by turning A_0 from its starting position until it enters robot's field of view, after which the robot can reliably track red color of the ball while driving toward it. In the environment without obstacles, the robot selects possible actions in sequence due visual tracking: A_0—turning from its starting position until the object is in robots field of view, A_1—turning left by 10°, A_2—turning right by 10°, A_3—translate straight away, A_4—stop moving.

The behavior mobile robot scheme consists of the following stages: (1) vision processing involves detecting features, such as color or spatial and temporal intensity gradients;

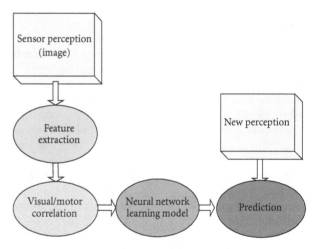

FIGURE 3: Behavior mobile robot scheme.

(2) obtaining the fundamental relationship between visual information and robot motions by correlating visual patterns and motion commands; (3) mobile robot behavior of learning to grip a target; (4) prediction of motor actions for new visual perceptions, Figure 3.

3. Visual Detection of Features

In the first phase, visual detection of features is made on the basis of a specific data set from the camera's streaming video sent to the mobile robot. Centre of the mass (RCVData(2)), number of pixels within the window (RCVData(8)), and data reliability regarding the color (RCVData(9)) are specific parameters from image.

When the object is positioned in middle of robot' camera window, the variable called RCVData(2) has value 45. Possible action selections are represented in (Pseudocode 1). For example, if we get RCVData(2) greater than 55 and data reliability regarding the color (RCVData(9)) greater than 25, the object is left of the centre. In that case, the robot needs to turn to the left.

```
Step 1: Start, Move = 0
Step 2: Send command "Track Color" in order to get back
the array of the data
if (RCVData(2) > 55 & RCVData(9) > 25) then
    Move = 1; A₁ action (move of the robot to the left)
else if (RCVData(2) < 35 & RCVData(9) > 25) then
    Move = 1; A₂ action (move of the robot to the right)
else if (RCVData(8) < 140 & RCVData(9) > 25) then
    Move = 1; A₃ action (move of the robot straight ahead)
else if RCVData(8) > 140 then
    Move = 1, A₄ action (stop the move)
else if Move = 0 then
    A₁ action (move of the robot to the left)
else go to Step 2.
```

PSEUDOCODE 1: Pseudocod of action creating.

4. Behavior Chain Model

The behaviors can be implemented as a Finite State Acceptor (FSA) [18], which describes aggregations and sequences of behaviors. They make explicit the behaviors active at any given time and the transitions between them. FSA is best used to specify complex behavioral control systems where entire sets of primitive behaviors are swapped in and out of execution during the accomplishment of some high-level goal.

We propose Behavior Chain Model (BCM) in order to generalize the form to cope with a variety of similar tasks in similar environment. Each change in action type presents a behavior changing. For example, each time, when the human starts to do something new, it starts to counter (we counter feet in one directions and then change direction or when cooking, we counter spoons, before mixing, etc.). This is inspiration for introducing a formal definition of this behavior model.

BCM consists of: (1) creating of behavior chain from a sequence of actions and (2) extracting physical variables using behavior transform function. We introduce next definitions:

Definition 1. The behavior of system S, which consists of sequence of N behavior actions

$$S_A = \left(A_i, A_i, A_j, A_j, \ldots, A_N\right) \tag{1}$$

with k_i repetitions of same action type in continuous sequence of N actions that can be described by Behavior Chain C_B, that is, with chain coefficients $k_i, i = 1, \ldots, m$:

$$C_B = (k_1, k_2, \ldots, k_m). \tag{2}$$

We introduce a formal definition of the behavior transform function, which give us variables from mathematical description of real problem.

Definition 2. The system behavior transform function F_B

$$F_B : C_B \longrightarrow \Psi \tag{3}$$

transforms chain coefficients $k_i, i = 1, \ldots, m$ in physical variables $(\xi_1, \ldots, \xi_J), J < m$

$$(\xi_1, \ldots, \xi_J) = F_B(k_1, k_2, \ldots, k_m), \tag{4}$$

where

$$\xi_1 = f_B^1(k_1, k_2, \ldots, k_m),$$

$$\xi_2 = f_B^2(k_1, k_2, \ldots, k_m)$$

$$\cdots \tag{5}$$

$$\xi_J = f_B^J(k_1, k_2, \ldots, k_m),$$

$$J < N.$$

For our behavior model, we introduce the coefficients, which counts changing actions:

(i) k_1 = sum of (numbers of repeated turns) in initial position, before (A_0) and after detecting the ball by camera $(A_1$ or $A_2)$;

(ii) k_2 = number of repeated translations straight away from the starting point to new point $(A_3$ in sequence);

(iii) k_3 = number of repeated new turns $(A_1$ or A_2 in sequence);

(iv) k_4 = number of repeated new translations straight away $(A_3$ in sequence).

In case of more changing of action repetitions (longer target distances or environment with obstacles), we can introduce more coefficients $k_1, k_2, \ldots, k_m$, with which we can describe a system's behavior.

One example of creating of behavior chain is presented in Figure 4.

Table 1 contains only one part of experimental results, with the coordinates of the ball position, number of turnings from its starting position until target is found in its field of view and a sequence of actions, which the mobile robot must take to target. Consider first example of action's sequence for

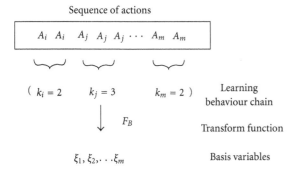

FIGURE 4: Creating of behavior chain.

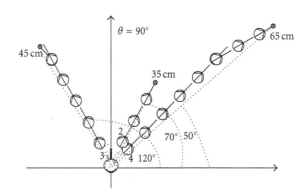

FIGURE 5: Experimental robot scenario.

TABLE 1: Examples of correlating behavior sequence of actions.

Position (ρ, θ)	Turning A_0	Sequence of actions
(55, 170)	6	$A_1 A_3 A_1 A_3 A_3 A_3 A_3 A_3 A_3$
(35, 160)	5	$A_1 A_1 A_3 A_3 A_3$
(15, 150)	3	$A_1 A_1$
(25, 140)	3	$A_1 A_3 A_1 A_3$
(45, 130)	2	$A_1 A_3 A_3 A_3 A_3 A_3$
(45, 120)	1	$A_1 A_1 A_3 A_3 A_3 A_3 A_3 A_1$
(65, 110)	1	$A_1 A_3 A_3 A_3 A_3 A_3 A_3 A_3 A_1 A_3 A_3$
(25, 100)	0	$A_1 A_3 A_3$
(65, 90)	0	$A_3 A_3 A_3 A_3 A_3 A_3 A_3 A_3 A_3$
(55, 80)	0	$A_2 A_3 A_3 A_3 A_3 A_3$
(35, 70)	0	$A_2 A_2 A_3 A_3 A_3$
(45, 60)	1	$A_2 A_2 A_3 A_3 A_3 A_3$
(65, 50)	3	$A_2 A_3 A_3 A_3 A_3 A_3 A_3 A_2 A_3 A_3$
(25, 40)	2	$A_2 A_2 A_3$
(15, 30)	3	$A_2 A_3$
(45, 20)	6	$A_2 A_2 A_3 A_3 A_3 A_3 A_2 A_3$
(65, 10)	6	$A_2 A_2 A_3 A_3 A_3 A_3 A_3 A_2 A_3 A_3 A_3$

ball position (55 cm, 170°) in polar coordinate system. First, the mobile robot made $A_0 = 6$ turning by 10° to the left until it detects the ball, then robot rotates again by 10° to the left, then goes straight away (action A_3), then turns again by 10° left (action A_1) and goes straight away (six repetition of action A_3).

A turn to the left has a positive value, while a turn to the right has a negative value in an action matrix. In the this example of ball position (55, 170°), a sequence of actions is presented with the following Behavior Chain:

$$C_B(50, 170) = (k_1, k_2, k_3, k_4) = (7, 1, 1, 6). \tag{6}$$

In the example of ball position (65, 50°), a sequence of actions is presented with the following Behavior Chain:

$$C_B(65, 50) = (k_1, k_2, k_3, k_4) = (-4, 6, -1, 2). \tag{7}$$

The examples of mobile robot's behaviors for some ball positions ((65 cm, 50°), (35 cm, 70°), and (45 cm, 120°)) are presented on Figure 5.

For example, the mobile robot position in polar system is presented with (d, α). We need transforming process which

gives us variables from the mathematical description of a real problem. This transforming process presents second phase of LBCM model.

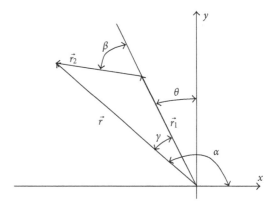

FIGURE 6: Mobile robot positioning.

5. Mathematical Model of Mobile Robot Positioning

In order to calculate the positions (d, α) where a mobile robot comes, we use the mathematical model of mobile robot positioning presented below. In an experiment, we got the sequence of robot motor actions, for given object positions (Figure 6).

In our approach, one turn is 10 degrees ($\theta = 10k_1$, $\beta = 10k_3$). For those object positions in environment, which a mobile robot need to recognize visualy, the vector distance of the mobile robot can be approximated by a superposition of two vectors $\vec{r_1}$ and $\vec{r_2}$, whose intensities are determined by the expressions $|\vec{r_1}| = 6k_2$, $|\vec{r_2}| = 6k_4$ (translation step is 6 cm):

$$d = \vec{r} = \sqrt{|\vec{r_1}|^2 + |\vec{r_2}|^2 - 2|\vec{r_1}||\vec{r_2}|\cos(180 - \beta)},$$
$$d = 6\sqrt{k_2^2 + k_4^2 + 2k_2 k_4 \cos 10k_3}. \tag{8}$$

Angle α is the sum of the angles of the initial turns, the turns after the initial displacement and 90°, that is,

$$\alpha = 90 + \theta + \gamma. \tag{9}$$

From Figure 5, the following relationship is valid:

$$\frac{|\vec{r_2}|}{\sin\gamma} = \frac{d}{\sin(180 - \beta)} \tag{10}$$

or

$$\sin\gamma = \frac{|\vec{r_2}|}{d}\sin(180 - \beta) = \frac{|\vec{r_2}|}{d}\sin\beta = \frac{6k_4}{d}\sin 10k_3. \tag{11}$$

Finally, angle α can be expressed with:

$$\alpha = 90 + 10k_1 + \arcsin\left(\frac{6k_4}{d}\sin 10k_3\right). \tag{12}$$

Using behavior transform function

$$(\xi_1, \xi_2) = (d, \alpha) = F_B(k_1, k_2, k_3, k_4), \quad J = 2, \tag{13}$$

where

$$d = f_B^1(k_2, k_3, k_4) = 6\sqrt{k_2^2 + k_4^2 + 2k_2k_4\cos 10k_3},$$

$$\alpha = f_B^2(k_1, k_3, k_4) = 90 + 10k_1 + \arcsin\left(\frac{6k_4}{d}\sin 10k_3\right). \tag{14}$$

Table 2 shows some examples of ball positions, for which the mobile robot positions (d, α) are calculated from above mathematical model.

The third phase in our approach is the learning of a sequence of actions, which establishes an appropriate correspondence between the perceived states and actions. The calculated mobile robot positions, based on coefficients extracted from the experimental patterns, will be compared with mobile robot positions (d_{NN}, α_{NN}), based on a neural learned coefficient, serving for prediction purposes.

6. Robot Behavior Learning

Based on artificial cognition, a robot system can simulate goal-directed human behavior and significantly increase the conformity with human expectations [19]. Our approach stresses the creation of behavior chain from a sequence of actions. To achieve visually guided pointing, our task learns mapping from ball coordinates (ρ, θ) to the mobile robot motor commands, presented with Behavior Chain $C_B = (k_1, k_2, k_3, k_4)$, necessary to achieve these locations. To simplify the dimensionality problems, mobile robot positions are specified as a linear combination of vector primitives, formed from S_A parameters. This form of mapping is exemplified by the neural learning, which leads a robot's prediction ability. After some experiments with different neural network's structures, trained with backpropagation learning algorithm, we used the feed-forward multilayer network with Levenberg-Marquardt (LM) learning algorithm.

A set of input data consists of $N = 102$ target samples (ρ, θ) and a sequence of actions from its starting position to a point from which it is possible to pick up the ball. The collected data are divided into three subsamples, train

TABLE 2: Description examples of behavior sequence of actions.

(ρ, θ)	k_1	k_2	k_3	k_4	d	α
(55, 170)	7	1	1	6	42	169
(35, 160)	7	3	0	0	18	160
(15, 150)	5	0	0	0	0	140
(25, 140)	4	1	1	1	12	135
(45, 130)	4	5	0	0	30	130
(45, 120)	3	5	1	0	30	120
(65, 110)	2	7	1	2	54	112
(25, 100)	1	2	0	0	12	100
(65, 90)	0	9	0	0	54	90
(55, 80)	−1	6	0	0	36	80
(35, 70)	−2	3	0	0	18	70
(45, 60)	−3	4	0	0	24	60
(65, 50)	−4	6	−1	2	47	45
(25, 40)	−5	1	0	0	6	40
(15, 30)	−6	1	0	0	6	30
(45, 20)	−8	4	−1	1	30	8
(65, 10)	−8	5	−1	3	48	6

TABLE 3: Results of error by different neural network training.

L	N_n	M_{ne}	L_r	Error test (MSE)		Error predict (MSE)		RMS
				E_d	E_α	EP_d	EP_α	
1	10	500	0.001	7.74	7.77	3.29	4.55	4.00
1	10	1000	0.001	5.18	8.48	2.45	4.44	3.76
1	20	500	0.01	5.57	10.5	7.13	3.11	4.07
1	30	500	0.001	38.13	13.6	29.7	8.88	7.30
2	30	500	0.001	5.99	8.65	4.20	14.43	3.89
2	20	500	0.01	5.01	7.77	2.43	4.63	3.63
2	20	1000	0.01	7.57	8.07	3.57	4.43	4.02
2	30	500	0.1	8.52	8.93	4.79	4.30	4.25
2	20	1500	0.1	8.86	736	3.04	4.43	3.80
2	30	1500	0.01	17.62	10.6	3.06	4.30	5.40

samples (63%), test samples (31%), and prediction samples (6%). The feed-forward multilayer network is used for training with one and two hidden layers, with tansig or purelin activation functions and with a total number of neurons in the hidden layers (10, 20, or 30). The output layer of neural network has 4 neurons, which present 4 coefficients of S_A used for calculating (d_{NN}, α_{NN}). A few results are listed in Table 3.

During neural network training, we changed the number of hidden layers (L), the number of neurons in hidden layers (N_n), the maximum number of epochs (M_{ne}), type of activation function in hidden and output layers, and the learning rate (L_r). For each neural network configuration, we calculated MSE (mean square error) between (d, α) and values from neural network learning (d_{NN}, α_{NN}) for both test set and for prediction set, as well as root mean square error (RMS) for the test set. According to the results from Table 3, the best network configuration with a minimum value of root mean square error RMS = 3.63 was selected.

TABLE 4: Selected set of mobile robot positions from experiments and predicted values from neural network learning process.

ρ	15	25	35	45	55	65
θ	160	140	120	100	80	60
Real values of coefficients k_i						
k_1	6	4	3	1	−1	−3
k_2	0	1	3	5	6	8
k_3	0	1	0	0	0	0
k_4	0	1	0	0	0	0
Real values of (d, α)						
d	0	12	18	30	36	48
α	150	135	120	100	80	60
Values of coefficients k_i gained from neural network learning process						
k_1	6.66	5.09	3.05	1.00	−0.68	−2.70
k_2	−0.06	2.10	3.34	4.68	4.92	5.71
k_3	−0.14	0.09	0.02	0.04	−0.22	−0.32
k_4	0.00	−0.34	−0.07	0.48	1.55	2.14
d_{NN} and α_{NN} gained from neural network learning process						
d_{NN}	0.37	10.57	19.65	30.99	38.83	47.09
α_{NN}	149.95	129.83	119.99	100.04	79.46	59.12

We got a minimum root mean square error (RMS) for the three-layer neural network with 20 neurons in hidden layers, learning coefficient 0.01, the activation functions of neurons in hidden and output layers were tansig and purelin, and the training was conducted through 500 epochs.

7. Results of Predictive Behavior

The data collected during the experiments are comprised of a large amount of information. Several analyses can be carried out over this data, especially those regarding the appropriateness and usefulness of the different features. However, we are more interested in the predictive capabilities that can be inferred from these data and the methods that can make the best use of it.

In the fourth phase of our approach, we present prediction results of selected input data using neural network configuration with minimal value of the error (RMS). For each target position from the prediction set, we calculated (d, α) from experiments using mathematical model and compared them with (d_{NN}, α_{NN}), gained from the neural network learning process (Table 4).

Using Table 4, we compare graphically mobile robot's position obtained through an experiment, using mathematical model and from neural network learning.

Figures 7 and 8 presents the different sequences of mobile robot actions towards the target. The path (presented with a red line) is a mobile robot path from mathematical model and the path (presented with blue line) is a mobile robot path, gained from parameters from neural network learning. The difference between the distance to the ball ρ and the distance d (where robot came) exists, because the length of

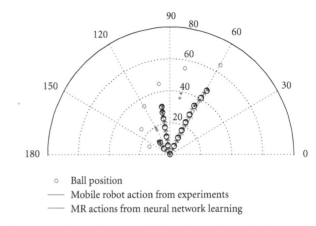

○ Ball position
— Mobile robot action from experiments
— MR actions from neural network learning

FIGURE 7: Experimental mobile robot with tracked target on position $(65, 60)$, $(45, 100)$, and $(25, 140)$.

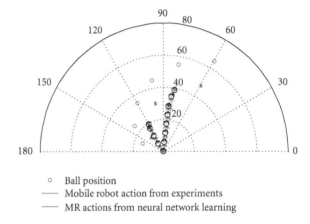

○ Ball position
— Mobile robot action from experiments
— MR actions from neural network learning

FIGURE 8: Experimental mobile robot with tracked target on position $(55, 80)$ and $(35, 120)$.

gripper specifies that robot must stop at 9–13 cm distance of in front of the target.

For example, the target is located at position $(45, 100)$, Figure 7. From its initial position, the mobile robot turned for angle of 10 degrees to the left, that is, $k_1 = 1$. Then, 4 translation actions were made (each by 6 cm), and 4 cm displacement. After that, a turn of $10k_3$ was made (it is an angle of 0.4 degrees), followed by 2.9 cm displacement, and it came in a position to grip a ball.

For example, the target is located at position $(55, 80)$, Figure 8. From its initial position, the mobile robot turned for angle of 6.8 degrees to the right, that is, $k_1 = -0.68$. Then, 4 translation actions (each by 6 cm) were made, including 5.5 cm displacement. After that, a turn of $10k_3$ was made (it is an angle of 2.2 degrees to the right), then 6 cm and 3.3 cm displacements, and then it came in a position to grip a ball.

8. Conclusion

We proposed a methodology which tries to emulate the human action of vision in a general-conceptual way that includes: primary recognition of object in environment, visual-based mobile robot behavior learning, and prediction of new situations. This form of robot learning does not need the knowledge about the environment or kinematics/dynamics of the robot itself, because such knowledge is implicitly embodied in structure of the learning process.

This approach is very flexible and can be applied to a wide variety of problems, because behavior description is "elastic" enough to adapt to various situations. In order to apply our approach to any kind of tasks, we have to solve two important problems. One is how to construct the behavior description of actions and other is how to generalize the learned form to cope with a variety of similar tasks in similar environment.

Although the neural network could theoretically adapt to different representations of sensor/actuator interfaces, it was necessary to find an interface with low cognitive complexity for neural network, which, in our case, was a simple polar representation of the sensors and intended robot movements through "k" parameters. Furthermore, we analyzed the influence of using different sizes and parameters of a multilayer perceptron. While the number of neurons had the smaller effect to the performance, the complete type of representation affected the neural network results.

We have implemented a prediction approach that uses such features to produce reliable output. Feature space data were obtained from real experiments with a mobile robot with camera and gripper. The obtained prediction results are satisfactory enough to suggest that the methodology is adequate and that further progress should be made in this direction. In future work, more involved strategies may be developed by expanding a set of new manipulation tasks, independent learning, adaptation in space, or involving multiagent behaviour learning.

References

[1] A. M. Howard and C. H. Park, "Haptically guided teleoperation for learning manipualtion tasks," in *Robotics: Science and Systems: Workshop on Robot Manipulation*, Atlanta, Ga, USA, June 2007.

[2] G. Taylor and L. Kleeman, *Visual Perception and Robotic Manipulation: 3D Object Recognition, Tracking and Hand-Eye Coordination*, Springer, 2006.

[3] Y. Wu, *Vision and learning for intelligent Human-Computer interaction [Ph.D. thesis]*, University of Illnois, 2001.

[4] M. V. Butz, O. Sigaud, and P. Gerard, "Internal models and anticipations in adaptive learning systems," in *Proceedings of the 1st Workshop on Adaptive Behavior in Anticipatory Learning Systems (ABiALS '06)*, 2006.

[5] A. Barrera, "Anticipatory mechanisms of human sensory-motor coordination inspire control of adaptive robots: a brief review," in *Robot Learning*, S. Jabin, Ed., InTech, 2010.

[6] L. Rozo, P. Jimenez, and C. Torras, "Robot learning of container-emptyng skills through haptic demonstration," Tech. Rep. IRI-TR-09-05, Institut de Robòtica i Informàtica Industrial, CSIC-UPC, 2009.

[7] C. Gaskett, L. Fletcher, and A. Zelinsky, "Reinforcement learning for visual servoing of a mobile robot," in *Proceedings of the Australian Conference on Robotics and Automation (ACRA '00)*, Melbourne, Australia, August 2000.

[8] M. Asada, T. Nakamura, and K. Hosoda, "Behavior acquisition via visual-based robot learning," in *Proceedings of the 7th International Symposium on Robotic Research*, 1996.

[9] A. Morales, E. Chinellato, A. H. Fagg, and A. P. del Pobil, "Experimental prediction of the performance of grasp tasks from visual features," in *Proceedings of the IEEE/RSJ International Conference on Intelligent Robots and Systems*, pp. 3423–3428, Las Vegas, Nev, USA, October 2003.

[10] H. Hoffmann, "Perception through visuomotor anticipation in a mobile robot," *Neural Networks*, vol. 20, no. 1, pp. 22–33, 2007.

[11] E. Datteri, G. Teti, C. Laschi, G. Tamburrini, P. Dario, and E. Guglielmelli, "Expected perception: an anticipation-based perception-action scheme in robots," in *Proceedings of the IEEE/RSJ International Conference on Intelligent Robots and Systems*, vol. 1, pp. 934–939, October 2003.

[12] D. A. Pomerleau, *Neural Network Perception for Mobile Robot Guidance*, Kluwer, Dordrecht, The Netherlands, 1993.

[13] L. A. Meeden, G. McGraw, and D. Blank, "Emergence of control and planning in an autonomous vehicle," in *Proceedings of the 50th Annual Meeting of the Cognitive Science Society*, p. 735, Lawrence Erlbaum Associates, Hillsdale, NJ, USA, 1993.

[14] T. Ziemke, "Remembering how to behave: recurrent neural networks for adaptive robot behavior," in *Recurrent Neural Networks, Design and Applications*, L. R. Medsker and L. C. Jain, Eds., CRC Press, 2001.

[15] J. Tani, R. Nishimoto, J. Namikawa, and M. Ito, "Codevelopmental learning between human and humanoid robot using a dynamic neural-network model," *IEEE Transactions on Systems, Man, and Cybernetics B*, vol. 38, no. 1, pp. 43–59, 2008.

[16] M. Peniak, D. Marocco, J. Taniy, Y. Yamashitay, K. Fischer, and A. Cangelosi, "Multiple time scales recurrent neural network for complex action acquisition," in *Proceedings of the International Joint Conference on Development and Learning (ICDL) and Epigenetic Robotics (ICDL-EPIROB '11)*, Frankfurt, Germany, August 2011.

[17] I. Fehervari and W. Elmenreich, "Evolving neural network controllers for a team of self-organizing robots," *Journal of Robotics Volume*, vol. 2010, Article ID 841286, 10 pages, 2010.

[18] R. C. Arkin, *Behavior-Based Robotics*, The MIT Press, Cambridge, Mass, USA, 1998.

[19] M. Mayer, B. Odenthal, and M. Grandt, "Task-oriented process planning for cognitive production systems using MTM," in *Proceedings of the 2nd International Conference on Applied Human Factors and Ergonomic*, USA Pub, 2008.

14

Estimation of Fuzzy Measures Using Covariance Matrices in Gaussian Mixtures

Nishchal K. Verma

Department of Electrical Engineering, Indian Institute of Technology Kanpur, Kanpur 208016, India

Correspondence should be addressed to Nishchal K. Verma, nishchal.iitk@gmail.com

Academic Editor: Enric Trillas

This paper presents a novel computational approach for estimating fuzzy measures directly from Gaussian mixtures model (GMM). The mixture components of GMM provide the membership functions for the input-output fuzzy sets. By treating consequent part as a function of fuzzy measures, we derived its coefficients from the covariance matrices found directly from GMM and the defuzzified output constructed from both the premise and consequent parts of the nonadditive fuzzy rules that takes the form of Choquet integral. The computational burden involved with the solution of λ-measure is minimized using Q-measure. The fuzzy model whose fuzzy measures were computed using covariance matrices found in GMM has been successfully applied on two benchmark problems and one real-time electric load data of Indian utility. The performance of the resulting model for many experimental studies including the above-mentioned application is found to be better and comparable to recent available fuzzy models. The main contribution of this paper is the estimation of fuzzy measures efficiently and directly from covariance matrices found in GMM, avoiding the computational burden greatly while learning them iteratively and solving polynomial equations of order of the number of input-output variables.

1. Introduction

Generalized fuzzy model (GFM) [1–3] is the backbone of this work that employs two norms for computing the strength of a rule: the multiplicative T-norm operator for determining the strength of a rule [4–6] and the additive S-norm operator for combining the outputs of all the rules. The effect of input fuzzy sets is taken into the defuzzified output in the form of rule strengths or weights. Gan et al. [7] have simplified the formulation of GFM by setting both the inputs and the output to be jointly Gaussian and proved that the input-output relation is as an expectation using the Bayesian framework. On simplification, this turns out to be the coveted Gaussian mixture model (GMM), which is linked by an additive function between the inputs and the output. The GMM, also known as cluster-weighted modeling (CWM) [8–12], is advocated by many researchers as means of statistical modeling of input-output systems [10, 13–15]. After the establishment of equivalence between GMM and GFM in [7], the difficult-to-compute index of fuzziness of GFM has become easy-to-compute prior probability [16–23]

in GMM. Further simplification of GFM will be explored when it is converted into nonadditive case.

The use of GMM in GFM has provided a generalized framework for additive fuzzy systems. A few existing additive fuzzy systems urging our attention are due to fuzzy models given in Kosko [24] and Wang and Mendel [25]. Using the framework of GMM, Abonyi et al. [26] have made a semblance of generalizing TS model [4, 27, 28] by attaching weight to each of its rules and subsequently treating it as the strength of the rule. However, nowhere they touched upon the concept of GFM that seeks to unify both Mamdani and TS models [4, 5].

Incorporation of the nonadditive property into the fuzzy sets is done so that the corresponding output of a non-additive fuzzy system is explored here. Let us throw some light on the additive and non-additive fuzzy systems [29–31]. Conventional evaluation with multiple attributes which are independent is based on the concept of additive fuzzy systems where importance of each attribute is given a weight.

Some important applications of fuzzy measures are now mentioned. A random generation of fuzzy measures have been introduced and some subfamilies of fuzzy measures tackled in [32]. A set of isometric fuzzy measures for any isometric transformation in each family of fuzzy measures (e.g., convex) is also studied. In [33] fuzzy measure is shown to be a unifying structure for modeling knowledge about an uncertain variable. Kim Le in [34] presents an expression to evaluate a fuzzy measure from set of aggregated evidences. Hierarchical autoregression model is presented in [34] using nonmonotonic fuzzy measures and the Choquet integral. Narukawa et al. in [35] discuss a space of fuzzy measures bearing the topology introduced by Choquet integral and the space of nonnegative fuzzy measure is shown to be locally convex. Fuzzy measures and integrals (e.g., Sugeno and Choquet) are used in decision making and modeling auctions [36, 37]. Fuzzy measures also find an application in [38] to track a moving object from a dynamic image sequence.

Fascinated by the ever growing importance of the fuzzy measure theory [39–45], the additive function of the GFM model in the consequent part is replaced by a nonadditive function satisfying certain axioms of the fuzzy measures. The defuzzified output of the resultant non-additive GFM is shown to be in the form of Choquet integral [41]. This formulation is intended for real-life applications in which the information from different sources needs not to be additive; hence our efforts in this work will go a long way in evolving different types of non-additive fuzzy systems, like dynamic, adaptive, and so forth, but here our attempt is only on a simple non-additive fuzzy system. To take account of the overlapping information in the fuzzy sets, Sugeno [40] has introduced the concept of λ-measure such that an appropriate value of λ can account for the interaction. In the proposed formulation, Q-measure takes the role of this λ-measure for reducing the computational complexity of the former.

Fuzzy integrals have come into vogue for the information fusion as they aggregate information from several sources. Out of all fuzzy integrals [40–44], the Choquet fuzzy integral [39, 41, 45] and Sugeno integral [46] are widely used. A handful of applications of fuzzy integrals include: handwriting recognition [47], landmine detection [48], pattern recognition [49], and decision making [37]. In the present study, the Choquet fuzzy integral is favored for it employs the non-additive property of fuzzy measures. The Choquet integral has not lost its luster even now; instead it is gaining prominence day by day and making inroads into new applications.

The main theme of the present work is the estimation of fuzzy densities, and hence fuzzy measures for the non-additive fuzzy model are derived from GFM; thus the fuzzy densities can be calculated straightaway from the covariance matrices used in GMM [50]. As the large number of input variables is increased for the purpose of fusion, the computational complexity grows exponentially [31, 51] with the λ-measure. To overcome this problem a new fuzzy measure known as Q-Measure is introduced in [52]. This new measure is just normalization of λ-measure, and with this modification, the fuzzy densities are decorrelated. In this λ is taken as a variable to be learned using the training data set. The proposed modeling technique considerably reduces the computational complexity in two steps: firstly finding fuzzy densities without learning them through iterative process

and secondly using Q-measure that eliminates the burden of solving the exponentially increasing polynomials.

This paper is organized as follows. Section 2 briefly describes the fuzzy measures. In Section 3, the formulation for the non-additive GFM is presented. An algorithm for non-additive fuzzy modeling based on Q-measure is given in Section 4. Two benchmark applications and one real-time electric load demand prediction application are provided in Section 5 to illustrate the proposed methodology. Finally conclusions are drawn in Section 6.

2. Fuzzy Measures

The fuzzy measure or fuzzy capacity is a subjective evaluation introduced by Choquet in 1953 and defined by Sugeno in 1974 for fuzzy integrals. Fuzzy measure includes a number of special class of measures like Sugeno's λ-measure and Q-measure. In this work, we make use of Fuzzy measures in quantifying the influence of the interactive inputs on the output function using the fuzzy measures. The resulting model is non-additive in the sense that the information from the interactive inputs is computed non-additively. For converting GFM into a non-additive fuzzy system, the relevant properties of the fuzzy measures [46].

Definition 1. Let us denote $X = \{x_1, x_2, \ldots, x_D\}$ as a finite set with its elements sorted from $\mathbf{x}$ and let χ be the power set of X, that is, set of all subsets of X. Then a fuzzy measure over a set X is a function given by

$$\zeta : \chi \longrightarrow [0, 1]. \tag{1}$$

Satisfying the two properties

(1) $\zeta(\phi) = 0, \zeta(X) = 1$.
(2) If $X_i, X_j \subset \chi$ and $X_i \subset X_j$, then $\zeta(X_i) \leq \zeta(X_j)$, which is the monotonicity relation in fuzzy measure. Next we invoke the third property, namely, the so-called λ-measure due to Sugeno [40] stated as follows:
(3) for all $X_i, X_j \subset \chi$ with $X_i \cap X_j = \phi$

$$\zeta(X_i \cup X_j) = \zeta(X_i) + \zeta(X_j) + \lambda\zeta(X_i)\zeta(X_j). \tag{2}$$

Example 2. Let $X_d = \{x_d, x_{d+1}, \ldots, x_D\}$ be the input sets satisfying the properties 1 and 2; then considering g as a fuzzy density satisfying the property 3, the values of fuzzy measure, $\zeta(X_d)$ can be computed recursively as

$$\begin{aligned} \zeta(X_d) &= \zeta(\{x_d\} \cup X_{d+1}) \\ &= g_d + \zeta(X_{d+1}) + \lambda g_d\zeta(X_{d+1}), \quad \text{for } 1 \leq d < D, \end{aligned} \tag{3}$$

starting with the one-input set to find the first measure as

$$\zeta(X_D) = \zeta(\{x_D\}) = g_D. \tag{4}$$

It is then combined with the next input set $\{x_{D-1}\}$ to compute their λ-measure since these two input sets are disjoint, that is, $\{x_D\} \cap \{x_{D-1}\} = \phi$, but their fuzzy sets A_D and A_{D-1} are dependent, that is, $A_D \cap A_{D-1} \neq \phi$. Equation (3) indicates that we must consider every time the fuzzy measure of two disjoint input sets, $\{x_d\}$ and X_{d+1}, which consists of inputs $x_{d+1}, \ldots, x_D$. It may be noted that a single element fuzzy measure is the fuzzy density itself. The following polynomial which arises from the condition $\zeta(X) = 1$ (see the appendix) needs to be solved for λ:

$$1 + \lambda = \prod_{d=1}^{D} (1 + \lambda g_d). \tag{5}$$

The solution of (5) is computationally intensive. We will now discuss the Q-measure to address this problem.

Q-Measure. The λ-measure is burdened with the problem of finding the roots of the polynomial equation in λ. As the number of dimensions, D increases, the complexity of the equation increases enormously. In order to surmount this problem, Q-measure is proposed in [52]. It derives its name from the word "Quotient." The Q-measure follows the same properties of λ-measure. For the finite X the Q-measure is defined as the ratio of two fuzzy measures:

$$Q(X_d) = \frac{\zeta(X_d)}{\zeta(X)} = \frac{\zeta(X_d)}{\zeta(X_1)}, \tag{6}$$

where $\zeta(X) = \zeta(X_1)$ is a function of fuzzy densities and is a polynomial in λ. The Q-measure [52] over a set X is similar to $\zeta(X)$ in (1):

$$Q : \chi \longrightarrow [0, 1], \tag{7}$$

with the two properties as follows:

(1)

$$Q(\phi) = 0, \qquad Q(X) = 1. \tag{8}$$

(2) If $X_i, X_j \subset \chi$ and $X_i \subset X_j$, then $Q(X_i) \leq Q(X_j)$, which is the monotonicity relation.

The third property is as follows:

(3) for all $X_i, X_j \subset \chi$ with $X_i \cap X_j = \phi$,

$$Q(X_i \cup X_j) = Q(X_i) + Q(X_j) + \lambda Q(X_i) Q(X_j) \text{ for } \lambda > -1. \tag{9}$$

Following (9), $Q(X_d)$ is evaluated from

$$Q(X_d) = Q(\{x_d\} \cup X_{d+1}) = g_d + Q(X_{d+1}) \\ + \lambda \cdot g_d \cdot Q(X_{d+1}) \quad \text{for } 1 \leq d < D. \tag{10}$$

The first measure is computed from

$$Q(X_D) = Q(\{x_D\}) = g_D. \tag{11}$$

Convergence Behavior of Q-Measure. Let $\{x_1\}$, $\{x_2, x_3, \ldots, x_D\} \subset X$ Such that, $\{x_1\} \cup \{x_2, x_3, \ldots, x_D\} = X$, and $\{x_1\} \cap \{x_2, x_3, \ldots, x_D\} = \phi$, that is, null. Supposing $G_1 = \zeta(\{x_1\})$ and

$$G_2 = \zeta(\{x_2, x_3, \ldots, x_D\}) \\ = \zeta(X_2) \quad \forall \lambda \geq -1, G_1 \geq 0, G_2 \geq 0. \tag{12}$$

Then the λ-measure of G_1 and G_2 is

$$\zeta(X_1) = G_1 + G_2 + \lambda \cdot G_1 \cdot G_2. \tag{13}$$

Using (10) the Q-measure is written as

$$Q(X_{D-1}) = g_{D-1} + Q(X_D) + \lambda \cdot g_{D-1} \cdot Q(X_D), \tag{14}$$

or

$$Q(X_{D-1}) = g_{D-1} + g_D + \lambda \cdot g_{D-1} \cdot g_D. \tag{15}$$

For $g_{D-1}, g_D \in [0, 1]$ and $\lambda \geq -1$, it is always assured that

$$g_{D-1} + g_D > \lambda \cdot g_{D-1} \cdot g_D. \tag{16}$$

Hence, $Q(X_{D-1}) > g_{D-1}$ and also $Q(X_{D-1}) > g_D$. Next, we have

$$Q(X_{D-2}) = g_{D-2} + Q(X_{D-1}) + \lambda \cdot g_{D-2} \cdot Q(X_{D-1}) \\ = Q(X_{D-1}) + g_{D-2}(1 + \lambda \cdot Q(X_{D-1})), \tag{17}$$

where $\lambda Q(X_{D-1}) < 1$. Therefore $g_{D-2}(1 + \lambda \cdot Q(X_{D-1})) > 0$ and the values lie in between 0 and 1. Hence we have

$$Q(X_{D-2}) > Q(X_{D-1}). \tag{18}$$

This will continue until $D = 3$ when we will have

$$Q(X_1) > Q(X_2). \tag{19}$$

But $Q(X_1) = 1$; this means that the Q-measure converges to unity.

3. From GMM to Nonadditive GFM with Q-Measure

The GFM [7] includes both the Mamdani and TS models. The Mamdani model (CRI-model) inhibits the property of fuzziness around the fixed centroid of the consequent part while the TS model gives a varying singleton for the consequent part in each fuzzy rule. The output of GFM is a fuzzy set, which is the output of Mamdani model with an index of fuzziness and with a varying centroid as the output of the TS model. To combine both of these properties, Azeem et al. [1, 53] have introduced a GFM fuzzy rule of the form

$$R^k : \text{IF } \mathbf{x}^k \text{ is } \mathbf{A}^k \text{ THEN } y_k \text{ is } \mathbf{B}^k(f_k(\mathbf{x}), v_k). \tag{20}$$

The fuzzy set $\mathbf{B}^k(f_k(\mathbf{x}), v_k)$ may also be in the linguistic form with the output function $f^k(\mathbf{x})$ which may be linear or nonlinear regression of inputs and the index of fuzziness v_k. The fuzzy output of the kth rule is y_k. The defuzzified output obtained by applying additive S-norm to the consequent parts of GFM rules is

$$\hat{y} = \sum_{k=1}^{K} \frac{\mu^k(\mathbf{x}).v_k}{\sum_{l=1}^{K} \mu^l(\mathbf{x}) \cdot v_l} f_k(\mathbf{x}), \tag{21}$$

with $f_k(\mathbf{x}) = b_0^k + b_1^k x_1 + \cdots + b_D^k x_D$. As noted in Section 1 on introduction, GFM represents the additive fuzzy system. Using the framework of GMM, we intend to generalize to the case when the input fuzzy sets have overlapping information, that is, $A_i^m \cap A_{i+1}^m \neq \phi$. So, we modify the above fuzzy rule to the nonadditive GFM as

$$R^m : \text{if } \mathbf{x}^m \text{ is } \mathbf{A}^m \text{ such that } A_i^m \cap A_{i+1}^m \neq \phi.$$
$$\text{Then } y_m \text{ is } B^m(f_m'(X), v_m) \text{ with } X \subseteq \mathbf{x}. \tag{22}$$

To take account of the above constraint, we form the input set X from which the fuzzy measures of subsets $X_d = (\{x_d\} \cup X_d)$ are found recursively using (10) and (11). Using the fuzzy measures as the coefficients the output function is expressed as [31]

$$f_m'(X) = \beta_0^m + \beta_1^m x_1 + \cdots + \beta_D^m x_D. \tag{23}$$

Equation (23) is an additive function of fuzzy measures as explained in the sequel. As the input fuzzy sets in (22) are overlapping, we take disjoint input sets from the power set χ and compute their fuzzy measure. The function $f_m'(X)$ combines the fuzzy measures from subsequent fuzzy sets, and the resulting system arising from the fuzzy rules is called nonadditive fuzzy system unlike the output function in TS model where each coefficient corresponds to its own fuzzy set and there is no concept of fuzzy measure in this model. We now impose three constraints for the model to be called non-additive:

(i) the input fuzzy sets A_i associated with the power set χ are overlapping,

(ii) the input sets X_i are disjoint,

(iii) the output function is additive in fuzzy measures.

We will now show that the above conditions are necessary to represent the defuzzified output of the nonadditive GFM in the Choquet integral form as follows:

$$\hat{y}_j = \sum_{m=1}^{M} \left(\frac{\mu^m(\mathbf{x}_j) \cdot p(c_m)}{\sum_{l=1}^{M} \mu^l(\mathbf{x}_j) \cdot p(c_l)} \right) \cdot f_m'(X)$$
$$= \sum_{m=1}^{M} \left(\frac{\mu^m(\mathbf{x}_j) \cdot p(c_m)}{\sum_{l=1}^{M} \mu^l(\mathbf{x}_j) \cdot p(c_l)} \right) \cdot \sum_{d=0}^{D} \beta_d^m \cdot x_{jd}, \tag{24}$$

where for jth set of the data we have

$$\mu^m(\mathbf{x}_j) = \prod_{d=1}^{D} \mu^m(\mathbf{x}_{jd})$$
$$= \prod_{d=1}^{D} N^1\left(\mathbf{x}_{jd}^m; \overline{\mathbf{x}}_d^m, \sum_{m,d}\right), N^1\left(\mathbf{x}_{jd}^m; \overline{\mathbf{x}}_d^m, \sum_{m,d}\right) \tag{25}$$
$$= \exp\left(-\frac{\left(\mathbf{x}_{jd}^m - \overline{\mathbf{x}}_d^m\right)^2}{2 \sum_{m,d}} \right),$$

with $\sum_{m,d}$ being the diagonal element. The firing strength of each rule is obtained by taking the multiplicative T-norm of the membership functions (by suppressing the subscripts "j") of the premise parts of the rules as $\mu^m(\mathbf{x}) = \mu^m(x_1)\Lambda\mu^m(x_2)\Lambda \cdots \Lambda\mu^m(x_D)$. We intend to compute the coefficients of the output function by reformulating (21) in the Choquet fuzzy integral form. The role of GMM is to facilitate the computation of M, $\mu^m(\mathbf{x})$ and $p(c_m)$.

3.1. Choquet Fuzzy Integral and Q-Measure. When a fuzzy measure is available on a finite set X, we can use a fuzzy integral as a computational scheme to integrate all values from χ, that is, the subsets X_i of X nonlinearly. In other words, a fuzzy integral relies on the concept of a fuzzy measure. A general definition is that given a class of functions $F \subseteq \{h : \chi \rightarrow \mathfrak{R}^+\}$ and a class of Q-measures $Q(\cdot)$, we have a functional $f : F \times Q = h \times Q \rightarrow \mathfrak{R}$, which is a fuzzy integral [42]. The Choquet integral is a particular fuzzy integral [41] that serves as an alternative computational scheme for aggregating information.

Definition 3. Let Q-measure over a set X be a function whose elements (discrete) are $x_1, x_2, \ldots, x_D$, then the Choquet integral of a positive function h with respect to Q is defined by [39]

$$f_g(h) = \sum_{d=1}^{D} ((h(x_d) - h(x_{d-1}))Q(X_d)), \tag{26}$$

or

$$f_g(h) = \sum_{d=1}^{D} h(x_d)(Q(X_d) - Q(X_{d+1})), \tag{27}$$

where $h(x_1) \leq h(x_2) \leq \cdots \leq h(x_D)$. We assume here that $Q(X_{D+1}) = 0$ and $h(x_0) = 0$. To convert (24) into the Choquet fuzzy integral form, we shall represent coefficients β_d^m in terms of Q-measures, $Q(X_d)$ as

$$\beta_d^m = Q^m(X_d) - Q^m(X_{d+1}) = g_d^m + \lambda^m g_d^m Q^m(X_{d+1}),$$
$$\text{for } d = 1, 2, 3 \ldots, D \text{ and } Q^m(X_{D+1}) = 0. \tag{28}$$

Interchanging the summations in (24) leads to

$$\hat{y}_j = \sum_{d=0}^{D} \left(\sum_{m=1}^{M} \left(\frac{\mu^m(\mathbf{x}_j) \cdot p(c_m) \cdot x_{jd}}{\sum_{l=1}^{M} \mu^l(\mathbf{x}_j) \cdot p(c_l)} \right) \right)$$
$$\cdot (Q^m(X_d) - Q^m(X_{d+1})). \tag{29}$$

Next separating out the $d = 0$ term yields,

$$\hat{y}_j = a_0 + \sum_{d=1}^{D} \left(\sum_{m=1}^{M} \left(\frac{\mu^m(\mathbf{x}_j) \cdot p(c_m) \cdot x_{jd}}{\sum_{l=1}^{M} \mu^l(\mathbf{x}_j) \cdot p(c_l)} \right) \right)$$
$$\cdot (Q^m(X_d) - Q^m(X_{d+1})), \tag{30}$$

where a_0 is a constant. Letting

$$h^m(x_{jd}) = \left(\frac{\mu^m(\mathbf{x}_j) \cdot p(c_m) \cdot x_{jd}}{\sum_{l=1}^{M} \mu^l(\mathbf{x}_j) \cdot p(c_l)} \right). \tag{31}$$

Equation (30) is simplified as

$$\hat{y}_j = a_0 + \sum_{d=1}^{D} \left(\sum_{m=1}^{M} h^m\left(x_{jd}\right) \cdot (Q^m(X_d) - Q^m(X_{d+1})) \right). \tag{32}$$

Denoting $[h(x_{jd})] = [h^1(x_{jd}) \quad h^2(x_{jd}) \quad \cdots \quad h^M(x_{jd})]$ and

$$[(Q(X_d) - Q(X_{d+1}))] = \begin{bmatrix} (Q^1(X_d) - Q^1(X_{d+1})) \\ (Q^2(X_d) - Q^2(X_{d+1})) \\ \vdots \\ (Q^M(X_d) - Q^M(X_{d+1})) \end{bmatrix} \tag{33}$$

allows us to write (32) compactly for D input variables as

$$\hat{y}_j = a_0 + \sum_{d=1}^{D} \left[h\left(x_{jd}\right) \right] \cdot [(Q(X_d) - Q(X_{d+1}))], \tag{34}$$

or

$$\hat{y}_j = a_0 + \sum_{d=1}^{D} \left[h\left(x_{jd}\right) - h\left(x_{j(d-1)}\right) \right] \cdot [Q(X_d)], \tag{35}$$

where $h^m(x_{j1}) \le h^m(x_{j2}) \le \cdots \le h^m(x_{jD})$ and $h^m(x_{j0}) = 0$ for $m = 1, 2, \ldots, M$, is the monotonicity condition. Note that $h^m(x_{j1}), h^m(x_{j2}), \ldots, h^m(x_{jD})$ are the evidences provided by the input sources $x_1, x_2, \ldots, x_D$, respectively, and $Q^m(X_1), Q^m(X_2), \ldots, Q^m(X_D)$ are the Q-measures for mth cluster. Here, we take $Q^m(X_{D+1})$ to be zero. Equations (34) and (35) similar to (26) and (27) are the two forms of Choquet fuzzy integral [42]. We have now proved that the defuzzified output of the non-additive GFM fuzzy rules is in the form of Choquet fuzzy integral. The underlying model is nonadditive GFM because both h and Q are nonlinear functions of x. Thus the Choquet integral provides the functionality of non-additive GFM. The functionality of the Choquet integral for GMM will be discussed later. We will now estimate the unknown Q-measures from fuzzy densities determined using (9). We then evaluate the performance of the fuzzy model with a measure, which is a function of mean square error [54], chosen as

$$E = \frac{\sum_{j=1}^{n} e_j^2}{n \cdot y_r}, \tag{36}$$

where n is the total number of test data vectors:

$$e_j = \hat{y}_j - y_j,$$
$$y_r = [\max(Y) - \min(Y)]^2, \tag{37}$$

where $\hat{y}_j$ is the estimated value, y_j is the actual output, and $Y = \{y_j\}$ is the output vector.

3.2. Determination of Fuzzy Densities.

The cluster-wise breakup of the estimated output of the additive fuzzy system [7] is given as

$$\hat{y}_j = \left(\frac{\mu^1\left(\mathbf{x}_j\right) \cdot p(c_1) \cdot f\left(\mathbf{x}_j, \alpha_1\right)}{\sum_{l=1}^{M} \mu^l\left(\mathbf{x}_j\right) \cdot p(c_l)} \right)$$
$$+ \left(\frac{\mu^2\left(\mathbf{x}_j\right) \cdot p(c_2) \cdot f\left(\mathbf{x}_j, \alpha_2\right)}{\sum_{l=1}^{M} \mu^l\left(\mathbf{x}_j\right) \cdot p(c_l)} \right) \tag{38}$$
$$+ \cdots$$
$$+ \left(\frac{\mu^M\left(\mathbf{x}_j\right) \cdot p(c_M) \cdot f\left(\mathbf{x}_j, \alpha_M\right)}{\sum_{l=1}^{M} \mu^l\left(\mathbf{x}_j\right) \cdot p(c_l)} \right),$$

where using GMM from [7] we estimate $f(\mathbf{x}_j, \alpha_m)$ as

$$f\left(\mathbf{x}_j, \alpha_m\right) = \overline{y}_j^m - \sum_{d=1}^{D} \left(\left(x_{jd} - \overline{x}_d^m\right) \cdot \frac{\sigma_m^{dy}}{\sigma_m^{yy}} \right). \tag{39}$$

Equation (38) can also be written as

$$\hat{y}_j = w_1 \cdot f\left(\mathbf{x}_j, \alpha_1\right) + w_2 \cdot f\left(\mathbf{x}_j, \alpha_2\right)$$
$$+ \cdots + w_M \cdot f\left(\mathbf{x}_j, \alpha_M\right), \tag{40}$$

where $w_m = ((\mu^m(\mathbf{x}_j) \cdot p(c_m))/(\sum_{l=1}^{M} \mu^l(\mathbf{x}_j) \cdot p(c_l)))$. Substituting $f(\mathbf{x}_j, \alpha_m)$ for $m = 1$ to M from (39) in (40), we have

$$w_1 \cdot \left(\overline{y}^1 - \sum_{d=1}^{D} \left(\left(x_{jd} - \overline{x}_d^1\right) \cdot \frac{\sigma_1^{dy}}{\sigma_1^{yy}} \right) \right)$$
$$+ w_2 \cdot \left(\overline{y}^2 - \sum_{d=1}^{D} \left(\left(x_{jd} - \overline{x}_d^2\right) \cdot \frac{\sigma_2^{dy}}{\sigma_2^{yy}} \right) \right)$$
$$\cdots$$
$$\cdots$$
$$+ w_M \cdot \left(\overline{y}^M - \sum_{d=1}^{D} \left(\left(x_{jd} - \overline{x}_d^M\right) \cdot \frac{\sigma_M^{dy}}{\sigma_M^{yy}} \right) \right)$$
$$= a_0^1 + w_1\left(x_{j1} \cdot g_1^1 + x_{j2} \cdot g_2^1 + \cdots + x_{jD} \cdot g_D^1\right)$$
$$+ a_0^2 + w_2\left(x_{j1} \cdot g_1^2 + x_{j2} \cdot g_2^2 + \cdots + x_{jD} \cdot g_D^2\right)$$
$$\cdots$$
$$\cdots$$
$$+ a_0^M + w_M\left(x_{j1} \cdot g_1^M + x_{j2} \cdot g_2^M + \cdots + x_{jD} \cdot g_D^M\right). \tag{41}$$

Using (32), for M rules, we have the cluster-wise estimates of the output for the non-additive fuzzy model written as

$$
\hat{y}_j = a_0^1 + \sum_{d=1}^{D} h^1\left(x_{jd}\right) \cdot \left(Q^1(X_d) - Q^1(X_{d+1})\right)
$$
$$
+ a_0^2 + \sum_{d=1}^{D} h^2\left(x_{jd}\right) \cdot \left(Q^2(X_d) - Q^2(X_{d+1})\right)
$$
$$
\cdots
$$
$$
\cdots
$$
$$
+ a_0^M + \sum_{d=1}^{D} h^M\left(x_{jd}\right) \cdot \left(Q^M(X_d) - Q^M(X_{d+1})\right). \tag{42}
$$

From (42) it is implied that $a_0 = a_0^1 + a_0^2 + \cdots + a_0^M$ in view of (34) and (35).

Equation (42) can also be written as

$$
\hat{y} = a_0^1 + w_1\left(x_{j1} \cdot g_1^1(1 + \lambda^1 Q^1(X_2))\right.
$$
$$
\left. + x_{j2} \cdot g_2^1(1 + \lambda^1 Q^1(X_3)) + \cdots + x_{jD} \cdot g_D^1\right)
$$
$$
+ a_0^2 + w_2\left(x_{j1} \cdot g_1^2(1 + \lambda^2 Q^2(X_2))\right.
$$
$$
\left. + x_{j2} \cdot g_2^2(1 + \lambda^2 Q^2(X_3)) + \cdots + x_{jD} \cdot g_D^2\right)
$$
$$
\cdots
$$
$$
\cdots
$$
$$
+ a_0^M + w_M\left(x_{j1} \cdot g_1^M\left(1 + \lambda^M Q^M(X_2)\right)\right.
$$
$$
+ x_{j2} \cdot g_2^M\left(1 + \lambda^M Q^M(X_3)\right)
$$
$$
\left. + \cdots + x_{jD} \cdot g_D^M\right) \tag{43}
$$

or

$$
\hat{y} = a_0 + w_1 \cdot f'\left(\mathbf{x}_j, \beta_1\right) + w_2 \cdot f'\left(\mathbf{x}_j, \beta_2\right)
$$
$$
+ \cdots + w_M \cdot f'\left(\mathbf{x}_j, \beta_M\right). \tag{44}
$$

Since (40) and (44) represent the estimated outputs for additive and non-additive fuzzy systems, respectively, and hence these must be equivalent to each other for $\lambda = 0$. Equating the right hand sides of (40) and (44), we have

$$
w_1 \cdot f\left(\mathbf{x}_j, \alpha_1\right) + w_2 \cdot f\left(\mathbf{x}_j, \alpha_2\right) + \cdots + w_M \cdot f\left(\mathbf{x}_j, \alpha_M\right)
$$
$$
= a_0 + w_1 \cdot f'\left(\mathbf{x}_j, \beta_1\right) + w_2 \cdot f'\left(\mathbf{x}_j, \beta_2\right)
$$
$$
+ \cdots + w_M \cdot f'\left(\mathbf{x}_j, \beta_M\right). \tag{45}
$$

Thus when the fuzzy measure $\lambda^m = 0, \alpha_i = \beta_i$. As $\alpha_i = g_i^m$ we can express the fuzzy densities in terms of the elements of covariance matrices of GMM as [7]

$$
g_1^m = \frac{\sigma_m^{1y}}{\sigma_m^{yy}}; \qquad g_2^m = \frac{\sigma_m^{2y}}{\sigma_m^{yy}}, \cdots g_D^m = \frac{\sigma_m^{Dy}}{\sigma_m^{yy}} \tag{46}
$$
$$
\text{for } m = 1, 2, \ldots, M.
$$

We are in a position to estimate λ and Q-measures and hence the β coefficients using the fuzzy densities. We will then use all these in the Choquet integral to estimate the output. For convenience of notation we start with fuzzy measure of one element set $X_d = \{x_D\}$ and move in backward direction to find the Q-measure of X_1. Since we are computing all Q-measures before the start of the Choquet integral, these become handy in computing the output. This is because in (32) the index d is in the forward direction from 1 to D.

3.3. Functionality of GMM. As we have already proved that the Choquet integral is the functionality of non-additive GFM, It is now easy to extend to this functionality the GMM case from the fact that the output is Gaussian in the nonadditive case too as per the expression

$$
p(\mathbf{y} \mid \mathbf{x}, c_m) = \frac{1}{\sqrt{2\pi \sum_{m,(D+1)}}}
$$
$$
\cdot \exp\left\{\frac{-\sum_j \left[y_j^m - f\left(\mathbf{x}_j^m, \beta_m\right)\right]^2}{2\sum_{m,(D+1)}}\right\}. \tag{47}
$$

From the above it may be noted that β_m is obtained from α_m using GMM by the choice of λ^m in the Q-measure. Hence $f(\mathbf{x}_j^m, \beta_m)$ is the mean of y_j^m in the non-additive case just as $f(\mathbf{x}_j^m, \alpha_m)$ is the mean of y_j^m in the additive case. We can conclude therefore that when β_m is evaluated from α_m, the Choquet integral also assures the functionality of GMM.

4. Algorithm for Estimating the Model Parameters of the Nonadditive Fuzzy Systems

The algorithm has the following steps.

Step 1. Normalize the input-output data, so that the data values lie in between 0 and 1:

$$
\mathbf{x}^{\text{normalized}} = \frac{(\mathbf{x} - \min(\mathbf{z}))}{(\max(\mathbf{z}) - \min(\mathbf{z}))}, \tag{48}
$$

where $\mathbf{z} = [\mathbf{x}, y]$ is the input-output data vector.

Step 2. Find the premise model parameters of GMM using the EM Algorithm.

Step 3. Determine fuzzy densities $g_1^m, g_2^m, \ldots, g_D^m$ for each input variable in mth cluster/rule using (47).

Step 4. Choose initial values of λ^m with the restriction $\lambda^m \geq -1$ for mth cluster.

Step 5. Compute $Q^m(X_d)$ by the recursive computation involving the following equations from (10) and (11):

$$
Q^m(X_D) = Q^m(\{x_D\}) = g_D^m,
$$
$$
Q^m(X_d) = g_d^m + Q^m(X_{d+1})
$$
$$
+ \lambda^m g_d^m Q^m(X_{d+1}), \quad \text{for } 1 \leq d < D. \tag{49}
$$

Step 6. Using (31) find $h^m(x_d)$ for each input variable d in the cluster/rule to obtain the matrix $[h(x_d)]$.

TABLE 1: Estimated parameters of A 4-component GMM using the EM algorithm.

Cluster or rule no. (m)	Weight of the rule $p(c_m)$	Mean ($\bar{\mathbf{z}}^m$)	Covariance (Σ_m)
Cluster or rule no. 1	$p(c_1) = 0.2991$	$\bar{\mathbf{z}}^1 = \begin{bmatrix} 0.4066 \\ 0.2897 \\ 0.4341 \\ 0.5321 \\ 0.2986 \end{bmatrix}$	$\Sigma_1 = \begin{bmatrix} 0.0246 & 0.0032 & 0.0114 & -0.0075 & 0.0095 \\ 0.0032 & 0.0150 & -0.0027 & -0.0106 & 0.0149 \\ 0.0114 & -0.0027 & 0.0161 & 0.0104 & 0.0004 \\ -0.0075 & -0.0106 & 0.0104 & 0.0427 & -0.0146 \\ 0.0095 & 0.0149 & 0.0004 & -0.0146 & 0.0170 \end{bmatrix}$
Cluster or rule no. 2	$p(c_2) = 0.1685$	$\bar{\mathbf{z}}^2 = \begin{bmatrix} 0.4372 \\ 0.6782 \\ 0.4676 \\ 0.2232 \\ 0.6904 \end{bmatrix}$	$\Sigma_2 = \begin{bmatrix} 0.0503 & 0.0056 & 0.0151 & -0.0124 & 0.0170 \\ 0.0056 & 0.0209 & 0.0062 & 0.0085 & 0.0180 \\ 0.0151 & 0.0062 & 0.0090 & -0.0019 & 0.0096 \\ -0.0124 & 0.0085 & -0.0019 & 0.0150 & 0.0025 \\ 0.0170 & 0.0180 & 0.0096 & 0.0025 & 0.0194 \end{bmatrix}$
Cluster or rule no. 3	$p(c_3) = 0.2166$	$\bar{\mathbf{z}}^3 = \begin{bmatrix} 0.5558 \\ 0.7100 \\ 0.5996 \\ 0.4178 \\ 0.7355 \end{bmatrix}$	$\Sigma_3 = \begin{bmatrix} 0.0198 & -0.0090 & 0.0049 & -0.0066 & -0.0039 \\ -0.0090 & 0.0234 & -0.0018 & -0.0034 & 0.0199 \\ 0.0049 & -0.0018 & 0.0098 & -0.0029 & 0.0004 \\ -0.0066 & -0.0034 & -0.0029 & 0.0140 & -0.0054 \\ -0.0039 & 0.0199 & 0.0004 & -0.0054 & 0.0181 \end{bmatrix}$
Cluster or rule no. 4	$p(c_4) = 0.3158$	$\bar{\mathbf{z}}^4 = \begin{bmatrix} 0.3211 \\ 0.5366 \\ 0.5265 \\ 0.5963 \\ 0.5065 \end{bmatrix}$	$\Sigma_4 = \begin{bmatrix} 0.0135 & -0.0057 & 0.0013 & 0.0016 & -0.0033 \\ -0.0057 & 0.0270 & 0.0069 & -0.0153 & 0.0256 \\ 0.0013 & 0.0069 & 0.0183 & 0.0064 & 0.0073 \\ 0.0016 & -0.0153 & 0.0064 & 0.0208 & -0.0152 \\ -0.0033 & 0.0256 & 0.0073 & -0.0152 & 0.0248 \end{bmatrix}$

Step 7. Compute the estimated output using (34).

Step 8. Learn the model. This requires the following two subtasks:

(a) set up an objective function [54] as the case required. For batch:

$$J_{\text{batch}} = \frac{1}{n} \sum_{j=1}^{n} \left(\hat{y}_j - y_j \right)^2$$
$$= \frac{1}{n} \sum_{j=1}^{n} e_j^2, \tag{50}$$

for incremental,

$$J_{\text{incr}} = \frac{1}{2} \left(\hat{y}_j - y_j \right)^2 = \frac{1}{2} e_j^2. \tag{51}$$

(b) Update the values of λ^m by the Gradient-descent learning law:

$$(\lambda^m)_{\text{new}} = (\lambda^m)_{\text{old}} - \eta \cdot \left(\frac{\partial J}{\partial \lambda^m} \right),$$
$$a_{0,\text{new}} = a_0 - \eta \cdot \left(\frac{\partial J}{\partial a_0} \right), \tag{52}$$

where J may refer to either J_{batch} or J_{incr} and η is a learning factor fixed at the value 0.9 for better performance. The parameter learning can be accomplished in either of the above two ways: batch or incremental. Derivatives required in the learning process are relegated to the Appendix.

Step 9. Repeat Step 1 to Step 8, till the model parameters are within the tolerance.

Step 10. Calculate E from (36).

TABLE 2: Fuzzy densities using GMM.

Rule (m)	g_1	g_2	g_3	g_4
Rule no. 1	0.2473	0.7760	0.0005	0.0000
Rule no. 2	0.5699	0.8204	0.0028	0.0003
Rule no. 3	0.6284	0.8671	0.0070	0.0001
Rule no. 4	0.4844	0.7330	0.0042	0.0012

TABLE 3: Estimated lambda (λ^m).

Rule 1	Rule 2	Rule 3	Rule 4
−0.1241	−0.8364	−0.9108	−0.6197

5. Experimental Results

5.1. Gas Furnace. Here, we take up the gas furnace data [55] to demonstrate the effectiveness of the proposed algorithm. In this gas furnace, the air at a feed rate of $u(t)$ is combined with methane to produce a mixture of gases with carbon dioxide of concentration $y(t)$. These are used to fit the Gaussian mixture density function with four components. The input vector after sorting is $\mathbf{x} = [x_1 \quad x_2 \quad x_3 \quad x_4] = [y(t-1) - y(t-2) y(t-1) u(t) - u(t-1) u(t)]$ and the output is $y = y(t)$. The composition of the input vector is arrived at using the fuzzy curve approach [56]. On applying the expectation maximization (EM) [57] clustering, the number of clusters is found to be 4; hence the model will have four components. The five-variable GMM using the EM algorithm yields the parameters of GMM as shown in Table 1. These parameters are also the premise model parameters of the non-additive GFM fuzzy rules.

Fuzzy densities and estimated fuzzy measures of the model are given in Tables 2 and 4, respectively. The estimated values of λ^m are given in Table 3. The estimated β-coefficient and Q-measures are given in Tables 5 and 6 respectively. Note that $\zeta(X_1)$ contains all input elements, hence its value is one. The β-coefficients constitute the consequent parameters of the GMM fuzzy rules. The performance measure is found to be 0.00208. The fuzzy measures of the constituent singleton

TABLE 4: Estimated fuzzy measures.

Rule (m)	$\zeta(X_1)$	$\zeta(X_2)$	$\zeta(X_3)$	$\zeta(X_4)$
Rule no. 1	1.0000	0.7923	0.0021	0.0009
Rule no. 2	0.9997	0.8214	0.0032	0.0003
Rule no. 3	0.9999	0.8686	0.0071	0.0001
Rule no. 4	0.9994	0.7359	0.0053	0.0012

TABLE 5: Estimated β coefficients.

Rule (m)	β_1	β_2	β_3	β_4
Rule no. 1	0.2077	0.7902	0.0012	0.0009
Rule no. 2	0.1783	0.8182	0.0029	0.0003
Rule no. 3	0.1313	0.8615	0.0070	0.0001
Rule no. 4	0.2635	0.7306	0.0041	0.0012

TABLE 6: Estimated Q-measures.

Rule (m)	$Q(X_1)$	$Q(X_2)$	$Q(X_3)$	$Q(X_4)$
Rule no. 1	1.0000	0.7823	0.0013	0.0000
Rule no. 2	1.0000	0.8541	0.0635	0.0001
Rule no. 3	1.0000	0.9175	0.0863	0.0003
Rule no. 4	1.0000	0.7230	0.0169	0.0002

sets satisfy the monotonic relations for $D = 4$ shown as a lattice in Figure 2.

For the training dataset containing the first 250 data vectors, $E = 6.12505 \times 10^{-4}$. For the remaining data vectors forming the validation data set, $E = 0.0021$. This is inferior to that of the training data set, as expected. The plots of actual output and model output for both training and prediction along with the prediction error of the model output are shown in Figure 1. The model output is very close to the actual output during training, but it displays small deviations from the actual output during the prediction period. Using the premise and consequent parameters of Table 1, we have constructed the membership functions for the four inputs and one output in Figure 3 where we depict the membership function of rules-1, 2, 3, and 4 using dashed lines, dotted lines, dots with dashes lines and solid lines, respectively.

The first rule R^1 consists of,

(i) the weight of the rule; 0.2991,

(ii) the membership functions of the premise parts

$$N^1(x_1; 104066, 0.0246), \quad N^1(x_2; 0.2897, 0.0150), \atop N^1(x_3; 0.4341, 0.0161), \quad N^1(x_4; 0.5321, 0.0427). \tag{53}$$

(iii) The consequent part of a rule can be found using Table 6.

Similarly other rules can also be formed.

5.2. Industrial Dryer. In this, we consider the industrial dryer data obtained from the *DaISy* database. Fuel is combusted to produce the hot gas, which is blown by an exhaust fan on the raw material fed into the dryer. It is desired to determine the relationship between the functional elements of the dryer with the moisture content of the raw material at the dryer output. The measurements are designated by

(i) fuel flow rate, $x_1(t)$,

(ii) hot gas exhaust-fan speed, $x_2(t)$,

(iii) rate of flow of raw material, $x_3(t)$,

(iv) moisture content of the raw material after drying which is $y(t)$.

Sampling period of 10 seconds is considered to generate a total of 867 samples. Input and output data are normalized using (40) to maintain compatibility in the range 0 to 1. The input variables $x_1(t)$, $x_2(t)$, $x_3(t)$, and $y(t-1)$ affect the current output $y(t)$. The input-output vectors are represented by $\mathbf{z}(t) = [x_1(t) \quad x_2(t) \quad x_3(t) \quad y(t-1) \quad y(t)]$. Out of these vectors 70% is taken as the training set. The remaining 30% is kept for prediction and evaluation of our proposed model.

The number of clusters is found to be 4 using EM clustering, which yields the parameters of GMM in Table 7, and these are also the premise model parameters of the non-additive GFM.

The estimated fuzzy densities, fuzzy measures, β-coefficients and Q-measure of the model are given in Tables 8, 10, 11, and 12, respectively. The monotonicity relations for $D = 4$ are also verified here for fuzzy measure values of the constituent singleton sets, shown as a lattice in Figure 5. Table 9 shows the estimated values of λ^m.

The training data set yields $E = 9.0005 \times 10^{-4}$ for training the model. The remaining 30% data vectors constitute the validation data set. The performance measure E over the prediction period is obtained as 0.0019. The results of the actual output and the model output during the training and the prediction periods are shown in Figure 4 which also includes the prediction error. The results demonstrate the effectiveness of the proposed non-additive fuzzy model using Q-measure. The membership functions associated with all the four rules can be obtained in the similar fashion as in Figure 3.

5.3. Electric Load Demand. In this, we consider the real time hourly electric load data, that is, hourly peak electric load consumption with uncertain weather information like hourly average temperature, humidity, and wind speed for the month of April 2003. The variables are designated as

(i) hourly average Temperature, $x_1(t)$,

(ii) hourly average Humidity, $x_2(t)$,

(iii) hourly average Wind speed, $x_3(t)$,

(iv) hourly peak electric load consumption which is $y(t)$.

A number of 720 samples of Input and output data are normalized using (40) to maintain the compatibility in the range 0 to 1. We consider 75% of the total input-output vectors of the form $\mathbf{z}(t) = [10 \cdot (y(t) - y(t-2)) \quad 10 \cdot (x_3(t) - x_2(t-2)) \quad 10 \cdot (x_2(t) - x_2(t-2)) \quad 50 \cdot (x_3(t-2) - x_3(t)) \quad 100 \cdot y(t)]$

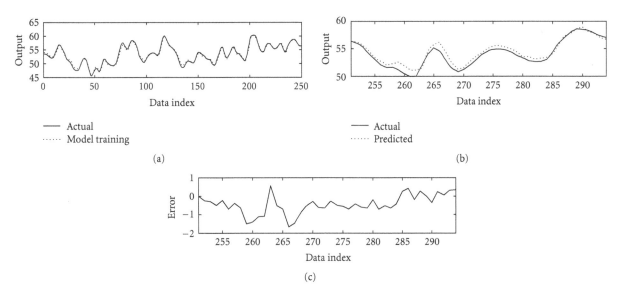

FIGURE 1: Plot of actual output and model output for training data set (uppermost plot) and plot of actual output and predicted output and the corresponding prediction error for Box and Jenkins's gas furnace data.

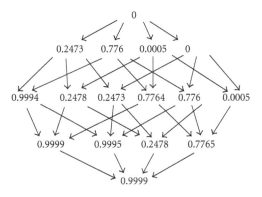

FIGURE 2: Lattice of fuzzy measure values of the constituent singleton sets [39] of rule 1 for Box and Jenkins's data.

as the training set. The remaining 25% is reserved for the prediction. The weights before the components in $\mathbf{z}(t)$ have been fixed for achieving better prediction capability. It may be noted that the criteria only facilitate the selection of proper inputs by trying out different combinations. But the final curtain falls on the selection with the verification through the performance measure.

The number of clusters in this example also is found to be 4 using the EM clustering after discarding a few datasets as outliers. Application of the EM algorithm yields the parameters of GMM in Table 13. These constitute the premise parameters of the GFM. The estimated fuzzy densities, lambda values, fuzzy measure, Q-measure and β-coefficients of the model are given in Tables 14, 15, 16, 17, and 18, respectively. The monotonicity relations can also be verified as in the previous applications

The training data set is found to give $E = 0.0034$. The remaining 25% data vectors constitute the validation data set. The performance measure E over this set is obtained as

0.00256. The results of the actual output and the model output during the training and the prediction periods are shown in Figure 6, which also includes the prediction error. The results demonstrate the effectiveness of the proposed non-additive fuzzy model using Q-measure for this application too (Figure 7).

The performance measures of the applications A and B are given in Table 19 for comparison with some of the existing well-known methods of fuzzy modeling. This table shows that E of the proposed nonadditive fuzzy model is better than those of the additive fuzzy systems of Gan et al. [7] and WM method [25].

6. Conclusions

This paper deals with an important issue of computing fuzzy measures directly from covariance matrices found in GMM. Use of EM algorithm in GMM provides us with the input clusters and their Gaussian memberships. The consequent parts of the fuzzy rules, that is, the output function, of GFM are altered for incorporating the non-additive property. It has to be noted that we have been still using the multiplicative T-norm in the premise part but the additive property of S-norm in the consequent part. For this the output function is defined as a linear function of fuzzy measures serving as coefficients. Computation complexity is reduced by replacing Sugeno's λ-measure with the Q-measure in the non-additive fuzzy model.

The defuzzified output of the non-additive GFM rules is then shown to be in the form of Choquet integral. By showing the Choquet fuzzy integral as the functionality of non-additive GFM, we have enhanced its capability to tackle a variety of real-life problems. We have also proved the corresponding non-additive functionality for GMM. This has been accomplished by showing that $f(\mathbf{x}, \beta_m)$ is the mean value of $\mathbf{y}$. The computation of fuzzy measures required in

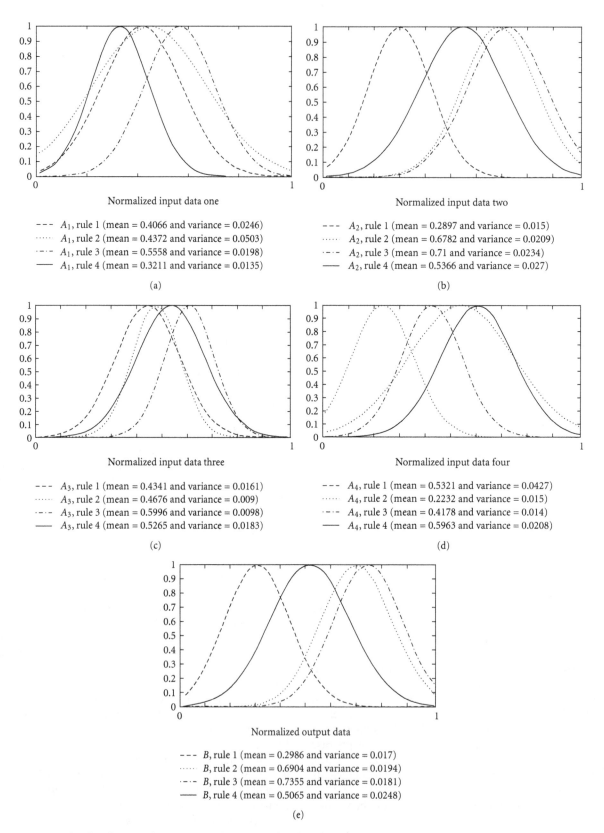

FIGURE 3: (a) Membership function for input one. (b) Membership functions for input two. (c) Membership function for input three. (d) Membership function for input four. (e) Membership function for output.

TABLE 7: Estimated parameters of A 4-component GMM using the EM algorithm.

Cluster or rule no. (m)	Weight of the rule $p(c_m)$	Mean ($\bar{\mathbf{z}}^m$)	Covariance ($\sum_m$)
Cluster or rule no. 1	$p(c_1) = 0.3564$	$\bar{\mathbf{z}}^1 = \begin{bmatrix} 0.3946 \\ -0.6119 \\ -0.0988 \\ -0.3346 \\ -0.3402 \end{bmatrix}$	$\sum_1 = \begin{bmatrix} 0.4246 & -0.0243 & 0.1174 & -0.0049 & 0.0066 \\ -0.0243 & 0.0983 & -0.0372 & -0.0558 & -0.0618 \\ 0.1174 & -0.0372 & 0.6188 & 0.0229 & 0.0355 \\ -0.0049 & -0.0558 & 0.0229 & 0.3952 & 0.3608 \\ 0.0066 & -0.0618 & 0.0355 & 0.3608 & 0.3933 \end{bmatrix}$
Cluster or rule no. 2	$p(c_2) = 0.2723$	$\bar{\mathbf{z}}^2 = \begin{bmatrix} -0.1952 \\ 0.1800 \\ -0.1897 \\ 1.5585 \\ 1.5501 \end{bmatrix}$	$\sum_2 = \begin{bmatrix} 0.5879 & -0.2083 & -0.0120 & -0.0916 & -0.1151 \\ -0.2083 & 0.7343 & -0.1670 & 0.0011 & -0.0073 \\ -0.0120 & -0.1670 & 0.8701 & 0.0702 & 0.1139 \\ -0.0916 & 0.0011 & 0.0702 & 0.2802 & 0.2227 \\ -0.1151 & -0.0073 & 0.1139 & 0.2227 & 0.2849 \end{bmatrix}$
Cluster or rule no. 3	$p(c_3) = 0.2046$	$\bar{\mathbf{z}}^3 = \begin{bmatrix} -1.1811 \\ 1.4027 \\ -0.4488 \\ -0.1763 \\ -0.1760 \end{bmatrix}$	$\sum_3 = \begin{bmatrix} 0.7008 & 0.1105 & -0.2400 & 0.0711 & 0.0582 \\ 0.1105 & 0.2471 & -0.0056 & -0.0244 & -0.0416 \\ -0.2400 & -0.0056 & 0.4133 & -0.1059 & -0.0953 \\ 0.0711 & -0.0244 & -0.1059 & 0.4661 & 0.4226 \\ 0.0582 & -0.0416 & -0.0953 & 0.4226 & 0.4704 \end{bmatrix}$
Cluster or rule no. 4	$p(c_4) = 0.1667$	$\bar{\mathbf{z}}^4 = \begin{bmatrix} -0.3041 \\ 1.0443 \\ 0.9807 \\ -0.0032 \\ 0.0179 \end{bmatrix}$	$\sum_4 = \begin{bmatrix} 0.4283 & 0.0685 & -0.2311 & -0.0418 & -0.0953 \\ 0.0685 & 0.6950 & -0.4111 & 0.0238 & -0.0029 \\ -0.2311 & -0.4111 & 0.7699 & 0.1282 & 0.1662 \\ -0.0418 & 0.0238 & 0.1282 & 0.3210 & 0.2911 \\ -0.0953 & -0.0029 & 0.1662 & 0.2911 & 0.3528 \end{bmatrix}$

TABLE 8: Fuzzy densities using GMM.

Rule (m)	g_1	g_2	g_3	g_4
Rule no. 1	0.4982	0.4295	0.3881	0.7989
Rule no. 2	0.4996	0.7368	0.6158	0.9027
Rule no. 3	0.4696	0.7543	0.3704	0.5916
Rule no. 4	0.4844	0.7330	0.0042	0.0012

TABLE 11: Estimated β coefficients.

Rule (m)	β_1	β_2	β_3	β_4
Rule no. 1	0.0354	0.0536	0.0790	0.7989
Rule no. 2	0.0199	0.0070	0.0009	0.8749
Rule no. 3	0.2971	0.0285	0.0326	0.5918
Rule no. 4	0.0000	0.0000	0.0019	0.9981

TABLE 9: Estimated lambda (λ^m).

Rule 1	Rule 2	Rule 3	Rule 4
-0.9970	-1.0000	-1.0000	-0.9947

TABLE 12: Estimated Q-measures.

Rule (m)	$Q(X_1)$	$Q(X_2)$	$Q(X_3)$	$Q(X_4)$
Rule no. 1	1.0000	0.7823	0.0013	0.0000
Rule no. 2	1.0000	0.8541	0.0635	0.0001
Rule no. 3	1.0000	0.9175	0.0863	0.0003
Rule no. 4	1.0000	0.7230	0.0169	0.0002

TABLE 10: Estimated λ-measures.

Rule (m)	$\zeta(X_1)$	$\zeta(X_2)$	$\zeta(X_3)$	$\zeta(X_4)$
Rule no. 1	0.9669	0.9315	0.8779	0.7989
Rule no. 2	0.9027	0.8828	0.8758	0.8749
Rule no. 3	0.9500	0.6529	0.6244	0.5918
Rule no. 4	1.0000	1.0000	1.0000	0.9981

the Choquet integral entails a lot of computational burden, as we need to solve a polynomial in λ. Using Q-measure this burden has been eliminated.

The non-additive fuzzy model is applied on the three benchmark applications, namely, Box and Jenkins's, Dryers' data and on the real time electric load demand data. The results demonstrate the superiority of this model over the additive fuzzy model of Gan et al. [7] and Wang and Mendel method [25]. Thus this work makes an important contribution to the field of fuzzy modeling by providing a transition from additive fuzzy systems to non-additive fuzzy systems for dealing with the real-life applications. This is done without learning the fuzzy densities and eliminating the computational complexity associated with solving the polynomial function in λ. In the non-additive fuzzy systems, it makes a novel contribution and will pave the way for several other applications and for further research.

Appendix

Formulation of the Learning Process

In this section we will find the derivatives required for the learning laws. To keep the thread going, we recall the relevant equations from Section 5.

For *incremental learning*, using (51), we obtain the derivatives in (52) as

$$\frac{\partial J_{\text{incr}}}{\partial a_0} = \left(\hat{y}_j - y_j\right) = e_j, \tag{A.1a}$$

$$\frac{\partial J_{\text{incr}}}{\partial \lambda^m} = \frac{\partial\left((1/2)\left(\hat{y}_j - y_j\right)^2\right)}{\partial \lambda^m} = \frac{\partial\left((1/2)e_j^2\right)}{\partial \lambda^m} = e_j \cdot \frac{\partial\left(\hat{y}_j\right)}{\partial \lambda^m}. \tag{A.1b}$$

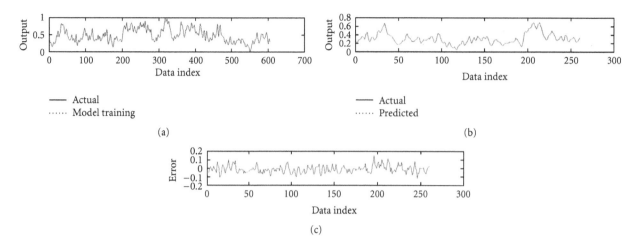

FIGURE 4: Plot of actual output and model output for training data set (uppermost plot) and plot of actual output and predicted output and the corresponding prediction error for industrial dryer data.

TABLE 13: Estimated parameters of A 4-component GMM using the EM algorithm (load).

Cluster or rule no. (m)	Weight of the rule $p(c_m)$	Mean ($\overline{\mathbf{z}}^m$)	Covariance ($\sum_m$)
Cluster or rule no. 1	$p(c_1) = 0.2646$	$\overline{\mathbf{z}}^1 = \begin{bmatrix} 0.4720 \\ 0.4500 \\ 0.4694 \\ 0.3820 \\ 0.5007 \end{bmatrix}$	$\sum_1 = \begin{bmatrix} 0.0031 & -0.0000 & -0.00107 & -0.0016 & 0.0026 \\ -0.0000 & 0.0306 & 0.0160 & -0.0051 & 0.0010 \\ -0.0017 & 0.0160 & 0.0246 & 0.0050 & -0.0005 \\ -0.0016 & -0.0051 & 0.0050 & 0.0227 & -0.0015 \\ 0.0026 & 0.0010 & -0.0005 & -0.0015 & 0.0029 \end{bmatrix}$
Cluster or rule no. 2	$p(c_2) = 0.2225$	$\overline{\mathbf{z}}^2 = \begin{bmatrix} 0.5226 \\ 0.7430 \\ 0.5564 \\ 0.4598 \\ 0.5269 \end{bmatrix}$	$\sum_2 = \begin{bmatrix} 0.0188 & -0.0007 & 0.0031 & -0.0004 & 0.0122 \\ -0.0007 & 0.0081 & 0.0031 & -0.0044 & -0.0001 \\ 0.0031 & 0.0031 & 0.0052 & 0.0034 & 0.0024 \\ -0.0004 & -0.0044 & 0.0034 & 0.0308 & 0.0009 \\ 0.0122 & 0.0001 & -0.0024 & 0.0009 & 0.0084 \end{bmatrix}$
Cluster or rule no. 3	$p(c_3) = 0.2474$	$\overline{\mathbf{z}}^3 = \begin{bmatrix} 0.2902 \\ 0.3000 \\ 0.6844 \\ 0.4393 \\ 0.3771 \end{bmatrix}$	$\sum_3 = \begin{bmatrix} 0.0228 & -0.0014 & -0.0035 & -0.0012 & 0.0137 \\ -0.0014 & 0.0154 & 0.0018 & 0.0003 & -0.0044 \\ -0.0035 & 0.0018 & 0.0065 & 0.0018 & -0.0025 \\ -0.0012 & 0.0003 & 0.0018 & 0.0054 & -0.0020 \\ 0.0137 & -0.0044 & -0.0025 & -0.0020 & 0.0142 \end{bmatrix}$
Cluster or rule no. 4	$p(c_4) = 0.2655$	$\overline{\mathbf{z}}^4 = \begin{bmatrix} 0.6474 \\ 0.5738 \\ 0.7372 \\ 0.4940 \\ 0.6013 \end{bmatrix}$	$\sum_4 = \begin{bmatrix} 0.0102 & 0.0011 & 0.0009 & -0.0023 & 0.0068 \\ 0.0011 & 0.0093 & -0.0004 & 0.0030 & 0.0037 \\ 0.0009 & -0.0004 & 0.0108 & -0.0033 & 0.0002 \\ -0.0023 & 0.0030 & -0.0033 & 0.0189 & 0.0024 \\ 0.0068 & 0.0037 & 0.0002 & 0.0024 & 0.0073 \end{bmatrix}$

For *batch learning*, using (50), (52), we obtain the derivative as

$$\frac{\partial J_{\text{batch}}}{\partial a_0} = \left(\frac{2}{n}\right) \cdot \sum_{j=1}^{n} \left(\hat{y}_j - y_j\right), \tag{A.2a}$$

$$\frac{\partial J_{\text{batch}}}{\partial \lambda^m} = \frac{\partial\left((1/n)\sum_{j=1}^{n}\left(\hat{y}_j - y_j\right)^2\right)}{\partial \lambda^m} = \frac{\partial\left((1/n)\sum_{j=1}^{n} e_j^2\right)}{\partial \lambda^m}$$

$$= \frac{2}{n} \cdot \sum_{j=1}^{n}\left(e_j \cdot \frac{\partial\left(\hat{y}_j\right)}{\partial \lambda^m}\right). \tag{A.2b}$$

In the two applications that we dealt with, we have used the incremental learning. Now the formulation of the learning process required in the above two types of learning is presented in the following. For jth set of D-inputs $\mathbf{x}_j = $ $[x_{j1} \quad x_{j2} \quad x_{j3} \quad \cdots \quad x_{jD}]$, the estimated output using (34) is

$$\hat{y}_j = a_0 + \sum_{d=1}^{D}\left(\sum_{m=1}^{M} h^m\left(x_{jd}\right) \cdot \left(Q^m(X_d) - Q^m(X_{d+1})\right)\right). \tag{A.3}$$

The partial derivatives of (A.3) with respect to λ^m and fuzzy densities g_d^m for $d = 1, 2, 3, \ldots, D$ required in (A.1b) and (A.2b) are obtained after rearranging as

$$\frac{\partial\left(\hat{y}_j\right)}{\partial \lambda^m} = 0 + \left(\frac{\mu^m\left(\mathbf{x}_j\right) \cdot p(c_m) \cdot x_{j1}}{\sum_{l=1}^{M} \mu^l\left(\mathbf{x}_j\right) \cdot p(c_l)}\right) \cdot \frac{\partial(Q^m(X_1))}{\partial \lambda^m}$$

$$+ \left(\frac{\mu^m\left(\mathbf{x}_j\right) \cdot p(c_m) \cdot \left(x_{j2} - x_{j1}\right)}{\sum_{l=1}^{M} \mu^l\left(\mathbf{x}_j\right) \cdot p(c_l)}\right) \cdot \frac{\partial(Q^m(X_2))}{\partial \lambda^m}$$

$$+ \cdots$$

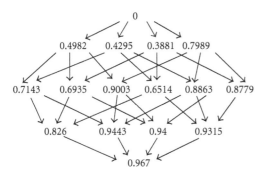

FIGURE 5: Lattice of fuzzy measure values of the constituent singleton sets of rule no.1 of Table 10 for industrial dryer's data.

TABLE 14: Fuzzy densities using GMM.

Rule (m)	g_1	g_2	g_3	g_4
Rule no. 1	0.8479	0.6488	0.5817	0.6735
Rule no. 2	0.0196	0.0633	0.0001	0.2634
Rule no. 3	0.0264	0.0100	0.0725	0.0255
Rule no. 4	0.0001	0.0469	0.0001	0.1708

TABLE 15: Estimated lambda (λ^m).

Rule 1	Rule 2	Rule 3	Rule 4
29.3843	−0.0776	−0.9995	0.2543

TABLE 16: Estimated λ-measures.

Rule (m)	$\zeta(X_1)$	$\zeta(X_2)$	$\zeta(X_3)$	$\zeta(X_4)$
Rule no. 1	1.0000	0.0877	0.0439	0.6735
Rule no. 2	1.0000	0.1200	0.0569	0.2634
Rule no. 3	1.0000	0.0910	0.0818	0.0255
Rule no. 4	1.0000	0.4718	0.1974	0.1708

TABLE 17: Estimated Q-measures.

Rule (m)	$Q(X_1)$	$Q(X_2)$	$Q(X_3)$	$Q(X_4)$
Rule no. 1	1.0000	0.0291	0.0145	0.0033
Rule no. 2	1.0000	0.1569	0.0744	0.0614
Rule no. 3	1.0000	0.1468	0.1320	0.0161
Rule no. 4	1.0000	0.3891	0.1628	0.1409

TABLE 18: Estimated β coefficients.

Rule (m)	β_1	β_2	β_3	β_4
Rule no. 1	0.9709	0.0146	0.0112	0.0033
Rule no. 2	0.8431	0.0825	0.0130	0.0614
Rule no. 3	0.8532	0.0148	0.1159	0.0161
Rule no. 4	0.6109	0.2263	0.0219	0.1409

$$+ \left(\frac{\mu^m(\mathbf{x}_j) \cdot p(c_m) \cdot \left(x_{jD} - x_{j(D-1)} \right)}{\sum_{l=1}^{M} \mu^l(\mathbf{x}_j) \cdot p(c_l)} \right)$$

$$\times \frac{\partial(Q^m(X_D))}{\partial \lambda^m}. \tag{A.4}$$

Using (6), we obtain the derivatives as follows:

$$\frac{\partial(Q^m(X_d))}{\partial \lambda^m} = \frac{\zeta^m(X_1) \cdot \partial \zeta^m(X_d)/\partial \lambda^m}{(\zeta^m(X_1))^2} - \frac{\zeta^m(X_d) \cdot \partial \zeta^m(X_1)/\partial \lambda^m}{(\zeta^m(X_1))^2}. \tag{A.5}$$

The polynomial for the general case of D-inputs using (3) and (4) is

$$\zeta^m(X_1) = \left((\lambda^m)^{D-1} \right)$$
$$\cdot \prod_{d=1}^{D} \left(g_d^m \right) + \cdots + (\lambda^m) \cdot \sum_{d=1}^{D-1} \sum_{k=d+1}^{D} g_d^m \cdot g_k^m + \sum_{d=1}^{D} g_d^m. \tag{A.6}$$

The polynomial in λ^m for $D = 4$ is found as

$$\zeta^m(X_1) = \varphi_3 \cdot (\lambda^m)^3 + \varphi_2 \cdot (\lambda^m)^2 + \varphi_1 \cdot \lambda^m + \varphi_0.$$
$$\zeta^m(X_2) = (\lambda^m)^2 \left(g_2^m \cdot g_3^m \cdot g_4^m \right)$$
$$+ \lambda^m \left(g_2^m \cdot g_3^m + g_3^m \cdot g_4^m + g_2^m \cdot g_4^m \right)$$

$$+ \left(g_2^m + g_3^m + g_4^m \right),$$
$$\zeta^m(X_3) = \lambda^m \left(g_3^m \cdot g_4^m \right) + \left(g_3^m + g_4^m \right),$$
$$\zeta^m(X_4) = g_4^m. \tag{A.7}$$

The derivatives of the above with respect to λ^m are

$$\frac{\partial \zeta^m(X_1)}{\partial \lambda^m} = 3\varphi_3 \cdot (\lambda^m)^2 + 2\varphi_2 \cdot (\lambda^m) + \varphi_1,$$
$$\frac{\partial \zeta^m(X_2)}{\partial \lambda^m} = 2\lambda^m \left(g_2^m \cdot g_3^m \cdot g_4^m \right)$$
$$+ \left(g_2^m \cdot g_3^m + g_3^m \cdot g_4^m + g_4^m \cdot g_2^m \right), \tag{A.8}$$
$$\frac{\partial \zeta^m(X_3)}{\partial \lambda^m} = g_3^m \cdot g_4^m,$$
$$\frac{\partial \zeta^m(X_4)}{\partial \lambda^m} = 0,$$

where

$$\varphi_3 = g_1^m \cdot g_2^m \cdot g_3^m \cdot g_4^m,$$
$$\phi_2 = \big(g_1^m \cdot g_2^m \cdot g_3^m + g_2^m \cdot g_3^m \cdot g_4^m$$
$$+ g_3^m \cdot g_4^m \cdot g_1^m + g_4^m \cdot g_1^m \cdot g_2^m \big),$$
$$\varphi_1 = \big(g_1^m \cdot g_2^m + g_2^m \cdot g_3^m + g_3^m \cdot g_4^m$$
$$+ g_4^m \cdot g_1^m + g_1^m \cdot g_3^m + g_2^m \cdot g_4^m \big),$$
$$\varphi_0 = \big(g_1^m + g_2^m + g_3^m + g_4^m \big). \tag{A.9}$$

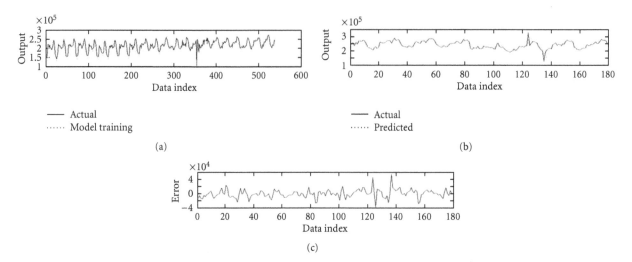

(a)

(b)

(c)

FIGURE 6: Plot of actual output and model output for training data set (uppermost plot) and plot of actual output and predicted output and the corresponding prediction error for hourly electric load data.

TABLE 19: Comparison of E.

Data	WM [25] method	Gan et al. [7]	Non-additive (using λ-measure)	Proposed algorithm (using fuzzy measure estimation)
Box & Jenkins's Gas Furnace data	0.0057	0.0032	0.0021	0.00208
Industrial Dryer's data	NA	0.0027	0.0019	0.00189

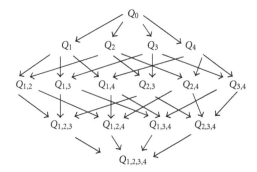

FIGURE 7: Lattice of Q-measure values of the constituent singleton sets with $D = 4$.

The above polynomial and their derivatives in (A.8) are used in (A.4) and (A.5) to obtain a solution. Thus, we can see a considerable simplification with Q-measure as the solution of λ^m-polynomials is not needed. On the other hand without Q-measure, the derivatives of λ^m with respect to g_d^m are required to learn λ^m.

References

[1] M. F. Azeem, M. Hanmandlu, and N. Ahmad, "Structure identification of generalized adaptive neuro-fuzzy inference systems," *IEEE Transactions on Fuzzy Systems*, vol. 11, no. 5, pp. 666–681, 2003.

[2] M. F. Azeem, M. Hanmandlu, and N. Ahmad, "Generalization of adaptive neuro-fuzzy inference systems," *IEEE Transactions on Neural Networks*, vol. 11, no. 6, pp. 1332–1346, 2000.

[3] N. K. Verma and M. Hanmandlu, "Adaptive non-additive generalized fuzzy systems," *Applied Soft Computing Journal*, vol. 10, no. 3, pp. 820–831, 2010.

[4] T. Takagi and M. Sugeno, "Fuzzy identification of systems and its applications to modeling and control," *IEEE Transactions on Systems, Man and Cybernetics*, vol. 15, no. 1, pp. 116–132, 1985.

[5] E. H. Mamdani and S. Assilian, "Experiment in linguistic synthesis with a fuzzy logic controller," *International Journal of Man-Machine Studies*, vol. 7, no. 1, pp. 1–13, 1975.

[6] J. S. R. Jang and C. T. Sun, "Functional equivalence between radial basis function networks and fuzzy inference systems," *IEEE Transactions on Neural Networks*, vol. 4, no. 1, pp. 156–159, 1993.

[7] M.-T. Gan, M. Hanmandlu, and A. H. Tan, "From a gaussian mixture model to additive fuzzy systems," *IEEE Transactions on Fuzzy Systems*, vol. 13, no. 3, pp. 303–316, 2005.

[8] R. L. Flood and E. R. Carson, *Dealing with Complexity: An Introduction to the Theory and Application of Systems Science*, Plenum, New York, NY, USA, 2nd. edition, 1993.

[9] G. J. McLachlan, "Cluster analysis and related techniques in medical research," *Statistical Methods in Medical Research*, vol. 1, no. 1, pp. 27–48, 1992.

[10] N. A. Gershenfeld, *The Nature of Mathematical Modeling*, Cambridge University Press, London, UK, 1999.

[11] B. S. Everitt, *Cluster Analysis*, Edward Arnold, London, UK, 3rd. edition, 1993.

[12] K. Y. Yeung, C. Fraley, A. Murua, A. E. Raftery, and W. L. Ruzzo, "Model-based clustering and data transformations for gene expression data," *Bioinformatics*, vol. 17, no. 10, pp. 977–987, 2001.

[13] D. V. Prokhorov, L. A. Feldkamp, and T. M. Feldkamp, "A new approach to cluster-weighted modeling," in *Proceedings of the International Joint Conference on Neural Networks (IJCNN'01)*, vol. 3, pp. 1669–1674, July 2001.

[14] L. A. Feldkamp, D. V. Prokhorov, and T. M. Feldkamp, "Cluster-weighted modeling with multiclusters," in *Proceedings of the International Joint Conference on Neural Networks (IJCNN'01)*, vol. 3, pp. 1710–1714, July 2001.

[15] B. Everitt, D. J. Hand et al., *Finite Mixture Distributions*, Chapman and Hall, London, UK, 1981.

[16] J. H. Wolfe, "A Monte-Carlo study of the sampling distribution of the likelihood ratio for mixtures of multinormal distributions," Technical Bulletin STB 72-2, US Navel Personnel and Training Research Activity, San Diego, Calif, USA, 1971.

[17] N. R. Mendell, H. C. Thode, and S. J. Finch, "The likelihood ratio test for the two-component normal mixture problem: power and sample size analysis," *Biometrics*, vol. 47, no. 3, pp. 1143–1148, 1991.

[18] G. J. McLachlan, "On bootstrapping the likelihood ratio test statistic for the number of components in a normal mixture," *Journal of the Royal Statistical Society, Series C*, vol. 36, no. 3, pp. 318–324, 1987.

[19] G. J. McLachlan, *Discriminant Analysis and Statistical Pattern Recognition*, Wiley-Interscience, New York, NY, USA, 1992.

[20] R. E. Walpole, R. H. Myers, and S. L. Myers, *Probability and Statistics for Engineers and Scientists*, Prentice Hall, 6th. edition, 1998.

[21] K. V. Mardia, J. T. Kent, and J. M. Bibby, *Multivariate Analysis*, Academic Press, 1979.

[22] W. H. Press, S. A. Teukolsky, W. T. Vetterling, and B. P. Flannery, *Numerical Recipes in C: The Art of Scientific Computing*, Cambridge University Press, London, UK, 2nd. edition, 1993.

[23] M. Aitkin, D. Anderson, and J. Hinde, "Statistical modelling of data on teaching styles," *Journal of the Royal Statistical Society A*, vol. 144, no. 4, pp. 419–461, 1981.

[24] B. Kosko, *Fuzzy Engineering*, Prentice Hall, London, UK, 1997.

[25] L. X. Wang and J. M. Mendel, "Generating fuzzy rules by learning from examples," *IEEE Transactions on Systems, Man and Cybernetics*, vol. 22, no. 6, pp. 1414–1427, 1992.

[26] J. Abonyi, R. Babuška, and F. Szeifert, "Modified Gath-Geva fuzzy clustering for identification of Takagi-Sugeno fuzzy models," *IEEE Transactions on Systems, Man, and Cybernetics, Part B*, vol. 32, no. 5, pp. 612–621, 2002.

[27] M. Sugeno and T. Yasukawa, "Fuzzy-logic-based approach to qualitative modeling," *IEEE Transactions on Fuzzy Systems*, vol. 1, no. 1, pp. 7–31, 1993.

[28] M. Sugeno and G. T. Kang, "Structure identification of fuzzy model," *Fuzzy Sets and Systems*, vol. 28, no. 1, pp. 15–33, 1988.

[29] M. Hanmandlu, N. K. Verma, N. Ahmad, and S. Vasikarla, "Cluster-weighted modeling as a basis for non-additive GFM," in *Proceedings of the IEEE International Conference on Fuzzy Systems, FUZZ-IEEE*, pp. 652–657, Reno, Nev, USA, May 2005.

[30] J. R. Chang, G. H. Tzeng, C. T. Hung, and H. H. Lin, "Non-additive fuzzy regression applied to establish flexible pavement present serviceability index," in *Proceedings of the IEEE International Conference on Fuzzy Systems*, pp. 1020–1025, May 2003.

[31] N. K. Verma and M. Hanmandlu, "From a gaussian mixture model to nonadditive fuzzy systems," *IEEE Transactions on Fuzzy Systems*, vol. 15, no. 5, pp. 809–827, 2007.

[32] P. Miranda and E. F. Combarro, "On the structure of some families of fuzzy measures," *IEEE Transactions on Fuzzy Systems*, vol. 15, no. 6, pp. 1068–1081, 2007.

[33] R. R. Yager, "Uncertainty representation using fuzzy measures," *IEEE Transactions on Systems, Man, and Cybernetics, Part B*, vol. 32, no. 1, pp. 13–20, 2002.

[34] K. Le, "Fuzzy measures of aggregated evidences," in *Proceedings of the Biennial Conference of the North American Fuzzy Information Processing Society (NAFIPS '96)*, pp. 572–576, Berkeley, Calif, USA, June 1996.

[35] Y. Narukawa, T. Murofushi, and M. Sugeno, "Space of fuzzy measures and convergence," *Fuzzy Sets and Systems*, vol. 138, no. 3, pp. 497–506, 2003.

[36] J.-H. Chiang, "Choquet fuzzy integral-based hierarchical networks for decision analysis," *IEEE Transactions on Fuzzy Systems*, vol. 7, no. 1, pp. 63–71, 1999.

[37] Y. Narukawa and V. Torra, "Fuzzy measures and integrals in evaluation of strategies," *Information Sciences*, vol. 177, no. 21, pp. 4686–4695, 2007.

[38] Z. Q. Liu, L. T. Bruton, J. C. Bezdek et al., "Dynamic image sequence analysis using fuzzy measures," *IEEE Transactions on Systems, Man, and Cybernetics, Part B*, vol. 31, no. 4, pp. 557–572, 2001.

[39] M. Grabisch, T. Murofushi, and M. Sugeno, *Fuzzy Measures and Integrals: Theory and Applications*, Physica, Heidelberg, Germany, 2000.

[40] M. Sugeno, "Fuzzy measures and fuzzy integrals: a survey," in *Fuzzy Automata and Decision Processes*, M. M. Gupta, G. N. Saridis, and B. R. Gaines, Eds., pp. 89–102, North-Holland, New York, NY, USA, 1977.

[41] T. Murofushi and M. Sugeno, "Some quantities represented by the choquet integral," *Fuzzy Sets and Systems*, vol. 56, no. 2, pp. 229–235, 1993.

[42] L. M. De Campos, M. T. Lamata, and S. Moral, "A unified approach to define fuzzy integrals," *Fuzzy Sets and Systems*, vol. 39, no. 1, pp. 75–90, 1991.

[43] M. Friedman, M. Ma, and A. Kandel, "Numerical methods for calculating the fuzzy integral," *Fuzzy Sets and Systems*, vol. 83, no. 1, pp. 57–62, 1996.

[44] M. Sugeno and T. Murofushi, "Pseudo-additive measures and integrals," *Journal of Mathematical Analysis and Applications*, vol. 122, no. 1, pp. 197–222, 1987.

[45] Z. Wang, G. J. Klir, and W. Wang, "Monotone set functions defined by choquet integral," *Fuzzy Sets and Systems*, vol. 81, no. 2, pp. 241–250, 1996.

[46] M. Sugeno, *Theory of fuzzy integrals and its applications*, Ph.D. thesis, Tokyo Institute of Technology, Tokyo, Japan, 1974.

[47] P. D. Gader, J. M. Keller, R. Krishnapuram, J. H. Chiang, and M. A. Mohamed, "Neural and fuzzy methods in handwriting recognition," *Computer*, vol. 30, no. 2, pp. 79–86, 1997.

[48] P. D. Gader, J. M. Keller, and B. N. Nelson, "Recognition technology for the detection of buried land mines," *IEEE Transactions on Fuzzy Systems*, vol. 9, no. 1, pp. 31–43, 2001.

[49] J. M. Keller, P. Gader, H. Tahani, J. H. Chiang, and M. Mohamed, "Advances in fuzzy integration for pattern recognition," *Fuzzy Sets and Systems*, vol. 65, no. 2-3, pp. 273–283, 1994.

[50] W. J. Krzanowski and F. H. C. Marriott, *Multivariate Analysis Part 2: Classification, Covariance Structures and Repeated Measurements*, Edward Arnold, London, UK, 1995.

[51] A. K. Hocaoğlu and P. Gader, "Comments on 'choquet fuzzy integral-based hierarchical networks for decision analysis,'" *IEEE Transactions on Fuzzy Systems*, vol. 7, no. 6, p. 767, 1999.

[52] M. A. Mohamed and W. Xiao, "Q-measures: an efficient extension of the sugeno λ-measure," *IEEE Transactions on Fuzzy Systems*, vol. 11, no. 3, pp. 419–426, 2003.

[53] M. F. Azeem, M. Hanmandlu, and N. Ahmad, "Parameter determination for a generalized fuzzy model," *Soft Computing*, vol. 9, no. 3, pp. 211–221, 2005.

[54] A. R. Barron, "Predicted squared error: a criterion for automatic model selection," in *Self-Organizing Methods in Modeling*, S. J. Farlow, Ed., vol. 54, pp. 87–103, Marcel Dekker, New York, NY, USA, 1984.

[55] E. P. Box and G. M. Jenkins, *Time Series Analysis: Forecasting and Control*, Holden-day, San Francisco, Calif, USA, 1970.

[56] M. F. Azeem, M. Hanmandlu, and N. Ahmad, "A new criteria for input variable identification of dynamical systems," in *Proceedings of the IEEE Region 10th International Conference on Global Connectivity in Energy, Computer, Communication and Control (TENCON '98)*, vol. 1, pp. 230–233, New Delhi, India, 1998.

[57] A. P. Dempster, N. M. Laird, and D. B. Rubin, "Maximum likelihood from incomplete data via the EM algorithm," *Journal of the Royal Statistical Society B*, vol. 39, no. 1, pp. 1–38, 1977.

15

A Fuzzy Logic Controller to Increase Fault Ride-Through Capability of Variable Speed Wind Turbines

Geev Mokryani, Pierluigi Siano, Antonio Piccolo, and Vito Calderaro

Department of Industrial Engineering, University of Salerno, Salerno, 84084 Fisciano, Italy

Correspondence should be addressed to Pierluigi Siano, psiano@unisa.it

Academic Editor: Anyong Qing

A fuzzy controller for improving Fault Ride-Through (FRT) capability of Variable Speed Wind Turbines (WTs) equipped with Doubly Fed Induction Generator (DFIG) is presented. The controller is designed in order to compensate the voltage at the Point of Common Coupling (PCC) by regulating the reactive and active power generated by WTs. The performances of the controller are evaluated in some case studies considering a different number of wind farms in different locations. Simulations, carried out on a real 37-bus Italian weak distribution system, confirmed that the proposed controller can enhance the FRT capability in many cases.

1. Introduction

Wind turbines (WTs) are typically located in remote and rural areas. In these areas, the feeders are long and operated at a medium voltage level characterized by a high R/X ratio and unbalanced voltage situations. Furthermore, weak grids are usually referred to have a "low short-circuit level" or "low fault level." In a weak network a change in the real and reactive power can cause a considerable change in the voltage. The impact relies on the strength of the network and the output power of the WTs [1]. Integration of WTs into weak grids can cause the steady-state voltage level to go outside of its acceptable limit. Therefore, it can limit the exploitation of wind energy resources. Another constraint is related to the effect of the power generated by WTs on the voltage quality. Voltage level limitations and accurate control systems are required to control the voltage variations as well as to improve the voltage quality [2], and variable speed WTs can be used as reactive power sources for voltage control.

In recent times, many researches have been carried out in this field. A proportional-integral- (PI-) based control algorithm to control the reactive power produced by WTs has been proposed in [3]. In [4], the authors have proposed a mathematical model of the Doubly Fed Induction Generator (DFIG) for the analysis of active and reactive power performances of a wind farm (WF). In [5], the relation between reactive and active power to maintain the DFIG's operation inside the maximum rotor and stator currents has been studied. In [6], the authors have proposed a fuzzy controller to manage the operation of a Flywheel Energy Storage System (ESS) connected to the DC bus.

Recently, the penetration of WTs into the grids increased, and the performance of the WTs under faults has became an important issue, especially for DFIGs. Several grid codes prescribed, in fact, that WTs should remain connected to the network during and after faults. The ability of WTs to stay connected to the grid during fault and voltage variations is defined as Fault Ride-Through (FRT) capability [7]. One of the common FRT capability improvement solutions is to set up a crowbar circuit across the rotor terminals [8]. Another common method is to insert an ESS [9], such as batteries or super capacitors at the DC bus inside the rotor side converter (RSC). A control strategy to improve FRT capability by using Flexible AC Transmission System (FACTS) devices and ESS has been proposed in [10]. In [11], the authors have proposed a new feed-forward transient current control (FFTCC) applied to RSC for improving the FRT capability. In [12], a fuzzy controller to manage the rotor speed oscillations and the DC-link voltage variations of the DFIG has been proposed.

In this paper, a fuzzy controller for improving FRT capability of variable-speed WTs in wind farms is presented.

The controller is designed in order to compensate the voltage at the point of common coupling (PCC) by controlling the reactive and active power generated by WFs. In previous research works, other authors have investigated the FRT capability improvement only considering voltage sag, while in this paper the voltage swell effect is also considered to investigate FRT capability improvement according to Danish grid code. The novelty of the proposed fuzzy controller consists in considering active and reactive power regulation simultaneously. In particular, if during a voltage swell, the absorbed reactive power is not adequate to lower the voltage at the PCC within its statutory limits, the reference signal for the active power production is decreased by the fuzzy controller. In this case the WT will not generate the maximum active power according to its power coefficient, but this will determine two positive effects of the voltage regulation at the PCC: firstly, due to the limited size of the power converters of DFIGs, the active power reduction will allow increasing the maximum reactive power that can be absorbed by WTs; moreover, in medium-voltage weak networks with long feeders characterized by a high R/X ratio, the active power decrease can also increase the voltage drop on the feeders thus contributing to lower the voltage at the PCC.

The performance of the controller is analyzed for both voltage sags and swells considering different load values. Different locations have been assumed for the WFs, and simulations have been carried out on a real 37-bus weak distribution network. The Danish grid code for the voltage levels below 100 kV is used in order to evaluate the FRT capability improvement.

The paper is organized as follows: grid code requirements and FRT capability are presented in Section 2. The WT generator system and the fuzzy controller designing are discussed in Sections 3 and 4, respectively. Case studies and simulation results are discussed in Section 5.

2. Grid Code Requirements and FRT Capability

In recent years, the increasing penetration of WTs into power systems has led power system operators to develop new grid code requirements for WTs in many countries. These requirements impose WTs operators to deal with some aspects such as FRT capability, reactive power control, and voltage control. This implies that the WTs connection into a distribution system requires coordination with voltage and reactive power control. Several countries have provided different grid codes depending on their system characteristics and operation standards such as the code from E.ON Netz Germany, Denmark, Belgium, the UK, Spain, the Netherlands, USA, and Canadian TSO Hydro-Quebec [13]. The Nordic grid code from Nordel [14] specifies the technical requirements that new WTs should have in order to be connected at the transmission network and provide acceptable safe operation and reliability. Belgium grid code [15], provided by the Belgian TSO, Elia, applies to the grids with the voltage levels 30–70 kV and 150–380 kV. This code discriminates different kinds of voltage disturbances. German grid code from E.ON Netz Germany [16] applies to the grids with the voltage levels of 110 kV, 220 kV, and 380 kV [17].

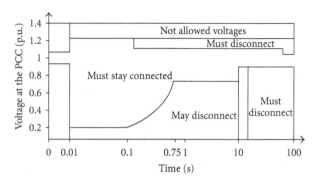

FIGURE 1: FRT requirements of the Danish grid code for grids below 100 kV [17].

Denmark grid code [17] relates to the WTs connected to the grids with the voltages below 100 kV. Figure 1 illustrates the FRT requirements of the Danish grid code. Apart from the FRT requirements shown in Figure 1, WFs must disconnect if the voltage increases above 1.2 p.u.

3. Description of Fuzzy Controller

Due to nonlinearity of power system and linearization problems, the control of variable wind speed WTs could not perform correctly with conventional control methods. For example, a Proportional Integral (PI) controller design requires identifying the WT transfer function, the linear model of the network, and defining an accurate tuning process.

The use of a fuzzy controller can overcome these problems and counterbalance the nonlinearities as well as time variances of the system under control of which an accurate model is not required. In the case of WTs control, for example, inaccurate aerodynamic calculations, tolerance in mounting the turbine, dirt or ice on blades, time-varying aerodynamic parameters, and other unpredictable parameter variations can make fuzzy logic control preferable if compared to conventional control methods [18].

The proposed fuzzy controller presents the many advantages if compared to a PI controller [19, 20]: (1) it is easy in obtaining variable gains depending on the error; (2) it is simple in solving problems affected by uncertain models, (3) it gives fast convergence, (4) it is parameter insensitive and accepts noisy and inaccurate signals.

Considering that, for a given combination of the active and the reactive power, the maximum reactive power that can be injected/absorbed by a WT depends on both the power converter size and the generated active power, the maximum reactive power that the WT can inject/absorb can be increased by decreasing the generated active power according to the following formula:

$$|Q| = \sqrt{S^2 - P^2}, \tag{1}$$

where S is the power converter size, given as maximum apparent power, P and Q are the generated active and reactive power, respectively. The proposed controller is designed in

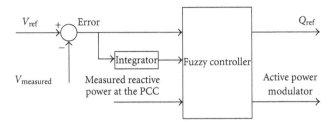

FIGURE 2: Fuzzy controller.

order to compensate the voltage at the PCC by injecting/absorbing the reactive power generated by both of grid side converter (GSC) and RSC as well as by regulating the active power modulator used to decrease the generated active power in the case of voltage swell.

In particular, when the absorbed reactive power reaches 80% of its maximum value and the measured voltage exceeds the reference value, the active power is decreased by the fuzzy controller in order to increase the maximum reactive power that the WT can absorb. Moreover, it is used in combination with a protection system for disconnecting the WTs from the grid when the controller is unable to compensate the voltage variations.

The fuzzy controller, as shown in Figure 2, presents three inputs: the error, the integral of error, and the measured reactive power at the PCC and two outputs that are the reference values for both the reactive power reference signal (Q_{ref}), varying in the range $[-1\ 1]$, and the reference signal for the active power modulator, varying in the range $[0\ 1]$, both sent by the fuzzy controller to the WT local controllers.

The error is defined as the difference between the reference voltage (V_{ref}) and the measured voltage at the PCC.

The third input, the reactive power measured at the PCC, is used in order to determine when the active power modulator is required to be regulated by the fuzzy controller.

The reactive power reference signal (Q_{ref}) is sent by the fuzzy controller to the WTs local controllers in order to inject/absorb reactive power. The active power modulator is the reference signal for the active power production and is sent by the fuzzy controller to the WTs local controllers in order to decrease the injected active power with the aim of increasing the absorbed reactive power according to (1).

The implementation of the fuzzy controller requires an adequate knowledge base and the ability to transform the latter in a set of fuzzy rules. The knowledge base has been coded in a set of rules consisting of linguistic statements linking a finite number of conditions with a finite number of conclusions. Such a knowledge can be collected and delivered by human experts and expressed by a finite number ($r = 1, 2, \ldots n$) of heuristic Multiple Input Single Output (MISO) fuzzy rules, written in the following form:

$$R_{MISO}^{(r)} : \text{IF } \left(x \text{ is } A_i^{(r)}\right), \left(y \text{ is } B_i^{(r)}\right), \ldots, \left(z \text{ is } C_i^{(r)}\right)$$
$$\text{THEN } \left(u \text{ is } U_j^{(r)}\right)'', \tag{2}$$

where $A_i^{(r)}, B_i^{(r)}, \ldots, C_i^{(r)}$ are the values of linguistic variables (conditions) $x, y, \ldots, z$, defined in the universes of discourse: $X, Y, \ldots, Z$, respectively, and $U_j^{(r)}$ is the value of independent linguistic variable u in the universe of discourse U.

Among all the parameters associated with a FLC, membership functions (MFs) have a dominant effect in changing its performance.

The type of MFs is frequently chosen to fit an expected input data distribution or clusters and can influence both the tracking accuracy and the execution time. Triangular, trapezoidal, and Gaussian membership functions are the common choice even if any convex shape can be adopted. Even though most researchers are inclined to design the input/output fuzzy membership sets using equal span mathematical functions, these do not always guarantee the best solution.

In the proposed approach, the selection of the best membership functions has been performed on the basis of a prior knowledge and on experimentation with the system and its dynamics. In particular, triangular and Gaussian membership functions have been compared. Moreover, in order to design a FLC, shrinking span MFs have been chosen: this guarantees smoother results with less oscillations, large and fast control actions when the system state is far from the set point, and moderate and slow adjustments when it is near to the set point. Thus, when the system is closer to its set point, the fuzzy MFs, for those specific linguistic terms, have narrower spans.

The fuzzy sets of the inputs and outputs assume the following names: NVB: Negative-Very-Big, NB: Negative-Big, NM: Negative-Medium, NS: Negative-Small, ZE: Zero, and so forth. Nine triangular membership functions have been selected for the inputs and outputs. The membership functions of inputs and outputs are shown in Figure 3.

Inference rules for the controller can be derived by the control surfaces and some of these rules are provided in Table 1. 86 rules are used in order to design the fuzzy controller. A Mamdani-based system architecture is realized; Max-Min and Centroid methods are used in the inference engine and defuzzification process, respectively.

Two control surfaces of the fuzzy controller are provided in Figure 4. According to Figure 4(a), in the case of voltage sag (error is positive) only Q_{ref} is sent by the fuzzy controller to the local controllers of the WTs in order to inject reactive power while in the case of voltage swell (error is negative), when the Q_{ref} is not enough to compensate the voltage swell effects, the active power modulator is sent by the fuzzy controller to the local controllers of WTs in order to decrease the active power, according to (1), and consequently increase the absorbed reactive power.

As evidenced from Figure 4(b), when the absorbed reactive power reaches 80% of its maximum value and the measured voltage exceeds the reference value, the active power is decreased by the fuzzy controller in order to increase the maximum reactive power that the WT can absorb. Moreover, it is used in combination with a protection system for disconnecting the WTs from the grid when the controller is unable to compensate the voltage variations.

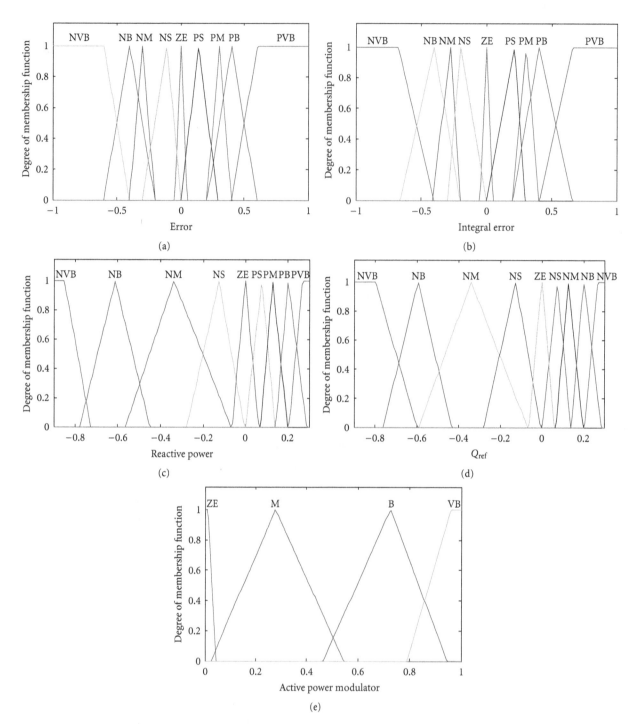

FIGURE 3: Membership functions of fuzzy controller. (a) Input signal error, (b) input signal integral error, (c) input signal reactive power measured at the PCC, (d) output reference reactive power, and (e) output active power modulator.

An easy understanding of the fuzzy controller can be summarized as in following considerations.

(1) If error is positive and integral of error is positive and reactive power measured at the PCC is positive, then reactive power should be injected by the WTs.

(2) If error is negative and integral of error is negative and reactive power measured at the PCC is not NVB, then reactive power should be absorbed by the WTs

and the active power modulator is zero. Note that in this case, the absorbed reactive power is enough in order to decrease the voltage swell effects and there is no need to also regulate the active power.

(3) If error is negative and integral of error is negative and reactive power measured at the PCC is NVB, both reactive and active power are regulated in order to decrease the voltage swell effects.

TABLE 1: Rules of fuzzy controller.

No.	Error	Integral error	Reactive power	Reference reactive power	Active power modulator
1	NVB	~PS	NVB	NB	B
2	NVB	~PVB	~NVB	NVB	ZE
3	NVB	NVB	~NVB	NVB	VB
4	NB	NS	~NVB	NVB	M
5	NM	PM	~NVB	NM	ZE
6	NS	PS	~NS	NS	ZE
7	ZE	ZE	ZE	ZE	ZE
8	PS	PVB	~PS	PS	ZE
9	PVB	NVB	~PB	PB	ZE

~ Means NOT.

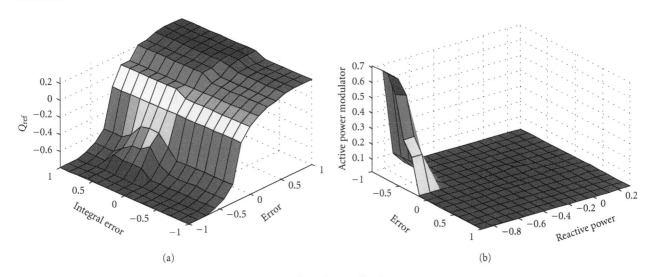

(a)   (b)

FIGURE 4: Fuzzy surface of controller for 1.5 MW WT.

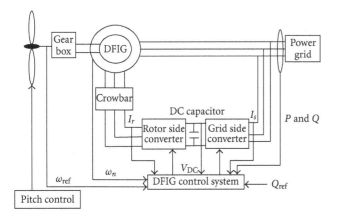

FIGURE 5: Configuration of DFIG-based WT connected to a grid.

4. Wind Turbine Generator System

A DFIG is a wound rotor induction generator with the stator directly connected to the grid and with the rotor connected to the network through a back-to-back converter. The schematic of DFIG-based WT is shown in Figure 5. The aim of the RSC is to control the active and reactive power on the grid autonomously, while the GSC has to maintain the DC-link voltage at a set value.

The relation between the wind speed and aerodynamic torque in a WT can be described by the following equation:

$$P_w = \frac{1}{2}\rho\pi R^2 V_w^3 C_p(\theta,\lambda),$$
$$T_w = \frac{1}{2}\rho\pi R^2 V_w^3 C_p\frac{(\theta,\lambda)}{\lambda}, \tag{3}$$

where P_w and T_w are the power and aerodynamic torque extracted from the wind in (W, N/m), respectively. ρ is the air density (kg/m^3), R is the wind turbine rotor radius (m), V_w is the equivalent wind speed (m/s), θ is the pitch angle wind turbine blade (deg.), $\lambda = (\omega_{\text{rot}}R)/V_w$ is the tip speed ratio, where ω_{rot} is the rotor speed of WT (rad/s) and C_P is the aerodynamic efficiency of the rotor. C_P can be expressed as a function of the tip speed ratio (λ) and pitch angle (θ) by the following equation:

$$C_P = 0.22\left(\frac{116}{\beta} - 0.4\theta - 5\right)^{e-12.5/\beta}, \tag{4}$$

where β is defined as follows:

$$\beta = \frac{1}{(1/(\lambda + 0.08\theta)) - (0.035/(\theta^3 + 1))}. \tag{5}$$

The induction generator converts the power captured by the WT into electrical power and transmits it into the grid. The AC/DC/AC converter consists of the RSC and the GSC. Both RSC and GSC are voltage source converters (VSCs) that use forced commutated power electronic devices to synthesize an AC voltage from a DC voltage source. A detailed description of the control systems for both the converters and the pitch angle command can be found in [21].

4.1. Capability Curve. The total active power of the DFIG fed into the grid is the sum of the stator and rotor active power.

$$P_T = P_S + P_R \tag{6}$$

taking into account that

$$P_R = -SP_S, \tag{7}$$

$$P_T = (1 - S)P_S, \tag{8}$$

where P_T is the total active power of the DFIG fed into the grid, P_S is the stator active power, and P_R is the rotor active power. The total reactive power fed into the grid is the sum of the reactive power of GSC and RSC. Usually, these inverters work with unity power factor, and consequently, the total reactive power will be equal to the reactive power of stator:

$$Q_T = Q_S. \tag{9}$$

The active and reactive power of stator can be expressed as a function of the maximum allowable current of rotor and stator [22]:

$$P_S^2 + Q_S^2 = (3U_S^2 I_S^2), \tag{10}$$

$$P_S^2 + \left(Q_S + 3\frac{U_S^2}{X_S}\right)^2 = \left(3\frac{X_M}{X_S}U_S I_R\right)^2. \tag{11}$$

Equation (10) represents a circumference centered equal to the stator rated apparent power. Equation (9) represents a circumference centered at $[-3(U_S^2)/X_S, 0]$. Substituting (8) and (9) into (10) and (11) can be expressed as

$$\left(\frac{P_T}{1-S}\right)^2 + Q_T^2 = (3U_S I_S)^2, \tag{12}$$

$$\left(\frac{P_T}{1-S}\right)^2 + \left(Q_T + 3\frac{U_S^2}{X_S}\right)^2 = \left(3\frac{X_M}{X_S}U_S I_R\right)^2. \tag{13}$$

The DFIG capability limits according to (12) and (13) can be achieved by taking into consideration the stator and rotor maximum currents $I_{S\max}$ and $I_{R\max}$, respectively. However, the reactive power delivered to the grid is limited by constraints imposed by the converter and expressed as rotor current limits to avoid an excessive heating of converters,

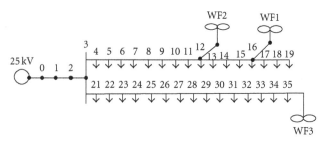

FIGURE 6: 25 kV weak distribution system.

rotor slip-rings, and brushes. The stator reactive power limits $Q_{S,\lim}$ depend on the stator active power P_S, the stator voltage U_S, and the maximum rotor current $I_{R\max}$. It is expressed as follows:

$$Q_{S,\lim} = -\frac{U_S^2}{X_S} \pm \sqrt{\left(\frac{X_M}{X_S}U_S I_{R\max}\right)^2 - P_S^2}. \tag{14}$$

Equation (14) expresses the maximum reactive power that can be delivered to the grid.

5. Case Study and Simulation Results

A DFIG-based WT, shown in Figure 5, has been considered [23]. In order to test the proposed controller, three 9-MW WFs (6 × 1.5 MW WTs) connected to a real 25 kV weak distribution system at buses 12, 16, and 35 are considered, as shown in Figure 6. The network is characterized by lines with high resistances and low X/R ratios. The base value for the power and voltage are 9/0.9 MVA and 575 V, respectively. According to the capability curve of the considered WFs, the limits of the reactive power that the WT can absorb or inject are 8 MVar and 2.50 MVar, respectively. Real wind data sets acquired by the Wind Engineering Research Field Laboratory [24] are considered. The wind speed time history consists of 17500 observations within 50-second interval with sampling rate 25 Hz.

In order to test the FRT capability of the WFs endowed with the proposed fuzzy controller considering minimum and maximum load, four different scenarios are studied for both load conditions as follows, with a total of eight case studies:

(1) Case study 1: a 30% voltage sag with a duration of 1 second starting at $t = 5$, considering

    (i) three WFs at buses 12, 16, and 35,

    (ii) two WFs at buses 16 and 35.

(2) Case study 2: a 15% voltage swell with a duration of 1 second starting at $t = 5$, considering

    (i) three WFs at buses 12, 16, and 35,

    (ii) two WFs at buses 16 and 35.

5.1. Minimum Load. The total network loads are 18 MW and 12.5 MVAr assumed as minimum load.

TABLE 2: Results obtained with PI controller and without controller for all WFs.

WF no.	Proposed controller		PI controller		Without controller	
	Voltage (p.u.)	WF's situation	Voltage (p.u.)	WF's situation	Voltage (p.u.)	WT's situation
1	0.745	Connected	0.698	Disconnected	0.688	Disconnected
2	0.740	Connected	0.695	Disconnected	0.685	Disconnected
3	0.715	Connected	0.715	Connected	0.691	Disconnected

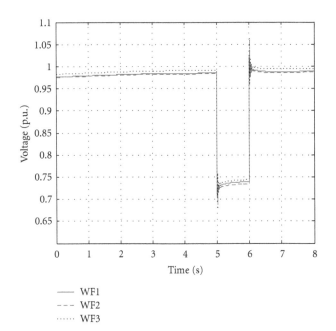

FIGURE 7: Voltage at the PCC.

TABLE 3: Results obtained with proposed controller in the case of 2 WFs.

WF no.	Voltage (p.u.)	WF's situation
1	0.690	Disconnected
3	0.721	Connected

in order to help lowering the voltage. The voltages, as shown in Figure 8(a), at buses 16, 12, and 35 are about 1.060, 1.070, and 1.076 p.u., respectively. The absorbed reactive power varies between about 7 MVAr for WF1 to about 8 MVAr for WF3, as shown in Figure 8(b), according to the voltages at the connection buses. Moreover, when the absorbed reactive power reaches 80% of its maximum value and is not enough for compensating voltage variations, the active power modulator is regulated in order to decrease the generated active power and consequently increase the reactive power absorbed by WFs (see Figure 8(c)). According to the capability curve of WTs and the limited size of the power converters, WFs cannot absorb reactive power more than 8 MVAr.

According to the fuzzy controller surface in Figure 4(b) and as shown in Figure 8(c), it can be observed that the active power modulator regulation starts at $t = 5.2$ s. The combined regulation of both active and reactive power generated by WFs allows reducing the voltage swell effects. According to the Danish grid code, all WFs can successfully fulfill the FRT requirement and, consequently, remain connected to the grid. In order to assess the effectiveness of the proposed controller, the performance of the fuzzy controller is compared with that of a PI controller as designed in [25] and without any controller. As shown in Table 4, with the PI controller, WF1 and WF2 can successfully fulfill the FRT requirement and remain connected to the grid while WF3 disconnects; moreover, without any controller, all WFs are disconnected.

(ii) When considering only WF1 and WF3, it can be observed that the absorbed reactive powers by the WFs increase if compared to the previous case, while more active power is reduced.

For example, for WF3, the absorbed reactive power is about 7.8 MVAr in case (i) while a reduction of about 55% of active power is achieved. In case (ii), instead these values are about 8 MVAr and 62%, respectively. According to Table 5, both WF1 and WF3 can successfully fulfill the grid code requirements and remain connected to the grid. It can be concluded that, by increasing the number of WFs, their probability of remaining connected is increased.

5.1.1. Case Study A1 (Voltage Sag). (i) When the voltage drops by 30%, each WF injects reactive power during the voltage sag in order to help in increasing the voltage to 0.725, 0.730, and 0.741 p.u. for WF2, WF1, and WF3, respectively (see Figure 7). The injected reactive power varies between about 2.25 MVAr for WF3 to about 2.40 MVAr for WF2 according to the voltages at the connection buses. According to Danish grid code, all WFs can successfully fulfill the FRT requirement and, consequently, remain connected to the grid.

In order to evaluate the effectiveness of the proposed controller, both of the cases without any controller and with a classical PI controller as designed in [25] are evaluated. The results are given in Table 2. It can be evidenced that with the fuzzy controller, all WFs can successfully fulfill the FRT requirement and remain connected to the grid while with the PI controller only WF3 can successfully fulfills the FRT requirement and remain connected to the grid while WF1 and WF2 disconnect. Moreover, without any controller, all WFs disconnect.

(ii) In this case, only WF1 and WF3 are considered. The reactive powers injected by the WFs increase if compared to the previous case and only WF3 can fulfill grid code requirements and remain connected to the grid (see Table 3).

5.1.2. Case Study A2 (Voltage Swell). (i) Considering three WFs during a 15% voltage swell, they absorb reactive power

5.2. Maximum Load. A total maximum load of 24 MW and 15 MVAr has been assumed. The same case studies

TABLE 4: Results obtained with PI controller and without controller For All WFs.

WF no.	Proposed controller		PI controller		Without controller	
	Voltage (p.u.)	WF's situation	Voltage (p.u.)	WF's situation	Voltage (p.u.)	WT's situation
1	1.056	Connected	1.085	Connected	1.112	Disconnected
2	1.059	Connected	1.090	Connected	1.115	Disconnected
3	1.067	Connected	1.111	Disconnected	1.125	Disconnected

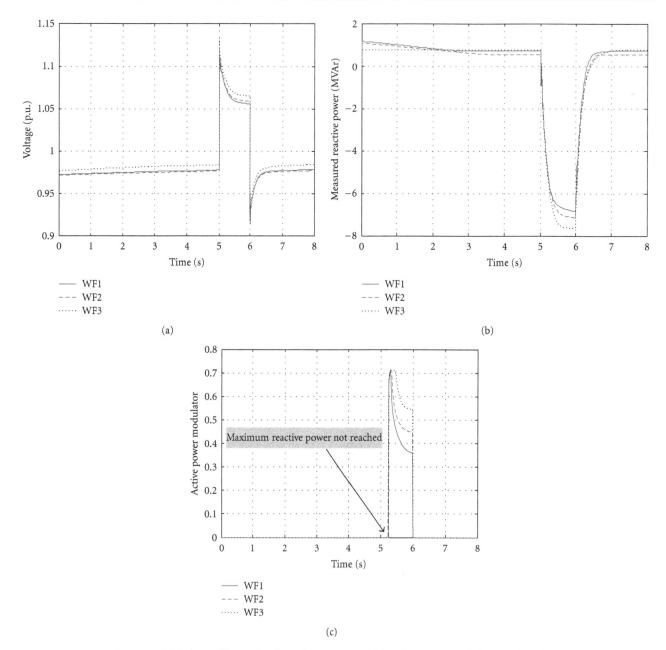

FIGURE 8: (a) Voltage, (b) measured reactive power, and (c) active power modulator at the PCC.

investigated in Section 5.1 for minimum load are also studied for maximum load.

5.2.1. Case Study B1 (Voltage Sag). (i) When the voltage drops by 30%, each WF injects reactive power during the voltage sag in order to help in increasing the voltage. The injected reactive power varies between about 2.35 MVAr for WF3 to about 2.50 MVAr for WF2 according to the voltages at the PCC. In correspondence with maximum load, the voltage at the PCC decreases and the reactive powers

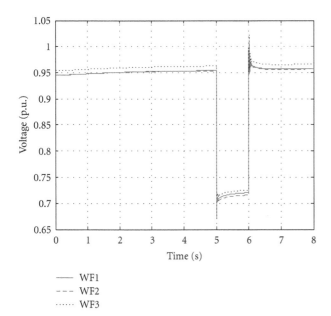

—— WF1
--- WF2
······ WF3

FIGURE 9: Voltage at the PCC.

TABLE 5: Results obtained with proposed controller in the case of 2 WFs.

WF no.	Voltage (p.u.)	WF's situation
1	1.071	Connected
3	1.062	Connected

TABLE 6: Results obtained with proposed controller in the case of 2 WFs.

WF no.	Voltage (p.u.)	WF's situation
1	0.684	Disconnected
3	0.705	Connected

injected by WFs increase if compared to the case of minimum load. As shown in Figure 9, all WFs can fulfill the grid code requirements and can remain connected to the grid.

(ii) By decreasing the number of WFs connected to the grid the injected reactive powers increase. According to Table 6, WF3 can fulfill the grid, code requirement and remain connected to the grid while WF1 disconnects from the grid.

5.2.2. *Case Study B2 (Voltage Swell)*. (i) Considering three WFs during a 15% voltage swell, the absorbed reactive power varies between about 6 MVAr for WF1 to about 7 MVAr for WF3. A reduction of about 28% and 46% of active power is achieved for WF1 and WF3, respectively. According to the Danish grid code, all WFs can successfully fulfill the FRT requirements and, consequently, remain connected to the grid.

(ii) In this case, both WF1 and WF3 can fulfill the grid code requirement and remain connected to grid.

6. Conclusion

In this paper, a fuzzy controller for improving the FRT capability of variable speed WTs is proposed. The controller is designed in order to compensate the voltage-sags and swells by regulating both the active and reactive power generated by WFs. The performances of the proposed controller are evaluated in several case studies considering a 37-bus Italian weak distribution network with WFs in different locations. Simulation results evidenced that the proposed controller can improve WTs' FRT capability in medium-voltage weak networks in many cases, thus improving wind energy exploitation.

References

[1] I. M. de Alegría, J. Andreu, J. L. Martín, P. Ibañez, J. L. Villate, and H. Camblong, "Connection requirements for wind farms: a survey on technical requierements and regulation," *Renewable and Sustainable Energy Reviews*, vol. 11, no. 8, pp. 1858–1872, 2007.

[2] J. O. G. Tande, "Exploitation of wind-energy resources in proximity to weak electric grids," *Applied Energy*, vol. 65, no. 1–4, pp. 395–401, 2000.

[3] G. Tapia, A. Tapia, and J. X. Ostolaza, "Proportional-integral regulator-based approach to wind farm reactive power management for secondary voltage control," *IEEE Transactions on Energy Conversion*, vol. 22, no. 2, pp. 488–498, 2007.

[4] G. Tapia, A. Tapia, and J. X. Ostolaza, "Two alternative modeling approaches for the evaluation of wind farm active and reactive power performances," *IEEE Transactions on Energy Conversion*, vol. 21, no. 4, pp. 909–920, 2006.

[5] W. Gao, G. Wang, and J. Ning, "Development of low voltage ride-through control strategy for wind power generation using real time digital simulator," in *Proceedings of the IEEE/PES Power Systems Conference and Exposition (PSCE '09)*, pp. 1–6, March 2009.

[6] L. Jerbi, L. Krichen, and A. Ouali, "A fuzzy logic supervisor for active and reactive power control of a variable speed wind energy conversion system associated to a flywheel storage system," *Electric Power Systems Research*, vol. 79, no. 6, pp. 919–925, 2009.

[7] M. Tsili and S. Papathanassiou, "A review of grid code technical requirements for wind farms," *IET Renewable Power Generation*, vol. 3, no. 3, pp. 308–332, 2009.

[8] S. M. Muyeen, R. Takahashi, T. Murata et al., "Low voltage ride through capability enhancement of wind turbine generator system during network disturbance," *IET Renewable Power Generation*, vol. 3, no. 1, pp. 65–74, 2009.

[9] J. Liang, W. Qiao, and R. G. Harley, "Feed-forward transient current control for low-voltage ride-through enhancement of DFIG wind turbines," *IEEE Transactions on Energy Conversion*, vol. 25, no. 3, pp. 836–843, 2010.

[10] M. Rahimi and M. Parniani, "Grid-fault ride-through analysis and control of wind turbines with doubly fed induction generators," *Electric Power Systems Research*, vol. 80, no. 2, pp. 184–195, 2010.

[11] H Karimi-Davijani, A. Sheikholeslami, H. Livani, and M. Karimi-Davijani, "Fuzzy logic control of doubly fed induction generator wind turbine," *World Applied Sciences Journal*, vol. 6, no. 4, pp. 499–508, 2009.

[12] F. Iov, A. Hansen, P. Soerensen, and N. Cutululis, "Mapping of grid faults and grid codes," Technical Report of the Research

Project 'Grid Fault and Design Basis for Wind Turbine', Riso National Laboratory, Roskilde, Denmark, 2007.

[13] Nordel, "Nordic grid code," January 2007.

[14] Grid code for the Local Transmission System Operator, "Arrêté du Gouvernement wallon relatif à la révision du règlement technique pour la gestion des réseaux de distribution d'électricité en Région wallonne et l'accès à ceux-ci," Walloon Energy Commission (Commission Wallone pour l' Energie-CWaPE),Wallonia, Belgium, May 2007.

[15] E.ON Netz GmbH, "Grid code–high and extra high voltage," Bayreut, Germany, April 2006.

[16] E.ON Netz GmbH, "Requirements for offshore grid connections in the E.ON Netz Network," E.ON Netz GmbH, Bayreuth, Germany, April 2008.

[17] Regulation TF 3.2.6, "Grid connection of wind turbines to networks with voltages below 100 kV," Energinet, Denmark, May 2004.

[18] V. Galdi, A. Piccolo, and P. Siano, "Exploiting maximum energy from variable speed wind power generation systems by using an adaptive Takagi-Sugeno-Kang fuzzy model," *Energy Conversion and Management*, vol. 50, no. 2, pp. 413–421, 2009.

[19] V. Calderaro, V. Galdi, A. Piccolo, and P. Siano, "A fuzzy controller for maximum energy extraction from variable speed wind power generation systems," *Electric Power Systems Research*, vol. 78, no. 6, pp. 1109–1118, 2008.

[20] A. J. Pujante-Lopez, E. Gomez-Lazaro, J. A. Fuentes-Moreno, A. Molina-Garca, and A. Vigueras-Rodriguez, "Performance comparison of a 2 MW DFIG wind turbine model under wind speed variations," in *Proceedings of the Europe's Premier Wind Energy Event (Ewec '09)*, pp. 1–6, 2009.

[21] J. M. Carrasco, L. G. Franquelo, J. T. Bialasiewicz et al., "Power-electronic systems for the grid integration of renewable energy sources: a survey," *IEEE Transactions on Industrial Electronics*, vol. 53, no. 4, pp. 1002–1016, 2006.

[22] A. Tapia, G. Tapia, J. Xabier Ostolaza, and J. R. Sáenz, "Modeling and control of a wind turbine driven doubly fed induction generator," *IEEE Transactions on Energy Conversion*, vol. 18, no. 2, pp. 194–204, 2003.

[23] V. Galdi, A. Piccolo, and P. Siano, "Designing an adaptive fuzzy controller for maximum wind energy extraction," *IEEE Transactions on Energy Conversion*, vol. 23, no. 2, pp. 559–569, 2008.

[24] http://www.winddata.com/.

[25] Mathwork, "SimPower system Toolbox of MATLAB," Mathwork, 2009.

16

Modeling Chaotic Behavior of Chittagong Stock Indices

Shipra Banik, Mohammed Anwer, and A. F. M. Khodadad Khan

School of Engineering and Computer Science, Independent University, Bangladesh, Dhaka 1212, Bangladesh

Correspondence should be addressed to Shipra Banik, shiprabanik@yahoo.com.au

Academic Editor: Yi-Chi Wang

Stock market prediction is an important area of financial forecasting, which attracts great interest to stock buyers and sellers, stock investors, policy makers, applied researchers, and many others who are involved in the capital market. In this paper, a comparative study has been conducted to predict stock index values using soft computing models and time series model. Paying attention to the applied econometric noises because our considered series are time series, we predict Chittagong stock indices for the period from January 1, 2005 to May 5, 2011. We have used well-known models such as, the genetic algorithm (GA) model and the adaptive network fuzzy integrated system (ANFIS) model as soft computing forecasting models. Very widely used forecasting models in applied time series econometrics, namely, the generalized autoregressive conditional heteroscedastic (GARCH) model is considered as time series model. Our findings have revealed that the use of soft computing models is more successful than the considered time series model.

1. Introduction

The stock index values play an important role in controlling dynamics of the capital market. As a result, the appropriate prediction of stock index values is a crucial factor for domestic/foreign stock investors, buyers and/or sellers, fund managers, policy makers, applied researchers (who want to improve the model specifications of this index), and many others. Many researchers, for example, [1–4] and others have found that the empirical distribution of stock is significantly nonnormal and nonlinear. Stock market data are also observed in practice chaotic and volatile by nature (e.g., see [5–8]). That is why stock values are hard to predict. Traditionally, the fundamental Box-Jenkins analysis has been the mainstream methodology that is used to predict stock values in applied literature. Due to continual studies of stock market experts, the use of soft computing models (such as artificial neural networks, fuzzy set, evolutionary algorithms, and rough set theory.) have been widely established to forecast stock market. Evidence [9, 10] suggests that the Box-Jenkins approach often fails to predict time series when the behavior of series is chaotic and nonlinear. Thus, soft computing systems have emerged to increase the accuracy of chaotic time series predictions. The reason is that these systems have the potential to provide a viable solution through the versatile approach to self-organization. Thus, in forecasting literatures [11–14], it has been found that soft computing systems yield better results compared to the statistical time series approaches when the series is chaotic. This paper compares forecasts of stock prices from soft computing forecasting models and the model introduced by [15]. Our motivation for this comparison lies in the recent increasing interest in the use of soft computing models for forecasting purposes of economic and finance variables. Thus, soft computing models are used to learn the nonlinear and chaotic patterns in the stock system. Several studies [7, 11, and many others] have compared soft computing models and the traditional Box-Jenkins model. However, there are only a few comparative analyses (according to our knowledge) between soft computing models and standard time series statistical models [13] in case of Bangladeshi stock indices. In this paper, we examine the performance of the daily Chittagong stock market indices using soft computing models and time series model. See [13] for prediction of the daily Dhaka stock market index values. Thus, we hope that findings of the study will be interesting to fund managers, many businesses investors, policy makers, academics, and others who are involved in this volatile

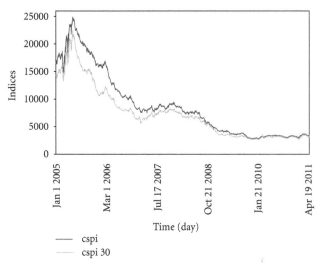

Figure 1: Time plots of the indices.

market. The structure of the paper is as follows: data and forecasting model is given in the next section. Statistical properties and various econometric noises are discussed in Section 3. A brief description of the considered forecasting models is described in Section 4. Performances of the different evaluation criterion are explained in Section 5. Finally, concluding remarks with some proposed future research are given in the final section.

2. Data and Forecasting Model

2.1. Data. The indices, the Chittagong Stock Exchange has been maintaining since October 10 1995, are the stock prices for all companies (cse-all) and for 30 selected companies (cse-30). Thus, we considered the daily cse-all and cse-30 [data source: http://www.cse.com.bd/] prices for the available periods (January 1, 2005 to May 5, 2011). For a description of the indices, see the above website.

It is true people trend to invest in stock market because it has high returns over time. Stock markets are generally affected by economic, social, political, and even psychological factors. These factors interact with each other in a very complicated manner. That is why stock data are observed, chaotic and volatile by nature. It is well known that chart is the best way to visualize trend and chaotic behavior if present in any price series. Thus, to understand the behaviors of considered indices, cse-all and cse-30 are plotted against time in Figure 1. It is very clear that there is a decreasing trend with respect to time. There are some reasons why these sorts of trend exist. See http://www.cse.com.bd/ for details. It is also observable from this plot the behaviors of these selected price series are not linear. This means series can appear volatile with moves that look chaotic. Some sort of nonlinearity can also be present in the selected series.

2.2. Forecasting Models. Since our series are time series, so we have selected the most commonly used time series model,

Table 1: Data description and proposed model.

Indices	Size	Proposed AR(p) model
cse-all	1540×1	AR(2)
cse-30	1540×1	AR(4)

namely, the autoregressive (AR) model of order p. The model is defined for each of considered series as follows:

$$\text{cse-all}_t = \alpha + \beta t + \rho_i \text{cse-all}_{t-i} + e_t, \quad t = 1, 2, 3, \dots, n, \tag{1}$$

$$\text{cse-30}_t = \alpha + \beta t + \rho_i \text{cse-30}_{t-i} + e_t, \quad t = 1, 2, 3, \dots, n, \tag{2}$$

where α is an intercept, β is the deterministic trend, t is the time variable, ρ_i are the lag orders of the AR(p) model, and $e_t \sim N(0, \sigma^2)$. The appropriate lags of the series are selected by the Bayesian Information Criterion (BIC). Other information criterions, for example, Akaike Information Criterion (AIC), Schwarz Information Criterion (SIC), and others can also be used to select the lag order of the AR components of our selected models. See Table 1 for data size and proposed AR(p) model.

3. Statistical Properties of Data

3.1. Numerical Summary. To understand the characteristics of the selected indices, summary statistics are tabulated in Table 2. It is clear from the above table, most of times, that cse-all and cse-30 indices are observed 8691 and 7259.9, respectively. Standard deviation measures confirm to us that the considered prices are not equal to 8691 and 7259.9. The expected range of cse-all and cse-30 prices can be estimated as 8691 ± 5883.3 and 7259.9 ± 4668.6, respectively. Skewness measures indicate to us that stock market indices display right skewed distributions. It means that most of prices are below the average prices. Kurtosis measures also indicate to us that price indices are not normal.

3.2. Time Series Properties. It is now a well-established stylized fact that most time series are nonstationary and contain a unit root (e.g., see [14]). The conventional approach of time series is based on the implicit assumption that the underlying data series is stationary. This assumption was rarely questioned until the early 1970s and numerical analysis proceeded if all-time series were stationary. Numerous studies (e.g., [14–16] and many others) have suggested that most time series are nonstationary and therefore, the assumption of stationarity is unrealistic. Thus, prior to model specifications and the estimations, the stationary property of the data series is routinely tested. Otherwise, the study can yield unrealistic results. That is why to select appropriate forecasting model for our study, we have tested first stationarity property of the considered series.

3.2.1. Stationarity Tests. There are many stationarity tests available in time series literature. For details, see [17–19] and

TABLE 2: Numerical properties of the selected indices.

Indices	Mean	Median	Standard deviation	Skewness	Kurtosis
cse-all	$8.6916e + 003$	$7.6318e + 003$	$5.8833e + 003$	0.5404	2.9063
cse-30	$7.2599e + 003$	$6.5434e + 003$	$4.6686e + 003$	0.4604	3.6754

TABLE 3: Stationarity test results.

Indices	ADF(p) statistic	P value (critical value) for the ADF test	PP(L) statistic	P value (critical value) for the PP test
cse-all	$-0.9888(2)$	$0.9434(-3.4144)$	$-1.13(12)$	$0.9227(-3.4144)$
cse-30	$-1.2330(4)$	$0.9022(-3.4144)$	$-1.29(10)$	$0.8877(-3.4144)$

"p" and "L" indicate lag order to remove serial correlation.
Decision rule: If P value < level of significance (α), then accept null hypothesis.

TABLE 4: Linearity test results.

Indices	cse-all	cse-30
Engle test statistic	53.52	54.35
P value	0.0	0.0

TABLE 5: GA options.

Step	Algorithm option
Creation	Uniform, normal
Fitness scaling	Rank, proportional, top (truncation), linear scaling, shift
Selection	Roulette, stochastic uniform selection, tournament, uniform
Crossover	Binary-valued (single-point, two-point, n-point, uniform) real-valued (intermediate, line)
Mutation	Gaussian, uniform
Reinsertion	Pure, uniform, elitist, fitness-based

others. To test the nonstationarity behavior of our considered models (1)-(2), we have used most commonly applied unit root tests, namely, the Augmented Dickey Fuller (ADF) test proposed by Said and Dickey [20] and the test proposed by Phillips and Perron (PP) [21]. For test procedures, see [17]. MATLAB commands that *Adftest* and *pptest* are used to compute the ADF and the PP statistics and results are reported in Table 3. Note that under the null hypothesis of the ADF and PP tests the series assumed nonstationary and that under the alternative hypothesis the series is stationary. Results show us all series are nonstationary (because P value $> \alpha, \alpha = 0.05$). Thus, null hypothesis of the tests is accepted. Then we have taken the first difference of the series to remove non-stationarity and applied then again the ADF test and the PP test. These test results show us in first differences that considered series are stationary. These results are not reported for spaces but are available on request. The effect of these tests will be shown when our forecasting model is used, the model is used in first differences.

3.3. Linearity Test. There are many statistical techniques available in literature to test whether the series is linear or nonlinear. To select appropriate forecasting method, we have tested also linearity of the considered models (1) and (2). These tests are based on the ordinary least square method residuals. The statistical test proposed by Engle [5] is used to test the presence of nonlinear dependence. For details of the test procedure, see [22]. Linearity test results are tabulated in Table 4. Results show that at the 5% level of significance (α), nonlinearity is present (check the P-value) in our considered series. Just a note here under the null hypothesis, the series are considered linear and under the alternative hypothesis, the series are considered nonlinear. Table 4 results show us P-value is less than α which indicates rejection of the null hypothesis. So Table 4 results confirm to us that our considered series are nonlinear.

4. Models Used for Prediction

Considered statistical tests results show that our selected series are nonstationary, nonlinear, and chaotic (Figure 1). To remove nonstationarity, we used the series in first differences. We have selected nonlinear forecasting models to forecast Chittagong stock indices, which has also the ability to capture chaotic behavior. We have chosen the following models to forecast considered indices. A brief description of the considered forecasting models is given below.

4.1. Soft Computing Model. We have chosen two very popular and widely used models, namely, the genetic algorithm (GA) model and the neuro-fuzzy model.

4.1.1. GA Model. Holland [23] introduces this technique. It is a technique based on the "Darwin's Principle of Natural Selection" and is used to solve optimization problems. The basic idea is to select the best, discard the rest. To handle the complex multidimensional behaviors of a system, this approach has been used efficiently in forecasting literature (e.g., [23–26] and others). See Figure 2, for the flowchart that illustrates the basic steps in a GA. See Table 5, for the standard GA options. A brief explanation of each step is as follows.

Step 1. Create an initial population consisting of random chromosomes. To understand the GA process, for example,

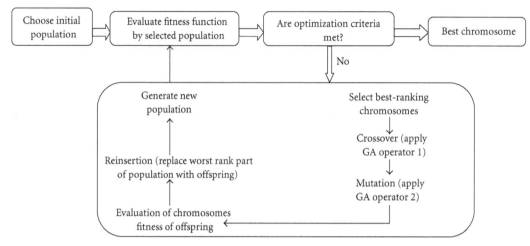

FIGURE 2: Flowchart of a GA model.

TABLE 6

RMSE:	26.19	32.09	53.75	20.18	18.67	66.64
Fit (RMSE):	1.2	0.8	0.4	1.6	2.0	0
pdf of RMSE:	0.2	0.13	0.06	0.26	0.33	0
cdf of RMSE:	0.2	0.33	0.39	0.65	0.98	1.0

for an AR(2) model, consider the following random population of 6 chromosomes with 4 parameters each: (0.13, 0.01, 0.84, 0.68), (0.20, 0.74, 0.52, 0.37), (0.19, 0.44, 0.20, 0.83), (0.60, 0.93, 0.67, 0.50), (0.27, 0.46, 0.83, 0.70), and (0.19, 0.41, 0.01, 0.42). Population size is chosen usually from 100–500. Larger population may produce more robust solution.

Step 2. Fitness scaling is used to provide a measure of how selected chromosomes perform in the problem domain. The AR(2) model fitness is evaluated through a criterion like RMSE (CC, MAE can be also used). For the AR(2) model, we get RMSE: 26.19, 32.09, 53.75, 20.18, 18.67, and 66.64. Using the linear-ranking process, for example, (details, see Pohlheim [27]), Fit(RMSE): 1.2, 0.8, 0.4, 1.6, 2.0, 0.

Step 3. Based on Step 2 results, choose parents for the next generation. To understand it, consider the distribution found in Tables 5 and 6.

It is observed that chromosome 5 is the fittest chromosome, because it occupies the largest interval, whereas chromosome 3 is the second least fit chromosome as the smallest interval. Chromosome 6 is the least fit interval that has a fitness value of 0 and gets no chance for reproduction. Using for example, the roulette wheel method (purpose is to eliminate the worst chromosomes and to regenerate better substitutes), selected 4 parents are: (0.20, 0.74, 0.52, 0.37), (0.13, 0.01, 0.84, 0.68), (0.27, 0.46, 0.83, 0.70), and (0.13, 0.01, 0.84, 0.68).

Next step is to produce offspring from selected parents by combining entries of a pair of parents (known as crossover) and also by making random changes to a single parent (known as mutation).

Step 4 (GA operator-1). Basic operator for producing new (improved) chromosomes is known as crossover (a version of artificial mating). It produces offspring that have some parts of both parents genetic material. Offspring are produced using the intermediate crossover method, because this is a method proposed to recombine for parents with real-valued chromosomes (see details, Pohlheim [27]). Thus, crossover offspring are (0.16, 0.16, 0.85, 0.57), (0.13, 0.22, 0.76, 0.43), (0.13, 0.15, 0.83, 0.69), and (0.26, 0.45, 0.84, 0.68).

Step 5 (GA operator-2). Offspring are mutated after producing crossover offspring and this GA operator increases the chance that the algorithm will generate better fittest RMSE than the Step 4. GA creates 3 types of offspring: elite offspring (number of best RMSE values in the current generation that are guaranteed to survive to the next generation), crossover offspring, and mutation offspring. To understand it, consider an example: suppose that the population size is 20 and the elite count is 2. If crossover fraction is 0.8, then the distribution of offspring is 2 elites, 14 (18*0.8) are crossover offspring, and the remaining 4 are mutation offspring. Just to know, a crossover fraction of 1 means all offspring other than elite are crossover offspring, while a crossover fraction of 0 means that all offspring are mutation offspring. How offspring are produced under the mutation process, see Pohlheim [27]. The mutation offspring are found (0.16, 0.17, 0.85, 0.56), (0.13, 0.22, 0.76, 0.43), (0.13, 0.14, 0.83, 0.69), (0.26, 0.45, 0.84, 0.68), respectively.

Step 6. Once offspring have been produced using Steps 4–5, offspring fitness (i.e., RMSE values) must be determined (procedure similar to Step 2). We get improved RMSE: 23.37, 28.13, 24.11, 18.62.

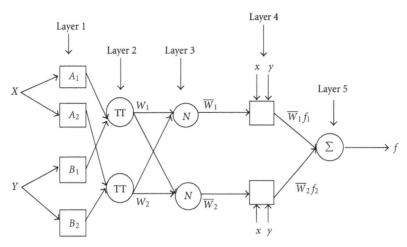

FIGURE 3: AN ANFIS system.

If less offspring are produced than the original population size, then to maintain size, offspring have to be reinserted into the old population. By this step, it is determined which chromosomes will be replaced by offspring. Using for example, the fitness-based reinsertion method, the following RMSE are found: 20.18, 18.67, 18.62, 23.37, 24.11, and 28.13.

If termination criteria are not defined, GA returns to Step 3 and continues up to Step 6. It is satisfied when either maximum number of generations is achieved or when all chromosomes in the population are identical (i.e., converge). The creator sets this number before running GA, which ensures that GA does not continue indefinitely.

4.1.2. Adaptive Network Fuzzy Integrated System (ANFIS) Model. The second widely used soft computing model we have selected is the ANFIS model. In computing the literature, Jang [8] proposed this model. This model is a combination of two intelligence systems: neural network (NN) system and fuzzy inference system (FIS). This is also known as NN-fuzzy integrated system, where the NN learning algorithm is used to determine parameters of FIS. NNs are nonlinear statistical data modeling tools and can capture and model any input-output relationships. FIS is the process of formulating the mapping from a given input to an output using the fuzzy logic. This mapping provides a basis from which decisions can be made or patterns can be discerned. The process of FIS involves membership functions (mfs), fuzzy logic operators, and if-then rules. The structure of ANFIS (see Figure 3 for its architecture) has 5 layers: (a) 1 input layer, (b) 3 hidden layers that represents mfs and fuzzy rules, and (c) 1 output layer. ANFIS uses the Sugeno-fuzzy inference model to be the learning algorithm. As an example, the fuzzy if-then rules for the first-order Sugeno-fuzzy model can be expressed as follows.

Rule 1. If x (input 1) is A_1 and y (input 2) is B_1, then f_1 (output) $= p_1x + q_1y + r_1$.

Rule 2. If x (input 1) is A_2 and y (input 2) is B_2, then f_2 (output) $= p_2x + q_2y + r_2$.

The learning algorithm of ANFIS is a hybrid algorithm, which combines the gradient descent (GD) method and the least square estimation (LSE) for an effective search of parameters. ANFIS uses a two-pass of learning algorithm to reduce error: forward pass and backward pass. The hidden layer is computed by the GD method of the feedback structure and the final output is estimated by the LSE method (for details, see [8]).

4.2. Time Series Model: GARCH Model. Since our considered series are time series, to compare the performances of the soft computing models, a very popular time series model, namely, generalized autoregressive conditional heteroscedastic (GARCH) model is selected from time series econometrics literature. A brief description of this model is discussed.

In 1986, Bollerslev invented the GARCH model. To understand it clearly, consider an AR(1) model:

$$\text{stockprice}_t = \text{Constant} + \text{stockprice}_{t-1} + e_t,$$
$$t = 1, 2, \ldots, n, \tag{3}$$

where stockprice_t is the observed cse-all and cse-30 prices. Here, the current volatility depends not only on the past errors, but also on the past volatilities. Suppose $e_t = \varepsilon_t\sigma_t$, where $\sigma_t = \beta_0 + \sum_{i=1}^{q} \beta_i e_{t-i}^2 + \sum_{j=1}^{p} \gamma_j \sigma_{t-j}$ with $\beta_0 > 0, \beta_i \geq 0$ ($i = 1, 2, \ldots, q$), $\gamma_j \geq 0$ ($j = 1, 2, \ldots, p$), and $\varepsilon_t \sim N(0, 1)$, known as an GARCH process of orders p and q. This model is widely used to know the volatility nature that exists generally in the time series data. For details, see [6].

5. Discussion of Results

Forecasting with 100% accuracy may be impossible, but we can do our best to reduce forecasting errors. Thus, to find the error level between observed and predicted stock series that means the forecasting performances of the considered models are evaluated against the following widely used statistical measures, namely, root mean square error (RMSE), correlation coefficient (CC), and coefficient of determination (R^2).

TABLE 7: Computational settings for selected forecasting models.

GA	ANFIS	GARCH
(1) Population size—3000, generated at random from the uniform probability distribution.	(1) Input—Lags of cse-all and cse-30	cse-all and cse-30: Fitted GARCH (2,1) and GARCH (1,1) Selection Process: BIC.
(2) Fitness function—RMSE of model (2.2.1-2.2.2); Fitness scaling—Linear ranking process.	(2) 2 mfs (type Gaussian) for each of input variables. Thus, 8 if-then fuzzy rules were learned.	
(3) Selection-Roulette wheel.		
(4) Crossover-fraction: 0.95; Intermediate method.		
(5) Mutation-fraction: 0.05; Uniform method.		
(6) Reinsertion: The fitness-based reinsertion method.		
(7) Termination Criteria—Maximum number of generations, assumed 200.		

TABLE 8: Performances for training data.

Forecasting models	cse-all			cse-30		
	RMSE	CC	R^2	RMSE	CC	R^2
GA	6.79	0.94	0.88	6.95	0.91	0.82
ANFIS	6.89	0.93	0.86	6.83	0.92	0.84
GARCH	7.34	0.91	0.82	7.56	0.88	0.77

Note: We considered January 1, 2005 to January 1, 2009 as a training period.

TABLE 9: Performances for testing data.

Forecasting models	cse-all			cse-30		
	RMSE	CC	R^2	RMSE	CC	R^2
GA	5.37	0.96	0.92	6.48	0.94	0.88
ANFIS	6.93	0.94	0.88	5.59	0.97	0.94
GARCH	8.58	0.89	0.79	7.89	0.90	0.81

Note: We considered February 1, 2005 to May 5, 2011 as a testing period.

Note that a smallest value of RMSE indicates higher accuracy in forecasting, and higher R^2 value indicates better prediction. All computational works were carried out using the programming code of MATLAB (version 7.0). We have selected January 1, 2005 to January 1, 2009 as the training periods and rest of periods as the testing periods. See Table 7 for computational parameters for all selected forecasting models. Tables 8 and 9 summarize the performances of different considered forecasting models where the training and testing data are achieved for prediction of stock values using the considered error measures RMSE, CC, and R^2. In terms of all measures, our training results show that for the cse-all price series, the GA forecasting model performed better (noted smallest RMSE values, highest CC, and R^2 values) than other forecasting models, followed by the ANFIS forecasting model and the GARCH forecasting model. For the cse-30 series, we found that the ANFIS forecasting model performed better than the other forecasting models. After the models are built using the training data, considered series forecasted over the testing data and performances are reported in Table 9. The testing results when compared to our considered forecasting models show again that the daily cse-all price series forecasting ability of the GA forecasting model is higher than the other forecasting models. We noted for the cse-30 price index, the ANFIS forecasting model performed (lowest value of RMSE, highest values of CC and R^2) better than the other forecasting models.

6. Conclusion and Future Works

It is well known that soft computing models pay particular attention to nonlinearties which in turn help to improve complex data predictions. In this paper, we forecasted Chittagong stock price index for all companies and stock price index for 30 selected companies for the period from January 1, 2005 to May 5, 2011. Recent time series literature suggests that most stock price series are nonstationary, contains a unit root. For this reason to make appropriate predictions, using unit root tests, first we tested nonstationarity properties because our considered series are time series. Our test results suggested that the series are nonstationary. To remove this noise from the series, we used the series in first differences. Then we tested linearity of the series using the statistical linear test. Test result showed us that the two considered series are nonlinear. Thus, we selected two very well-known soft computing models, namely, the GA forecasting model and the ANFIS forecasting model. To compare the performances of these two models, we also selected most popular nonlinear time series forecasting model. According to our findings, we would like to conclude that applied workers should select the GA forecasting model to forecast future daily stock price index for all selected companies. In case of daily stock price index for 30 selected companies, the ANFIS forecasting model is more successful than the other considered forecasting models. We believe our findings will be helpful for researchers who are planning to make appropriate decisions with this complex variable. Our next step is to improve and compare the predictions with other recently proposed model, for example, rough set theory and other. This is left for future research.

Acknowledgments

The authors are grateful to the participants of the 17th International Mathematics conference held on 22–24 December 2011 and organized by the Bangladesh Mathematical Society and the Department of Mathematics, Jahangirnagar University, Dhaka, Bangladesh. They greatly acknowledge comments and very useful suggestions from anonymous referees, which improved greatly the presentation of the paper. They are also very thankful to the Editor Yi-Chi Wang and editorial staff Badiaa Sayed for their very valuable cooperation. They greatly acknowledge it.

References

[1] B. Mandelbrot, "The variation of certain speculative prices," *Journal of Business*, vol. 36, pp. 394–419, 1963.

[2] E. F. Fama, "The behavior of stock market prices," *Journal of Business*, vol. 38, pp. 34–105, 1965.

[3] D. A. Hsu, R. B. Miler, and D. W. Wichern, "On the stable paretian behavior of stock market prices," *Journal of the American Statistical Association*, vol. 69, pp. 108–113, 1974.

[4] D. Kim and S. J. Kon, "Alternative models for the conditional heteroskedasticity of stock returns," *Journal of Business*, vol. 67, pp. 563–598, 1994.

[5] R. F. Engle, "Autoregressive conditional heteroscedasticity with estimates of the variance of UK Inflation," *Econometrica*, vol. 50, pp. 987–1008, 1982.

[6] T. Bollerslev, "Generalized autoregressive conditional heteroskedasticity," *Journal of Econometrics*, vol. 31, no. 3, pp. 307–327, 1986.

[7] S. Banik, M. Anwer, K. Khan, R. A. Rouf, and F. H. Chanchary, "Neural network and genetic algorithm approaches for forecasting bangladeshi monsoon rainfall," in *Proceedings of the 11th International Conference on Computer and Information Technology (ICCIT '08)*, December 2008.

[8] J. S. R. Jang, "ANFIS: adaptive-network-based fuzzy inference system," *IEEE Transactions on Systems, Man and Cybernetics*, vol. 23, no. 3, pp. 665–685, 1993.

[9] D. F. Cook and M. L. Wolfe, "A back-propagation neural network to predict average air temperatures," *AI Applications in Natural Resource Management*, vol. 5, no. 1, pp. 40–46, 1991.

[10] A. Abraham, N. S. Philip, and P. Saratchandran, "Modeling chaotic behavior of stock indices using intelligent paradigms," *International Journal of Neural, Parallel and Scientific Computations*, vol. 11, no. 1-2, pp. 143–160, 2003.

[11] J. Kamruzzaman and R. A. Sarker, "Comparing ANN based models with ARIMA for prediction of forex rates," *Bulletin of the American Schools of Oriental Research*, vol. 22, no. 2, pp. 2–11, 2003.

[12] G. E. P. Box and G. Jenkins, *Time Series Analysis: Forecasting and Control*, Cambridge University Press, Cambridge, UK, 1970.

[13] S. Banik, F. H. Chanchary, R. A. Rouf, and K. Khan, "Modeling chaotic behavior of Dhaka Stock Market Index values using the neuro-fuzzy model," in *Proceedings of the 10th International Conference on Computer and Information Technology (ICCIT '07)*, pp. 80–85, December 2007.

[14] C. R. Nelson and C. R. Plosser, "Trends and random walks in macroeconmic time series. Some evidence and implications," *Journal of Monetary Economics*, vol. 10, no. 2, pp. 139–162, 1982.

[15] W. F. Mitchell, "Testing for unit roots and persistence in OECD unemployment rates," *Applied Economics*, vol. 25, no. 12, pp. 1489–1501, 1993.

[16] R. S. McDougall, "The seasonal unit root structure in New Zealand macroeconomic variables," *Applied Economics*, vol. 27, pp. 817–827, 1995.

[17] W. H. Greene, *Econometric Analysis*, Prentice Hall, Upper Saddle River, NJ, USA, 7th edition, 2008.

[18] S. Banik, *Testing for Stationarity, Seasonality and Long Memory in Economic and Financial Time Series [Ph.D. thesis]*, School of Business, La Trobe University, Bundoora, Australia, 1999, Unpublished.

[19] S. Banik and P. Silvapulle, "Testing for seasonal stability in unemployment series: international evidence," *Empirica*, vol. 26, no. 2, pp. 123–139, 1999.

[20] S. E. Said and D. A. Dickey, "Testing for unit roots in autoregressive-moving average models of unknown order," *Biometrika*, vol. 71, no. 3, pp. 599–607, 1984.

[21] P. C. B. Phillips and P. Perron, "Testing for a unit root in time series regression," *Biometrika*, vol. 75, no. 2, pp. 335–346, 1988.

[22] R. L. Thomas, *Modern Econometrics: An Introduction*, Addision-Wesley, New York, NY, USA, 1997.

[23] J. N. Holland, *Adaptation in Natural and Artificial Systems*, The University of Michigan Press, Ann Arbor, Mich, USA, 1975.

[24] Y. H. Lee, S. K. Park, and D. E. Chang, "Parameter estimation using the genetic algorithm and its impact on quantitative precipitation forecast," *Annales Geophysicae*, vol. 24, no. 12, pp. 3185–3189, 2006.

[25] J. R. Koza, *Genetic Programming: On the Programming of Computers by Means of Natural Selection*, MIT Press, Cambridge, Mass, USA, 1992.

[26] Z. Wei, W. U. Zhi-ming, and Y. Gen-Ke, "Genetic programming-based chaotic time series modeling," *Journal of Zhejiang University*, vol. 5, no. 11, pp. 1432–1439, 2004.

[27] H. Pohlheim, *Documentation for Genetic and Evolutionary Algorithm Toolbox for Use with MATLAB*, 2005.

17

A Nanotechnology Enhancement to Moore's Law

Jerry Wu,[1,2] Yin-Lin Shen,[1,2] Kitt Reinhardt,[3] Harold Szu,[1,2] and Boqun Dong[1,2]

[1] School of Engineering and Applied Science, The George Washington University, Washington, DC 20052, USA
[2] School of Engineering, The Catholic University of America, Washington, DC 20064, USA
[3] Air Force Laboratory, US Air Force Office of Scientific Research, Arlington, VA, USA

Correspondence should be addressed to Jerry Wu; clwu@gwu.edu

Academic Editor: Liyi Dai

Intel Moore observed an exponential doubling in the number of transistors in every 18 months through the size reduction of transistor components since 1965. In viewing of mobile computing with insatiate appetite, we explored the necessary enhancement by an increasingly maturing nanotechnology and facing the inevitable quantum-mechanical atomic and nuclei limits. Since we cannot break down the atomic size barrier, the fact implies a fundamental size limit at the atomic/nucleus scale. This means, no more simple 18-month doubling, but other forms of transistor doubling may happen at a different slope. We are particularly interested in the nano enhancement area. (i) 3 Dimensions: If the progress in shrinking the in-plane dimensions is to slow down, vertical integration can help increasing the areal device transistor density. As the devices continue to shrink into the 20 to 30 nm range, the consideration of thermal properties and transport in such devices becomes increasingly important. (ii) Quantum computing: The other types of transistor material are rapidly developed in laboratories worldwide, for example, Spintronics, Nanostorage, HP display Nanotechnology, which are modifying this Law. We shall consider the limitation of phonon engineering fundamental information unit "Qubyte" in quantum computing, Nano/Micro Electrical Mechanical System (NEMS), Carbon Nanotubes, single-layer Graphenes, single-strip Nano-Ribbons, and so forth.

1. Introduction

There have been numerous papers and scientists' experiments about the lives and deaths of Moore's Law which are dealing with several technological issues and economics barriers. Indeed, looking at the history of integrated circuits from 1975 to 2011, a doubling of transistor counts every twenty-four months was a good estimation. This prediction, known as Moore's Law, has become a business dictum for the whole semiconductor industry. However, "what the Moore's Law is" and "how did it came about" are not clear. We observe that Moore's Law has expanded beyond its original intentions/meaning. The definition of Moore's Law has come to refer to almost anything related to the semiconductor industry that, when plotted on semilog paper, approximates a straight line [1].

In this work, by reviewing Moore's Law history, investigating possible barriers for Moore's Law, and predicting potential nanotechnologies to enhance Moore's Law, we define a roadmap of future key technologies. In addition, we also estimate the end of Moore's Law, assuming we focus on technical capabilities.

2. Moore's Law History

Alan Turing in his 1950 paper [2] "Computing machinery and intelligence" had predicted that by the turn of the millennium, we would have "computers with a storage capacity of about 10^9" what today we would call 128 megabytes processing speed, memory capacity, sensors, and even the number and size of pixels in digital cameras, for example, smartphone. After him, Gordon Earle Moore (born January 3, 1929; UC Berkeley BS Chemistry, 1950; Caltech PhD. major in Chemistry and minor Physics, 1954) is the cofounder and Chairman Emeritus of Intel Corporation. In 1965, Moore, a founder of Fairchild Semiconductor (later Intel), observed in his famous paper [3] that "the complexity for minimum component costs has increased at a rate of roughly a factor of two per year". Extrapolating this trend for a decade,

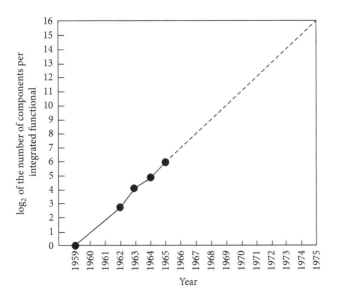

FIGURE 1: Moore's prediction, in 1965, of the doubling of the number of minimum cost components on a chip per year, with extrapolated to 1975 [3].

Moore predicted that chips with 65,000 components would be available by 1975. This observation of exponential growth in circuit density has proven to be one of the greatest examples of prescience in modern era.

Moore then refined his component count estimation, in 1975, to a doubling every twenty-four months, and thus a reduced exponential growth compared to his initial estimation in 1965 [4]. Based on the history of integrated circuits from 1975 to 2008, a doubling of transistor counts every two years was a good estimation.

This prediction known as *Moore's Law* has become a remarkable evolutionary trend for the whole semiconductor industry.

Indeed, Moore himself already observed, in 1995, that the semiconductor industry cannot continue its fast exponential growth indefinitely, since it would exceed the gross world product (GWP) at some time. In the meantime, lots of publications deal with technological limitations to Moore's Law, for example, [5].

3. Current Barrier of Moore's Law

Gordon Moore's prediction is that the density of transistors and computing power doubles every twenty-four months, which has held since there were fewer than 100 transistors in an integrated circuit. Up to today's many millions of transistors on a single-integrated computer chip are still followed this trend. This amazing prediction has encouraged some authors to state that "periodically, people predict the death of Moore's Law. They state that Moore's Law eventually will end because of some future technological or scientific barrier. However, to date, engineers and scientists have found a way around these problems, and Moore's Law continues to be an accurate means of predicting the future development of technology" [6].

In this paper, we discuss the possible barrier of Moore's Law then follow by the possible technologies that may enhance Moor's Law.

3.1. Performance Demand of Processor. Intel CTO Justin Rattner recently stated in an interview with Network World that Moore's Law will likely be the rule for many decades to come. "If Moore's Law is simply a measure of the increase in the number of electronic devices per chip, then Moore's Law has much more time to go, probably decades"; he is quoted as saying.

Figure 2 shows the technology node from 130 nm to 22 nm announced recently versus the performance of the semiconductor chips. The gate length keeps on shrinking as the technology node decreases. As what most people expected for past few decades, the performance or the speed of the designed semiconductor chips should be increased as well. However, we can observe from this figure that the performance was, in contrast, decreased after technology node reached 65 nm.

The major reasons for this result are mainly from the following: current leakage, power consumption, and heat sink. These factors will limit the modern consumer demand products such as smartphone, laptop, and flat-panel device.

The drivers for technology development fall into two top-level categories: push and pull. As the electronics have grown to become a $2 trillion USA industry as well as an enabler for productivity and growth in all areas of economic activity, the mobile devices are obviously the major push drivers for the economic. However, these push drivers, in contract, become the pull drivers for performance of the semiconductor chips due to the following major factors: low cost, mobility, and low power. First of all, the major characters of modern mobile devices are huge amount of end user and short recycle time. This will limit the unit cost of the mobile device. Hence, the cost of research and development, manufacture, texting, and packing will also be limited. Secondly, the other character of modern mobile devices is mobility. This will limit the weight of the mobile device. However, it increases the requirements for wireless communication module, such as WiFi, Bluetooth, GPS, and 3G/4G communication, inside these devices. Therefore, a complex tradeoff between cost, weight, and performance will need to be seriously considered in modern mobile device industry. In other words, when we discuss Moore's Law, it is not just simply a measure of the increase in the number of electronic devices per chip.

3.2. Power Source/Consumption and Heat Sink. As mobile device industry keeps growing up, energy is always one of the most important issues in this century. Therefore, research and development of new energy storage materials and devices are receiving worldwide concern and increasing research interest [7]. Graphene, a unique two-dimensional carbon material, is predicted to be an excellent electrode material candidate for energy conversion/storage systems because of its high-specific surface area, good chemical stability, excellent electrical, and thermal conductivity as well as remarkably high mechanical strength and Young's modulus.

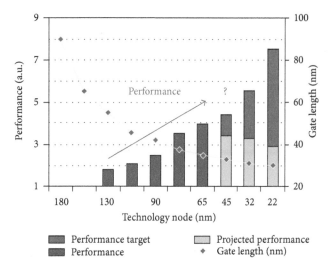

FIGURE 2: Performance demand of processor [5].

Indeed, increasing the battery performance can provide more room for the performance of processor. However, the generated heat will become another barrier for the mobile device development, especially for the smartphone, flat-panel PC, and Ultra-Book which do not allow a build-in fan structure. These limitations will become another factor to further limit Moore's Law in the future.

3.3. Tunneling Effect.

Semiconductor manufacturers will be able to produce chips on the 14 nm manufacturing process, expected by conservative estimates to arrive in 2018. However, semiconductor makers will not be able to shrink transistors much, if at all, beyond 2021, according to a new paper from Intel [8]. Transistors are essentially microscopic on/off switches that consist of a source (S), where electrons come from, a drain (D), where the electrons target to, and a gate (G) that mainly controls the flow of electrons through a channel that connects the source and the drain. When the length of the gate gets smaller than 5 nanometers, however, tunneling effect will begin to kick into play. Electrons will simply pass through the channel on their own without any driver voltage, because the source and the drain will be extremely close. Therefore, a transistor becomes unreliable as a source of basic data, because the probability of spontaneous transmission is about 50 percent. In other words, Heisenberg's uncertainty principle is in action, because the location of the electrons cannot be accurately predicted based on Heisenberg's uncertainty principle.

On a two-year cycle based on Moore's Law, this would mean that 16-nanometer chips would appear in 2013 with the barriers preventing new, smaller chips in 2015.

Semiconductor manufacturers, however, have had to delay the introduction of new processes recently, around 2012. Using a three-year calendar, 5-nanometer chips will not hit until 2018 or 2019 based on the new technology progress update history, putting a barrier generation at about 2021. The ITRS timetable will provide more details about the different manufacturing technologies for a given year.

However, the tunneling effects will occur regardless of the chemistry of the transistor materials. Several researchers over the years have predicted the end of Moore's Law but made the mistake of extrapolating on the basis of existing materials.

3.4. The Quantum Limit to Moore's Law.

Gordon Moore himself stated during an interview September 18, 2007, at Intel's twice-annual technical conference that we will soon be bumping against the laws of physics: "another decade, a decade and a half I think we'll hit something fairly fundamental."

Since this involves a physics limit (in his words), he went on to quote Stephen Hawking during his visit to Intel in 2005. "When Stephen Hawking was asked what are the fundamental limits to microelectronics, he said the speed of light and the atomic nature of matter" [9]. Determining an ultimate physics limit to Moore's Law would mark out a future boundary to electronics miniaturization.

A calculation of the quantum limit to Moore's Law was conducted by writing Moore's Law in equation form as [5]

$$n_2 = n_1 2^{[(y_2 - y_1)/2]}. \tag{1}$$

This equation predicts the number n_2 of transistors or equivalent computing power in any given year y_2 from the number n_1 of transistors in any other earlier year y_1 [5].

From the definition of Moore's Law, we know that the characteristic dimension or length L of a transistor is inversely proportional to the number of transistors n on an IC. If the measurement of n is in "number per meter," then, from dimensional analysis, the measurement of L is in meters (m), or, equivalently, $1 = L$ is the number per meter just as in (1).

We can then rewrite (1) as

$$\frac{1}{L_2} - \left(\frac{1}{L_1}\right) 2^{[(y_2 - y_1)/2]}. \tag{2}$$

The characteristic dimension of an electron from Heisenberg uncertainty is the Compton wavelength [10] $\lambda_c = h/m_e c = 2.4263 \times 10^{-12}$ m based on Planck's constant h, the mass of the electron m_e, and the speed of light c.

The Compton wavelength of the electron is the fundamental limit to measuring its position based on quantum mechanics and special relativity, or the length scale where a relativistic quantum field theory is necessary for an adequate description [11]. The Compton wavelength is therefore the fundamental boundary to determining the position (or spin) of a particle, which satisfies the Stephen Hawking prediction that this limit would be based on the speed of light and the atomic nature of matter since c is determined by λ_c, m_e, and h [5]. Rewriting (2) using the year of 2008 with available technology, transistor feature size, and Compton wavelength, 2.4263×10^{-12} m or 0.00243 nm:

$$\left(2.4263 \times 10^{-12}\,\text{m}\right)^{-1} = \left(0.045 \times 10^{-6}\,\text{m}\right)^{-1} 2^{[(y_2 - 2008)/2]}. \tag{3}$$

Solving for the exponent $\Delta y = (y_2 - 2008)$ using the natural log function, we end up to have

$$y_1 = 28.36y + 2008 = \text{year } 2036. \qquad (4)$$

This is the quantum limit year predicted by Moore's Law if electrons were implemented as the smallest quantum computing transistor elements [5].

3.5. The Economic Limit to Moore's Law. The higher component density has led to a decrease in end consumer prices. However, the costs for producers follow a converse trend: research and development, manufacture, and tests become more and more expensive with each new generation. This observation is known as *Rock's Law* and sometimes also referred to as Moore's Second Law [12]; fabrication facility (fab) costs also follow an exponential growth. Despite this exponential growth of facility costs, the cost per shipped unit decreases at an exponential rate. Karl Rupp first investigated economic limitations to the semiconductor business. A summary of their results has already been published in [13]. Karl then found out If costs for a single fab are at most 0.02% of the GWP (i.e., $\varepsilon = 0.0002$), a reduced growth of transistor counts per chip for economic reasons is likely to happen around 2020 as shown in Figure 3.

3.6. On-Board Limit to Moore's Law. There have been numerous papers and discussions about the lives and deaths of Moore's Law, all of them dealing with several technological questions inside semiconductor chip. However, any semiconductor chip cannot exist along without PCB board, no matter flexible or not.

Higher bandwidth has become more important than ever in today's computing systems. Personal computers, routers, switches, and game consoles all require higher bandwidth to meet the increasing performance demand of new applications. Moreover, the continuous scaling of integrated circuit technology, confirming Moore's prediction, over the recent years has resulted in massive computational capacity and hence data processing capability which in turn has created the demand for high-speed communication across different components in a system [14]. These systems extend to optical communication networks spanning across the globe, but all come down to chip-to-chip communication in a single board [15]. The massive flux of information in and out of the chip has caused simple input/output (I/O) drivers to be replaced with sophisticated high-speed circuits which in turn depend on reliable high bandwidth channels.

Channel design, which was conveniently and justifiably ignored at lower frequencies, has become a major bottleneck for high-speed communication. The increase in data rates to the tens of Giga bits per second (Gbps) region has prompted more careful signal integrity considerations in the design of the channel from the transmitter of one chip to the receiver on the next. The decrease in wavelength size due to higher frequency signaling has caused the once short electrical lengths of different components to become significant due to transmission line delays, loss, and signal coupling in these components [16].

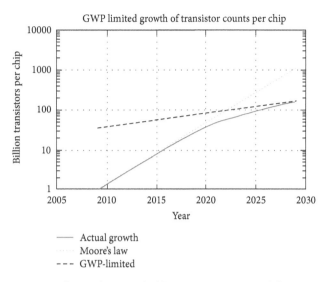

FIGURE 3: If costs for a single fab are at most 0.02% of the GWP (i.e., $\varepsilon = 0.0002$), a reduced growth of transistor counts per chip for economic reasons is likely to happen around 2020 [13].

Therefore, on-board transmission line would become a remarkable bottleneck for the input/output of the semiconductor design.

In addition, another possible on-board barrier would be on the other end of the transmission line as we discussed above, that is, the state-of-the-art analog to digital conversion (ADC) devices.

ADC devices translate physical information into a stream of numbers, enabling digital processing by sophisticated software algorithms. The ADC task is inherently intricate: its hardware must hold a snapshot of a fast-varying input signal steady, while acquiring measurements. Since these measurements are spaced in time, the values between consecutive snapshots are lost. In general, therefore, there is no way to recover the analog input unless some prior on its structure is incorporated [17]. A common approach in engineering is to assume that the signal is bandlimited, meaning that the spectral contents are confined to a maximal frequency f-max. Bandlimited signals have limited (hence slow) time variation and can therefore be perfectly reconstructed from equispaced samples with a rate at least 2 times f-max, termed the Nyquist rate. This fundamental result is often attributed in the engineering community to Shannon-Nyquist [18].

Uniform sampling ADC devices are the most common technology in the market. Figure 4 maps off-the shelf ADC devices according to their sampling rate. The ADC industry has perpetually followed the Nyquist paradigm—the datasheets of all the devices that are reported in the figure highlight the conversion speed, referring to uniform sampling of the input. The industry is continuously striving to increase the possible uniform conversion rates.

Therefore, the ADC devices on the user input/output sides could become another possible barrier of the semiconductor design. This barrier may happen sooner when the higher quality of video and audio is demanded as well as

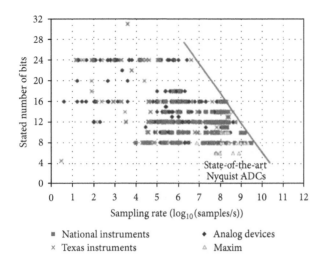

FIGURE 4: ADC technology: stated number of bits versus sampling rate. A map of more than 1,200 ADC devices from four leading manufacturers, according to online datasheets [17].

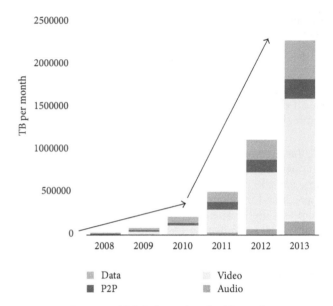

FIGURE 5: Mobile device bandwidth trend.

the higher speed requirement for wireless communication of mobile device such as smartphone, flat-panel PC, and laptop.

3.7. Mobile Device-Driven Industry. With the developing of the mobile devices, especially smartphones and multimedia Mobile (MMM) phones, more functionalities, faster download speed are becoming the main demands of customers. As the result, mobile market does not only depend on better hardware but also matter of bandwidth and frequencies. It is shown in Figure 5 below that mobile bandwidth (TB per month) grows extremely fast since 2011 [19]. We can find that different media share the whole bandwidth usage. So the sharing and cross talk among billions of users require bandwidth sharing strategies.

In addition, video will account for 64% of mobile traffic by 2013 and mobile data traffic will be more than double every year through 2013. In 2013, most important, mobile data traffic will be more than 66 times greater than mobile data traffic in 2008.

With the fast development of new technology, electronic devices tend to be smaller and more efficient. The market developed from PC to laptop and palm, all the way to cell phone and smart phone. Mobile devices, such as smartphone and tablet computers, are becoming more popular than ever. In most countries, the occupation ratio of mobile device is much higher than that of PC. As shown in Figure 6, global Internet users will double over the next few years, most of which will be mobile devices [20].

Due to the global Internet devices sales research, in a few years, the number of the mobile devices will dwarf the number of PCs. It is shown in Figure 7 that PC sales curve will become flat few years later, while smartphone and tablet sales will go up straight to the top [21].

The total global mobile phone market is expected to be worth $341.4 billion by 2015, while smartphone will occupy 75.8% of the overall mobile sales market in the same year.

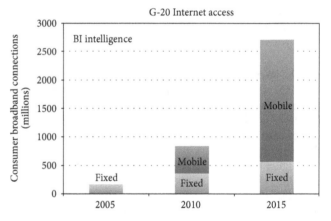

FIGURE 6: Global Internet connections in million.

However, the fast development of mobile devices will have impact on Moore's Law, which is a crucial factor in electronic manufactory fields. What is actually happening is that there is a race for mobile devices market in demand now versus the realities of Moore's Law. The law which states that the number of transistors that can be placed inexpensively on an integrated circuit doubles approximately every two years, and the performance will double in the same period. This law has remained true over the last 40 years, driven the technology industry, and has enabled computing devices to get cheaper, smaller, and more powerful and hence deliver more functionality. By prediction, Moore's Law will not remain fully precise in next decades due to the restriction of power consumption, size, and price.

3.7.1. Mobile Device-Driven Industry: Size/Weight. Today, mobile device is becoming smaller and lighter to meet the users' requirements and the most advanced logic technology node in production is 22 nm in 2012 and the target for

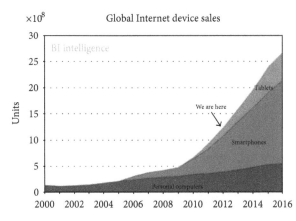

FIGURE 7: Global Internet device sales.

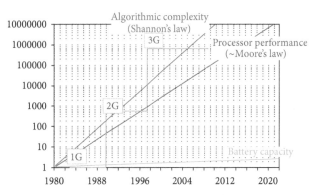

FIGURE 8: Shannon's Lay versus Moore's Law.

2013 will be 14 nm. With feature sizes below 100 nm, silicon technology has entered the realm of nanotechnology and continuing true Moore's Law becomes more and more difficult and requires new structures, materials, and technology.

The three important factors to reduce size are lithography, scalability of the planar CMOS transistor, and performance degradation due to pitch scaling. But we can predict that the trend of pitch will slow and stop during the next 10 years because the size cannot be half separated infinitely due to the physical rules. Addressing the lithography tool roadmap here, the classical pitch size for a given lithography single exposure is a straight-forward consequence of the diffraction-limited resolution of the projection optics. The lateral optical resolution is given by the quotient of the illumination wavelength, λ, and the numerical aperture, NA, of the projection optics according to the famous Rayleigh formula $\Delta x = k_1(\lambda/NA)$, where k_1 is a process factor determined by the exact details of the optical system.

In the past years, each of these factors has been addressed to increase the attainable resolution of a photolithography system and finally reached their limitations [22]. To pattern finer pitch, the industry solution is now either double pattering or DUV. However, for double pattering, it will cost extra processing challenging when smaller than 22 nm, which results in a cost issue. Also, for DUV (deep-UV) method, it has approached a technology limit of 193 nm [23]. As a result, Moore's Law will not be continuing forever due to these limitations.

3.7.2. Mobile Device-Driven Industry: Market Price.
As discussed above in Section 3.5, smaller size will cause cost issues. At the same time, to secure the market of mobile devices, economic factors must be considered for each vendor. This means that if cost continues to grow for cooler functionalities, the growing market price will limit the development predicted by Moore's Law. This is because there is a relationship between supply and demand in economic area. For example, if price increases, the number of consumers will decrease, and then the number of products will reduce. In his research, as discussed in Section 3.5, Karl Rupp pointed out that Moore's Law would be slowed down due to the limitation of GWP (gross world product) around 2020, as shown in Figure 3.

3.7.3. Mobile Device Driven Industry: Power Consumption and Shannon's Law.
According to Moore's Law, the size of transistor should be half every 2 years as discussed above. But when getting minimized, the physical characters will be changed a lot for nanoscale transistors. It will introduce a lot of new leakage mechanisms such as gate tunneling leakage, junction tunneling leakage, and subthreshold leakage. In this situation, to control the leakage power and dynamic power, power management IC will be introduced to SoC [24]. It is inferred here that the total number of functional transistors will not be to double due to the involved power management circuit.

For mobile system, the freedom fully depends on the energy provided by the batteries. As batteries can store a fixed amount of energy, the devices' operation time is limited as well [25] and the operation time becomes a significant factor for users because of the crammed up functionalities. So the main limiting factor in many portable device designs is not hardware or software, but instead how much power can be delivered by a battery.

However, research [26] states that although in the past 20 years system power consumption stays the same in every transistor-double technology generation cycle, in the next 20 years, power consumption will become a critical issue which will limit transistor's performance. As a result, if we use power management technology to reduce power consumption, as discussed above, the total number of functional transistors will not be doubled. If we do not use low-power design to solve this issue, then the fact that battery energy capacity for a given volume doubles only once per decade, as shown in Figure 8, will conflict with Moore's Law. In a word, no matter which solution we choose, it will make Moore's Law trend goes down in the future.

Figure 8 summarizes the key challenges facing the mobile device industry, which describes the gap among algorithmic complexity, processor performance, and the prediction of battery capacity. Algorithmic complexity, which is defined by Shannon's Law, tells the maximum rate at which information can be transmitted over a communications channel of a specified bandwidth in the presence of noise. It predicts that the transmission performance improves two times in 8.5 months, while processor performance improves two times in 18 months. In addition, it takes battery makers 5 to 10 years to achieve comparable increase in power density.

TABLE 1: Cellular system: 1G to 4G.

Decade	Generation	Efficiency: bps/Hz/sector
1980s	1G Analog cellular	0.016
1990s	2G Digital (TDMA → CDMA)	0.05 → 0.2
2000s	3G Enhanced CDMA	0.4 → 0.6
2010s	4G OFDM/M1MO	>1.0

To discuss the characteristics of mobile bandwidth, Nyquist-Shannon sampling theorem describes a worldwide sampling method in relation to bandwidth and frequency. The theorem states as if a function $x(t)$ contains no frequencies higher than bandwidth B Hz, it is completely determined by giving its ordinates at a series of points spaced $1/(2B)$ seconds apart. It is now used by mainstream information technology such as world's famous Code Division Multiplex (CDMA), the Orthogonal Frequency Division Multiplex (OFDM) with Multiple Input Multiple Output (MIMO). CDMA, which in one of several manifestations has been chosen for virtually all third-generation cellular systems, and OFDM with MIMO, which seems to be the most favored for a future generation [27].

CDMA is a spread spectrum multiple-access technique which spreads the bandwidth of the data uniformly for the same transmitted power and spread spectrum uses a transmission bandwidth that is several orders of magnitude greater than the minimum required signal bandwidth. OFDM is a method of encoding digital data on multiple carrier frequencies with all the carrier signals being orthogonal to each other. The orthogonality also allows high spectral efficiency, with a total symbol rate near the Nyquist rate for the equivalent baseband signal as compared in Table 1.

Although most of nowadays technologies are following Nyquist-Shannon sampling theorem, the theorem itself is meeting its limitation in regard with Moore's law. In fact, with the increasing data capacity and bandwidth, the number of I/O will grow with the sampling theorem which has a different speed with Moore's Law. The increasing size of the Shannon-Moore gap with time means that incremental transistors and MHz alone are not sufficient to close the gap between them. Furthermore, it is shown in Figure 9 below that if bandwidth capacity develops with Nyquist-Shannon sampling theorem, it will be hard to meet customers' demand [28].

A conclusion can be drawn from above that Nyquist-Shannon sampling theorem is increasingly incommensurate the technology demand. In this situation, compressed sensing, an alternative to Shannon/Nyquist sampling for acquisition of sparse or compressible signals that can be well approximated by just $K \ll N$ elements from an N-dimensional basis. Instead of taking periodic samples, it measures inner products with $M < N$ random vectors and then recovers the signal via a sparsity-seeking optimization or greedy algorithm [27]. So compressed sensing just obtains few compressed sparse sensing information of the sampling signals. At the same time, the sensing wave, unlike CDMA or OFDM, is irrelevant to the sparse space of signals. These characteristics will make I/O reduced compared to the

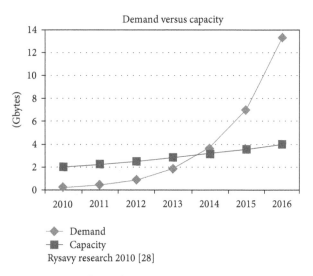

Rysavy research 2010 [28]

FIGURE 9: Average demand per user versus average capacity per user.

Shannon-Nyquist sampling and will also fit Moore's Law. As a result, the impact on Moore's Law which is due to Shannon-Nyquist theory will be eliminated.

4. Nanoenhancement to Moore's Law

4.1. DNA Scaffolding Tiny Circuit Board. As what we discussed previously, any semiconductor chip cannot exist along without PCB board, no matter flexible or not. Due to the on-board transmission line effect for high speed communication, its the time for us to start thinking about new materials for the circuit board.

IBM researchers, working with the California Institute of Technology, claimed they have collaborated in combining lithographic patterning with self-assembly to devise a method of arranging DNA "origami" structures on surfaces compatible with current semiconductor manufacturing equipment. IBM's developed chip-building technology that uses a DNA-like structure as a "scaffold." As shows in Figure 10, low concentrations of triangular DNA origami are binding to wide lines on a lithographically patterned surface, built by IBM scientists.

This technology could be a major breakthrough in enabling the semiconductor industry to pack more power and speed into tiny computer chips, while making them more energy efficient and less expensive to manufacturer.

As we discussed previously in this paper, the semiconductor industry is faced with the challenges of developing lithographic technology for feature sizes smaller than 22 nm and exploring new classes of transistors that employ carbon nanotubes or silicon nanowires. IBM's approach of using DNA molecules as scaffolding—where millions of carbon nanotubes could be deposited and self-assembled into precise patterns by sticking to the DNA molecules—may provide a way to reach sub-22 nm lithography [29]. The cost involved in shrinking features to improve performance is a limiting factor in keeping pace with Moore's Law and a concern across the semiconductor industry.

FIGURE 10: IBM tiny circuit boards [14].

4.2. 3D Tri-Gates Transistor. For more than four decades, Intel has delivered the challenge of Moore's Law. However, a fundamental barrier which is emerging technology is approaching atomic dimensions. Intel is already working on technologies to overcome this.

Intel shrank the fabrication process to use 22 nanometer (nm = billionths of a meter) nodes. Next, Intel departed from traditional planar (2-D) gates, using instead 3-D Tri-Gate technology. Let us look at the reduction in circuit size first. In order to double the number of transistors, scientists need the fabrication process to use 22 nm nodes, which means circuit paths not much thicker than single atoms.

By using 3-D Tri-Gate technology, Gate electrode controls silicon fin from three sides providing improved sub-threshold slope. Therefore, inversion layer area increased for higher drive current. In addition, Intel development team claimed that the process cost adder is only 2-3%. As shown in Figures 1 and 11(c), the 22 nm 3-D Tri-Gate transistors provide improved performance at high voltage and an unprecedented performance gain at low voltage.

The measurement results show 40% increase in performance at low voltage when compared to 32 nm 2D transistors and consume half the power at the same performance level as 32 nm 2-D transistors.

Intel expects to have the first microprocessor using 22 nm 3-D Tri-Gate transistors (The code named Ivy Bridge) in production by late 2012. One can only imagine what the digital future will hold when technology surrounding something ubiquitous as a transistor leapfrogs.

When Intel got the 22 nm fabrication process to work, getting the right number of transistors to fit in a useable form factor, Moore's Law is safe for another two years, when the fabrication process will use 14 nm nodes.

4.3. Spintronics. In conventional electronics theory, charge of electron is used to achieve functionalities for diodes, transistors, electrooptic devices. However, the spintronics technology manipulates electron spin, or resulting magnetism, to achieve new/improved functionalities spin transistors Figure 12(b) [30], memories as shown in Figure 12(a) [31], higher speed, lower power, tunable detectors, and lasers,

bits (Q-bits) for quantum computing. Spintronics has actually been around for years. IBM produced disk drive heads, using giant magnetoresistive (GMR) technology, taking advantage of these properties in 1997. Magnetic random access memory (MRAM) could become the next area where spintronics is incorporated. Ideally, MRAM would be able to store a substantial amount of data, consume little energy, operate at a much faster rate than conventional flash memory, and last forever. Figure 12(b) shows the inject polarized spin from one FM contact; other FM contact is analyzer, and modulates current by modifying spin precession via Rashba effect, Asymmetry-spin-orbit interact.

Finding a replacement for flash technology, which is used in cell phones, memory cards in digital cameras, and other devices, is an urgent business in the semiconductor market. Demand for flash is growing extremely rapidly.

4.4. Carbon Nanotube (CNT). As we discuss in the previous section, IBM's approach of using DNA molecules as scaffolding—where millions of carbon nanotubes (CNT) could be deposited and self-assembled into precise patterns by sticking to the DNA molecules—may provide a way to reach sub-22 nm lithography.

In our previous works [32], we elucidated the quantum mechanical nature of the Einstein photoelectric effect in terms of a field-effect transistor (FET) made of Carbon Nanotube (CNT) semiconductors. Consequently, we discovered a surprising low-pass band gap property as shown in Figure 13(a), as opposed to the traditional sharp band-pass band gaps. In other words, there exists a minimum amount of photon energy $n\hbar\omega$ shining on CNT which is necessary to excite the semiconductor CNT into free electrons. Applying a static magnet along the longitudinal direction as shown in (Figure 13(b), (c)), the conduction electron and holes will be spiral in the opposite direction over the surface reducing the current density and the collision recombination chance will therefore be reduced when travelling from the cathode end to the anode end, driven internally by the asymmetric semiconductor-metal (using Ag & Pd) work functions (Schottky interface effect) for an automatic triode read out.

Our previous works [32] show that CNT semiconductors have band-gap-like characteristics different from the traditional semiconductor. CNT semiconductors have a low-pass band gap, rather than band passing, according to Low Pass Band Gap Theorem of CNT (Szu et al. 2008) [33]:

$$\lambda_{\text{de Broglie}} = \frac{h}{P_{\text{electron}}} = n\pi d_{\text{CNT}} = \lambda_{\text{MWIR}}, \quad n = 1, 2, 3, \ldots.$$

$$(5)$$

The combination of micron scale circuit board revolution design and field-effect transistor (FET) made of Carbon NanoTube (CNT) semiconductors is an excellent candidate to further enhance Moor's Law in the next few decades.

4.5. Single-Atom Transistor. As the size of transistor keeps shrinking based on what we discuss in this paper, where/when could be the end of Moore's Law?

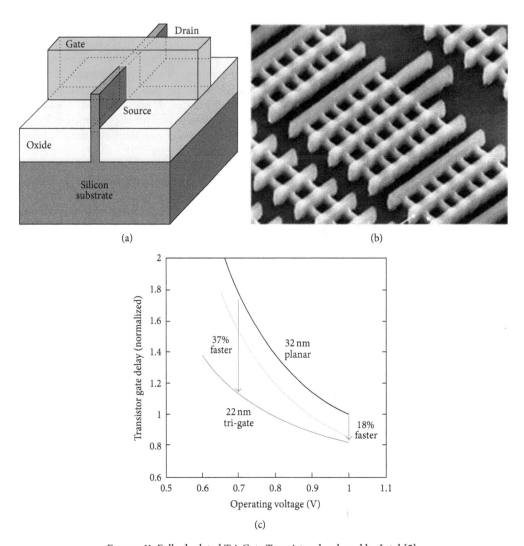

(a)

(b)

(c)

FIGURE 11: Fully depleted Tri-Gate Transistor developed by Intel [5].

Scientists in Australia [34] claim to have created a transistor the size of a single atom, opening the way for the next generation of nanotechnology. The microscopic device is made of a single phosphorus atom embedded into silicon with "gates" to control electrical flow and metallic contacts that are also on an atomic scale. The single atom creation in Australia could radically alter Moore's prediction, redefining the possible size of future gadgets and their applications. This research team demonstrated a working transistor comprised of a single atom—nearly 100 times smaller than the 22-nanometer cutting-edge transistors fabricated by Intel, as we discussed previously. More importantly, the research team led by Michelle Simmons of the University of New South Wales in Sydney was able to show a method for repeating the process with great accuracy and in a fashion that is compatible with the CMOS technology used in transistor fabrication today.

The work of Simmons and her colleagues could show a way to keep making microprocessor circuitry smaller and smaller through 2020 and beyond. In recent years, advances in quantum computing have offered a viable path to smaller and smaller transistors. But the new research might be the first strong sign that atomic-level transistor fabrication can

be done in keeping with the part of Moore's Law that is often forgotten amidst the wonderment over tinier and tinier computer chips—that it be done cheaply.

4.6. Quantum Computers. Quantum electronic devices and this effect will be more obvious as the transistors are going to have molecular scale.

The theory of quantum computation is one of the possible solutions to move the computation to a different computing paradigm, which is based on the theory of using quantum mechanics to perform computations instead of classical physics [35]. In the quantum world we are faced with a probability density, spread all over the world without a detecting operation, it will be impossible to understand whether that value is zero or one.

As a mathematical definition a Qbit is a vector, a linear combination of two fundamental bases states known as $|0\rangle = I$ and $|1\rangle = j$. A vector presentation is shown as [35]

$$|\varphi \geq \alpha |0\rangle + \beta |1\rangle, \quad \text{where } \alpha^2 + \beta^2 = 1, \quad (6)$$

where the term $|x\rangle$ called ket is another representation of a vector, also $\langle x|$ known as bra is a transposed vector, and

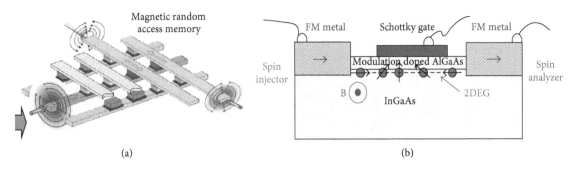

FIGURE 12: (a) Magnetic radom access memory (IBM), (b) spin transistor.

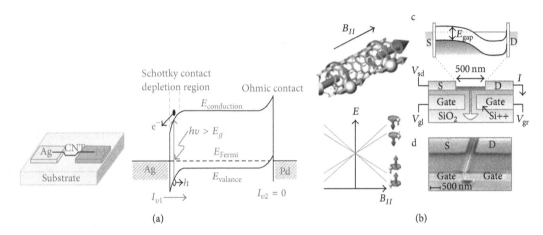

FIGURE 13: (a) 1D CNT has double-bond carbon rigid lattice suffering less thermal noise, which is about 0.5 KT, 1/3 of the thermal noise of CCD dark current liquid nitrogen coolant (LNC). (b) Axial magnetic field increases the surface area as the phase space and avoids the collision recombination of photoelectric carriers (after Rice, Cornel Univ).

$\langle x \mid y \rangle$ called braket is the inner product of these two vectors. A vector space with this inner product is called Hillbert Space.

This linear combination is called a Quantum Superposition of the basis states $|0\rangle$ and $|1\rangle$. The only condition with this definition is $\alpha^2 + \beta^2 = 1$. This is because α^2 and β^2 are quantum probability densities. A sample Qbit model is shown in Figure 14.

Quantum computers are still in the beginning of their way. It has also been suggested that quantum mechanics may be playing a role in consciousness, if a quantum mechanical model of mind and consciousness was developed, this would have significant impact on computational and artificial intelligence. If the brain handles quantum-type transformations somewhere in its neural network this could lead to future quantum computers being biological/biochemical in nature [35].

Although quantum computing can bring our logic element down to molecular scale, however, quantum computers are still faced with the following challenges: (a) interconnection across long distance, (b) room-temperature operation, (c) lack of classical efficient algorithms, (d) setting the initial state of the system, and (e) single defect in line of dots will stop propagation.

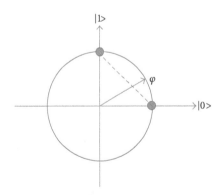

FIGURE 14: Qbit model in state: $(1/\sqrt{2})|0\rangle + (1/\sqrt{2})|1\rangle$.

5. Summary of Key Technologies

Table 2 shows the summary of key future nanotechnologies with known advantages/disadvantages and application.

6. Future of Moore's Law

There have been numerous papers and discussions regarding the lives and deaths of Moore's Law [36]. Before we get into this type of endless debate, we found that we can compare

TABLE 2: Key future nanotechnologies.

Device	Applications	Advantages	Disadvantages
3D transistor	Logic element	Small size	Will still face tunneling effect issue.
	Memory	Low power	Clock tree routing.
Spintronics	Memory	Small size	Control of magnetic field versus spin-polarized current.
	Logic element	Low power	Drivability.
Carbon nanotube FET/graphene	Logic element	Ballistic transport (high speed)	Placement of nanotubes/graphene in a circuit is difficult and not yet production.
		Small size	Control of electrical properties of carbon nanotube (size, chirality) difficult and not yet stably achieved.
Single-electron transistors (SET)	Logic element	Small size Low power	Sensitive to background charge instability.
			High resistance and low drive current.
			Cannot drive large capacitive (wiring) loads.
			Requires geometries 10 nm for room-temperature operation.
Quantum dot (quantum cellular automata, QCA)	Logic element	Small size	Multiple levels of interconnection across long distance difficult.
			Room-temperature operation difficult.
			New computation algorithms required.
			Method of setting the initial state of the system not available.
			Single defect in line of dots will stop propagation.
DNA computing	Logic element	High parallelism	Imperfect yield.
			General-purpose computing not possible.
Quantum computing	Logic element	High computing speed for some certain problem	The coherence in some highly promising concepts for qubits will disappear after about a second. Moreover, the smaller the qubits the faster that process occurs. The information exists may not be long enough to be processed.

the Moore's Law, semiconductor history up to today, and the Dow Jones Industrial Average Curves as shown in Figure 15. What we can learn from this comparison is that people tried their best on both semiconductor developments and the stock market investment in the past few decades. It seems like their curves/trends show us that they are highly related, at least from 1971 up to today (of course we took log on number of transistor). In addition, if we compare that Moore's prediction for the past four decades against the semiconductor industry, we have to admit Moore is a visionary!, no matter what is going to happen in the future.

Looking forward, in this work, we further identify the future transistor counts and places on the following decades, 2020, 2030, and so on. Then, we estimate the sizes of the key technologies that we investigated in this work and locate them on the same chart, assuming Moore's Law is still live. Figure 15 shows that we will face key challenges almost every single decade if we want to meet Moore's Law up to year 2050.

When will Moore's Law end? This is a popular question that scientists keep on asking. To answer this question, we may need to review the original definition of Moore's Law. If we consider Moore's Law as simply just a transistor/component count in a chip, then we can easily break this law today, by making the semiconductor area bigger or

stacking multiple dies in one. Hence, in this work, we consider Moore's Law as a matter of transistor/component density in a chip and focus on the technologies barriers of this law. Based on our calculations along the Moore's Law curve shown in Figure 15, by 2060, our technology node will get into a subatomic scale. In other words, we have nothing to improve on the transistor/component density in a chip. The only thing we can do is extending the chip in 2-D or 3-D (stack) and make the die size larger, unless we find a way to make a switch inside an atom and solve the signal drivability issue also in atom scale in the future! Otherwise, to discuss Moore's Law beyond that point, in Figure 15, will become meaningless.

7. Conclusion

Whether there is an ultimate limit to Moore's Law is an open debate dependent upon future electronic innovations, material science, and physics. Moore's prediction as early as 1965 proves since Turing that he is a unique technological visionary who quietly led the silicon revolution with his own law. We have estimated that the potential future nanotechnologies will enhance the current known barriers for Moore's Law. Based on our estimations on the scale of these

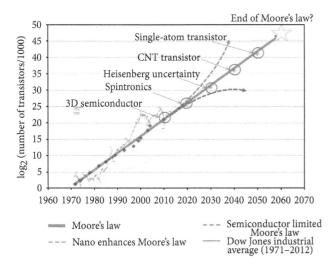

FIGURE 15: Moore's Law history, future, limited factors, and Nanotechnology-Enhance factors for Moore's Law and compared with Dow Jones industrial average in the same period of time (1971–2011).

nanotechnologies, we further forecast the major milestones and key technologies that confront us in the near future in Figure 14. The computing industry and the world population have enjoyed five remarkable decades of Moore's Law. Up to the next half-millennium, our discussion of Moore's Law in turn of density of discrete computing elements will become meaningless from quantum mechanical uncertainty and entanglement technologies point of view. As before those days, the economic limit will continue playing the key role, despite of the fact that we know we cannot break the fundamental limits of the atomic and nucleus nature of matter. The ubiquitous computing in the future might be in an entirely different form of the information representation and nonlocal manipulation. However, the bottleneck might be in the transformation between the classical Moore's Law localized computing and a modern Moore's Law-distributed computing that remains to be formulated by some other visionaries.

Acknowledgment

This work is supported by US Air Force Scientific Research Office, Grant 2010–2012, and a partial support to CUA.

References

[1] P. K. Bondyopadhyay, "Moore's law governs the silicon revolution," *Proceedings of the IEEE*, vol. 86, no. 1, pp. 78–81, 1998.

[2] A. Turing, "Computing Machinery and Intelligence," *Mind*, vol. 59, pp. 433–460, 1950.

[3] G. E. Moore, "Cramming more components onto integrated circuits," *Electronics*, vol. 38, no. 8, pp. 114–117, 1965.

[4] G. E. Moore, "Progress in digital integrated electronics," *Proceedings of the International Electron Devices Meeting (IEDM '75)*, vol. 21, pp. 11–13, 1975.

[5] J. R. Powell, "The quantum limit to Moore's law," *Proceedings of the IEEE*, vol. 96, no. 8, pp. 1247–1248, 2008.

[6] G. C. Orsak et al., *Engineering Our Digital Future*, Prentice-Hall, Upper Saddle River, NJ, USA, 2004.

[7] H. M. Cheng, "Development of graphene-based materials for energy storage," in *Proceedings of the 8th International Vacuum Electron Sources Conference (IVESC '10)*, p. 49, October 2010.

[8] V. V. Zhirnov, R. K. Cavin, J. A. Hutchby, and G. I. Bourianoff, "Limits to binary logic switch scaling—a gedanken model," *Proceedings of the IEEE*, vol. 91, no. 11, pp. 1934–1939, 2003.

[9] D. Martell, "BIntel's Moore Muses on End of Technology Maxim," 2007.

[10] Fundamental physical constants, National Institute of Standards and Technology (NIST)/Committee on Data for Science and Technology (CODATA), 2006.

[11] J. Baez, *Length Scales in Physics*, University of California, Riverside, Calif, USA, 2005.

[12] P. E. Ross, "5 commandments," *IEEE Spectrum*, vol. 40, no. 12, pp. 30–35, 2003.

[13] K. Rupp and S. Selberherr, "The economic limit to moore's law," *Proceedings of the IEEE*, vol. 98, no. 3, pp. 351–353, 2010.

[14] R. R. Schaller, "Moore's law: past, present, and future," *IEEE Spectrum*, vol. 34, no. 6, pp. 52–57, 1997.

[15] K.-Y. K. Chang, S. T. Chuang, N. McKeown, and M. Horowitz, "50 Gb/s 32 × 32 CMOS crossbar chip using asymmetric serial links," in *Proceedings of the Symposium on VLSI Circuits*, pp. 19–20, June 1999.

[16] Graham, H. Johnson, and M. s. l, *High-Speed Signal Propagation: Advanced Black Magic*, Prentice Hall, New York, NY, USA, 2003.

[17] M. Mishali and Y. C. Eldar, "Wideband spectrum sensing at sub-nyquist rates," *IEEE Signal Processing Magazine*, vol. 28, no. 4, pp. 102–135, 2011.

[18] C. E. Shannon, "Communication in the presence of noise," in *Proceedings of the Institute of Radio Engineers (IRE '49)*, vol. 37, pp. 10–21, January 1949.

[19] G. Kim, "How Fast is Mobile Bandwidth Demand Growing?" Razorsight Corp., 2012, http://www.razorsight.com/.

[20] M. Meeker, K. Perkins, and M. Stanley, Research, Berg Insight, http://www.berginsight.com/.

[21] Gartner, IDC, Strategy Analytics, BI Intelligence.

[22] M. Totzeck, W. Ulrich, A. Göhnermeier, and W. Kaiser, "Semiconductor fabrication: pushing deep ultraviolet lithography to its limits," *Nature Photonics*, vol. 1, no. 11, pp. 629–631, 2007.

[23] P. Zimmerman, *Double Patterning Lithography: Double the Trouble or Double the Fun?*, 2009.

[24] E. Scott, "Thompson; power, cost and circuit IP reuse: the real limiter to moore's law over the next 10 years," in *International Symposium on VLSI Technology Systems and Applications (VLSI-TSA '10)*, April 2010.

[25] G. P. Perrucci, F. H. P. Fitzek, and J. Widmer, "Survey on energy consumption entities on the smartphone platform," in *Proceedings of the IEEE 73rd Vehicular Technology Conference (VTC Spring)*, May 2011.

[26] S. Borkar and A. A. Chien, "The future of microprocessors," *Communications of the ACM*, vol. 54, no. 5, pp. 67–77, 2011.

[27] A. Viterbi, *Shannon Capacity Limits of Wireless Networks, Sequences, Subsequences, and Consequences*, Lecture Notes in Computer Science, 2007.

[28] Rysavy Research, "Mobile Broadband Capacity Constraints and the Need for Optimization," Rysavy Research, LLC, http://www.rysavy.com/.

[29] R. J. Kershner, L. D. Bozano, C. M. Micheel et al., "Placement and orientation of individual DNA shapes on lithographically patterned surfaces," *Nature Nanotechnology*, vol. 4, no. 9, pp. 557–561, 2009.

[30] D. Bruce McCombe, Department of Physics, University at Buffalo State University of New York, http://www.csequin.buffalo .edu/Lectures/SemicondSpintronics.ppt.

[31] IBM Corporation, http://www.ibm.com/.

[32] H. Szu, Y. L. Shen, J. Wu, and K. Reinhardt, "Non-cryogenic cooled MWIR with swap-limited carbon nanotubes," in *Proceedings of the Independent Component Analyses, Wavelets, Neural Networks, Biosystems, and Nanoengineering IX*, vol. 8058 of *Proceedings of SPIE*, June 2011.

[33] H. Szu, L. H. Ya, and K. Reinhardt, "Nano-Surgeon targeted at tumor cells mediated with CNT at NIR band-gap," in *Presented in US/Taiwan Nanotech Workshop*, Dr. Weinstock, AFOSR, San Francisco, Calif, USA, 2008.

[34] Centre for Quantum Computation and Communication at the University of New South Wales, http://www.cqc2t.org/.

[35] S. Jafarpour, "Introduction to the world of Quantum Computers," in *Proceedings of the 5th IEEE International Conference on Cognitive Informatics (ICCI '06)*, pp. 760–764, July 2006.

[36] H. Huff, *Into The Nano Era: Moore's Law Beyond Planar Silicon CMOS*, Springer, 2008.

18

A Nonlinear Programming and Artificial Neural Network Approach for Optimizing the Performance of a Job Dispatching Rule in a Wafer Fabrication Factory

Toly Chen

Department of Industrial Engineering and Systems Management, Feng Chia University, No. 100 Wenhwa Road, Seatwen, Taichung 407, Taiwan

Correspondence should be addressed to Toly Chen, tcchen@fcu.edu.tw

Academic Editor: Yi-Chi Wang

A nonlinear programming and artificial neural network approach is presented in this study to optimize the performance of a job dispatching rule in a wafer fabrication factory. The proposed methodology fuses two existing rules and constructs a nonlinear programming model to choose the best values of parameters in the two rules by dynamically maximizing the standard deviation of the slack, which has been shown to benefit scheduling performance by several studies. In addition, a more effective approach is also applied to estimate the remaining cycle time of a job, which is empirically shown to be conducive to the scheduling performance. The efficacy of the proposed methodology was validated with a simulated case; evidence was found to support its effectiveness. We also suggested several directions in which it can be exploited in the future.

1. Introduction

This study attempts to optimize the performance of a job dispatching rule in a wafer fabrication factory. The production equation required by a wafer fabrication factory is very expensive and must be fully utilized. For this purpose, to ensure that the capacity does not substantially exceed the demand is a perquisite. Subsequently, how to plan the use of the existing capacity to shorten the cycle time and maximize the turnover rate is an important goal. In this regard, scheduling is undoubtedly a very useful tool.

However, some studies [1–4] noted that job dispatching is very difficult task in a semiconductor manufacturing factory. Theoretically, it is an NP-hard problem. In practice, many semiconductor manufacturing factories suffer from lengthy cycle times and are not able to improve on their delivery promises to their customers.

Semiconductor manufacturing can be divided into four stages: wafer fabrication, wafer probing, packaging, and final testing. The most important stage is wafer fabrication. It is also the most time-consuming one. In this study, we investigated the job dispatching for this stage. This field includes many different methods, including dispatching rules, heuristics, data-mining-based approaches [5, 6], agent technologies [5, 7–9], and simulation. Among them, dispatching rules (e.g., first-in first out (FIFO), earliest due date (EDD), least slack (LS), shortest processing time (SPT), shortest remaining processing time (SRPT), critical ratio (CR), the fluctuation smoothing rule for the mean cycle time (FSMCT), and the fluctuation smoothing rule for cycle time variation (FSVCT), FIFO+, SRPT+, and SRPT++) all have received a lot of attention over the last few years [5–7] and are the most prevalent methods used in practical applications. For details on the traditional dispatching rules, please refer to Lu et al. [10].

Some advances in this field are as follows. Altendorfer et al. [11] proposed the work in parallel queue (WIPQ) rule targeting maximizing throughput at a low level of work in process (WIP). Zhang et al. [12] proposed the dynamic bottleneck detection (DBD) approach by classifying workstations into several categories and then applied different dispatching rules to these categories. They used three dispatching rules including FIFO, the shortest processing time until the next bottleneck (SPNB), and CR. Based on the current conditions in the wafer fabrication factory, Hsieh et al. [6] chose one approach from FSMCT, FSVCT, largest deviation first (LDF), one step ahead (OSA), or FIFO. Chen [13] modified FSMCT and proposed the nonlinear FSMCT (NFSMCT) rule, in which he smoothed the fluctuation in the estimated remaining cycle time and balanced it with that of the release time or the mean release rate. To diversify the slack, he applied the "division" operator instead. This was followed by Chen [14], in which he proposed the one-factor-tailored NFSMCT (1f-TNFSMCT) rule and the one-factor-tailored nonlinear FSVCT (1f-TNFSVCT) rule. Both rules contain an adjustable parameter to allow them to be customized for a target wafer fabrication factory. Chen [15] used more parameters and proposed 2f-TNFSMCT and 2f-TNFSVCT.

In a multiple-objective study, Chen and Wang [16] proposed a biobjective nonlinear fluctuation smoothing rule with an adjustable factor (1f-biNFS) to optimize both the average cycle time and the cycle time variation at the same time. More degrees of freedom seem to be helpful in the performance of customizable rules. For this reason, Chen et al. [17] extended 1f-biNFS to a biobjective fluctuation smoothing rule with four adjustable factors (4f-biNFS). For a summary of these rules please refer to Table 1. One drawback of these rules is that only static factors are used, and they must be determined in advance. To this end, most studies (e.g., [13–17]) performed extensive simulations. This is not only time-consuming but it also fails to consider enough possible combinations of these factors. Chen [18] established a mechanism that was able to adjust the values of the factor in 1f-biNFS dynamically (dynamic 1f-biNFS). However, even though satisfactory results were obtained in his experiment, there was no theoretical basis supporting the proposed mechanism. Chen [19] attempted to relate the scheduling performance to the factor values using a back propagation network (BPN). If that would have worked, then the factor values contributing to the optimal scheduling performance could have been found. However, the explanatory ability of the BPN was not good enough.

At the same time, Chen [18] stated that a nonlinear fluctuation smoothing rule uses the divisor operator instead of the subtraction operator, which diversifies the slack and makes the nonlinear fluctuation smoothing rule more responsive to changes in the parameters. Chen and Wang [16] proved that the effects of the parameters are balanced better in a nonlinear fluctuation smoothing rule than in a traditional one if the variation in the parameters is large. In addition, there will be fewer ties since the slack values are very different. Further, magnifying the difference in the slack seems to improve the scheduling performance, especially with respect to the average cycle time [20]. For these reasons, a slack-diversifying fuzzy-neural rule is used in chen et al. [20] for job dispatching in a wafer fabrication factory, in order to further improve the performance of job dispatching in a wafer fabrication factory. The slack-diversifying nonlinear fluctuation smoothing rule is modified from 1f-TNFSVCT by maximizing the difference in the slack measured with the standard deviation of the slack.

This study adopts several treatments to further improve Wang et al.'s approach.

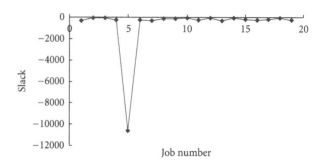

FIGURE 1: The extreme cases.

(1) In nonlinear fluctuation smoothing rules, it is common that some jobs have very large or small slack values, that is the extreme case (see Figure 1), which usually distorts the results of calculating the standard deviation of slacks. In this study, the extreme cases are excluded before calculation.

(2) Two objectives, the average cycle time and cycle time standard deviation, are considered at the same time by fusing the results from 2f-TNFSMCT and 2f-TNFSVCT.

(3) A nonlinear programming problem is solved to find the optimal values of parameters in 2f-TNFSMCT and 2f-TNFSVCT.

(4) On the other hand, the remaining cycle time of a job needs to be estimated in 2f-TNFSMCT and 2f-TNFSVCT. For this reason, we also propose a more effective fuzzy-neural approach to estimate the remaining cycle time of a job. The fuzzy-neural approach is a modification of the fuzzy c-means and back propagation network (FCM-BPN) approach [17] by incorporating in the concept of principal component analysis (PCA). According to Chen and Wang [3], with more accurate remaining cycle time estimation, the scheduling performance of a fluctuation smoothing rule can be significantly improved. In the original study, Chen and Wang used a gradient search algorithm for training the BPN, which is time-consuming and not very accurate. In this study, we use the Levenberg-Marquardt algorithm to achieve the same purpose, which is more efficient than that in Chen and Wang's study and can produce more accurate forecasts.

The differences between the proposed methodology and the previous methods are summarized in Table 1.

The remainder of this paper is arranged as follows. Section 2 provides the details of the proposed methodology. In Section 3, a simulated case is used to validate the effectiveness of the nonlinear programming and artificial neural network approach. The performances of some existing approaches in this field are also examined using the simulated data. Finally, we draw our conclusions in Section 4 and provide some worthwhile topics for future work.

A Nonlinear Programming and Artificial Neural Network Approach for Optimizing the Performance of a Job
Dispatching Rule in a Wafer Fabrication Factory

175

TABLE 1: The differences between the proposed methodology and the previous methods.

Rule	Number of objectives	Objectives	Number of adjustable parameters	Optimized?	How to derive the rule?
NFSMCT	1	Average cycle time	1	No	(i) Generalizing FSMCT
1f-TNFSVCT	1	Cycle time standard variation	1	No	(i) Generalizing FSVCT (ii) Adding adjustable parameters
1f-TNFSMCT	1	Average cycle time	1	No	(i) Generalizing FSMCT (ii) Adding adjustable parameters
2f-TNFSVCT	1	Cycle time standard deviation	2	No	(i) Generalizing FSVCT (ii) Adding adjustable parameters
4f-biNFS	2	Average cycle time, cycle time standard deviation	2	Yes	(i) Fusing FSVCT and FSMCT (ii) Adding adjustable parameters
The proposed methodology	2	Average cycle time, cycle time standard deviation	2	Yes	(i) Fusing 2f-TFSMCT and 2f-TNFSVCT (ii) Nonlinear programming

2. Methodology

The variables and parameters that will be used in the proposed methodology are defined in the following.

(1) R_j: the release time of job j; $j = 1 \sim n$.

(2) BQ_j: the total queue length before bottlenecks at R_j.

(3) CR_{ju}: the critical ratio of job j at step u.

(4) CT_j: the cycle time of job j.

(5) CTE_j: the estimated cycle time of job j.

(6) D_j: the average delay of the three most recently completed jobs at R_j.

(7) DD_j: the due date of job j.

(8) FQ_j: the total queue length in the whole factory at R_j.

(9) Q_j: the queue length on the processing route of job j at R_j.

(10) $RCTE_{ju}$: the estimated remaining cycle time of job j from step u.

(11) RPT_{ju}: the remaining processing time of job j from step u.

(12) SCT_{ju}: the step cycle time of job j until step u.

(13) SK_{ju}: the slack of job j at step u.

(14) U_j: the average factory utilization before job j is released. If the utilization of the factory is reported on a daily basis, then U_j is the utilization of the day before job j is released.

(15) WIP_j: the factory work in progress (WIP) at R_j.

(16) λ: mean release rate.

(17) x_p: inputs to the three-layer BPN, $p = 1 \sim 6$.

(18) h_l: the output from hidden-layer node l, $l = 1 \sim L$.

(19) w_l^o: the connection weight between hidden-layer node l and the output node.

(20) w_{pl}^h: the connection weight between input node p and hidden-layer node l, $p = 1 \sim 6$; $l = 1 \sim L$.

(21) θ_l^h: the threshold on hidden-layer node l.

(22) θ^o: the threshold on the output node.

The proposed methodology includes the following seven steps.

Step 1. Replacing parameters using PCA.

Step 2. Use FCM to classify jobs. The required inputs for this step are the new variables determined by PCA. To determine the optimal number of categories, we use the S-test. The output of this step is the category of each job.

Step 3. Use the BPN approach to estimate the cycle time of each job. Jobs of different categories will be sent to different three-layer BPNs. The inputs to the three-layer BPN include the new variables of a job, while the output is the estimated cycle time of the job.

Step 4. Derive the remaining cycle time of each job from the estimated cycle time.

Step 5. Incorporate the estimated remaining cycle time into the new rule that is composed of two subrules–2f-TNFSMCT and 2f-TNFSVCT.

Step 6. Find out the optimal value of parameters in the new rule by solving a nonlinear programming problem.

The remaining cycle time of a job being produced in a wafer fabrication factory is the time still needed to complete the job. If the job is just released into the wafer fabrication factory, then the remaining cycle time of the job is its cycle time. The remaining cycle time is an important input for the scheduling rule. Past studies (e.g., [21–24]) have shown that the accuracy of the remaining cycle time forecasting can be improved by job classification. Soft computing methods (e.g., [3, 20, 25, 26]) have received much attention in this field.

2.1. PCA Analysis. First, PCA is used to replace the inputs to the FCM-BPN. The combination of PCA and FCM has been shown to be a more effective classifier than FCM alone. Although there are more advanced applications of PCA, in this study PCA is used to enhance the efficiency of training the FCM-BPN. PCA consists of the four following steps:

(1) Raw data standardization: to eliminate the difference between the dimensions and the impact of large numerical difference in the original variables $\{U_j, Q_j, BQ_j, FQ_j, WIP_j, D_j\}$, the original variables are standardized:

$$x_{ij}^* = \frac{x_{ij} - \bar{x}_j}{\sigma_j},$$

$$\bar{x}_j = \frac{\sum_{i=1}^n x_{ij}}{n}, \tag{1}$$

$$\sigma_j = \sqrt{\frac{\sum_{i=1}^n \left(x_{ij} - \bar{x}_j\right)^2}{n - 1}},$$

where $\bar{x}_j$ and σ_j indicate the mean and standard deviation of variable j, respectively,

(2) Establishment of the correlation matrix R:

$$R = \frac{1}{n-1} X^{*T} X^*, \tag{2}$$

where X^* is the standardized data matrix. The eigenvalues and eigenvectors of R are calculated and represented as $\lambda_1 \sim \lambda_m$ and $u_1 \sim u_m$, respectively; $\lambda_1 \geq \lambda_2 \geq \cdots \geq \lambda_m$.

(3) Determination of the number of principal components: the variance contribution rate is calculated as:

$$\eta_i = \frac{\lambda_i}{\sum_{i=1}^m \lambda_i} \cdot 100\%, \tag{3}$$

and the accumulated variance contribution rate is

$$\eta_\Sigma(q) = \sum_{i=1}^q \eta_i. \tag{4}$$

Choose the smallest q value such that $\eta_\Sigma(q) \geq 85\% \sim 90\%$.

(4) Formation of the following matrixes:

$$U_{m \times q} = \left[u_1, u_2, ..., u_q\right],$$
$$Z_{n \times q} = X_{n \times m}^* U_{m \times q}. \tag{5}$$

After PCA, examples are then classified using FCM.

2.2. The FCM Approach.
In the proposed methodology, jobs are classified into K categories using FCM. If a crisp clustering method is applied, then it is possible that some clusters will have very few examples. In contrast, an example belongs to multiple clusters to different degrees in FCM, which provides a solution to this problem.

FCM classifies jobs by minimizing the following objective function:

$$\text{Min} \sum_{k=1}^K \sum_{j=1}^n \mu_{j(k)}^m e_{j(k)}^2, \tag{6}$$

where K is the required number of categories; n is the number of jobs; $\mu_{j(k)}$ indicates the membership that job j belongs to category k; $e_{j(k)}$ measures the distance from job j to the centroid of category k; $m \in [1, \infty)$ is a parameter to adjust the fuzziness and is usually set to 2. The procedure of FCM is as follows.

(1) Produce a preliminary clustering result.

(2) (Iterations) Calculate the centroid of each category as

$$\bar{x}_{(k)} = \left\{\bar{x}_{(k)p}\right\}; \quad p = 1 \sim q,$$

$$\bar{x}_{(k)p} = \frac{\sum_{j=1}^n \mu_{j(k)}^m x_{jp}}{\sum_{j=1}^n \mu_{j(k)}^m},$$

$$\mu_{j(k)} = \frac{1}{\sum_{q=1}^K \left(e_{j(k)}/e_{j(q)}\right)^{2/(m-1)}}, \tag{7}$$

$$e_{j(k)} = \sqrt{\sum_{\text{all } p} \left(x_{jp} - \bar{x}_{(k)p}\right)^2},$$

where $\bar{x}_{(k)}$ is the centroid of category k. $\mu_{j(k)}^{(t)}$ is the membership that job i belongs to category k after the tth iteration.

(3) Remeasure the distance from each job to the centroid of each category, and then recalculate the corresponding membership.

(4) Stop if the following condition is met. Otherwise, return to step (2):

$$\max_k \max_j \left| \mu_{j(k)}^{(t)} - \mu_{j(k)}^{(t-1)} \right| < d, \tag{8}$$

where d is a real number representing the threshold for the convergence of membership.

Finally, the separate distance test (S-test) proposed by Xie and Beni [24] can be applied to determine the optimal number of categories K:

$$\text{Min } S \tag{9}$$

subject to

$$J_m = \sum_{k=1}^K \sum_{j=1}^n \mu_{j(k)}^m e_{j(k)}^2,$$

$$e_{\min}^2 = \min_{k1 \neq k2} \left(\sum_{\text{all } p} \left(\bar{x}_{(k1)p} - \bar{x}_{(k2)p}\right)^2 \right), \tag{10}$$

$$S = \frac{J_m}{n \times e_{\min}^2},$$

$$K \in Z^+.$$

The K value minimizing S determines the optimal number of categories.

2.3. The BPN Approach.

After clustering, a portion of the jobs in each category is input as the "training examples" to the three-layer BPN to determine the parameter values. The configuration of the three-layer BPN is set up as follows. First, inputs are the six parameters associated with the jth example/job including the q new variables. These parameters have to be normalized before feeding into the three-layer BPN. Subsequently, there is only a single hidden layer with neurons that are twice that in the input layer. Finally, the output from the three-layer BPN is the (normalized) estimated cycle time (CTE_j) of the example. The activation function used in each layer is Log Sigmoid function:

$$f(x) = \frac{1}{(1 + e^{-x})}. \tag{11}$$

The procedure for determining the parameter values is now described. Two phases are involved at the training stage. At first, in the forward phase, inputs are multiplied with weights, summated, and transferred to the hidden layer. Then activated signals are outputted from the hidden layer as

$$h_l = \frac{1}{1 + e^{-n_l^h}}, \tag{12}$$

where

$$n_l^h = I_l^h - \theta_l^h$$
$$I_l^h = \sum_{p=1}^{q} w_{pl}^h \cdot x_{jp}. \tag{13}$$

h_l's are also transferred to the output layer with the same procedure. Finally, the output of the BPN is generated as

$$o_j = \frac{1}{1 + e^{-n^o}}, \tag{14}$$

where

$$n^o = I^o - \theta^o,$$
$$I^o = \sum_{l=1}^{L} w_l^o \cdot h_l. \tag{15}$$

Subsequently, in the backward phase, some algorithms are applicable for training a BPN, such as the gradient descent algorithms, the conjugate gradient algorithms, and the Levenberg-Marquardt algorithm. In this study, the Levenberg-Marquardt algorithm is applied. The Levenberg-Marquardt algorithm was designed for training with second-order speed without having to compute the Hessian matrix. It uses approximation and updates the network parameters in a Newton-like way, as described below.

The network parameters are placed in vector $\boldsymbol{\beta} = [w_{11}^h, \ldots, w_{qL}^h, \theta_1^h, \ldots, \theta_L^h, w_1^o, \ldots, w_L^o, \theta^o]$. The network output o_j can be represented with $f(\mathbf{x}_j, \boldsymbol{\beta})$. The objective function of the BPN is to minimize the root mean-squared error (RMSE) or equivalently the sum of squared error (SSE):

$$\mathrm{SSE}(\boldsymbol{\beta}) = \sum_{j=1}^{n} \left(N\left(\mathrm{CT}_j\right) - f\left(\mathbf{x}_j, \boldsymbol{\beta}\right) \right)^2. \tag{16}$$

The Levenberg-Marquardt algorithm is an iterative procedure. In the beginning, the user should specify the initial values of the network parameters $\boldsymbol{\beta}$. Let $\boldsymbol{\beta}^{\mathrm{T}} = (1, 1, \ldots, 1)$ is a common practice. In each step, the parameter vector $\boldsymbol{\beta}$ is replaced by a new estimate $\boldsymbol{\beta} + \boldsymbol{\delta}$, where $\boldsymbol{\delta} = [\Delta w_{11}^h, \ldots, \Delta w_{qL}^h, \Delta \theta_1^h, \ldots, \Delta \theta_L^h, \Delta w_1^o, \ldots, \Delta w_L^o, \Delta \theta^o]$. The network output becomes $f(\mathbf{x}_j, \boldsymbol{\beta} + \boldsymbol{\delta})$ that is approximated by its linearization as

$$f\left(\mathbf{x}_j, \boldsymbol{\beta} + \boldsymbol{\delta}\right) \approx f\left(\mathbf{x}_j, \boldsymbol{\beta}\right) + \mathbf{J}_j \boldsymbol{\delta}, \tag{17}$$

where

$$\mathbf{J}_j = \frac{\partial f\left(\mathbf{x}_j, \boldsymbol{\beta}\right)}{\partial \boldsymbol{\beta}} \tag{18}$$

is the gradient vector of f with respect to $\boldsymbol{\beta}$. Substituting (17) into (16),

$$\mathrm{SSE}(\boldsymbol{\beta} + \boldsymbol{\delta}) \approx \sum_{j=1}^{n} \left(N\left(CT_j\right) - f\left(\mathbf{x}_j, \boldsymbol{\beta}\right) - \mathbf{J}_j \boldsymbol{\delta} \right)^2. \tag{19}$$

When the network reaches the optimal solution, the gradient of SSE with respect to $\boldsymbol{\delta}$ will be zero. Taking the derivative of $\mathrm{SSE}(\boldsymbol{\beta} + \boldsymbol{\delta})$ with respect to $\boldsymbol{\delta}$ and setting the result to zero gives

$$\left(\mathbf{J}^{\mathrm{T}} \mathbf{J}\right) \boldsymbol{\delta} = \mathbf{J}^{\mathrm{T}} \left(N\left(CT_j\right) - f\left(\mathbf{x}_j, \boldsymbol{\beta}\right) \right), \tag{20}$$

where $\mathbf{J}$ is the Jacobian matrix containing the first derivative of network error with respect to the weights and biases. Equation (20) includes a set of linear equations that can be solved for $\boldsymbol{\delta}$.

Finally, the BPN can be applied to estimate the cycle time of a job, and then the remaining cycle time of the job can be derived as

$$\mathrm{RCTE}_{ju} = \mathrm{CTE}_j - \mathrm{SCT}_{ju}, \tag{21}$$

2.4. The New Rule.

In traditional fluctuation smoothing (FS) rules there are two different formulation methods, depending on the scheduling purpose [22]. ne method is aimed at minimizing the average cycle time with FSMCT:

$$\mathrm{SKM}_{ju} = \frac{j}{\lambda} - \mathrm{RCTE}_{ju}. \tag{22}$$

The other method is aimed at minimizing the variance of cycle time with FSVCT:

$$\mathrm{SKV}_{ju} = R_j - \mathrm{RCTE}_{ju}. \tag{23}$$

Jobs with the smallest slack values (SKM_{ju} or SKV_{ju}) will be given higher priority. These two rules and their variants have been proven to be very effective in shortening the cycle time in wafer fabrication factories [10, 14–17].

Chen [15] normalized the parameters and used the division operator instead and derived the 2f-TNFSVCT rule:

$$SKM_{ju} = \left(\frac{\beta}{\alpha\left(RCTE_{ju} - \min\left(RCTE_{ju}\right)\right)} \right)^{\xi}$$
$$\cdot \left(R_j - RCTE_{ju} + \zeta\left(RCTE_{ju} - \min\left(R_j\right)\right) \right), \tag{24}$$

and the 2f-TNFSMCT rule:

$$SKV_{ju} = \left(\frac{\lambda\beta}{(n-1)\left(RCTE_{ju} - \min\left(RCTE_{ju}\right)\right)} \right)^{\xi}$$
$$\cdot \left(\frac{j}{\lambda} - RCTE_{ju} + \zeta\left(RCTE_{ju} - \frac{1}{\lambda}\right) \right), \tag{25}$$

where

$$\alpha = \max\left(R_j\right) - \min\left(R_j\right),$$
$$\beta = \max\left(RCTE_{ju}\right) - \min\left(RCTE_{ju}\right), \tag{26}$$

$0 \le \xi, \zeta \le 1$. There are many possible models to form the combination of ξ and ζ. For example,

(Linear model) $\xi = \zeta$,

(Nonlinear model) $\xi = \zeta^k, \quad k \ge 0,$ \tag{27}

(Logarithmic model) $\xi = \frac{\ln(1 + \zeta)}{\ln 2}$.

The new rule is composed of two rules. The first rule is derived by diversifying the slack in the 2f-TNFSVCT rule, aimed at minimizing the variation of cycle time [22]. To diversify the slack, the standard deviation of the slack is to be maximized as follows:

$$\sigma_{SKM_{ju}} = \sqrt{ \frac{\sum_{j=1}^{N} \left(SKM_{ju} - \overline{SKM_{ju}}\right)^2}{N-1} }. \tag{28}$$

However, in nonlinear fluctuation smoothing rules, it is common that two of the jobs will have very large or small slack values, that is, the extreme cases, which distort the sequencing results. For this reason, such jobs are put in a set EC that will be excluded from calculating the standard deviation:

$$\overline{SKM'_{ju}} = \frac{\sum_{j=1}^{N} {}_{j \notin EC} SKM_{ju}}{N-2},$$
$$\sigma'_{SKM_{ju}} = \sqrt{ \frac{\sum_{j=1, j \notin EC}^{N} \left(SKM_{ju} - \overline{SKM'_{ju}}\right)^2}{N-3} }. \tag{29}$$

The second rule is derived by diversifying the slack in the 2f-TNFSMCT rule, aimed at minimizing the mean cycle time:

$$SKV_{ju} = \left(\frac{\lambda\beta}{(n-1)\left(RCTE_{ju} - \min\left(RCTE_{ju}\right)\right)} \right)^{\xi}$$
$$\cdot \left(\frac{j}{\lambda} - RCTE_{ju} + \zeta\left(RCTE_{ju} - \frac{1}{\lambda}\right) \right). \tag{30}$$

To diversify the slackness, the standard deviation of the slack is to be maximized:

$$\overline{SKV'_{ju}} = \frac{\sum_{j=1, j \notin EC}^{N} SKV_{ju}}{N-2}, \tag{31}$$
$$\sigma'_{SKV_{ju}} = \sqrt{ \frac{\sum_{j=1, j \notin EC}^{N} \left(SKV_{ju} - \overline{SKV'_{ju}}\right)^2}{N-3} }. \tag{32}$$

To generate a biobjective rule, the two rules need to be combined into a single one, for which the following nonlinear programming model is to be optimized:

$$\text{Max } Z = \omega_1 \sigma'_{SKM_{ju}} + (1 - \omega_1)\sigma'_{SKV_{ju}} \tag{33}$$

s.t.

$$\overline{SKM'_{ju}} = \frac{\sum_{j=1, j \notin EC}^{N} SKM_{ju}}{N-2},$$
$$\sigma'_{SKM_{ju}} = \sqrt{ \frac{\sum_{j=1, j \notin EC}^{N} \left(SKM_{ju} - \overline{SKM'_{ju}}\right)^2}{N-3} },$$
$$\overline{SKV'_{ju}} = \frac{\sum_{j=1, j \notin EC}^{N} SKV_{ju}}{N-2},$$
$$\sigma'_{SKV_{ju}} = \sqrt{ \frac{\sum_{j=1, j \notin EC}^{N} \left(SKV_{ju} - \overline{SKV'_{ju}}\right)^2}{N-3} },$$
$$SKM_{ju} = \left(\frac{\beta}{\alpha\left(RCTE_{ju} - \min\left(RCTE_{ju}\right)\right)} \right)^{\xi}$$
$$\cdot \left(R_j - RCTE_{ju} + \zeta\left(RCTE_{ju} - \min\left(R_j\right)\right) \right),$$
$$SKV_{ju} = \left(\frac{\lambda\beta}{(n-1)\left(RCTE_{ju} - \min\left(RCTE_{ju}\right)\right)} \right)^{\xi}$$
$$\cdot \left(\frac{j}{\lambda} - RCTE_{ju} + \zeta\left(RCTE_{ju} - \frac{1}{\lambda}\right) \right),$$
$$0 \le \xi, \quad \zeta \le 1 \tag{34}$$

which is an NP problem.

3. A Simulation Study

To evaluate the effectiveness of the proposed methodology, simulated data were used to avoid disturbing the regular operations of the wafer fabrication factory. Simulation is a widely used technology to assess the effectiveness of a scheduling policy, especially when the proposed policy and the current practice are very different. This investigation is not possible to implement in the actual production environment. The real-time scheduling systems will input information very rapidly into the production management information systems (PROMIS). To this end, a real wafer fabrication factory located in Taichung Scientific Park of Taiwan with a monthly capacity of about 25,000 wafers was simulated. The simulation program has been validated and verified by comparing the actual cycle times with the simulated values and by analyzing the trace report, respectively. The wafer fabrication factory is producing more than 10 types of memory products and has more than 500 workstations for performing single-wafer or batch operations using 58 nm~110 nm technologies. Jobs released into the fabrication factory are assigned three types of priorities, that is, "normal," "hot," and "super hot." Jobs with the highest priorities will be processed first. Such a large scale accompanied with reentrant process flows make job dispatching in the wafer fabrication factory a very tough task. Currently, the longest average cycle time exceeds three months with a variation of more than 300 hours. The wafer fabrication factory is therefore seeking better dispatching rules to replace first-in first-out (FIFO) and EDD, in order to shorten the average cycle times and ensure the on-time delivery to its customers. One hundred replications of the simulation are successively run. The time required for each simulation replication is about 30 minute using a PC with Intel Dual CPU E2200 2.2 GHz and 1.99G RAM. A horizon of twenty-four months is simulated.

To assess the effectiveness of the proposed methodology and to make comparison with some existing approaches– FIFO, EDD, SRPT, CR, FSVCT, FSMCT, Justice [27], NFS [16], 2f-TNFSMCT, and 2f-TNFSVCT all of these methods were applied to schedule the simulated wafer fabrication factory to collect the data of 1000 jobs, and then we separated the collected data by their product types and priorities. That is about the amount of work that can be achieved with 100% of the monthly capacity. In some cases, there was too little data, so they were not discussed.

To determine the due date of a job, the PCA-FCM-BPN approach was applied to estimate the cycle time, for which the Levenberg-Marquardt algorithm rather than the gradient descent algorithm was applied to speed up the network convergence. Then, we added a constant allowance of three days to the estimated cycle time, that is, $\kappa = 72$, to determine the internal due date.

Jobs with the highest priorities are usually processed first. In FIFO, jobs were sequenced on each machine first by their priorities, then by their arrival times at the machine. In EDD, jobs were sequenced first by their priorities, then by their due dates. In CR, jobs were sequenced first by their priorities, then by their critical ratios. In the proposed methodology, the nonlinear model with $k = 2$ is used. In Justice, jobs were sequenced on each machine first by their priorities, then according to the job speed matrix (Table 2).

TABLE 2: The job speed matrix.

| | | Machine's bottleneck status | | |
		Hungry	Proper	Crowded
Work progress status	Behind	Rapid	Rapid	Normal
	Just in time	Rapid	Normal	Suspended
	Advanced	Normal	Normal	Suspended

Subsequently, the average cycle time and cycle time standard deviation of all cases were calculated to assess the scheduling performance. With respect to the average cycle time, the FIFO policy was used as the basis for comparison, while FSVCT was compared in evaluating cycle time standard deviation. The results are summarized in Tables 3 and 4.

According to the experimental results, the following points can be made:

(1) For the average cycle time, the proposed methodology outperformed the baseline approach, the FIFO policy. The average advantage was about 16%.

(2) In addition, the proposed methodology surpassed the FSVCT policy in reducing cycle time standard deviation. The most obvious advantage was 59%.

(3) As expected, SRPT performed well in reducing the average cycle times, especially for product types with short cycle times (e.g., product A), but might give an exceedingly bad performance with respect to cycle time standard deviation. If the cycle time is long, the remaining cycle time will be much longer than the remaining processing time, which leads to the ineffectiveness of SRPT. SRPT is similar to FSMCT. Both try to make all jobs equally early or late.

(4) The performance of EDD was also satisfactory for product types with short cycle time. If the cycle time is long, it is more likely to deviate from the prescribed internal due date, which leads to the ineffectiveness of EDD. That becomes more serious if the percentage of the product type is high in the product mix (e.g., product type A). CR has similar problems.

(5) The proposed rule was also compared with the traditional one without slack diversification. Taking product type A with normal priority as an example, the comparison results are shown in Figure 2. Obviously, the proposed rule dominated most of the traditional rules without slack diversification. According to these results, slack diversification did indeed improve the performances of the fluctuation smoothing policies.

4. Conclusions and Directions for Future Research

For capital-intensive industries like wafer fabrication, efficient use of expensive equipment is very important. To this end, job dispatching is a challenging but important task. However, for such a complex production system, to optimize the scheduling performance is a tough task.

TABLE 3: The performances of various approaches in the average cycle time.

Avg. cycle time (hrs)	A (normal)	A (hot)	A (super hot)	B (normal)	B (hot)
FIFO	1254	400	317	1278	426
EDD	1094	345	305	1433	438
SRPT	948	350	308	1737	457
CR	1148	355	300	1497	440
FSMCT	1313	347	293	1851	470
FSVCT	1014	382	315	1672	475
NFS	1456	407	321	1452	421
Justice	1126	378	322	1576	489
2f-TNFSMCT	1369	379	306	1361	399
2f-TNFSVCT	1465	416	318	1551	500
The proposed methodology	1076	289	269	1132	388

TABLE 4: The performances of various approaches in cycle time standard deviation.

Cycle time standard deviation (hrs)	A (normal)	A (hot)	A (super hot)	B (normal)	B (hot)
FIFO	55	24	25	87	51
EDD	129	25	22	50	63
SRPT	248	31	22	106	53
CR	69	29	18	58	53
FSMCT	419	33	16	129	104
FSVCT	280	37	27	201	77
NFS	87	49	19	44	47
Justice	120	26	20	69	32
2f-TNFSMCT	75	37	17	47	19
2f-TNFSVCT	38	38	29	33	24
The proposed methodology	86	26	15	54	21

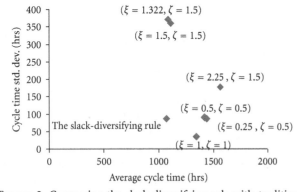

FIGURE 2: Comparing the slack-diversifying rule with traditional rules without slack diversification.

As an innovative attempt, this study presents a nonlinear programming and artificial neural network approach to optimize the performance of a slack-diversifying dispatching rule in a wafer fabrication factory, to optimize the average cycle time, and to optimize cycle time standard deviation.

The proposed methodology merges two existing rules—2f-TNFSMCT and 2f-TNFSVCT, and constructs a nonlinear programming model to choose the best values of parameters in the two rules. A more effective approach is also applied to estimate the remaining cycle time of a job, which is empirically shown to be conducive to the scheduling performance.

To further enhance the accuracy of the remaining cycle time estimation, other dynamic parameters must be considered. In addition, some advanced methods for the cycle time estimation, such as data mining methods [28], can be applied as well.

After a simulation study, we observed the following phenomena.

(1) Through improving the accuracy of estimating the remaining cycle time, the performance of a scheduling rule can indeed be strengthened.

(2) Optimizing the adjustable factors in the two rules appears as an appropriate tool to enhance the scheduling performance of the rule.

(3) Slack diversification is indeed conducive to the performance of a fluctuation smoothing rule.

However, to further assess the effectiveness and efficiency of the proposed methodology, the only way is to apply it to an actual wafer fabrication factory. In addition, other rules can be optimized in the same way in future studies.

Acknowledgment

This work was supported by the National Science Council of Taiwan.

References

[1] C. N. Wang and C. H. Wang, "A simulated model for cycle time reduction by acquiring optimal lot size in semiconductor manufacturing," *International Journal of Advanced Manufacturing Technology*, vol. 34, no. 9-10, pp. 1008–1015, 2007.

[2] T. Chen and Y. C. Lin, "A fuzzy-neural fluctuation smoothing rule for scheduling jobs with various priorities in a miconductor manufacturing factory," *International Journal of Uncertainty, Fuzziness and Knowlege-Based Systems*, vol. 17, no. 3, pp. 397–417, 2009.

[3] T. Chen and Y. C. Wang, "A nonlinear scheduling rule incorporating fuzzy-neural remaining cycle time estimator for scheduling a semiconductor manufacturing factory-a simulation study," *International Journal of Advanced Manufacturing Technology*, vol. 45, no. 1-2, pp. 110–121, 2009.

[4] T. Chen, "Optimized fuzzy-neuro system for scheduling wafer fabrication," *Journal of Scientific and Industrial Research*, vol. 68, no. 8, pp. 680–685, 2009.

[5] D. A. Koonce and S. C. Tsai, "Using data mining to find patterns in genetic algorithm solutions to a job shop schedule," *Computers and Industrial Engineering*, vol. 38, no. 3, pp. 361–374, 2000.

[6] B. W. Hsieh, C. H. Chen, and S. C. Chang, "Scheduling semiconductor wafer fabrication by using ordinal optimization-based simulation," *IEEE Transactions on Robotics and Automation*, vol. 17, no. 5, pp. 599–608, 2001.

[7] H. J. Yoon and W. Shen, "A multiagent-based decision-making system for semiconductor wafer fabrication with hard temporal constraints," *IEEE Transactions on Semiconductor Manufacturing*, vol. 21, no. 1, pp. 83–91, 2008.

[8] Y. Harrath, B. Chebel-Morello, and N. Zerhouni, "A genetic algorithm and data mining based meta-heuristic for job shop scheduling problem," in *Proceedings of the IEEE International Conference on Systems, Man and Cybernetics*, pp. 280–285, October 2002.

[9] K. Sourirajan and R. Uzsoy, "Hybrid decomposition heuristics for solving large-scale scheduling problems in semiconductor wafer fabrication," *Journal of Scheduling*, vol. 10, no. 1, pp. 41–65, 2007.

[10] S. C. H. Lu, D. Ramaswamy, and P. R. Kumar, "Efficient scheduling policies to reduce mean and variance of cycle-time in semiconductor manufacturing plants," *IEEE Transactions on Semiconductor Manufacturing*, vol. 7, no. 3, pp. 374–388, 1994.

[11] K. Altendorfer, B. Kabelka, and W. Stöcher, "A new dispatching rule for optimizing machine utilization at a semiconductor test field," in *Proceedings of the IEEE/SEMI Advanced Semiconductor Manufacturing Conference (ASMC '07)*, pp. 188–193, June 2007.

[12] H. Zhang, Z. Jiang, and C. Guo, "Simulation-based optimization of dispatching rules for semiconductor wafer fabrication system scheduling by the response surface methodology," *International Journal of Advanced Manufacturing Technology*, vol. 41, no. 1-2, pp. 110–121, 2009.

[13] T. Chen, "Fuzzy-neural-network-based fluctuation smoothing rule for reducing the cycle times of jobs with various priorities in a wafer fabrication plant: a simulation study," *Proceedings of the Institution of Mechanical Engineers Part B, Journal of Engineering Manufacture*, vol. 223, no. 8, pp. 1033–1043, 2009.

[14] T. Chen, "A tailored non-linear fluctuation smoothing rule for semiconductor manufacturing factory scheduling," *Proceedings of the Institution of Mechanical Engineers Part I, Journal of Systems and Control Engineering*, vol. 223, no. 2, pp. 149–160, 2009.

[15] T. Chen, "Intelligent scheduling approaches for a wafer fabrication factory," *Journal of Intelligent Manufacturing*, vol. 23, no. 3, pp. 897–911, 2012.

[16] T. Chen and Y. C. Wang, "A bi-criteria nonlinear fluctuation smoothing rule incorporating the SOM-FBPN remaining cycle time estimator for scheduling a wafer fab—a simulation study," *International Journal of Advanced Manufacturing Technology*, vol. 49, no. 5–8, pp. 709–721, 2010.

[17] T. Chen, Y.-C. Wang, and Y.-C. Lin, "A bi-criteria four-factor fluctuation smoothing rule for scheduling jobs in a wafer fabrication factory," *International Journal of Innovative Computing, Information and Control*, vol. 6, pp. 4289–4303, 2010.

[18] T. Chen, "Dynamic fuzzy-neural fluctuation smoothing rule for jobs scheduling in a wafer fabrication factory," *Proceedings of the Institution of Mechanical Engineers. Part I: Journal of Systems and Control Engineering*, vol. 223, no. 8, pp. 1081–1094, 2009.

[19] T. Chen, "An optimized tailored nonlinear fluctuation smoothing rule for scheduling a semiconductor manufacturing factory," *Computers and Industrial Engineering*, vol. 58, no. 2, pp. 317–325, 2010.

[20] T. Chen, Y. C. Wang, and H. C. Wu, "A fuzzy-neural approach for remaining cycle time estimation in a semiconductor manufacturing factory—a simulation study," *International Journal of Innovative Computing, Information and Control*, vol. 5, no. 8, pp. 2125–2139, 2009.

[21] Y. C. Wang, T. Chen, and C. W. Lin, "A slack-diversifying nonlinear fluctuation smoothing rule for job dispatching in a wafer fabrication factory," *Robotics & Computer Integrated Manufacturing*. In press.

[22] T. Chen and T. Wang, "Enhancing scheduling performance for a wafer fabrication factory: the bi-objective slack-diversifying nonlinear fluctuation-smoothing rule," *Computational Intelligence and Neuroscience*. In press.

[23] T. Chen and M. Huang, "A fuzzy-neural slack-diversifying NFS rule for job dispatching in a wafer fabrication factory," *ICIC Express Letters*, vol. 6, no. 9, pp. 2243–2248, 2012.

[24] X. L. Xie and G. Beni, "A validity measure for fuzzy clustering," *IEEE Transactions on Pattern Analysis and Machine Intelligence*, vol. 13, no. 8, pp. 841–847, 1991.

[25] T. Chen and Y. C. Lin, "A fuzzy back propagation network ensemble with example classification for lot output time prediction in a wafer fab," *Applied Soft Computing Journal*, vol. 9, no. 2, pp. 658–666, 2009.

[26] T. Chen, Y. C. Wang, and H. R. Tsai, "Lot cycle time prediction in a ramping-up semiconductor manufacturing factory with a SOM-FBPN-ensemble approach with multiple buckets and partial normalization," *International Journal of Advanced Manufacturing Technology*, vol. 42, no. 11-12, pp. 1206–1216, 2009.

[27] T. Nakata, K. Matsui, Y. Miyake, and K. Nishioka, "Dynamic bottleneck control in wide variety production factory," *IEEE Transactions on Semiconductor Manufacturing*, vol. 12, no. 3, pp. 273–280, 1999.

[28] T. Chen, "Job cycle time estimation in a wafer fabrication factory with a bi-directional classifying fuzzy-neural approach," *International Journal of Advanced Manufacturing Technology*, vol. 56, pp. 1007–1018, 2011.

19

A Novel Algorithm for Feature Level Fusion Using SVM Classifier for Multibiometrics-Based Person Identification

Ujwalla Gawande,[1] **Mukesh Zaveri,**[2] **and Avichal Kapur**[3]

[1] *Department of Computer Technology, Yeshwantrao Chavan College of Engineering, Nagpur 441110, India*
[2] *Department of Computer Engineering, Sardar Vallabhbhai National Institute of Technology, Surat, India*
[3] *Nagar Yuwak Shikshan Sanstha, Nagpur, India*

Correspondence should be addressed to Ujwalla Gawande; ujwallgawande@yahoo.co.in

Academic Editor: Zhang Yi

Recent times witnessed many advancements in the field of biometric and ultimodal biometric fields. This is typically observed in the area, of security, privacy, and forensics. Even for the best of unimodal biometric systems, it is often not possible to achieve a higher recognition rate. Multimodal biometric systems overcome various limitations of unimodal biometric systems, such as nonuniversality, lower false acceptance, and higher genuine acceptance rates. More reliable recognition performance is achievable as multiple pieces of evidence of the same identity are available. The work presented in this paper is focused on multimodal biometric system using fingerprint and iris. Distinct textual features of the iris and fingerprint are extracted using the Haar wavelet-based technique. A novel feature level fusion algorithm is developed to combine these unimodal features using the Mahalanobis distance technique. A support-vector-machine-based learning algorithm is used to train the system using the feature extracted. The performance of the proposed algorithms is validated and compared with other algorithms using the CASIA iris database and real fingerprint database. From the simulation results, it is evident that our algorithm has higher recognition rate and very less false rejection rate compared to existing approaches.

1. Introduction

With the advantage of reliability and stability, biometric recognition has been developing rapidly for security and personal identity recognition. Protecting resources from an intruder is a crucial problem for the owner. The multimodal biometric system integrates more biometrics to improve security and accuracy and hence is capable of handling more efficiently the nonuniversality problem of human traits. In fact, it is very common to use a variety of biological characteristics for identification. In fact, it is very common to use a variety of biological characteristics for identification because different biological characteristics are knowingly/unknowingly used by people to identify a person.

Fusion of multiple biometric traits provides more useful information compared to that obtained using unimodal biometric trait. Use of different feature extraction techniques from each modality possibly covers some features those are not captured by the first method. Supplementary information on the same identity helps in achieving high performance [1]. Prevailing practices in multimodal fusion are broadly categorized as prematching and postmatching fusion [2]. Feature level fusion is prematching activity. Fusion at the feature level includes the incorporation of feature sets relating to multiple modalities. The feature set holds richer information about the raw biometric data than the match score or the final decision. Integration at feature level is expected to offer good recognition results. But fusion at this level is hard to accomplish. The information obtained from different modalities may be so heterogeneous that process of fusion is not so easy. The sequential and parallel feature fusion results in high-dimensional feature vector. The lesser the number of biometric traits, the lesser the time required for future fusion. The more number of traits covers more information. To achieve an increased recognition rate with reduced processing time is the primary objective of this work (feature fusion). The time required to fuse the feature vectors from different traits is directly proportional to the number of modalities. In the light of these facts it is better to have as less traits as possible, but the fusion of the features extracted from these traits must provide a higher recognition rate for having successful usage of multiple biometrics for recognition system compared to the unimodal-based system.

Fingerprint and iris are widely used biometric traits. In this work these traits are used for feature level fusion. Haar wavelet is known for its reduced computational complexity. The Haar wavelet technique is employed for feature extraction in both the cases. A new method of feature level fusion is proposed, implemented, and tested with this work. The viewpoint in this fusion is obtaining relatively better performance than the unimodal features. The proposed algorithm fuses the features of individual modalities accurately and efficiently. This is evident from simulation results. Ongoing similar research in this (multimodal) area has been focused on postclassification or matching score-level biometric fusion because of its simplicity [3, 4]. However the large-scale biometric identification applications still require performance improvements. Identification is more computational and time demanding application than the identity verification. Therefore a more specialized classification-based biometric system should be approached in order not only to achieve the desired performance improvement, but also to decrease the execution time [1, 2]. Commonly used classifiers for different biometrics are support vector machines (SVMs) with different kernels (especially Gaussian and polynomials), Gaussian mixture models-based classifiers, neural networks and multilayer perceptron [5–8]. Most of them provided significant performance improvements, but their results are strongly dependent on the available datasets [6]. Feature level fusion trained by the SVM-based classifier is used in the proposed work for evaluating the performance of the proposed system. The idea behind the SVM is to map the input vectors into a high-dimensional feature space using the "kernel trick" and then to construct a linear decision function in this space so that the dataset becomes separated with a maximum margin [6–9]. Quite often numbers of feature extraction techniques implemented by multimodal systems are generally equal to the number of biometrics under consideration. Use of single feature extraction technique for extracting features of both contributing traits makes the framework stronger. This research work aims at reducing the false rejection, false acceptance, and training and testing time for reliable recognition.

The remainder of this paper is organized as follows. Section 2 briefly presents the review of existing multimodal biometric systems. Section 3 describes the extraction of features from fingerprint and iris using Haar wavelet-based technique, their fusion using novel algorithm, and classification using SVM. Section 4 presents results of experimentation. Section 5 summarizes the recognition performance of the proposed algorithms with existing recognition and fusion algorithms. Finally Section 6 concludes our research and proposes a scope for future work.

2. Literature Review

In recent times, multimodal biometric systems have attracted the attention of researchers. A variety of articles can be found, which propose different approaches for unimodal and multimodal biometric systems which are [1, 2, 10–14]. Multimodal fusion has the synergic effect enhancing the value of information. First multimodal biometric was proposed by Jain and Ross 2002 [10]. Later, many scientists thrive for plenty of research in multimodal biometric system. A great deal of academic research was devoted to it. A number of published works demonstrate that the fusion process is effective, because fused scores provide much better discrimination than individual scores [1, 2]. Voluminous literature deals with a variety of techniques making the features more informative [9–12]. Single input and multiple algorithms for feature extraction [9] or multiple samples and single feature extraction algorithm [15] or utilizing two or more different modalities [16] are commonly discussed in recent times. It was found in [17] that the empirical relation in multimodal biometrics can improve the performance. But these improvements involve the cost of multiple sensors or multiple algorithms, which ultimately reflects higher installation and operational cost.

In most cases, multimodal fusion can be categorized into two groups: prematching fusion and postmatching fusion. Fusion prior to matching integrates pieces of evidence before matching. It includes sensor level fusion [10] and feature level fusion [18, 19]. Fusion after matching integrates pieces of evidence after matching. It includes match score level [20–22], rank level [23, 24], and decision level [3]. Fusion at the decision level is too rigid since only a limited amount of information is available at this level [25]. Integration at the matching score level is generally preferred due to the ease in accessing and combining matching scores. Since the matching scores generated by different modalities are heterogeneous, it is essential to normalize the scores before combining them. Normalization is computationally expensive [17]. Choosing inappropriate normalization technique may result in low recognition rate. For harmonious and effective working of the system, careful selection of different environments, different set of traits, different set of sensors, and so forth are necessary [17]. The features contain richer information about the input biometric data than the matching and decision scores. Integration at the feature level should provide better recognition results than other levels of integration [18, 19, 25]. However feature space and scaling differences make it difficult to homogenize features from different biometrics. Fused feature vector sometimes may result in increased dimension, compared to unimodal features. For example, fused vector is likely to end up with twice the dimension of unimodal features. For fusion to achieve the claimed performance enhancement, fusion rules must be chosen based on the type of application, biometric traits, and level of fusion. Biometric systems that integrate information at an early stage of processing are believed to be more effective than those systems which perform integration at a later stage.

In what follows, we introduce a brief review of some recent researches. The unimodal iris system, unimodal palm-print system, and multibiometric system (iris and palmprint) are presented in [20]. They worked on the matching score on the basis of similarity of the query feature vector with the template vector. Besbes et al. [3] proposed a multimodal biometric system using fingerprint and iris features. They use a hybrid approach based on (1) fingerprint minutiae extraction and (2) iris template encoding through a mathematical representation of the extracted Iris region. This approach was based on two recognition modalities, and every part provides its own decision. The final decision was obtained by ANDing the unimodal decision. Experimental verification of the theoretical claim is missing in their work. Aguilar et al. [26] worked on multibiometric using a combination of fast Fourier transform (FFT), and Gabor filters enhance fingerprint imaging. Successively, a novel stage for recognition using local features and statistical parameters was used. They used the fingerprints of both thumbs. Each fingerprint was separately processed, and the unimodal results were combined to obtain final fused result. Yang and Ma [22] used fingerprint, palm print, and hand geometry to implement personal identity verification. The three images were derived from the same image. They implemented matching score fusion to establish identity, performing first fusion of the fingerprint and palm-print features, and later a matching-score fusion between the multimodal system and the unimodal palm geometry. An approach suggested in [27] shows improved data fusion for face, fingerprint, and iris images. The approach was based on the eigenface and the Gabor wavelet methods, incorporating the advantages of the single algorithm. They recommended a new fusion system that exhibited improved performance. Baig et al. [4] worked on the state-of-the-art framework for multimodal biometric identification system. It is adaptable to any kind of biometric system. Faster processing was benefits of their system. A framework for fusion of the iris and fingerprint was developed for verification. Classification was based on single Hamming distance. An authentication method presented by Nagesh Kumar et al. [21] focuses on multimodal biometric system with two features, that is, face and palm print. Integrated feature vector resulted in the robustness of the person authentication. The final assessment was done by fusion at the matching score level. Unimodal scores were fused after matching. Maurer and Baker have presented a fusion architecture based on Bayesian belief networks for fingerprint and voice [28]. The features were modelled using statistical distributions.

A frequency-based approach resulting in a homogeneous biometric vector, integrating iris and fingerprint data, is worked out in [25]. Successively, a hamming-distance-based matching algorithm dealt with the unified homogenous biometric vector. Basha et al. [23] implemented fusion of iris and fingerprint. They used adaptive rank level fusion directly at verification stage. Ko [29] worked on the fusion of fingerprint, face, and iris. Various possibilities of multimodal biometric fusion and strategies were discussed for improving accuracy. Evaluation of image quality from different biometric and their influence on identification accuracy was also discussed.

Jagadeesan et al. [18] prepared a secured cryptographic key on the basis of iris and fingerprint features. Minutiae points were extracted from fingerprint. Similarly texture properties were extracted from iris. Feature level fusion was further employed. 256-bit cryptographic key was the outcome of the fusion. Improvement in authentication and security, using 256-bit encryption, was claimed as a part of their result in [18]. A multimodal biometric-based encryption scheme was proposed by [19]. They combine features of the fingerprint and iris with a user-defined secret key.

As far as multimodal biometric-based encryption schemes are concerned, there are very few proposals in the literature. Nandakumar and Jain [30] proposed a fuzzy vault-based scheme that combines iris with fingerprints. As expected, the verification performance of the multi-biometric vault was better than the unimodal biometric vaults. But the increase in entropy of the keys is only from 40 bits (for individual fingerprint and iris modalities) to 49 bits (for the multibiometric system). Nagar et al. [31] proposed a feature-level fusion framework to simultaneously protect multiple templates of a user as a single secure sketch. They implemented framework using two well-known biometric cryptosystems, namely, fuzzy vault and fuzzy commitment.

In contrast to the approaches found in the literature and detailed earlier, the proposed approach introduces an innovative idea to fuse homogenize size feature vector of fingerprint and iris at the feature level. A fusion process implemented in this work is based on the Mahalanobis distance. This fusion has the advantage of reduction in fused feature vector size, which is the main issue (of high dimensions) in feature level fusion. Our proposed approach of feature fusion outperforms the suggested technique by [3] and related comparisons against the unimodal elements. Extraction of features from multimodalities, their fusion using distinct process, and classification using SVM are the core of this work. The proposed fusion method is not used earlier in any research. The novelty of the work is to create a single template from two biometric modalities and the use of SVM for recognition purpose.

3. Proposed Multimodal Biometric System

The proposed approach implements an innovative idea to fuse the features of two different modalities—fingerprint and iris. The proposed system functions are grouped in the following basic stages:

(i) preprocessing stage which obtains region of interest (ROI) for further processing;

(ii) feature extraction stage which provides the resulting features using Haar wavelet from ROI;

(iii) fusion stage which combined the corresponding feature vectors of unimodal. The features so obtained are fused by innovative technique using the Mahalanobis distance. These distances are normalized using hyperbolic and are fused by applying the average sum rule tanh.

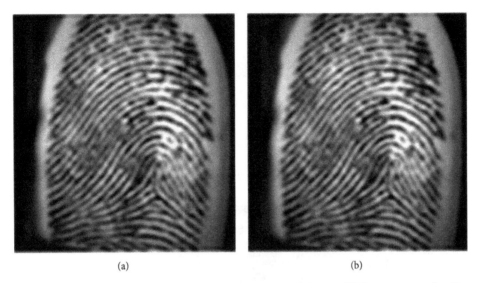

(a)   (b)

FIGURE 1: Preprocessing of Fingerprint Image (a) Input Fingerprint Image. (b) Histogram equalized Image.

(iv) the classification stage which operates on fingerprint feature vector, iris feature vector, and fused feature vector for an entire subject separately. We applied an SVM strategy for classification to get the results of acceptance/rejection or identification decision.

These techniques are explained as follows.

3.1. Fingerprint Feature Extraction. Fingerprint image is made available from the image acquisition system. Real fingerprint images are rarely of perfect quality. They may be degraded by noise due to many factors including variations in skin, impression condition, and noise of capturing devices. Quality of some images is really bad; preprocessing improves them to the extent required by feature extraction. Basically fingerprint recognition is performed by minutiae-based method and image-based method. Most of the minutiae-based methods require extensive preprocessing operations such as normalization, segmentation, orientation estimation, ridge filtering, binarization, and thinning [32]. Minutiae detection is then performed to reliably extract the minutiae features. For extracting the features of fingerprint we used a Haar wavelet-based technique. This image-based technique has its roots in frequency analysis (wavelet). An important benefit of this technique is less computational time, thereby making it more suitable for real-time applications. This technique requires less preprocessing and works fine even with low-quality images.

In this paper, the fingerprint image was first preprocessed using normalization, histogram equalization, and average filtering, to improve the image quality. Normalization of the input fingerprint image has prespecified mean and variance. Histogram equalization (HE) technique has the basic idea to map the gray levels based on the probability distribution of the input gray levels. HE flattens and stretches the dynamic range of the image's histogram [11]. This results in the overall contrast improvement of the image as shown in Figure 1. It produces an enhanced fingerprint image that is useful for feature extraction.

3.1.1. Haar Wavelet-Based Technique for Extracting Fingerprint Features. The wavelet transform is a mathematical tool based on many-layer function decomposition. After applying wavelet transform, a signal can be described by many wavelet coefficients which represent the characteristics of the signal. If the image has distinct features with some frequency and direction, the corresponding subimages have larger energies in wavelet transform. For this reason wavelet transform has been widely used in signal processing, pattern, recognition and texture recognition, [33]. By applying wavelet transform, vital information of original image is transformed into a compressed image without much loss of information. Haar wavelet decomposed the fingerprint image by mean and deviation. Wavelet coefficients of the image consist of four subbands each with a quarter of the original area. The up left subimage, composed of the low-frequency parts for both row and column, is called approximate image. The remaining three images, containing vertical high frequencies (down left), horizontal high frequencies (up right), and high frequencies in both directions (down right), are detailed images [34].

If $f(x, y)$ represents an image signal, its Haar wavelet transform is equal to two 1D filters (x-direction and y-direction). As shown in Figure 2(a), where LL represents low-frequency vectors (approximate), HL represents high-frequency vectors in horizontal direction, LH represents high-frequency vectors in vertical direction, and HH represents diagonal high-frequency vectors. After first decomposition LL quarter, that is, approximate component, is submitted for next decomposition. In this manner the decomposition is carried out four times, as shown in Figure 2(b). This reduces array size by 1×60 along x- as well as y-direction. The original image of 160×96 is reduced to 10×6 after fourth decomposition. From this image a single 1×60 feature vector

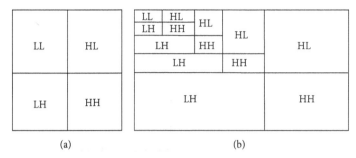

LL		HL				

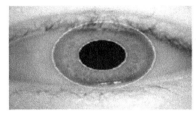  

FIGURE 2: (a) Wavelet decomposition and (b) 4-level wavelet decomposition.

(a) Iris after boundaries detected (b) Iris image after noise removal (c) Normalized Image

FIGURE 3: Iris Localization, segmentation, and normalization.

is extracted by row-wise serialization. This itself is treated as extracted feature vector for fingerprint.

3.2. Iris Feature Extraction.
The process of extracting features from the iris image is discussed in this section. The iris image must be preprocessed before using it for the feature extraction purpose. The unwanted data including eyelid, pupil, sclera, and eyelashes in the image should be excluded. Therefore, the preprocessing module for iris is required to perform iris segmentation, iris normalization and image enhancement. Segmentation is an essential module to remove nonuseful information, namely, the pupil segment and the part outside the iris (sclera, eyelids, and skin). It estimates the iris boundary. For boundary estimation, the iris image is first fed to the canny algorithm which generates the edge map of the iris image. The detected edge map is then used to locate the exact boundary of pupil and iris using Hough transforms [12]. The next step is to separate eyelid and eyelashes. The horizontal segmentation operator and image binarization were used to extract the eyelid edge information. The eyelids span the whole image in the horizontal direction. The average of vertical gradients is larger in the area with eyelid boundary. The longest possible horizontal line is demarking line for eyelids. This is used as the separator, segmenting it into two parts. The eyelid boundaries were modelled with the parabolic curves according to the determined edge points. In the process of normalization the polar image of iris is translated into the Cartesian frame depicting it as rectangular strip as shown in Figure 3. It is done using Daugman's rubber sheet model [13]. Finally, histogram equalization was used for image enhancement.

3.2.1. Haar Wavelet-Based Technique for Extracting Iris Features.
The enhanced normalized iris image is then used to extract identifiable features of iris pattern, using three-level decomposition by Haar wavelet transform. Haar wavelet is selected in this work because of its ability of capturing approximate information along with retention of detailed texture. The normalized image of 240×20 is decomposed first along the row (for each row) and then the column (for each column). It produces four regions—left-up quarter (approximate component), right-up (horizontal component), bottom-left (vertical component), and bottom-right (diagonal component). The mean and deviations of the coefficients are available after decomposition. We again decompose approximate quarter into four subquarters. This decomposition is employed three times. Four sub images of size 30×2 are obtained. The approximate component after 3rd decomposition is representative feature vector. The first row of 1×30 is appended by second row of 1×30 for getting the feature vector of 1×60.

3.3. Fusion of Iris and Fingerprint Feature Vectors.
The feature vectors extracted from encoded input images are further combined to the new feature vector by proposing a feature level fusion technique. The present work includes an innovative method of fusion at the feature level. The Mahalanobis distance technique is at the core of this fusion. This makes it distinct from different methods reported in the literature. The extracted features from fingerprint and iris are homogeneous; each vector is of size 1×60 elements. These two homogenous vectors are processed pragmatically to produce the fused vector of same order, that is, 1×60 elements. As most of the feature fusion in the literature is performed serially or parallel, it ultimately results in a high-dimensional vector. This is the major problem in feature level fusion. The proposed algorithm generates the same size fused vector as that of unimodal, and hence nullified the problem

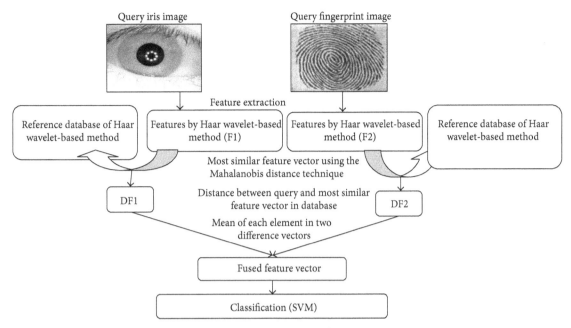

FIGURE 4: Architecture for feature fusion.

of high dimension. The fusion process is depicted in Figure 4 and is explained as follows.

(1) Features fingerprint and iris of the query images are obtained.

(2) The nearest match for query feature vectors of fingerprint and iris is selected from 4×100 reference feature vectors of fingerprints and iris using and Mahalanobis distance.

(3) The Mahalanobis distance (M_d) between a sample x and a sample y is calculated using the following equation:

$$M_d(x, y)^2 = (x - y)' S^{-1} (x - y), \tag{1}$$

where S is the within-group covariance matrix. In this paper, we assume a diagonal covariance matrix. This allows us to calculate the distance using only the mean and the variance. The minimum distance vector is considered as the most similar vector.

(4) The difference between query and its most similar vector is computed for fingerprint and iris, which are again of size 1×60.

(5) The elements of these difference vectors are normalized by Tanh to scale them between 0 and 1. Scaling of the participating (input) features to the same scale ensures their equal contribution to fusion.

(6) The mean value is calculated for these two difference vectors for each component. This yields a new vector of 1×60. That itself is the fused feature vector.

This fused vector is used for training using SVM. This method saves training and testing time, while retaining the benefits of fusion.

3.4. Support Vector Machine Classifier. SVM has demonstrated superior results in various classification and pattern recognition problems [35, 36]. Furthermore, for several pattern classification applications, SVM has already been proven to provide better generalization performance than conventional techniques especially when the number of input variables is large [37, 38]. With this purpose in mind, we evaluated the SVM for our fused feature vector.

The standard SVM takes a set of input data. It is a predictive algorithm to pinpoint the class to which the input belongs. This makes the SVM a nonprobabilistic binary linear classifier [39]. Given a set of training samples, each marked as belonging to its categories, an SVM training algorithm builds a model that assigns new sample to one category or another. For this purpose we turn to SVM for validating our approach. To achieve better generalization performance of the SVM, original input space is mapped into a high-dimensional dot product space called the feature space, and in the feature space the optimal hyperplane is determined as shown in Figure 5. The initial optimal hyperplane algorithm proposed by Vapnik [40] was a linear classifier. Yet, Boser et al. [39] suggested a way to create nonlinear classifiers by applying the kernel trick to extend the linear learning machine to handle nonlinear cases. We aimed to maximize the margin of separation between patterns to have a better classification result. The function that returns a dot product of two mapped patterns is called a kernel function. Different kernels can be selected to construct the SVM. The most commonly used kernel functions are the polynomial, linear, and Gaussian radial basis kernel functions (RBF). We employed two types of kernels for experimentation, namely radial basis function kernel and polynomial kernel.

The separating hyperplane (described by w) is determined by minimizing the structural risk instead of the empirical error. Minimizing the structural risk is equivalent

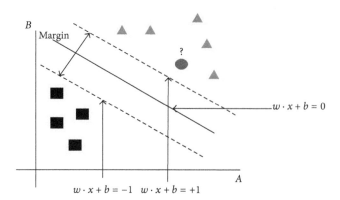

FIGURE 5: Linearly separable patterns.

to seeking the optimal margin between two classes. The optimal hyperplane can be written as a combination of a few feature points, which are called support vectors of the optimal hyperplane. SVM training can be considered as the constrained optimization problem which maximizes the width of the margin and minimizes the structural risk:

$$\min_{w,b} \quad \frac{1}{2}w^T w + C\sum_{i=1}^{N}\varepsilon_i$$

$$\text{subject to} \quad y_i\left(W^T\varphi\left(x_i\right)+b\right) \geq 1 - \varepsilon_i, \tag{2}$$

$$\varepsilon_i \geq 0, \ \forall i,$$

where b is the bias, C is the trade-off parameter, ε_i is the slack variable, which measures the deviation of a data point from the ideal condition of pattern, and $\varphi(\cdot)$ is the feature vector in the expanded feature space. The penalty parameter "C" controls the trade-off between the complexity of the decision function and the number of wrongly classified testing points. The correct C value cannot be known in advance, and a wrong choice of the SVM penalty parameter C can lead to a severe loss in performance. Therefore the parametric values are usually estimated from the training data by cross-validation and exponentially growing sequences of C:

$$w = \sum_{SV=1}^{N_{SV}} \alpha_{SV} y_{SV} \varphi\left(x_{SV}\right), \tag{3}$$

where N_{SV} is the number of SVs, $y_{SV} \in \{-1, +1\}$ is the target value of learning pattern x_{SV}, and α_{SV} is the Lagrange multiplier value of the SVs. Given a set of training samples, each marked as belonging to its categories, an SVM training algorithm builds a model that assigns new sample to one of the two available zones.

Classification of the test sample z is performed by

$$y = \text{sgn}\left(\sum_{SV=1}^{N_{SV}} \alpha_{SV} y_{SV} K\left(x_{SV}, z\right)\right), \tag{4}$$

where $K(x_{SV}, z)$ is the functional kernel that maps the input into higher-dimensional feature space. Computational

complexity and classification time for the SVM classifiers using nonlinear kernels depend on the number of support vectors (SVs) required for the SVM.

The effectiveness of SVM depends on the kernel used, kernel parameters, and a proper soft margin or penalty C value [41–43]. The selection of a kernel function is an important problem in applications, although there is no theory to tell which kernel to use. In this work two types of kernels are used for experimentation, namely, radial basis function kernel and Polynomial kernel. The RBF requires less parameters to set than a polynomial kernel. However, convergence for RBF kernels takes longer than for the other kernels [44].

RBF kernel has the Gaussian form of

$$K\left(x_i, x_j\right) = e\left\{-\frac{\left[\left(x_i - x_j\right)^2\right]}{2\sigma^2}\right\}, \tag{5}$$

where $\sigma > 0$ is a constant that defines the kernel width.

The polynomial kernel function is described as

$$K\left(x_i, x_j\right) = \left(x_i \cdot x_j + 1\right)^d, \tag{6}$$

where d is a positive integer, representing the constant of polynomial degree.

Before training, for SVM radial basis function, two parameters need to be found, C and γ. C is the penalty parameter of the error term and γ is a kernel parameter. By cross-validation, the best C and γ values are found to be 8.0 and 0.1, respectively. Similarly polyorder value needs to be found for p, for polynomial SVM. After regress parameter tuning the best p found was 8.0. Research has found that the RBF kernel is superior to the polynomial kernel for our proposed feature level fusion method.

4. Experimental Results

Evaluation of proposed algorithm is carried out in three different sets of experiments. The database is generated for 100 genuine and 50 imposter sample cases. Four images of iris as well as fingerprint are stored for each person in the reference database. Similarly one image of each iris and fingerprint for all 100 cases is stored in query database. In the same manner data for 50 cases in reference and 50 cases in the query is appended for imposters. Fingerprint images are real and iris images are from CASIA database. The mutual independence assumption of the biometric traits allows us to randomly pair the users from the two datasets. First, we report all the experiments, based on the unimodal. Then, the remaining experiments are related to the fused pattern classification strategy. Two kernels, RBFSVM and PolySVM, are used for classification in separate experiments. Three types of feature vectors, first from fingerprints, second from iris, and third as their fusion, are used as inputs in separate experimental setups. Combination of input features with classifier makes six different experiments. The objective of all these experiments is to provide a good basis for comparison. By using kernels the classification performance or the data

TABLE 1: Average GAR (%), FAR (%), and response time (mean) in seconds for unimodal and multimodal techniques.

Algorithm	Number of support vectors	Testing set	Identification accuracy (GAR%)		FAR%		Training time (mean in seconds)		Testing time (mean in seconds)	
			RBF Kernel	Polynomial Kernel	RBF Kernel	Polynomial Kernel	RBF Kernel	Polynomial Kernel	RBF Kernel	Polynomial Kernel
Fingerprint	400	100	87	85	4	8	5.22	4.78	0.2	0.21
Iris	400	100	88	84	2	4	3.25	4.94	0.25	0.16
Fusion	400	100	94	93	0	0	3.27	3.98	0.12	0.19

separability in the high-dimensional space gets improved. Since this is a pattern recognition approach, the database is divided into two parts: training and testing. This separation of the database into training and test sets was used for finding the average performance rating. For unimodal biometric recognition 4 features per user were used in training and one image per user is used for testing the performance of the system. For multimodal, four fused features per user were used in training and one is used for testing. This separation of the database into training and test sets was used for finding the average performance results of genuine acceptance rate (GAR), false acceptance rate (FAR), training and testing time.

The results obtained are tabulated in Table 1. The results indicate that the average rate of correct classification for fused vector is found to be 94%, in case of RBF kernel for 100 classes. The GAR of 87% and 88% for unimodal fingerprint and iris, respectively, is obtained. Also the average rate of correct classification for fused vector is found to be 93%, in case of polykernel for the same dataset. It is found to be 85% and 84% for unimodal fingerprint and iris, respectively. False acceptance rate (FAR) reached atoneable minima, that is, 0, using fused feature vector with both kernel classifiers. We can also observe that the RBF-SVM with fused data is the best combination for both GAR and FAR.

Moreover, the results reported here will help us to better assess the results produced by unimodal, and multimodal in terms of training and testing time. Time in seconds required for this training and testing for unimodal and multimodal is also tabulated in Table 1. The best performing method, that is, fused feature, required training time of 3.27 s by RBFSVM and 3.98 s by PolySVM. The minimum time required for training is for iris by Haar wavelet-based method (3.25 s). The results revealed that the mean training time for RBFSVM, and for fused data is slightly greater than unimodal iris. Fused feature vector outperforms unimodal features in both cases for testing. It took 0.12 s using RBFSVM and 0.19 s using PolySVM. Our experimental results provide adequate support for recommending fused feature vector with RBFSVM as the best combination for high recognition. It has highest GAR of 94% and FAR of 0%. It has least testing time of 0.12 s. This combination is the best performer amongst six different experiments carried out. The GAR of 93% and FAR of 0% with testing time of 0.19 s for PolySVM is the second best performer. The training time for fused data lacks behind unimodal iris, but it should be tolerated as the training is to be carried out only once. From Table 1, it can be easily concluded that feature level performs better compared to unimodal biometric systems.

5. Discussion and Comparison

This paper presents a feature level fusion method for a multimodal biometric system based on fingerprints and irises. The proposed approach for fingerprint and iris feature extraction, fusion, and classification by RBFSVM and PolySVM has been tested for unimodal as well as multimodal identification systems using the real fingerprint database and CASIA iris database. In greater detail, the proposed approach performs fingerprint and iris feature extraction using the Haar wavelet based method. These codified features are the representation of unique template. We compare our approach with Besbes et al.[3], Jagadeesan et al. [18], and Conti et al. [25].

Besbes et al. [3] worked on the same modalities (fingerprint and iris), but fusion is at the decision level. They claimed the improvement in results because of their fusion. The claim is not supported by experimental findings. The procedure followed by them is explained here. Features of fingerprint were extracted by minutiae-based method. The iris pattern was encoded by 2D Gabor filter. Matching was done by hamming distance. Each modality is processed separately to obtain its decision. The final decision of the system uses the operator "AND" between decision coming from the fingerprint recognition step and that coming from the iris recognition one. This ANDing operation is fusion at decision level. Hence, nobody can be accepted unless both of the results are positive. To compare their approach with our work, we fused their features sequentially and train these vectors by RBFSVM and PolySVM for two separate experiments.

Similar attempt made by Jagadeesan et al. [18] extracts the features, minutiae points, and texture properties from the fingerprint and iris images, respectively. Then, the extracted features were combined together with their innovative method, to obtain the fused multi-biometric template. A 256-bit secure cryptographic key was generated from the multibiometric template. For experimentation, they employed the fingerprint images obtained from publicly available sources (so we used our real fingerprint database) and the Iris images from CASIA iris database. Training and testing aspects were not covered in their literature. In our work we implemented this system separately and train by SVM, for comparison.

The feature level fusion proposed by Conti et al. [25] was based on frequency-based approach. Their generated fused vector was homogeneous biometric vector, integrating iris and fingerprint data. A hamming-distance-based matching algorithm was used for final decision. To compare our approach we train their fused vector with SVM. Results

TABLE 2: Comparison of the proposed approach with Besbes et al. [3], Jagadeesan et al. [18], and Conti et al. [25] (FAR, FRR, and response time (mean) in seconds).

Author	Methods	Modalities	FAR (RBF SVM)	FRR (RBF SVM)	FAR (Poly SVM)	FRR (Poly SVM)	Training time (RBF SVM)	Testing time (RBF SVM)	Training time (Poly SVM)	Testing time (Poly SVM)
Besbes et al. [3]	Feature level fusion	Fingerprint	14%	22%	16%	22%	5.7	0.35	5.89	0.29
		Iris	12%	15%	14%	18%	4.82	0.28	5.2	0.32
		Fusion	4%	10%	4%	10%	4.3	0.20	4.98	0.24
Jagadeesan et al. [18]	Feature level fusion	Fingerprint	2%	17%	8%	18%	6.02	0.31	6.88	0.34
		Iris	1%	12%	6%	15%	4.34	0.26	5.20	0.28
		Fusion	0%	9%	0%	9%	4.98	0.20	5.01	0.21
Conti et al. [25]	Feature level fusion	Fingerprint	2%	17%	8%	19%	5.47	0.28	5.90	0.30
		Iris	1%	10%	6%	16%	5.69	0.25	5.76	0.27
		Fusion	0%	8%	0%	9%	4.58	0.19	4.69	0.22
Proposed system	Feature level fusion	Fingerprint	4%	13%	8%	15%	5.22	0.2	4.78	0.21
		Iris	2%	12%	4%	16%	3.25	0.25	4.94	0.16
		Fusion	0%	6%	0%	7%	3.27	0.12	3.98	0.19

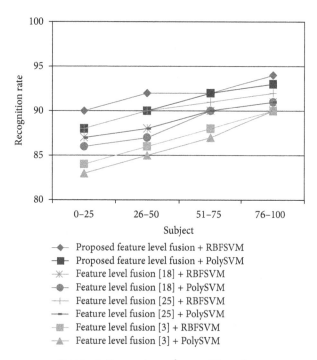

- ◆ Proposed feature level fusion + RBFSVM
- ■ Proposed feature level fusion + PolySVM
- ✳ Feature level fusion [18] + RBFSVM
- ● Feature level fusion [18] + PolySVM
- + Feature level fusion [25] + RBFSVM
- ▬ Feature level fusion [25] + PolySVM
- ▦ Feature level fusion [3] + RBFSVM
- ▲ Feature level fusion [3] + PolySVM

FIGURE 6: Comparison of recognition rates.

obtained for FAR and FRR are now available for comparison. We tested their technique on our database for 100 genuine and 50 imposter cases. The comparison chart of FAR and FRR and response time are tabulated in Table 2. Improved performance is exhibited by proposed feature level fusion compared to the fusion methods used by other researchers. From Table 2, it can be easily concluded that feature level performs better compared to unimodal biometric systems.

This section is the comparison of results between our proposed method and the approach recommended by [3, 18, 25].

Here the results of feature level fusion are compared. Results indicate GAR of 80% at the decision level fusion by ANDing of unimodal decision. By fusing their features sequentially and training by RBFSVM, we found the results of GAR = 90%, FAR = 4%, training time of 4.3 s, and testing time of 0.20 s. Also, we obtained the results of GAR = 90%, FAR = 4%, training time of 4.98 s, and testing time of 0.24 s for polySVM. On the basis of the experimental results it is proved that the feature level fusion is better than the decision level fusion for the concept proposed by [3]. The results also reveal that the feature level fusion gives better performance than the individual traits. The fused feature vector of Jagadeesan et al. [18] achieves 0% FAR and 9% FRR with both kernel of SVM. The training time of 4.98 s and testing time of 0.20 s are required by RBFSVM and training time of 5.01 s and testing time of 0.21 s are required by PolySVM in [18] for fused vector of one subject. Also, the results obtained by Conti et al. [25] achieved 0% FAR by both kernels of SVM. The FRR of 8% and 9% is obtained by RBFSVM and PolySVM, respectively. The mean training time for training the fused feature sets of [25] is 4.58 s and 4.69 s by RBFSVM and PolySVM, respectively. The testing time required by fused vector is 0.19 s by RBFSVM and 0.22 s by PolySVM of of [25]. In our case, GAR is 94%, FAR is 0%, training time is 3.27 s and testing time is 0.12 s by RBFSVM. Also GAR is 93%, FAR is 0%, training time is 3.98 s, and testing time is 0.19 s by PolySVM. The recognition rates and error rates comparison of the proposed approach with [3, 18, 25] is shown in Figures 6 and 7. Results obtained from our method of fusion are superior to those of Besbes et al. [3], Jagadeesan et al. [18], and Conti et al. [25]. The results obtained by our method are best competing the results of the reference work for all the four performance indicators. Of the two classifiers used in our work RBFSVM stands superior to PolySVM. Experimental results substantiate the superiority of feature level fusion and our proposed method over the approach of [3, 18, 25].

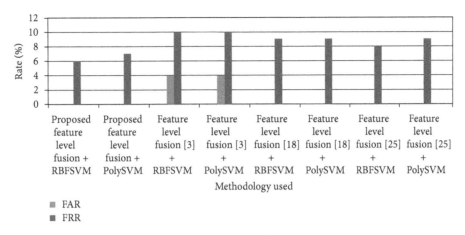

FIGURE 7: Comparison of error rates.

6. Conclusion

Content of information is rich with multimodal biometrics. It is the matter of satisfaction that multimodalities are now in use for few applications covering large population. In this paper a novel algorithm for feature level fusion and recognition system using SVM has been proposed. Intention of this work were to evaluate the standing of our proposed method of feature level fusion using the Mahalanobis distance technique. These fused features are trained by RBFSVM and PolySVM separately. The simulation results show clearly the advantage of feature level fusion of multiple biometric modalities over single biometric feature identification. The superiority of feature level fusion is concluded on the basis of experimental results for FAR, FAR, and training and testing time. Of the two RBFSVM performs better than PolySVM. The uniqueness of fused template generated also outperforms the decision level fusion. The improvement in performance of FAR, FRR, and response time is observed as compared to existing researches. From the experimental results it can be concluded that the feature level fusion produces better recognition than individual modalities. The proposed method sounds strong enough to enhance the performance of multimodal biometric. The proposed methodology has the potential for real-time implementation and large population support. The work can also be extended with other biometric modalities also. The performance analysis using noisy database may be performed.

References

[1] S. Soviany and M. Jurian, "Multimodal biometric securing methods for informatic systems," in *Proceedings of the 34th International Spring Seminar on Electronic Technology*, pp. 12–14, Phoenix, Ariz, USA, May 2011.

[2] S. Soviany, C. Soviany, and M. Jurian, "A multimodal approach for biometric authentication with multiple classifiers," in *International Conference on Communication, Information and Network Security*, pp. 28–30, 2011.

[3] F. Besbes, H. Trichili, and B. Solaiman, "Multimodal biometric system based on fingerprint identification and iris recognition," in *Proceedings of the 3rd International Conference on Information and Communication Technologies: From Theory to Applications (ICTTA '08)*, pp. 1–5, Damascus, Syria, April 2008.

[4] A. Baig, A. Bouridane, F. Kurugollu, and G. Qu, "Fingerprint—Iris fusion based identification system using a single hamming distance matcher," *International Journal of Bio-Science and Bio-Technology*, vol. 1, no. 1, pp. 47–58, 2009.

[5] L. Zhao, Y. Song, Y. Zhu, C. Zhang, and Y. Zheng, "Face recognition based on multi-class SVM," in *IEEE International Conference on Control and Decision*, pp. 5871–5873, June 2009.

[6] T. C. Mota and A. C. G. Thomé, "One-against-all-based multiclass svm strategies applied to vehicle plate character recognition," in *IEEE International Joint Conference on Neural Networks (IJCNN '09)*, pp. 2153–2159, New York, NY, USA, June 2009.

[7] R. Brunelli and D. Falavigna, "Person identification using multiple cues," *IEEE Transactions on Pattern Analysis and Machine Intelligence*, vol. 17, no. 10, pp. 955–966, 1995.

[8] S. Theodoridis and K. Koutroumbas, *Pattern Recognition*, Elsevier, 4th edition, 2009.

[9] B. Gokberk, A. A. Salah, and L. Akarun, "Rank-based decision fusion for 3D shape-based face recognition," in *Proceedings of the 13th IEEE Conference on Signal Processing and Communications Applications*, pp. 364–367, Antalya, Turkey, 2005.

[10] A. Jain and A. Ross, "Fingerprint mosaicking," in *IEEE International Conference on Acoustics, Speech, and Signal Processing (ICASSP '02)*, pp. IV/4064–IV/4067, Rochester, NY, USA, May 2002.

[11] M. Sepasian, W. Balachandran, and C. Mares, "Image enhancement for fingerprint minutiae-based algorithms using CLAHE, standard deviation analysis and sliding neighborhood," in *IEEE Transactions on World Congress on Engineering and Computer Science*, pp. 1–6, 2008.

[12] B. S. Xiaomei Liu, *Optimizations in iris recognition [Ph.D. thesis]*, Computer Science and Engineering Notre Dame, Indianapolis, Ind, USA, 2006.

[13] J. Daugman, "How iris recognition works," *IEEE Transactions on Circuits and Systems for Video Technology*, vol. 14, no. 1, pp. 21–30, 2004.

[14] L. Hong and A. Jain, "Integrating faces and fingerprints for personal identification," *IEEE Transactions on Pattern Analysis and Machine Intelligence*, vol. 20, no. 12, pp. 1295–1307, 1998.

[15] J. Fierrez-aguilar, L. Nanni, J. Ortega-garcia, and D. Maltoni, "Combining multiple matchers for fingerprint verification: a

case study," in *Proceedings of the International Conference on Image Analysis and Processing (ICIAP '05)*, vol. 3617 of *Lecture Notes in Computer Science*, pp. 1035–1042, Springer, 2005.

[16] A. Lumini and L. Nanni, "When fingerprints are combined with Iris—a Case Study: FVC2004 and CASIA," *International Journal of Network Security*, vol. 4, no. 1, pp. 27–34, 2007.

[17] L. Hong, A. K. Jain, and S. Pankanti, "Can multibiometrics improve performance?" in *IEEE Workshop on Automatic Identification Advanced Technologies*, pp. 59–64, New Jersey, NJ, USA, 1999.

[18] A. Jagadeesan, T. Thillaikkarasi, and K. Duraiswamy, "Protected bio-cryptography key invention from multimodal modalities: feature level fusion of fingerprint and Iris," *European Journal of Scientific Research*, vol. 49, no. 4, pp. 484–502, 2011.

[19] I. Raglu and P. P. Deepthi, "Multimodal Biometric Encryption Using Minutiae and Iris feature map," in *Proceedings of IEEE Students' International Conference on Electrical, Electronics and Computer Science*, pp. 94–934, Zurich, Switzerland, 2012.

[20] V. C. Subbarayudu and M. V. N. K. Prasad, "Multimodal biometric system," in *Proceedings of the 1st International Conference on Emerging Trends in Engineering and Technology (ICETET '08)*, pp. 635–640, Nagpur, India, July 2008.

[21] M. Nagesh kumar, P. K. Mahesh, and M. N. Shanmukha Swamy, "An efficient secure multimodal biometric fusion using palmprint and face image," *International Journal of Computer Science*, vol. 2, pp. 49–53, 2009.

[22] F. Yang and B. Ma, "A new mixed-mode biometrics information fusion based-on fingerprint, hand-geometry and palm-print," in *Proceedings of the 4th International Conference on Image and Graphics (ICIG '07)*, pp. 689–693, Jinhua, China, August 2007.

[23] A. J. Basha, V. Palanisamy, and T. Purusothaman, "Fast multimodal biometric approach using dynamic fingerprint authentication and enhanced iris features," in *Proceedings of the IEEE International Conference on Computational Intelligence and Computing Research (ICCIC '10)*, pp. 1–8, Coimbatore, India, December 2010.

[24] M. M. Monwar and M. L. Gavrilova, "Multimodal biometric system using rank-level fusion approach," *IEEE Transactions on Systems, Man and Cybernetics B*, vol. 39, no. 4, pp. 867–878, 2009.

[25] V. Conti, C. Militello, F. Sorbello, and S. Vitabile, "A frequency-based approach for features fusion in fingerprint and iris multimodal biometric identification systems," *IEEE Transactions on Systems, Man and Cybernetics C*, vol. 40, no. 4, pp. 384–395, 2010.

[26] G. Aguilar, G. Sánchez, K. Toscano, M. Nakano, and H. Pérez, "Multimodal biometric system using fingerprint," in *International Conference on Intelligent and Advanced Systems (ICIAS '07)*, pp. 145–150, Kuala Lumpur, Malaysia, November 2007.

[27] L. Lin, X.-F. Gu, J.-P. Li, L. Jie, J.-X. Shi, and Y.-Y. Huang, "Research on data fusion of multiple biometric features," in *International Conference on Apperceiving Computing and Intelligence Analysis (ICACIA '09)*, pp. 112–115, Chengdu, China, October 2009.

[28] D. E. Maurer and J. P. Baker, "Fusing multimodal biometrics with quality estimates via a Bayesian belief network," *Pattern Recognition*, vol. 41, no. 3, pp. 821–832, 2008.

[29] T. Ko, "Multimodal biometric identification for large user population using fingerprint, face and IRIS recognition," in *Proceedings of the 34th Applied Imagery and Pattern Recognition Workshop (AIPR '05)*, pp. 88–95, Arlington, Va, USA, 2005.

[30] K. Nandakumar and A. K. Jain, "Multibiometric template security using fuzzy vault," in *IEEE 2nd International Conference on Biometrics: Theory, Applications and Systems*, pp. 198–205, Washington, DC, USA, October 2008.

[31] A. Nagar, K. Nandakumar, and A. K. Jain, "Multibiometric cryptosystems based on feature-level fusion," *IEEE Transactions on Information Forensics and Security*, vol. 7, no. 1, pp. 255–268, 2012.

[32] K. Balasubramanian and P. Babu, "Extracting minutiae from fingerprint images using image inversion and bi-histogram equalization," in *SPIT-IEEE Colloquium and International Conference on Biometrics*, pp. 53–56, Washington, DC, USA, 2009.

[33] Y.-P. Huang, S.-W. Luo, and E.-Y. Chen, "An efficient iris recognition system," in *Proceedings of the International Conference on Machine Learning and Cybernetics*, pp. 450–454, Beijing, China, November 2002.

[34] N. Tajbakhsh, K. Misaghian, and N. M. Bandari, "A region-based Iris feature extraction method based on 2D-wavelet transform," in *Bio-ID-MultiComm, 2009 joint COST 2101 and 2102 International Conference on Biometric ID Management and Multimodal Communication*, vol. 5707 of *Lecture Notes in Computer Science*, pp. 301–307, 2009.

[35] D. Zhang, F. Song, Y. Xu, and Z. Liang, *Advanced Pattern Recognition Technologies with Applications to Biometrics*, Medical Information Science Reference, New York, NY, USA, 2008.

[36] C. J. C. Burges, "A tutorial on support vector machines for pattern recognition," *Data Mining and Knowledge Discovery*, vol. 2, no. 2, pp. 121–167, 1998.

[37] M. M. Ramon, X. Nan, and C. G. Christodoulou, "Beam forming using support vector machines," *IEEE Antennas and Wireless Propagation Letters*, vol. 4, pp. 439–442, 2005.

[38] M. J. Fernández-Getino García, J. L. Rojo-Álvarez, F. Alonso-Atienza, and M. Martínez-Ramón, "Support vector machines for robust channel estimation in OFDM," *IEEE Signal Processing Letters*, vol. 13, no. 7, pp. 397–400, 2006.

[39] B. E. Boser, I. M. Guyon, and V. N. Vapnik, "Training algorithm for optimal margin classifiers," in *Proceedings of the 5th Annual ACM Workshop on Computational Learning Theory (COLT '92)*, pp. 144–152, Morgan Kaufmann, San Mateo, Calif, USA, July 1992.

[40] V. N. Vapnik, *The Nature of Statistical Learning Theory*, Springer, New York, NY, USA, 1999.

[41] C.-W. Hsu and C.-J. Lin, "A simple decomposition method for support vector machines," *Machine Learning*, vol. 46, no. 1–3, pp. 291–314, 2002.

[42] J. Bhatnagar, A. Kumar, and N. Saggar, "A novel approach to improve biometric recognition using rank level fusion," in *IEEE Conference on Computer Vision and Pattern Recognition*, pp. 1–6, Hong Kong, China, June 2007.

[43] J. Manikandan and B. Venkataramani, "Evaluation of multiclass support vector machine classifiers using optimum threshold-based pruning technique," *IET Signal Processing*, vol. 5, no. 5, pp. 506–513, 2011.

[44] R. Noori, M. A. Abdoli, A. Ameri Ghasrodashti, and M. Jalili Ghazizade, "Prediction of municipal solid waste generation with combination of support vector machine and principal component analysis: a case study of mashhad," *Environmental Progress and Sustainable Energy*, vol. 28, no. 2, pp. 249–258, 2009.

20

Variance Entropy: A Method for Characterizing Perceptual Awareness of Visual Stimulus

Meng Hu and Hualou Liang

School of Biomedical Engineering, Science and Health Systems, Drexel University, Philadelphia, PA 19104, USA

Correspondence should be addressed to Hualou Liang, hualou.liang@drexel.edu

Academic Editor: Cheng-Hsiung Hsieh

Entropy, as a complexity measure, is a fundamental concept for time series analysis. Among many methods, sample entropy (SampEn) has emerged as a robust, powerful measure for quantifying complexity of time series due to its insensitivity to data length and its immunity to noise. Despite its popular use, SampEn is based on the standardized data where the variance is routinely discarded, which may nonetheless provide additional information for discriminant analysis. Here we designed a simple, yet efficient, complexity measure, namely variance entropy (VarEn), to integrate SampEn with variance to achieve effective discriminant analysis. We applied VarEn to analyze local field potential (LFP) collected from visual cortex of macaque monkey while performing a generalized flash suppression task, in which a visual stimulus was dissociated from perceptual experience, to study neural complexity of perceptual awareness. We evaluated the performance of VarEn in comparison with SampEn on LFP, at both single and multiple scales, in discriminating different perceptual conditions. Our results showed that perceptual visibility could be differentiated by VarEn, with significantly better discriminative performance than SampEn. Our findings demonstrate that VarEn is a sensitive measure of perceptual visibility, and thus can be used to probe perceptual awareness of a stimulus.

1. Introduction

Over the past decades, entropy [1] has been widely used for analysis of dynamic systems. Among many measures, sample entropy (SampEn) is thought of as an effective, robust method due to its insensitivity to data length and its immunity to noise [2]. Until now, SampEn has been successfully applied for discriminant analysis of cardiovascular data [3], electroencephalogram data [4], and many others [5]. In addition, SampEn has been used in multiscale analysis for computing entropy over multiple time scales inherent in time series. For example, multiscale entropy [6] and adaptive multiscale entropy (AME) [7] both use SampEn to estimate entropy over multiple scales of time series.

Despite its popularity, it is not well recognized that there is an inherit drawback of SampEn used for discriminant analysis, that is, the calculation of SampEn is routinely based on the normalized data where the variance of data that may provide additional information for discrimination is discarded [8]. The normalization is essentially to rescale the data, which is appropriate if the analysis is driven by the search for order in the dynamics, but is otherwise inappropriate for discriminant analysis of two data sets as the rescaling can make them appear identical when they clearly are not. In fact, the variance and SampEn represent different aspects of the data: the variance measures concentration only around the mean of the data, whereas the entropy measures diffuseness of the density irrespective of the location of concentration of the data. In this paper, we proposed a new complexity measure, variance entropy (VarEn), to take into account both SampEn and the variance for improved discriminant analysis. Not only can it be used as a single-scale measure, but it can also be adapted for studying nonstationary data over multiple time scales. We applied VarEn to analyze cortical local field potential (LFP) data collected from a macaque monkey while performing a generalized flash suppression task [9], in which physical stimulation is dissociated from perceptual experience, to probe perceptual awareness of a visual stimulus. We showed that VarEn performed better than SampEn for both the whole time series (single-scale) and multiscale analysis of LFP data in terms of discriminative ability in distinguishing different perceptual conditions (Visible versus Invisible). Our results suggest that the proposed VarEn measure is a useful technique for discriminant analysis of neural data and can be used to uncover perceptual awareness of a stimulus.

2. Method

2.1. Sample Entropy. Entropy describes the complexity or irregularity of system, which can be used to classify systems. So far, many attempts have been made for estimation of entropy, such as Kolmogorov entropy [10] and Eckmann-Ruelle entropy [11]. However, these methods usually require very long time series that is not always available. Approximate entropy can be efficiently computed for short and noisy time series [1], but introduces a bias via counting self-match when calculating the pairs of similar epochs. Sample entropy (SampEn) provides a refined version of approximate entropy to reduce the bias [2]. It is defined as the negative natural logarithm of conditional probability that two sequences similar for m points remain similar at the next $m + 1$ point in the data set within a tolerance r, where self-matches are excluded in calculating the probability.

In order to compute SampEn, a time series $I = \{i(1), i(2), \ldots, i(N)\}$ is embedded in a delayed m-dimensional space, where the m-dimensional vectors are constructed as $x_m(k) = (i(k), i(k+1), \ldots, i(k+m-1))$, $k = 1 \sim N - m + 1$. The match of two vectors in the embedded space is defined as their distance lower than the tolerance r. $B^m(r)$ is the probability that two sequences of m points match within r, whereas $A^m(r)$ is similarly defined for an embedded dimension of $m + 1$. The SampEn is then calculated as

$$\text{SampEn}(I, m, r) = -\ln\left(\frac{A^m(r)}{B^m(r)}\right). \tag{1}$$

In practice, it is common to set the tolerance r as a fraction of the standard deviation of the data, which effectively rescales the data to have similar dynamic scales. As a result, the normalization process obscures the difference in the scales of data sets, thus rendering the analysis inappropriate if the goal is chiefly to discriminate between data sets. We therefore introduce a variance entropy measure in the following section to rectify this shortcoming.

2.2. Variance Entropy. Variance entropy (VarEn) measure is designed for discriminant analysis by combining SampEn and the variance of data. Specifically, VarEn can be treated as inverse-variance weighted entropy to represent system complexity. For a time series x, VarEn is defined as

$$\text{VarEn}(x, m, r) = \frac{\sum_{i=1}^{p} \text{SampEn}(x_i, m, r) \times w_i}{\sum_{i=1}^{p} w_i}, \tag{2}$$

where x_i is the ith segment of x, obtained with a window that slides over time, p is the number of sliding windows, w_i is inverse variance of x_i, m and r are the parameters for calculation of $\text{SampEn}(x_i, m, r)$. Specifically, to calculate VarEn, we first apply a sliding window over time series x. For a given window (e.g., ith time window, x_i), we compute its SampEn, variance, and w_i. After computing all p time windows, we then apply above formula to obtain VarEn of this time series x. A schematic representation of the processing steps is shown in Figure 1. It is also straightforward to extend our VarEn measure to the analysis of multitrial neural data in which x_i is the ith trial of x, and p is the number of trials. In this study, the parameters m and r were chosen as 2 and 0.2 for minimizing the standard error of entropy estimation [3]. We note that there is no pronounced difference with automatic selection of r [12].

Similar to SampEn, VarEn can also be applied to non-stationary data by considering multiple time scales inherent in the data, on which the entropy can be calculated. By multiple-scale entropy analysis, we compute the VarEn in adaptive multiscale entropy (AME) [7] to demonstrate its performance in comparison with the use of SampEn. AME is a multiscale analysis method in which the scales are adaptively derived directly from the data by virtue of multivariate empirical mode decomposition [13], which is fully data driven, well suited for the analysis of nonlinear/nonstationary neural data. Depending on the consecutive removal of low-frequency or high-frequency components, AME can be estimated at either coarse-to-fine (preserving high-frequency oscillations by progressively removal of low-frequency components) or fine-to-coarse scales (preserving low-frequency oscillations by progressively removal of high-frequency components) over which the sample entropy is performed. The coarse-to-fine and fine-to-coarse AME can be used separately or used in tandem to reveal the underlying dynamics of complex neural data. In this study, we use the VarEn to replace SampEn to perform multiscale analysis.

3. Results

In this section, we apply VarEn to analyze local field potentials (LFPs) collected from visual cortex of a macaque monkey while performing a visual illusion task, to characterize neural dynamics of perceptual awareness of a visual stimulus.

The visual illusion task used here is called generalized flash suppression (GFS) task, where a salient visual stimulus can be rendered invisible despite continuous retinal input, thus providing a rare opportunity to study neural mechanisms directly related to perception [9]. In the task, as soon as a monkey gained fixation for about 300 msec, the target stimulus indicated by a red disk was presented. At 1400 msec after the target onset, small random-moving dots appeared as the surroundings. With the immediate presence of the surroundings, the red disk could be rendered subjectively invisible. If the target stimulus disappeared from perception, the monkey was trained to release a lever; otherwise, monkey was to hold the lever. Therefore, based on the responses of the animal, the trial was classified as either "Visible" or "Invisible." Note that the stimuli in these two conditions were physically identical. Multielectrode LFP recordings were simultaneously collected from multiple cortical areas V1, V2, and V4 while monkeys performed the GFS task [14]. The data were obtained by band-pass filtering the full bandwidth

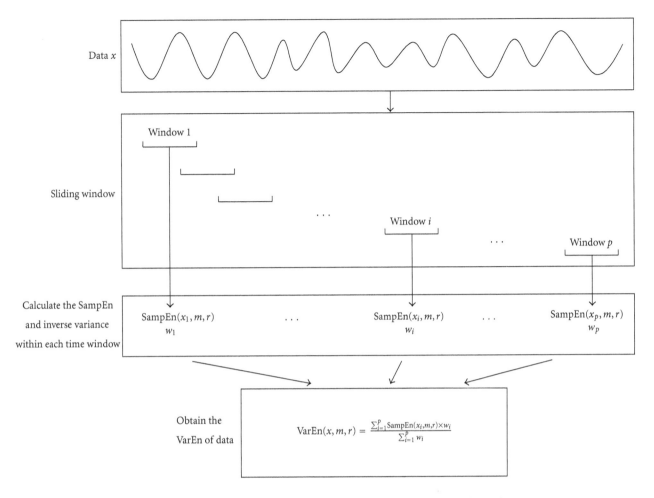

FIGURE 1: Schematic representation of the proposed variance entropy (VarEn).

signal between 1 and 500 Hz, and then resampled at 1 KHz. In this study, the LFPs of one second long after surrounding onset on a typical channel of area V4 over 87 trials were used in the analysis.

VarEn is first directly applied to the LFP data to discriminate two perceptual conditions: Visible versus Invisible. In Figure 2, we can see that the VarEn of the invisible condition is significantly greater than that of the visible condition ($P <$ 0.05). As a comparison, SampEn is applied to the same LFP data. However, the result reveals that there is no significant difference between two perceptual conditions (Figure 2). This result suggests that VarEn carries more discriminative information by integrating SampEn and the variance of data.

Next, VarEn is applied to the LFP data for performing multiple-scale entropy analysis. As described in the Method, we herein apply the VarEn-based adaptive multiscale analysis (AME) to the LFP data for discriminating two perceptual conditions over different LFP scales. As a comparison, the original AME is also applied to the LFP data, where the SampEn is applied to calculate the AME entropy measure. Figure 3 shows the comparison of two methods at the coarse-to-fine scales. We can see from Figures 3(a) and 3(b) that both methods exhibit dominantly increasing trend

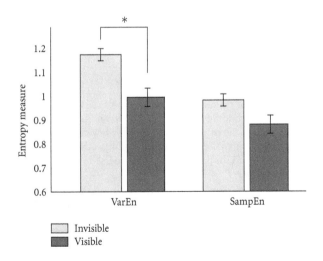

FIGURE 2: Comparison of the proposed variance entropy (VarEn) and sample entropy (SampEn) in discriminating the different perceptual conditions (Invisible versus Visible). Shown are the means and the standard errors of means of VarEn (left) and SampEn (right). As a result, the VarEn exhibits significant difference between two perceptual conditions ($p = 7.69e-4$, indicated by the sign "*"), but the SampEn does not ($P = 0.056$).

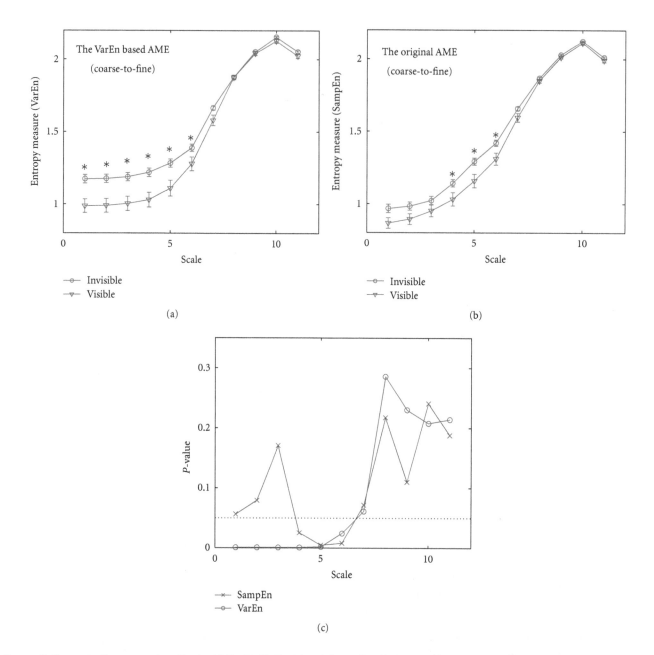

FIGURE 3: Coarse-to-fine comparison for the AME with VarEn (a) and the AME with SampEn (b) for discriminating the Invisible (red circle) and the Visible conditions (blue triangle) over multiple scales. The error bar refers to the standard error of mean. The leftmost red circle and blue triangle are the entropy measures of the raw data. For the AME with VarEn (a), significant differences occur at the 1st–6th scales, while the significant differences only occur at the 4th–6th scales for the AME with SampEn (b). The sign "*" refers to $P < 0.05$. The P values based on our VarEn and the SampEn along the coarse-to-fine scales are also compared (c), in which the horizontal black dotted line refers to the significance level ($P = 0.05$).

as the scale increases. However, the VarEn-based AME (Figure 3(a)) clearly provides significantly larger separation between two perceptual conditions than the original AME with SampEn (Figure 3(b)). Specifically, the VarEn-based AME at six significant scales (i.e., scale 1–6) shows significant differences between two perceptual conditions ($P < 0.05$) (Figure 3(a)), whereas the original AME differs only at three scales, that is, scales 4–6 (Figure 3(b)). A detailed comparison of P values between our VarEn and the SampEn along the

coarse-to-fine scales is shown in Figure 3(c). These results indicate that VarEn is more sensitive than SampEn to detect perceptual difference between two conditions.

Similarly, the improvement of discrimination by VarEn occurs at the fine-to-coarse scales as well (Figure 4), in which AME with VarEn significant different at scales 1–3 (Figure 4(a)) while AME with SampEn only exhibits significant difference at scale 2 (Figure 4(b)). Detailed comparison of P values between our VarEn and the SampEn along the

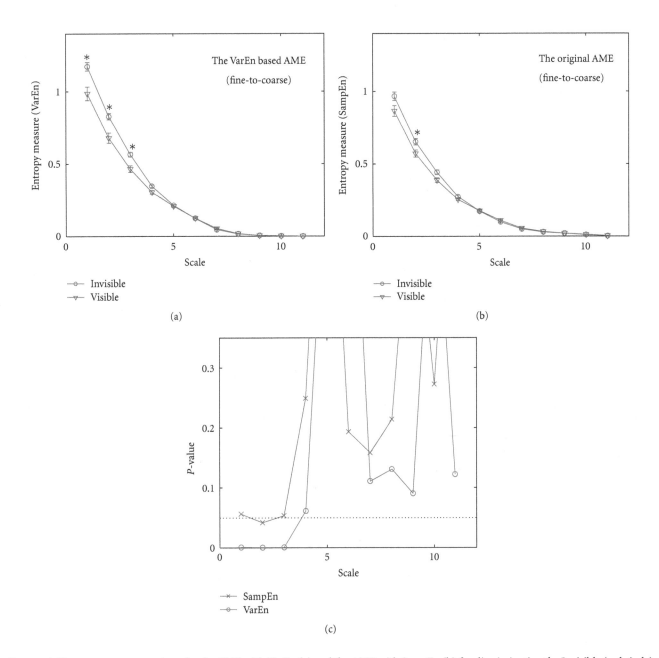

FIGURE 4: Fine-to-coarse comparison for the AME with VarEn (a) and the AME with SampEn (b) for discriminating the Invisible (red circle) and the Visible conditions (blue triangle) over multiple scales. For the AME with VarEn (a), significant differences occur at the 1st–3rd scales, whereas for the AME with SampEn (b) significant difference only occurs at the 2nd scale. Conventions are the same as in Figure 3. The P values based on our VarEn and the SampEn along the fine-to-coarse scales are also compared (c), in which the horizontal black dotted line refers to the significance level ($P = 0.05$). Note that the P values greater than 0.35 are truncated.

fine-to-coarse scales is also shown in Figure 4(c) to support our findings. These results, taken together, suggest that our VarEn can be used to obtain improved discriminative information for discriminant analysis of neural data.

In comparison of the coarse-to-fine AME (Figure 3) with the fine-to-coarse AME (Figure 4), the coarse-to-fine AME focuses on the high-frequency oscillations, whereas the fine-to-coarse AME emphasizes the low-frequency oscillations. When applied to the LFP data, we can see that the AME at coarse-to-fine scales exhibit more discriminative scales than

those at the fine-to-coarse scales, indicating that the low-frequency scales may not contain as much discriminative information as the high-frequency scales. The low-frequency oscillations mainly correspond to evoked potentials, which are presumably the same as the stimuli in the GFS task are identical; this explains why the fine-to-coarse scales exhibit less discriminative ability for separating two perceptual conditions. Furthermore, among all the significant differences, the AME measure in the invisible condition is higher than that in the visible condition, which suggests that perceptual suppression is likely to be related to more complex neural processes than the normal visible condition.

4. Discussion and Conclusion

In this paper, we proposed a simple complexity measure, variance entropy (VarEn), by combining SampEn and the variance to achieve improved discriminant analysis. Our measure was motivated by the observation that the calculation of SampEn is based on the normalized data where the variance is routinely discarded, which may otherwise provide the additional information for discrimination analysis. We applied VarEn to the analysis of cortical local field potential data collected from visual cortex of monkey performing a generalized flash suppression task. We showed that VarEn performed better than SampEn for both the whole time series (single-scale) and multiscale analysis of LFP data in terms of discriminative ability in distinguishing different perceptual conditions. The results suggest that our proposed VarEn measure is a useful measure for discriminant analysis of neural data and can be used to uncover perceptual awareness of a stimulus.

To quantify the complexity of a system, our proposed VarEn measure is defined as inverse-variance weighted SampEn. Inverse-variance weighting is typically used in statistical meta-analysis to combine several estimates of an unknown quantity to obtain an estimate of improved precision [15]. While other forms of weights (e.g., amplitude) could be used, such a choice of weight is optimal in providing the unbiased and minimum variance estimator. In comparison of VarEn to SampEn, the key difference is that SampEn discards the variance of the data, whereas VarEn combines the variance with SampEn via inverse-variance weighting. As such, if the main objective is for discriminant analysis, VarEn is preferred as it incorporates the variance information into its estimation. On the other hand, SampEn is appropriate if the analysis is driven by the search for order in the dynamics.

Acknowledgments

This work is partially supported by NIH. The authors thank Dr. Melanie Wilke for providing the data, which were collected at the laboratory of Dr. Nikos Logothetis at Max Planck Institute for Biological Cybernetics in Germany.

References

[1] S. M. Pincus, "Approximate entropy as a measure of system complexity," *Proceedings of the National Academy of Sciences of the United States of America*, vol. 88, no. 6, pp. 2297–2301, 1991.

[2] J. S. Richman and J. R. Moorman, "Physiological time-series analysis using approximate and sample entropy," *American Journal of Physiology*, vol. 278, no. 6, pp. H2039–H2049, 2000.

[3] D. E. Lake, J. S. Richman, M. Pamela Griffin, and J. Randall Moorman, "Sample entropy analysis of neonatal heart rate variability," *American Journal of Physiology*, vol. 283, no. 3, pp. R789–R797, 2002.

[4] E. N. Bruce, M. C. Bruce, and S. Vennelaganti, "Sample entropy tracks changes in electroencephalogram power spectrum with sleep state and aging," *Journal of Clinical Neurophysiology*, vol. 26, no. 4, pp. 257–266, 2009.

[5] S. Ramdani, B. Seigle, J. Lagarde, F. Bouchara, and P. L. Bernard, "On the use of sample entropy to analyze human postural sway data," *Medical Engineering and Physics*, vol. 31, no. 8, pp. 1023–1031, 2009.

[6] M. Costa, A. L. Goldberger, and C. K. Peng, "Multiscale entropy analysis of complex physiologic time series," *Physical Review Letters*, vol. 89, no. 6, Article ID 068102, 4 pages, 2002.

[7] M. Hu and H. Liang, "Adaptive multiscale entropy analysis of multivariate neural data," *IEEE Transactions on Biomedical Engineering*, vol. 59, no. 1, pp. 12–15, 2012.

[8] J. S. Richman, D. E. Lake, and J. R. Moorman, "Sample entropy," *Methods in Enzymology*, vol. 384, pp. 172–184, 2004.

[9] M. Wilke, N. K. Logothetis, and D. A. Leopold, "Generalized flash suppression of salient visual targets," *Neuron*, vol. 39, no. 6, pp. 1043–1052, 2003.

[10] P. Grassberger and I. Procaccia, "Estimation of the Kolmogorov entropy from a chaotic signal," *Physical Review A*, vol. 28, no. 4, pp. 2591–2593, 1983.

[11] J. P. Eckmann and D. Ruelle, "Ergodic theory of chaos and strange attractors," *Reviews of Modern Physics*, vol. 57, no. 3, pp. 617–656, 1985.

[12] S. Lu, X. Chen, J. K. Kanters, I. C. Solomon, and K. H. Chon, "Automatic selection of the threshold value r for approximate entropy," *IEEE Transactions on Biomedical Engineering*, vol. 55, no. 8, pp. 1966–1972, 2008.

[13] N. Rehman and D. P. Mandic, "Multivariate empirical mode decomposition," *Proceedings of the Royal Society A*, vol. 466, no. 2117, pp. 1291–1302, 2010.

[14] M. Wilke, N. K. Logothetis, and D. A. Leopold, "Local field potential reflects perceptual suppression in monkey visual cortex," *Proceedings of the National Academy of Sciences of the United States of America*, vol. 103, no. 46, pp. 17507–17512, 2006.

[15] L. V. Hedges and I. Olkin, *Statistical Methods for Meta-Analysis*, Academic Press, Orlando, Fla, USA, 1985.

21

Analyzing Ferroresonance Phenomena in Power Transformers Including Zinc Oxide Arrester and Neutral Resistance Effect

Hamid Radmanesh[1,2] and Fathi Seyed Hamid[2]

[1] *Electrical Engineering Department, Islamic Azad University, Takestan Branch, Takestan, Ghazvin 1995755681, Iran*
[2] *Electrical Engineering Department, Amirkabir University of Technology, Tehran, Iran*

Correspondence should be addressed to Hamid Radmanesh, hamid.nsa@gmail.com

Academic Editor: F. Morabito

This paper studies the effect of zinc oxide arrester (ZnO) and neutral earth resistance on controlling nonconventional oscillations of the unloaded power transformer. At first, ferroresonance overvoltage in the power system including ZnO is investigated. It is shown this nonlinear resistance can limit the ferroresonance oscillations but it cannot successfully control these phenomena. Because of the temperature dissipation of ZnO, it can withstand against overvoltage in a short period and after that ferroresonance causes ZnO failure. By applying neutral earth resistance to the system configuration, mitigating ferroresonance has been increased and chaotic overvoltage has been changed to the smoother behavior such as fundamental resonance and periodic oscillation. The simulation results show that connecting the neutral resistance exhibits a great mitigating effect on nonlinear overvoltage.

1. Introduction

Ferroresonance is a complex electromagnetic phenomenon which may be neglected in power system studies which is carried out for routine designs, planning, and operations [1]. A stability domain calculation of period-1 ferroresonance in nonlinear resonant circuit power system elements is given in [2]. In this case, quasistatic analytical approaches can be used to give a quick indication of the locations of domains of different ferroresonant states as a function of a set of parameters. Fast ferroresonance suppression of coupling capacitor voltage transformers (CCVT) is studied in [3]. This paper describes a procedure for fast suppression of the phenomenon of ferroresonance in CCVT without major change in the design. The design of a hall effect current transformer and examination of the linearity with real time parameter estimation is given in [4]. The aim of "blind source separation" (BSS) is to recover mutually independent unknown source signals only from observations obtained through an unknown linear mixture system [5]. Sensitivity studies on power transformer ferroresonance of a 400 kV double circuit are given in [6]. Novel analytical solution to fundamental ferroresonance in [7] investigated a major problem with the traditional excitation characteristic of

nonlinear inductors. Application of wavelet transform and MLP neural network for ferroresonance identification was done in [8]. Impacts of transformer core hysteresis formation on stability domain of ferroresonance modes were done in [9]. The principle of AC current transformers (CT) based on the magnetic coupling principle is given in [10]. Current paper studies the effect of neutral resistance on the global behavior of a ferroresonance circuit including ZnO in parallel to the transformer with linear core losses. Then, neutral earth resistance effect is discussed.

2. Power System Modeling Connecting ZnO

Transformer is connected to the power system while one of the three switches are open and only two phases of it are energized, which induced voltage in the open phase. This voltage back feeds the distribution line. Ferroresonance phenomenon is occurring if the distribution line is capacitive.

Base system model is adopted from [1] while ZnO is added to the initial ferroresonance circuit. Linear approximation of the peak current of the magnetization reactance can be presented by the following:

$$i_L = a\lambda, \tag{1}$$

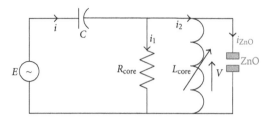

FIGURE 1: Final reduced model of power system for ferroresonance studies.

TABLE 1: Typical value of q and its coefficients.

q	(a)	(b)
11	0.0028	0.0072
7	3.14	0.41

TABLE 2: Power system parameters considered for simulation.

Parameters	Actual value	Per unit value
S_{base}	50 MVA,	—
V_{base}	635.1 kv	—
I_{base}	78.2 A	—
R_{base}	8121.4 Ω	—
C	4.9 μF	0.07955 pu
R_{core}	4.5 MΩ	554.09 pu
ω	377 (rad/sec)	1 pu
K	—	2.5101 pu
α	—	25

where λ is flux of the transformer coil and q is transformer nonlinear curve index. However, for very high currents λ-i characteristic of the transformer can be demonstrated by the polynomial in the following:

$$i_L = a\lambda + b\lambda^q. \tag{2}$$

The differential equation for the circuit in Figure 1 can be derived as follows. Polynomial coefficient of (2) is tabulated in Table 1:

$$v_l = \frac{d\lambda}{dt},$$

$$\frac{dv_l}{dt} = \frac{dE}{dt} - \frac{1}{RC}\frac{d\lambda}{dt} - \frac{1}{C}(a\lambda + b\lambda^q) - \frac{1}{C}\left(\frac{v_l}{k}\right)^\alpha, \tag{3}$$

$$\frac{dv_l}{dt} = \frac{d^2\lambda}{dt^2},$$

where $v_l = d\lambda/dt$, ω represents the power frequency and E is the peak value of the voltage source. Also, α and k are ZnO parameters as shown in Figure 1.

3. Simulation Results

Case 1 (Power System Behavior Connecting ZnO). In this section, effect of ZnO on mitigating ferroresonance phenomenon is investigated. Power system parameters values are tabulated in Table 2.

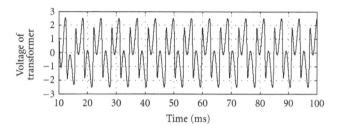

FIGURE 2: Time domain simulation for $q = 7$ (ZnO effect).

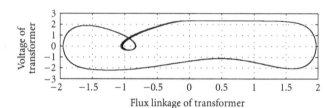

FIGURE 3: Phase plan diagram for $q = 7$ (ZnO effect).

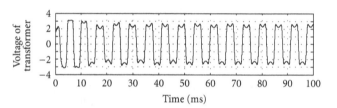

FIGURE 4: Time domain simulation for $q = 11$ (ZnO effect).

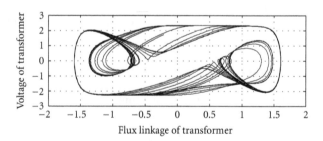

FIGURE 5: Phase plan diagram for $q = 11$ (ZnO effect).

It was shown that for proper representation of the saturation characteristics of a power transformer the values of q are 5, 7, and 11 [1].

Behavior of the system is analyzed by considering q degrees 7 and 11.

Figures 2 and 3 show time domain and phase plan simulation of the system behavior considering ZnO effect. By connecting ZnO chaotic ferroresonance is changed to fundamental resonance for $q = 7$ and subharmonic behavior for $q = 11$. ZnO clamps this overvoltage successfully. ZnO effect is shown in Figures 2 and 3 for $q = 7$ and in Figures 4 and 5 for $q = 11$.

Changing subharmonic resonance and ferroresonance overvoltage in the purpose power system by connecting ZnO

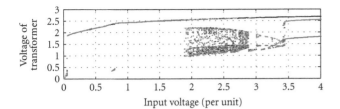

FIGURE 6: Bifurcation diagram with $q = 7$ (ZnO effect).

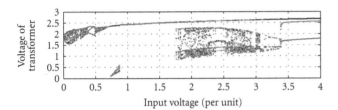

FIGURE 7: Bifurcation diagram with $q = 7$ (ZnO effect).

is clearly shows by using phase plan diagrams in Figures 4 and 5. Effect of ZnO surge arrester is clearly obvious, ZnO limit the ferroresonance overvoltage.

By increasing degree of q, amplitude of overvoltage remains in 2 p.u. Some sudden changes in nonlinear systems parameters may cause to the chaotic behavior. The noun "chaos" is used to describe the time behavior of a system when the behavior is nonperiodic and it never exactly repeats. In fact, most of the systems that will be studying are completely deterministic. In general we need these three factors to determine the behavior of the proposed power system. The time equations which are derived from ferroresonance equivalent circuit are given in (4) and (5). The value of parameters describing the system which all parameters values are tabulated in Table 2, then the initial conditions are most important factor for initiating ferroresonance and given in (6).

For studying the nonlinear dynamical systems as like power system, we need some tools such as time domain simulation, phase plan, and bifurcation diagrams. So, one of the most useful nonlinear dynamical tools is the bifurcation diagram [11]. To produce this diagram, we record the value of the peak voltage of the transformer as a function of control parameter being varied [11]. Here, control parameter is input voltage of the power system. In practice, a computer records the sampled values and then plotted as a function of the value of the control parameter. Two of these bifurcation diagrams are shown in Figures 6 and 7, where we have recorded sampled value of transformer voltage as a function of input voltage applied to the ferroresonance circuit with the frequency fixed.

According to the bifurcation diagram, it shows the ferroresonance overvoltage has been begun after 3 p.u. Tendency to chaos exhibited by the system voltage increases while q increases too.

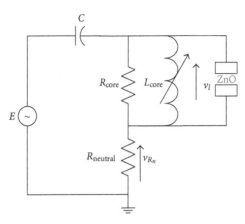

FIGURE 8: Equivalent circuit of the power system connecting ZnO and earth resistance.

4. Power System Modeling Considering Earth Resistance Effect

The main purpose of connecting resistance to the star point of a transformer is to limit ferroresonance. Low impedance is conventionally defined as impedance that limits the prospective ferroresonance to the no load of the transformer. The value of impedance required is easily calculated to a reasonable approximation by dividing the rated phase voltage by the rated phase current of the transformer. Neutral earthing resistance is achieved using resistors so as to limit the tendency for the ferroresonance to persist due to inductive energy storage. These resistors will limit heat when ferroresonance current flows and are usually only short term rated (typically 30 secs) so as to achieve an economic design.

So the typical values for various system parameters which have been considered for simulation were kept the same by Case 1, while earth resistance is added to the system and its value is given below and new system configuration is shown in Figure 8:

$$R_{\text{natural}} = 40 \, \text{k}\Omega. \tag{4}$$

The differential equation for the circuit in Figure 8 is given by the following:

$$\frac{dv_l}{dt} = \frac{dE}{dt} - \frac{1}{RC}\frac{d\lambda}{dt} - \frac{1}{C}(a\lambda + b\lambda^q) - \frac{R_n}{R}\frac{d^2\lambda}{dt^2} - R_n \cdot a\frac{d\lambda}{dt} - R_n q b\lambda^{q-1}\frac{d\lambda}{dt} - \alpha\left(\frac{1}{k}\right)^\alpha\left(\frac{d^2\lambda}{dt^2}\right)^{\alpha-1}. \tag{5}$$

For the initial conditions, we have:

$$\lambda(0) = 0.0; \qquad v_l = \frac{d\lambda}{dt}(0) = \sqrt{2}, \tag{6}$$

where R_n is the neutral earth resistance.

5. Simulation Results

Case 2 (Power System Behavior Considering Neutral Earth Resistance Effect). Figures 9 and 10 show the corresponding

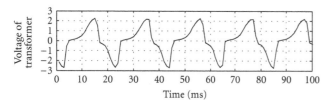

FIGURE 9: Time domain simulation for $q = 7$ (neutral resistance effect).

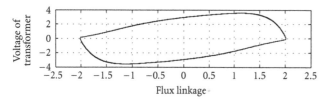

FIGURE 10: Time domain simulation for $q = 11$ (neutral resistance effect).

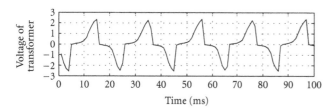

FIGURE 11: Phase plan diagram with $q = 7$ (neutral resistance effect).

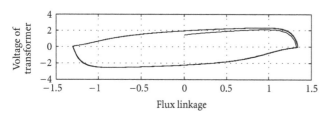

FIGURE 12: Phase plan diagram with $q = 11$ (neutral resistance effect).

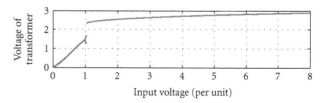

FIGURE 13: Bifurcation diagram with $q = 7$ (neutral resistance effect).

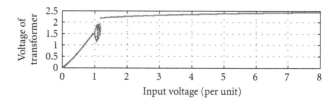

FIGURE 14: Bifurcation diagram with $q = 11$ (neutral resistance effect).

6. Conclusions

The nonlinear behavior of ferroresonance falls into two main categories. In the first, the response is a distorted periodic waveform, containing the fundamental harmonics of the fundamental frequency. The second type is a chaotic response. In both cases response's phase plan diagram contains fundamental and odd harmonic frequency components. In the chaotic response, there is also distributed subharmonics frequency. The simulation results confirm that system goes to chaos and bifurcation occurs in the proposed power system. The presence of the neutral resistance causes to clamp the ferroresonance overvoltage. The neutral resistance successfully, reduces the chaotic region for higher exponents of q. Simulation of system consists of two cases, at first, system modeling of power transformer including ZnO arrester and second, system contains ZnO and neutral earth resistance. Finally we compare the result of these two cases.

References

[1] S. Mozaffari, S. Henchel, and A. C. Soudack, "Chaotic ferroresonance in power transformers," *IEE Proceedings—Generation, Transmission and Distribution*, vol. 142, no. 3, pp. 247–250, 1995.

[2] D. A. N. Jacobson, P. W. Lehn, and R. W. Menzies, "Stability domain calculations of period-1 ferroresonance in a nonlinear resonant circuit," *IEEE Transactions on Power Delivery*, vol. 17, no. 3, pp. 865–871, 2002.

[3] M. Graovac, R. Iravani, X. Wang, and R. D. McTaggart, "Fast ferroresonance suppression of coupling capacitor voltage transformers," *IEEE Transactions on Power Delivery*, vol. 18, no. 1, pp. 158–163, 2003.

[4] G. Gokmen and K. Tuncalp, "The Design of a hall effect current transformer and examination of the linearity with real time parameter estimation," *Electronics and Electrical Engineering*, no. 5(101), pp. 3–8, 2010.

time domain simulation which shows the effect of earth resistance. Also Figures 11 and 12 show the phase plan diagrams for corresponding system including earth resistance effect. It is shown that subharmonic regions mitigates by applying earth resistance. It is shown that tendency to chaos reduce in this case. In the big degree of q, system has been simulated when neutral resistance is considered. It shows the ferroresonance carried out and there are no abnormal phenomena and chaotic region mitigates by applying neutral resistance.

By increasing in the degree of q, there is no more change in the system behavior. By comparing this case of bifurcation diagram with the previous case, it is clearly obvious that neutral resistance successfully clamps the ferroresonance overvoltage. This effect is shown in Figures 13 and 14.

[5] K. Pukėnas, "Blind separation of noisy pseudo periodic chaotic signals," *Electronics and Electrical Engineering*, no. 3(91), pp. 31–34, 2009.

[6] C. Charalambous, Z. D. Wang, M. Osborne, and P. Jarman, "Sensitivity studies on power transformer ferroresonance of a 400 kV double circuit," *IET Generation, Transmission & Distribution*, vol. 2, no. 2, pp. 159–166, 2008.

[7] Y. Li, W. Shi, and F. Li, "Novel analytical solution to fundamental ferroresonance—Part I: power frequency excitation characteristic," *IEEE Transactions on Power Delivery*, vol. 21, no. 2, pp. 788–793, 2006.

[8] G. Mokryani and M.-R. Haghifam, "Application of wavelet transform and MLP neural network for Ferroresonance identification," in *Proceedings of IEEE Power and Energy Society General Meeting—Conversion and Delivery of Electrical Energy in the 21st Century*, vol. 3, no. 4, pp. 1–6, Pittsburgh, Pa, USA, July 2008.

[9] A. Rezaei-Zare, R. Iravani, and M. Sanaye-Pasand, "Impacts of transformer core hysteresis formation on stability domain of ferroresonance modes," *IEEE Transactions on Power Delivery*, vol. 24, no. 1, pp. 177–186, 2009.

[10] P. Rafajdus, P. Braciník, and V. Hrabovcová, "The current transformer parameters investigation and simulations," *Electronics and Electrical Engineering*, no. 4(100), pp. 29–32, 2010.

[11] H. Radmanesh, G. B. Gharehpetian, and H. Fathi, "Ferroresonance of power transformers considering non-linear core losses and metal oxide surge arrester effects," *Electric Power Components and Systems*, vol. 40, no. 5, pp. 463–479, 2012.

Permissions

The contributors of this book come from diverse backgrounds, making this book a truly international effort. This book will bring forth new frontiers with its revolutionizing research information and detailed analysis of the nascent developments around the world.

We would like to thank all the contributing authors for lending their expertise to make the book truly unique. They have played a crucial role in the development of this book. Without their invaluable contributions this book wouldn't have been possible. They have made vital efforts to compile up to date information on the varied aspects of this subject to make this book a valuable addition to the collection of many professionals and students.

This book was conceptualized with the vision of imparting up-to-date information and advanced data in this field. To ensure the same, a matchless editorial board was set up. Every individual on the board went through rigorous rounds of assessment to prove their worth. After which they invested a large part of their time researching and compiling the most relevant data for our readers. Conferences and sessions were held from time to time between the editorial board and the contributing authors to present the data in the most comprehensible form. The editorial team has worked tirelessly to provide valuable and valid information to help people across the globe.

Every chapter published in this book has been scrutinized by our experts. Their significance has been extensively debated. The topics covered herein carry significant findings which will fuel the growth of the discipline. They may even be implemented as practical applications or may be referred to as a beginning point for another development. Chapters in this book were first published by Hindawi Publishing Corporation; hereby published with permission under the Creative Commons Attribution License or equivalent.

The editorial board has been involved in producing this book since its inception. They have spent rigorous hours researching and exploring the diverse topics which have resulted in the successful publishing of this book. They have passed on their knowledge of decades through this book. To expedite this challenging task, the publisher supported the team at every step. A small team of assistant editors was also appointed to further simplify the editing procedure and attain best results for the readers.

Our editorial team has been hand-picked from every corner of the world. Their multi-ethnicity adds dynamic inputs to the discussions which result in innovative outcomes. These outcomes are then further discussed with the researchers and contributors who give their valuable feedback and opinion regarding the same. The feedback is then collaborated with the researches and they are edited in a comprehensive manner to aid the understanding of the subject.

Apart from the editorial board, the designing team has also invested a significant amount of their time in understanding the subject and creating the most relevant covers. They scrutinized every image to scout for the most suitable representation of the subject and create an appropriate cover for the book.

The publishing team has been involved in this book since its early stages. They were actively engaged in every process, be it collecting the data, connecting with the contributors or procuring relevant information. The team has been an ardent support to the editorial, designing and production team. Their endless efforts to recruit the best for this project, has resulted in the accomplishment of this book. They are a veteran in the field of academics and their pool of knowledge is as vast as their experience in printing. Their expertise and guidance has proved useful at every step. Their uncompromising quality standards have made this book an exceptional effort. Their encouragement from time to time has been an inspiration for everyone.

The publisher and the editorial board hope that this book will prove to be a valuable piece of knowledge for researchers, students, practitioners and scholars across the globe.

List of Contributors

Kehinde Agbele and Ademola Adesina
Department of Computer Science, Soft Computing and Intelligent Systems Research Group, University of the Western Cape, Private Bag X17, Bellville, Cape Town, South Africa

Daniel Ekong
Department of Mathematical Sciences (Computer Science Option), Ekiti State University, Ado-Ekiti, PMB 5363, Ado-Ekiti, Ekiti State, Nigeria

Oluwafemi Ayangbekun
College of Information and Communication Technology, Crescent University, Abeokuta, Ogun-State, Nigeria

Jhing-Fa Wang, Bo-Wei Chen, Wei-Kang Fan and Chih-Hung Li
Department of Electrical Engineering, National Cheng Kung University, Tainan 70101, Taiwan

Masao Yokota
Department of System Management, Fukuoka Institute of Technology, Fukuoka 811-0295, Japan

V. Rajinikanth
Department of Electronics and Instrumentation Engineering, St. Joseph's College of Engineering, Chennai 600 119, India

K. Latha
Department of Instrumentation Engineering, MIT Campus, Anna University, Chennai 600 044, India

Harold Szu and Binh Q. Tran
Department of Biomedical Engineering, The Catholic University of America, Washington, DC 20064, USA

Charles Hsu
Trident Systems Inc., Fairfax, VA 22030, USA

Gyu Moon
Department of Electronic Engineering, Hallym University, Chuncheon, Gangwon-do 200-702, Republic of Korea

Takeshi Yamakawa
Fuzzy Logic System Institute, Semiconductor Center, Kitakyushu Science and Research Park, Kitakyushu 808-0135, Fukuoka, Japan

Tzyy Ping Jung
Swartz Center, University of California, San Diego, CA 92093, USA

Joseph Landa
Briartek Inc., Alexandria, VA 22301, USA

I. G. Damousis and S. Argyropoulos
Informatics and Telematics Institute, Centre for Research and Technology Hellas, 57001 Thessaloniki, Greece

Anna Lekova
Institute of System Engineering and Robotics, Bulgarian Academy of Sciences, Acad. G. Bonchev Street, Block 2, 1113 Sofia, Bulgaria

Hisateru Kato, Goutam Chakraborty and Basabi Chakraborty
Faculty of Software and Information Science, Iwate Prefectural University, Iwate, Takizawamura 020-0193, Japan

V. Rajinikanth
Department of Electronics and Instrumentation Engineering, St Joseph's College of Engineering, Chennai 600 119, India

K. Latha
Division of Avionics, Department of Aerospace Engineering, MIT Campus, Anna University, Chennai 600 044, India

Mauricio Guevara-Souza and Edgar E. Vallejo
ITESM-CEM, Carretera a Lago de Guadalupe km 3.5, Col. Margarita Maza de Juarez, 52956 Atizapan de Zaragoza, MEX, Mexico

Witold Pedrycz
Department of Electrical and Computer Engineering, University of Alberta, Edmonton, Canada
Systems Research Institute, Polish Academy of Sciences, 01-447 Warsaw, Poland

S. Sakinah S. Ahmad
Department of Electrical and Computer Engineering, University of Alberta, Edmonton, Canada

Kurosh Madani, Dominik M. Ramik and Cristophe Sabourin
Images, Signals and Intelligence Systems Laboratory (LISSI/EA 3956) and Senart-FB Institute of Technology, University Paris-EST Creteil (UPEC), Bat.A, avenue Pierre Point, 77127 Lieusaint, France

Lejla Banjanovic-Mehmedovic
Faculty of Electrical Engineering, University of Tuzla, 75000 Tuzla, Bosnia and Herzegovina

Dzenisan Golic
Infonet, 75000 Tuzla, Bosnia and Herzegovina

Fahrudin Mehmedovic
ABB, 75000 Tuzla, Bosnia and Herzegovina

Jasna Havic
General Secretariat Council of Ministers of B&H, 71000 Sarajevo, Bosnia and Herzegovina

Nishchal K. Verma
Department of Electrical Engineering, Indian Institute of Technology Kanpur, Kanpur 208016, India

Geev Mokryani, Pierluigi Siano, Antonio Piccolo and Vito Calderaro
Department of Industrial Engineering, University of Salerno, Salerno, 84084 Fisciano, Italy

Shipra Banik, Mohammed Anwer and A. F. M. Khodadad Khan
School of Engineering and Computer Science, Independent University, Bangladesh, Dhaka 1212, Bangladesh

Jerry Wu, Yin-Lin Shen, Harold Szu and Boqun Dong
School of Engineering and Applied Science, The George Washington University, Washington, DC 20052, USA
School of Engineering, The Catholic University of America, Washington, DC 20064, USA

Kitt Reinhardt
Air Force Laboratory, US Air Force Office of Scientific Research, Arlington, VA, USA

Toly Chen
Department of Industrial Engineering and Systems Management, Feng Chia University, No. 100 Wenhwa Road, Seatwen, Taichung 407, Taiwan

Ujwalla Gawande
Department of Computer Technology, Yeshwantrao Chavan College of Engineering, Nagpur 441110, India

Mukesh Zaveri
Department of Computer Engineering, Sardar Vallabhbhai National Institute of Technology, Surat, India

Avichal Kapur
Nagar Yuwak Shikshan Sanstha, Nagpur, India

Meng Hu and Hualou Liang
School of Biomedical Engineering, Science and Health Systems, Drexel University, Philadelphia, PA 19104, USA

Hamid Radmanesh
Electrical Engineering Department, Islamic Azad University, Takestan Branch, Takestan, Ghazvin 1995755681, Iran

Fathi Seyed Hamid
Electrical Engineering Department, Amirkabir University of Technology, Tehran, Iran

Printed in the USA
CPSIA information can be obtained
at www.ICGtesting.com
JSHW051439221024
72173JS00006B/1523